GLASS HOUSE

GLASS HOUSE

The 1% Economy and
the Shattering of the
All-American Town

BRIAN ALEXANDER

St. Martin's Press

New York

Frontispiece photograph by Shelley Metcalf
Map of Lancaster by Amanda Allen

www.stmartins.com

Designed by Susan Walsh

Cataloging-in-Publication Data is available from the Library of Congress.

ISBN 9781250085801 (hardcover)
ISBN 9781250085818 (e-book)

Our books may be purchased in bulk for promotional, educational, or business use. Please contact your local bookseller or the Macmillan Corporate and Premium Sales Department at 1-800-221-7945, extension 5442, or by e-mail at MacmillanSpecial Markets@macmillan.com.

First Edition: February 2017

10 9 8 7 6 5 4

To the memories of:

Thomas Alexander
immigrant, master tool and die maker
Cleveland, Ohio

Edward "E. B." Stern
office boy/sales manager, McKee Glass/Thatcher Glass
Jeannette, Pennsylvania

Robert Alexander
salesman/vice president, Lancaster Glass,
independent manufacturers' representative
Lancaster, Ohio

Agnes "Bobby" Alexander
Fairfield Heritage Association, Fairfield County Hospital Twig 3,
Miller for Congress co-chairwoman, League of Women Voters, poll worker
Lancaster, Ohio

"The nation-state at best is based on the social contract that is also an emotional contract, stamped by the charisma of the past."

—SVETLANA BOYM, *The Future of Nostalgia*

CONTENTS

PREFACE

The Cop

Eric Brown's chin trembled. He stopped talking, because if he kept going he was going to cry, and, by God, he wasn't going to cry. But then he did—a little—and then I found myself tearing up, too. So there we were, two middle-aged men, a cop and a reporter, sitting in a booth inside the Cherry Street Pub, clearing our throats, dabbing the backs of our fingers to our eyes, hoping nobody would notice.

By now I was used to people fighting the urge to cry. At first I was surprised: The Lancaster, Ohio, I remembered was not a teary sort of place. But in the months before Brown and I sat down together, I'd frequently had to pause to let people gather themselves.

A gnarly old union man was the first, when he told me a story about a toolbox his mentor in Anchor Hocking Plant 1 presented to him on the day the senior glassmaker retired. The older man had fashioned the toolbox out of steel, used it for over thirty years, and was now passing it on.

Most others choked up when they struggled to properly explain how much they loved their town. Getting the explanation right was important to them because they felt obliged to defend that love to an outsider—which was what I was now—in the face of so many seemingly obvious reasons to leave.

I didn't expect it from Brown, though. Maybe because he was a cop. He said, "I felt I carried the weight of this community on my shoulders." Ostensibly, he was referring to his efforts to rid the community of heroin—which, he was quick to point out, plagued not only Lancaster but every small city from the east side of the Appalachians through Indiana, though Lancaster had somehow gotten the reputation of being heroin heaven, a reputation Brown tended to blame on the reporters who popped down U.S. 33—"Heroin Highway," as many called it—from Columbus on slow news days to do ninety-second stand-ups in front of police headquarters.

Brown had run the Fairfield-Hocking Major Crimes Unit. About 90 percent of "major crimes" in the two counties were somehow connected to drugs. And so, he continued, "when you look around our community, all the bad things that are happening seem to be centered around drugs. Man, that's a lotta weight to carry."

For years Brown carried that weight like a Trojan. Well-known by his fellow task force officers and administrators around the state of Ohio, he had earned a reputation for being smart and sophisticated. His peers selected him to go to Washington, D.C., to plead for funding. Yet he sensed he'd become cynical.

Cynicism wasn't a natural fit for Brown. Born and raised in Lancaster, he made a name for himself as a star football player at Lancaster High, and he was still a solid guy with a palimpsest of golden-boy looks under the tempering that decades of policing had laid down. After trying big-time college ball, Brown returned to become a local policeman because he wanted to help protect his town. Coming from anybody else, that would sound corny. But for Brown, who could swear if he needed to, "Gosh!" and "My goodness!" were the natural defaults. Eventually, he married a Hajost, and so into a prominent local family. (As a teenager, I'd suffered through an unrequited crush on another Hajost girl.)

But it was these very hometown bonds that nurtured his cynicism. He'd come to the conclusion that he and his fellow cops could arrest drug users and dealers all day, every day, without making much of a dent in the problems that nagged Lancaster. He wasn't unique in this. After forty years of drug warring, police all over the country were chanting "We can't arrest ourselves out of this." Unlike many of his fellow officers, though, Brown understood that the bad things that had so altered his town from the days of his childhood weren't really grounded in drugs.

Some in Lancaster didn't notice (or they chose not to notice or refused to accept) just how much the foundation of the town they once knew had crumbled. The few with money could leave to play golf at the Greenbrier, go to the beach on Hilton Head, winter-hibernate in Florida, and still see their town as charming and full of history and nice people. They didn't have to venture across Memorial Drive and into the west side or cross the railroad tracks to the south side. Often, when people did talk about it, heroin and the "outsiders" who showed up to take advantage of social services provided conveniently simple explanations. Lancaster would go back to normal if only those two problems would go away.

Brown didn't have the luxury of blinders. He saw too clearly that whatever was going on was so much bigger—and so much more mysterious—than anything he could possibly control. It had to do with the economy, of course—with the decimation of downtown, with the fact that, every morning, Route 33 was packed with cars making the hour commute to Columbus because there weren't any good jobs in Lancaster. Sometimes it seemed like the only adult males left during the day were heavily tattooed and skinny, hoodies drawn up over their heads, riding little girls' bikes with pink banana seats or walking down Main Street, tugging at their jeans and often accompanied by girlfriends dressed in Hello Kitty pajama pants who pushed strollers. There were so many girls dragging dirty flannel hems across the sidewalks that local cops called Lancaster "the pajama pants capital of Ohio." What was he supposed to do about them? There was something in the culture, too—not just of Lancaster, but of America. The parks, a source of local pride, never seemed to have any kids in them. Who was he supposed to arrest for that? And yet, people expected him to do something.

"The people from here, roots here: I'm arresting them and dealing not only with them, but a distraught parent, distraught grandparents, sister, aunt, uncle." They were not outsiders, but people he knew—people he grew up with, played football with, saw right then in Cherry Street Pub. They'd call him up and plead with him to be not just a cop but a counselor, a corrections officer, a judge.

"The weight of it, the pressure, wanting to make things right, wanting Lancaster . . ." And that's when the chin started. He paused. "My mom and dad are still here. My son's here. He's raising his son here, him and his wife . . ."

People can become so frustrated, so discouraged, so mystified about what happened to the communities they love and about what they can do about them, they can't help but cry. Even a cop.

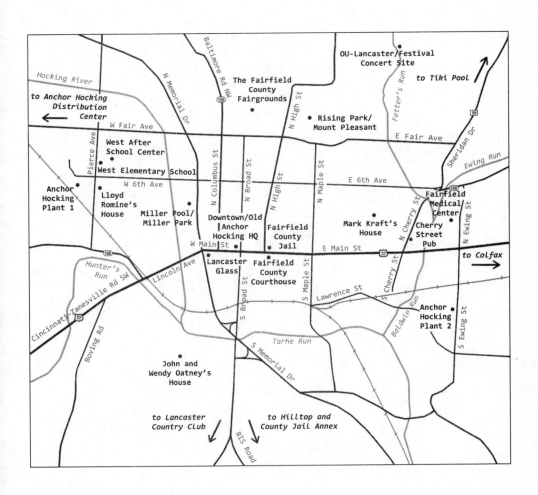

INTRODUCTION

The CEO

Sam Solomon drove his rental car through the west side, pulled into the rutted parking lot across the street from the offices on Pierce Avenue, opened his door, and heard air compressors whooshing, machines clanking, furnaces roaring. The factory adjacent to the offices groaned and heaved like an old man getting up out of his Barcalounger.

This was the heart and soul of EveryWare Global, a company with a name of pretend grandiosity that managed to be both redundant and generic. Solomon was about to start his first day as interim CEO.

He'd signed his new employment contract a few days before, on February 21, 2014: a Friday. That Sunday, he flew in from Chicago to Every-Ware's headquarters in Lancaster, Ohio, because he wanted to get an early Monday morning start. But upon arriving in Ohio, Solomon received a call waving him off: *Don't come in Monday.* Officials from Monomoy Capital Partners, the New York private equity outfit that owned most of Every-Ware's stock, told Solomon that the CEO they'd just fired, John Sheppard, wasn't quite fired yet. Certain documents and deals and signings were yet to be obtained.

The Monomoy guys were Manhattan finance pros for whom attention to detail is a creed. Solomon thought flubbing the transition to a new CEO was a strange bit of corporate statecraft.

Naturally, Solomon had done some due diligence before taking the job. He knew that EveryWare Global was the mash-up of two old, unrelated companies—the glassmaker Anchor Hocking and the flatware company Oneida, of Sherrill, New York.

Anchor Hocking was the much bigger operation. Founded in Lancaster in 1905, the Hocking Glass Company merged with New York-based Anchor Cap and Closure in 1937. By the late 1960s, it was the world's leading manufacturer of glass tableware, the second-largest maker of glass containers—beer bottles, baby food jars, coffee jars, liquor bottles—and employed more than five thousand people in Lancaster, a town of about twenty-nine thousand back then. Now it employed about one thousand people in Lancaster and about four hundred in a second plant in Monaca, Pennsylvania. Nobody in town called it EveryWare Global. To do so felt vaguely like betrayal. Back when the PE firm Cerberus Capital Management owned Anchor Hocking and tried to meld it with a couple of other, smaller companies, Cerberus called it Global Home Products, another dumbass name imposed by interlopers, that nobody in Lancaster ever used. Lancaster always was slow to change. Into the 1970s, some old-timers stubbornly called it "the Hockin'," partly out of loyalty to the Hocking River, which coursed nearby, and partly because the "Anchor" was new and alien. Now most people referred to it simply as "Anchor."

EveryWare was "distressed," a finance euphemism that evokes the delicacy of a blushing Victorian ingénue but could mean anything from "about to collapse" to "needs a shot of cash." EveryWare was a public company, so Solomon read what he could before accepting the job. But the numbers in annual reports, prospectuses, and Securities and Exchange Commission filings don't tell the whole story. Sometimes not anything like a real story.

Solomon was born in 1959, at North Carolina's Warren County Hospital, into an extended family of black farmhands who worked tobacco fields. He'd come a very long way since then by using his brains. But as smart as he was, he did not know—and could not know—how intertwined Anchor Hocking and Lancaster had been for more than a century. And while Solomon was used to being the only black man in a roomful of whites, he didn't know he was now the CEO of the biggest private employer in Fairfield County, and that Lancaster, at one time proudly, and now with chagrin, was reputed to be "the whitest town in America" and had a complicated racial history.

Finally, on the following Tuesday, Solomon was cleared to enter the offices and assume his duties. He could not have foreseen what awaited him as he walked across Pierce Avenue that morning toward the modest, low-slung one-story building. His new working home was a windowless, concrete cell of a room. Big photos of Anchor Hocking glasses and cake dishes and Oneida forks and knives didn't help much, nor did the agitated group of people who greeted him.

John Stewart, a Monomoy managing director, stood at a whiteboard, where he juggled some numbers on a chart with a couple of consultants from Alvarez & Marsal—an international "professional services" firm that deploys a gaggle of fix-its and charges enormous sums of money to tell companies how to get out of whatever swamp they've steered themselves into.

Solomon was a corporate gypsy with brands like Procter & Gamble, Coleman, and Sears on his résumé. He knew his way around a chart. So, within minutes of entering the room, he understood that EveryWare was in deeper trouble than he'd expected. Solomon came to find challenges: He was a challenges guy. This, though, was a shit storm.

Solomon could have turned around and walked out. The mess he found wasn't his mess. Besides, by any reasonable measure, he was rich. He could afford to go back to Illinois and wait for the inevitable—and probably better—next job offer.

But Anchor Hocking was an old brand, and Solomon had an affinity for old brands. An ambition to become the world's greatest brand manager drove him through Duke University's business school. The fact that anybody still recognized the anchor at the bottom of an Anchor Hocking measuring cup meant that generations of people had laid down geological layers of value. Anchor Hocking had survived two world wars, a depression, and a recession just short of another depression. Solomon wasn't sentimental about companies, and especially not about Anchor Hocking: His own corporate counsel would later call him Machiavellian, and would mean it as a compliment. Anchor Hocking appealed to his business aesthetic.

Flash was easy. No matter how useless a product, any bozo could make it flashy and fast and sexy, so that some venture capitalist in Silicon Valley would give you millions. It would trend on Twitter. And a year later—maybe two—when the product tanked? You'd still be rich. How hard could it really be to sell the Apple Watch? But a measuring cup? A pie dish? As a marketing guy, Solomon believed he could take a boring old industrial company, one still imbued with brand value, and get consumers, as well as businesses like restaurants and cruise ships and hotels, to flock to it again. If he could pull that off, he'd be a hero. Much more than a company depended on his success.

Solomon wasn't responsible for or to Lancaster. He was responsible to shareholders. At the moment, the majority shareholder was Monomoy Capital Partners. But as was true in a hundred other towns across the nation, Lancaster was a web of a community. Like it or not, the anchor thread in Lancaster was Anchor Hocking.

ONE

Glass House

December 2014

Brian Gossett worked the late shift, running an H-28 job: football-size vases, about the most difficult ware he made. A 2,400-degree lava-like ribbon of glass flowed out of Tank 3, a refractory furnace, and down a steel sluice to a pair of opposing automated blades shaped like prone V's. The two V's sliced together to pinch off a gob of glass from the ribbon. The gob dropped into a mold. Brian wore heat-resistant overalls, steel-toed boots, safety glasses over his own retro horn-rims, earplugs, and ear cups over the earplugs. Even with the hearing protection, his head filled with the hiss of air compressors and the rhythmic clanging rotation of the H-28 as it presented one mold after another to the gob feeder. *Ka-chunk plop, ka-chunk plop, ka-chunk plop,* each mold closed. A plunger forced the gob against the sides. Air blew into the mold so the glass was both pressed and blown. The combination made it look more polished than, say, a pressed-glass baking dish. Then the molds opened, each in its turn, to regurgitate the still-glowing ware onto a steel conveyor line.

Brian walked along a narrow platform that ringed the machine at about a foot off the concrete floor. Operators like Brian prepared new molds, reached into the moving merry-go-round, grabbed a mold from its spindle, and replaced it with the fresh one. They tried to do all this quickly, without losing a finger or a hand or burning an arm. The glass in a mold was about 1,600 degrees, and the H-28 wouldn't stop unless Brian fumbled and took

too much time, walked too far around that platform, and hit an emergency body gate.

Stopping an H-28 by hitting a body gate was not a trivial matter. It
meant you'd screwed up and that everybody would know it. And just
because the machine stopped didn't mean the glass would. It kept flowing
down the sluice, then diverted into the basement. Restarting the machine
was a hassle, because some of the ware coming out of the molds for the
first few rotations was sure to be flawed. Producing good ware required
constant temperature and timing, along with exact gob weight, so if you
had your ware running well, an emergency stop was the last thing you
wanted.

Brian was the fourth generation of his family to work at Anchor Hocking. He was twenty-six years old. Some guys had a Flint Glass journeyman
card by twenty-six, but Brian didn't. Technically, he was an apprentice, but
there really wasn't much of an apprenticeship program—not anymore. An
older man named Brant had taken Brian under his wing and helped out
now and then, but Brian operated the H-28 on his own most of the time.

Like most operators, Brian started as a floor boy, the worker ant of a
glass plant. Armed with a custom-made steel rake, a shovel, and a broom,
floor boys collected all the broken ware that accumulated under machines
during the course of a shift. They scouted for spilled fluids. They helped
clean the machines. Brian hadn't been a floor boy for long when he was
called to help scrape a burned man's skin from a machine.

On his first day in the plant, Brian was awed by what he saw. Giant
refractory-brick-lined furnace tanks measuring roughly forty feet long by
twenty feet wide and filled to a depth of about four feet with molten glass
blazed a story above the machine shops at the head of the hot end. Each
tank fed several shops. Each shop consisted of a machine and operators.
Shop 3-3—Tank 3, Shop 3—could be an H-28 making a tumbler. Shop
1-5—Tank 1, Shop 5—might be a press to make a pie dish. In just twenty-
four hours, more than 170 tons of glass could flow out of one tank. The
plant could produce more than 600,000 pieces of ware every day.

The machines in the hot end were black from years of glassmaking.
Standing by one of them, it seemed as if the whole plant was on fire. Flames
shot out of the burn-off station (where, for example, a tumbler's rim would
be given its "bead"). Blasts of blue and yellow torched ware in the anneal-

ing lehrs, where the glass was strengthened. Small explosions of flame erupted from the presses. The men were shadows silhouetted by fire.

When his buddy Swink, a fellow floor boy who had since become an operator like Brian, showed him the basement, Brian "saw all these big trash hoppers full of water, molten glass fucking streaming down, and I was like, 'This is like a water park for bad kids . . .' Everything in there looked like *The Addams Family,* where it's, like, metal hooks and chains."

The ware made its way from the hot end to the cold end, where it was inspected and then sent through to select-pack. There it was given a quick look again before being packed into boxes. Most people called this area the sluer. Generations of Lancaster mothers, some of whom worked in the sluer, motivated sandbagging schoolchildren not with "You wanna be a ditch digger?" but with "You'll wind up working in the sluer."

Brian respected the factory in the same way a young man might respect a wise veteran. He entered it more as boy than man. But Plant 1 was a place of manly work, where temperatures in the hot end during summer months could reach 130 degrees and where dangerous machines stamped and rotated and hissed. And there was all that annealing fire.

Longtime glass company employees, whether factory workers or executives, were called "glassmen," an honorific that meant you'd spent many years in the business, making glass, selling glass. Brian was on his way to becoming a glassman.

But Brian didn't think either he or Plant 1 were being treated with the respect they deserved. That's why he said he hated his job. "The people who own the place don't give a shit about us," he said. "The whole place is a piece of shit. Nothing works in there; they just put Band-Aids on it. It's embarrassing how that place is operated."

In January 2014, just as workers were returning from the annual Christmas shutdown, Tank 3, years overdue for a total rebuild, failed. Igneous glass ate through the bottom of the tank. A tide of fire spawned flames and smoke as it made its way into the basement. Some of the glass hit a natural gas line. That was the loudest boom Brian had ever heard other than the Fourth of July fireworks at the fairgrounds. The only thing you can do with all that glass is wait for it to cool into a solid mass and then break it up with jackhammers.

"I went from the only wrench I used bein' on my skateboard to having a toolbox 'n' shit, and they hand me a jackhammer. I lugged that up there," atop the feet-deep slab. "I just had my wisdom teeth taken out, so I'm spitting blood clots out, and I about fell off the motherfucker. That place is such a mess."

Brian had a reputation as a complainer. His union boss, Chris Nagle, headman of Local 51 of the United Steelworkers—a man who spent a good part of his life listening to complaints—thought so. But Brian wasn't saying anything a lot of other workers weren't also saying.

"That place is run . . . let's say jerry-rigged, to be polite," a veteran supervisor told me. "Everything is jerry-rigged."

Tank 2 had largely been torn down in anticipation of a rebuild. The rebuild never came. It sat cold and empty, the scorched, cracked yellow brick still in place. Nobody knew when or if it would ever come back to life. Body gates sometimes failed. Five of the nine air compressors powering pneumatic machines didn't function at all. Plant 1 was so decrepit it had a reputation around the industry for being a "shit hole."

Brian dreamed of one day leaving the shit hole. He'd never intended to be a glassman. He wanted to be an artist. He looked a little like a beatnik artist, too, with his neatly trimmed blond beard, his short blond hair, and those horn-rims. His mother had inherited a house on East Main Street, practically next door to a dive tavern called Leo's Bier Haus, and though the house itself was destroyed by a fire and the lot sat vacant, Brian and his parents had a deal. He'd keep the lot mowed and at least a little tidy. In return, he could transform the upstairs room of the antique wooden garage in the back, by the alley, into a studio.

The studio was tiny, a low-ceilinged room with a floor that sagged alarmingly to the west. An old drum set sat in the deepest corner. Brian sometimes practiced on it, but he mostly made art. He drew. He traced pictures to create stencils. He arranged repeated patterns of colored geometrical shapes on eight-by-ten pieces of paper. He clipped pop-culture detritus from his former teen life—anime cartoons like *Cowboy Bebop*, video game and book characters like Mega Man and Cosmic Camel, Pikachu from the *Pokémon* game, and Anna Nicole Smith—to make collages.

The collages especially were cultural commentaries. "Anna Nicole Smith is my hero," Brian said.

Brian had a lot to say about culture, though he sometimes had a rough time saying it. His mind had a tendency to jump two places ahead of his mouth. He'd trail off into vocal ellipses in the middle of sentences: "When I was a floor boy, me and Swink used to go down there and hide. You know, to get out of work—'cause if we sat in the break room too long, they called us lazy, and you didn't wanna be out on the floor, because it was clean. So we were just 'outta sight, outta mind.' So we'd go walk through the factory together, you know. At least we went together, so that way, if something bad happened, at least we were together. So we'd go exploring . . . I loved exploring that factory. As soon as you found the end, there'd be another hallway. It's real neat in there. It's a real dinosaur. So anyways, we'd go down there and hide and be like, 'This would be a great place to play paintball,' because about every ten yards there's, like, big pillars, you know. It's like the Afghanistan terrorist mission on *Counter-Strike* because of all the mortar and sand around."

But Brian's real problem wasn't organizing his thoughts. It was that he was plagued by so many of them. He thought about smartphones, TV, religion, pop music, business, politicians, capitalism, movies, America, truth. Mainly, he thought about *The System*. All these subtopics, and many more things, were just elements of The System. His friends seemed willing to—even happy to—buy into The System, but Brian was atavistic.

He was often annoyed to see his fellow operators sitting in chairs and looking at their smartphones instead of at their machines. When Tank 3 failed, the scene inside Plant 1 looked like Armageddon. Meanwhile, "everyone's got their phones out! And I'm just like, 'Okay, you guys fuckin' text. I'm going out to my truck. And that's when I about ran out of the fucking factory. I was just about ready to say, 'Fuck y'all, I'm going home.'"

The System was corrupt. The System didn't work for him. It didn't work for his parents. It didn't work for Anchor Hocking, nor for Lancaster, nor for America. He couldn't understand why anybody would obey The System. Fuck The System.

As Brian made vases on the H-28 in Plant 1 on one side of Pierce Avenue, Lloyd Romine was moving, little by little, into a gray two-story box of a house on the other. The house stood by itself, abutting an Anchor Hocking parking lot, its clapboard siding crumbling away, the yard dead in some patches and overgrown in others. A satellite dish connected the box to the wide world of TV. An old recliner, upholstered in gray velour, sat on the concrete front stoop. Above it, a plastic sign announced to anybody who cared that the premises were under surveillance. There was no sign of surveillance: no cameras, no motion lights, nothing. The sign was a poor man's security system.

Every cop in town—and a few county sheriff's deputies, too—knew Lloyd. He was first arrested when he was eight, a few years after his father left. He hid next to a garage to sneak a cigarette. He tossed the match over his shoulder. Pretty soon his back felt hot. Lloyd turned around and saw fire, so he ran as fast as he could. But this was Lancaster, and people notice little kids running from flames. So, of course, the police picked him up, and eight-year-old Lloyd had a juvie record.

He was forty now. His record grew with him. His reputation among Lancaster's bad boys grew, too, partly because Lloyd looked the part. He acquired a lot of ink—from his neck down over his arms—and he had a dark goatee, and hollow cheeks, and a wiry frame that gave him the scary aspect of a man who just didn't care how much punishment you could inflict in a fight.

Lloyd was friendly, though. If you hadn't cheated him in a drug deal or screwed him over stolen property, he was very congenial. Cops would stop him as he walked down the street and say, "Hey, Lloyd!" And he'd say, "Hey, Jimmy!" and ask about the family, and they'd chat for a while as Lloyd gripped a tiny ball of heroin in his jacket pocket. His own lawyer liked him so much he loaned him money. Lloyd paid back every cent.

Lloyd dropped out of high school in his sophomore year, but he could be a hard worker. He sold Kirby vacuum cleaners door to door. Wore a tie and everything. He had a job in the Lancaster Glass factory for a while and liked it okay, but it was only temporary. After about six months it was over. And Lancaster Glass shut down not long after anyway. He once skipped out on bail and took off to Florida. In short order he found a job laying pipe. He got good at it. His employer liked him and started giving him more responsibilities. Lloyd even filed a tax return. Not long after he filed, a small posse of police cars, their lights flashing, the dust flying, streamed onto a job site. Lloyd was in a backhoe. The boss shouted, "What the hell's going on?" "I think that's my ride," Lloyd said.

Lloyd was agnostic about drugs. He used and sold a little of whatever was flowing through Lancaster: meth, bath salts, Xanax, Perc 30s, moon rocks, cocaine, weed, Valium, heroin. Some of his clientele already lived, more or less, at the house on Pierce Avenue, but he also had customers inside the factory across the street. Now all they had to do was walk over after a shift. The mailman who'd bought drugs from Lloyd would no longer have to go knocking on a door in a part of town where houses were close together and everybody knew everybody's business. He could come over to the west side, fifteen yards from the Anchor gate, where people came and went twenty-four hours a day.

Lloyd never made much money. He used about as many drugs as he sold, worked legit jobs now and then, living hand to mouth. But those days were about to end. Lloyd Romine was about to make more money than he'd ever imagined.

M eanwhile, somebody knocked on the door of Mark Kraft's house in the 700 block of King Street, on the east side of Lancaster. Mark was working, but Carly Bowman was there.

Carly lived (also more or less) downstairs, rent-free, in the old house. Mark stayed upstairs, mainly. They were both twenty-five. Mark's grandparents raised a family in that house. His father inherited it, then essentially gave the house to Mark.

He had a pretty sweet deal. He didn't do much to keep it up, and it showed, though the white, two-story wood-sided house fit in with most of the others on the block. They were small and modest and had seen better times. Having Carly stay there off and on provided certain benefits for a junkie like Mark. The way Mark understood it, Carly's connect was an ex-boyfriend in Columbus, some black dude named Tayvon, from whom she bought most of her dope. Every other day she drove to Columbus, paid $600, and returned with about twelve grams, almost half an ounce.

Carly shot a lot of that into her legs—about half a gram every hit, four hits a day: a pretty big payload. Sometimes Mark would walk downstairs to find Carly laid out on the floor, her exposed legs bruised and scarred from all the needles she had shoved into them. Carly was a pretty enough girl, with brown hair and big eyes, but the bruises kind of grossed Mark out.

Mark took his hits in his arms. That's why he wore long sleeves all the time, even on the hottest August days. But other than the scars on his arms and a nagging fear of hepatitis, Mark thought he had his shit together. He was painfully thin, but he'd always been skinny. One front tooth was broken and he needed some other dental work, but he felt pretty healthy. He wore his dark hair short and often accessorized with an undersize hipster fedora.

He worked for his mom and dad at a small service business, showed up to work on time, did a decent job, and had more money to carry around than a lot of the other twenty-five-year-olds in town. So he could afford to drive up to Columbus every two weeks or so, hand over two or three thousand dollars to his own connect—some Mexicans—without having to break into somebody's garage and steal their golf clubs or shoplift from the Walmart up on 33.

When Mark was younger, he wanted to be a pilot. He took lessons at the county airport and racked up twenty-eight hours in the air. He liked school, too, earning good grades, and came close to winning a student council election.

But when he was a sophomore in high school, Mark called a teacher a "cunt." There was talk of expelling him, but his parents pleaded. Mark wound up being assigned to Occupational Work Experience (OWE). The program was intended to provide work training in addition to school for some trade-oriented students. Mark was not a trade-oriented student, but his parents said he could work in their business. So Mark attended school for part of the day and worked the other part.

Mark thought OWE was a joke: He was no longer really in high school at all. Most mornings, he'd hang out with other OWE kids in the parking lot where he started buying weed. Later, it was OxyContin. When Oxy went away, it was Percocet. When Percs went away, it was dope.

At first Mark bought all his dope in town. Once he started making acquaintances, he was amazed at how many junkies there were in Lancaster. Their presence hadn't been obvious to him before; it wasn't like the city was pocked with crack houses, opium dens, or street-corner drug markets. Many of the people he met were like the people he'd known all his life. Eventually he caught on that dope was cheaper in Columbus, so he paid his Lancaster dealer $200 to cough up the name of his Columbus supplier.

While Mark had a regular job, dope had become Carly's main source of income. Her dad was once a supervisor at Anchor Hocking, but that was a while ago. Now he was in business for himself, and things were tough. The family declared bankruptcy—partly because of the Great Recession and the conditions around town, and partly because it cost them a lot to buy Suboxone, a heroin-replacement drug used in rehab, for Carly. She went off Suboxone when they could no longer afford it. Carly sold roughly half her buy to her own customers. She taxed the dope by adding a surcharge to what she paid her connect, charging about $10 a point—one-tenth of a gram. In Columbus, you could buy dope for five bucks a point.

When Mark first started buying, he paid about $25 a point, but the law of supply and demand crashed the price: There was a shitload of dope around. Getting clean needles was easy, too. At first he bought needles off someone he knew with diabetes. Then he met a guy who worked in a drugstore and would sell a box of five hundred syringes for a hundred bucks.

The other sweet part was that when Mark's own supply was low, or when he couldn't make his regular run to Columbus, Carly would sell him a few grams without the tax. Mark figured Carly was his insurance policy. Her dope was a little better, too. Rarely, she'd fuck him, but her dope was the main attraction. Mark had a pretty sweet deal all the way around.

Whoever knocked on the door of Mark's house could have been any one of Carly's regulars, or perhaps somebody new sent by a regular. Carly took the money; the customer took the heroin. There wasn't any reason for suspicion.

Wendy Oatney was working the late shift at Taco Bell. She'd been working there for about a month, after stints at McDonald's and Sonic. Taco Bell was okay. Wendy usually liked the customers, though some of them could be ornery at two in the morning. She made about $8.50 an hour. She took home about $563 every two weeks. She was thirty-eight years old. Her husband, John, was forty-five. John's father had worked at Anchor. So had Wendy's dad. So had Wendy, in the sluer. That didn't last long, though.

John wasn't working. He'd had a series of jobs, mainly in warehouses or stocking shelves: at Home Depot, at a forklift company about twenty minutes up 33 in Canal Winchester, at the Goodwill. He especially liked the forklift company, Princeton Delivery Systems, where he worked in a manufacturing and parts warehouse when he and Wendy were first married, eight years before.

"I promised her when we got married that I would go ahead and take her places and show her some of the things I done, 'cause right before we was engaged, I went to Hawaii—four islands—and come back, and it was real nice, and she never got to go anywhere. I told her we'd be able to do stuff like that, but then I lost my job."

Cargotec, a Finnish company, bought Princeton and moved the jobs to Kansas. (Cargotec subsequently moved the jobs again, sourcing parts from "low-cost" countries and assembling the machines in Ireland.) Finding a new job was proving difficult. John had some behavioral problems, mainly a short temper. He had recently accepted Jesus Christ as his savior—a large tattoo of a cross covered most of one forearm—and strove every day to be a better Christian. That helped calm him some. So did his talks with the counselor a social service agency supplied. But some days were harder than others, and if a coworker got on John's nerves, he'd make an issue of it. So what work he could find didn't tend to last.

Also, John had a record, though he felt his arrest had been a little unfair. The Oatneys lived on the south side, in a tiny bungalow at the end of a lane on the south bank of the Hocking. About half a mile from their home, a former sheriff and his wife had gone into the halfway house business by establishing one in an old grocery store warehouse. Community Transition Center (CTC) was a place where felons spent weeks before being released into the community. Like many in the neighborhood, John resented the CTC. And someone had broken into the Oatneys' little house a while back. The front door still bore the scars from a crowbar. So, like many in Lancaster, John kept a loaded gun handy.

One day while John was sitting in the living room, he heard some sounds outside. He picked up his semiautomatic and charged out of the house, waving his gun at what turned out to be a family trying to find its way across the river to the park nearby.

"One cop that come down here and stuff . . . Me and Wendy had those Nextel phones . . . two-way, that was like walkie-talkies? I was in here, and she was in the bathroom. Heard all these sirens. *What in the hell's going on?* I go ahead, and thought I heard my phone chirp, so I picked my phone up and say, 'Hey, Wendy, where you at? What's goin' on?' She wouldn't answer me. I throwed the phone back down and took one step outside that door, and a cop had a .45 to my head." Aggravated menacing with a hand-gun was not a charge many employers were willing to overlook.

Their money troubles were amplified by a debt Wendy owed to one of the many car-title and payday lending offices that had sprung up all over town. John paid off Wendy's debt, but that left them short and owing other debts. A minister suggested they contact a new service in town called Loving Lending, a bank-backed, church-based charity set up to combat the high-interest money shops. Loving Lending helped pay their debts in return for a commitment to a program of financial counseling and saving strategies. They had just completed the program. Both were hopeful they could now catch a break.

Brian, the budding glassman, grew up in this new Lancaster. He made $14.55 an hour at Anchor Hocking. As of his late November paycheck, he had taken home a little over $21,000 in 2014. He had no pension plan, no 401(k). He lived with his parents. He didn't see any way he could avoid living with his parents next year, too, and the year after that. "I'm poor as shit," he said. His younger brother, Mike, was a full-time student at Ohio University, down in Athens, but he came home nearly every weekend to work at a Kroger gas station. Mike was Brian's best friend, but Brian rooted for him to become the first in his family to graduate from college, knowing that a degree would keep Mike out of Lancaster. Brian fantasized about starting a skateboard graphics business with Mike. When Brian brought it up, Mike smiled, nodded, said nothing. He couldn't wait to leave Lancaster behind. He wasn't sure where he would go, but it would be far away. Maybe Europe. He'd never been to Europe, but from where he stood in the glass booth of a gas station in Lancaster, Ohio, Europe looked better than America.

A few people over forty admitted that the whole town felt defeated. "Lancaster's been beaten up," Dave Bailey, the police chief, told me. Most, though, tended to avoid ruminating on Brian's Lancaster. Sure, they knew that Anchor Hocking had been slipping down a long, embarrassing slide for more than a generation. Few saw any point in trying to understand why. Some even used the past tense when talking about the company—"When Anchor was here . . ."—though Anchor was still there. Others regarded it as a shaggy uncle living out of a 1978 LeBaron, the relative who is no longer discussed at Thanksgiving. Anchor Hocking had become an uncomfortable metaphor.

They viewed Carly and Mark and Lloyd and the Oatneys in the same way they viewed Anchor Hocking. They were aware. It was a small town; they couldn't help but be aware. But they found consolation in thinking how aberrant it all was, how it wasn't the real Lancaster. Possessing the memories of Brian's parents, not the memories of Brian, they grasped at every positive development to support their view that one of these days Lancaster would return to normal.

The vacant restaurant over on Cherry Street was getting a makeover. Billy and Lorena Smith, who'd run another little place everybody liked before they moved to Florida, were back. They hoped to have the Cherry Street Pub open by the end of January. That would be the third new place to open in the space of a year. And Paul Hoch had bought the Pink Cricket, a tavern/restaurant on East Main, a Lancaster landmark since Prohibition.

Downtown, Brad and Penny Hutchinson, who owned a heavy-equipment-leasing business called Company Wrench, bought the Mithoff Building, an abandoned nineteenth-century wreck in such disrepair it was falling into itself. Two old buildings had been gutted by fire a few years back, leaving a big gap in the middle of downtown. The city wanted to yank the Mithoff in order to avoid a similar episode. But the Hutchinsons promised to spend whatever it took to resurrect it. Construction was about to begin on new elementary schools. Some of the schools they would replace were nearly a century old. The new ones would have the latest technology, which was thought to be very important.

And Lancaster still had what it had always had: the Fairfield County Fair, the Lancaster Festival—a music and art fair held every July since 1985—William Tecumseh Sherman's house, a decorative arts museum, and a new glass museum. Lancaster had beautiful antebellum homes.

Brian and Mike didn't buy into any of this optimism. They watched their parents struggle to provide a middle-class life for them after their father, Greg, lost his job at Anchor. Greg found another job with a company in Columbus, but their mother, Melinda, had to go to work, too, as a customer service rep at the Anchor Hocking distribution center. Brian hated that his mother was forced to work. To him, that was one more piece of evidence that The System had failed.

He'd been a skate punk all through high school and for some years after, and the music and the ideas still appealed to him. A thrash punk/ska outfit, Leftöver Crack, was a longtime favorite band of his, for lyrics like this from their song "Nazi White Trash":

eugenics, social darwinism, an excuse for yer positioning

Brian liked many kinds of music, as long as it had integrity. Lately he'd been raiding his father's large collection of LPs and had come to appreciate funk from the 1970s, rhythm and blues, classic rock, soul—sounds that almost nobody he knew, other than his father and sometimes Mike, appreciated.

At the moment, he was especially taken with Harry Nilsson. He thought Nilsson's "Me and My Arrow" was brilliant. Nilsson's song was tonic for a broken heart. Brian's girlfriend Renee had been his best friend, aside from Mike. But she wrecked a car in 2013, and that precipitated questions of her own about where she was going, or, more accurately, not. Her decision to leave was hard—at least, Brian believed her when she told him so. She joined the air force, and they rarely communicated after that.

Renee was still a raw subject. Brian would tell a story and, in the course of it, would say her name without really thinking about it, because Renee was part of most every story. He'd stop himself with a pause while he chased away the thought of her, then pick up the story further down the timeline, as if he were reading a document poorly redacted by the FBI.

One gray day I rode with Brian and Mike out to a spot they called Hilltop. It was warmer than usual for December, about forty-five, a good day to work on a project Brian had started the previous summer. We piled into

Brian's white Ford F-150. He'd bought the truck used, and it needed a little work, but it was fine for hauling rocks.

More than a hundred years ago, a Gossett ancestor owned land by the banks of Clear Creek, about ten miles southeast of town. The creek burbled through a hollow in the Appalachian foothills. The ancestor farmed along the bottomland at the base of a wooded hill. Almost all the acreage around had long since become a nature park, but the Gossetts still possessed a small inholding, Hilltop, crowning the hill. The land wasn't good for much except enjoying the woods and hunting deer. Brian had decided to start building a cabin on it. So far, he'd laid out the beginnings of a sandstone foundation made from rocks he'd collected. He'd cleared a few shrubby trees. He hoped to make good progress over the coming year. Maybe, he said, he'd become a back-to-the-land hillbilly.

We drove south, out Broad Street, across the railroad tracks, across the Hocking River—about five yards wide there—and veered onto BIS Road. The road was named after the Boys Industrial School (called the Ohio Reform Farm at its founding in 1856), a reformatory that in 1980 was turned into a state prison for adults, the Southeastern Correctional Institution. Everyone still called it BIS.

Brian slowed his truck to navigate the twists in the road as it wound through the prison campus. Mike looked out at the razor wire and asked Brian if he thought they knew anybody behind the fences.

They couldn't be sure, but it was possible. They talked about friends who'd overdosed, about the girl who appeared in a homemade porno for her drug dealer boyfriend, about the tweakers in town. It wasn't like he and his friends all came from lousy homes, either. His own parents cared. The parents of his friends cared.

"But they don't want to know how it really is," Brian interjected. "Dad sort of gets it, but Mom, she wants to stick her head in the sand and act like it's not there."

"Yeah," Mike agreed. "It's way different from when they were kids."

That night, after we cut some trees and piled a ton of rocks, Brian, Mike, and I hung out in the studio listening to a bootleg Sex Pistols album and rummaging through Brian's art. Brian lit a cigarette and stood by the open door to smoke it, because he hated the smell of cigarettes. While blowing a cloud out into the cold night air, he spotted a friend, Aaron Shonk, over by Leo's. Aaron was one leaf on a complex Lancaster family tree; there were scores of Shonks around town. He was in a funky folk-bluegrass band, the Shonk Brothers, with his brother and a couple of other guys. He was headed to practice when Brian called out to him by raising a fist in the air and shouting, "White power!" It was a joke he and Aaron had been acting out for years to make fun of people who said asshole stuff like "White power," like those guys from the Klan who had come through Lancaster a few months before and handed out flyers to kids. The flyers had lollipops attached.

Aaron and a friend walked up the shaky stairs that clung to the outside of the garage. Aaron was a good-looking young man with a black beard. He was so tall, he nearly had to hunch over to avoid hitting his head on the low ceiling. Brian brought out three bottles: Jägermeister, Bushmills, and Johnnie Walker Black Label. He showed off some stencil work. "I have so many projects I wished I'd finished," he said.

Brian sometimes joked about being ADD. Maybe he was, a little. But his self-diagnosis was more fecklessness than ADD. He'd gone to a technical college in Nelsonville, a town to the southeast, to study music engineering in an effort to combine his attraction to craftsmanship with his love of music, but he didn't complete the courses. He took some art classes at the Lancaster branch of Ohio University, but he stopped attending. His relationship with Renee had fizzled. He could pound out some good beats on the drums, but he lacked follow-though. He hated his inability to complete things. He felt pressure to pick a path in life and stick with it, but what path? Where could he fit, find meaning, not sell out to The System?

He held up a piece of stencil work, admiring it. He'd done a good job on the image. It depicted a dandelion, the flower head turned to puffs of dry seed and tiny puffs flying off into the air, where, far away, they morphed into birds.

Anchor Hocking was not going to be his longtime career, he said. He was sure of that much. Five years, maybe, then he was gone. But he also liked to say of the H-28, "For eight hours, she's my bitch. I run her. Sometimes she runs me." He boasted that he made some of the best ware of any operator. So I asked him to show me how he worked.

He stood up, comparing the machine to the size of the room. He stretched his arms out wide and shuffled around an imaginary H-28. Brian had played JV football and was still a little stocky, but he was light on his feet. We all watched as he stood on his tiptoes and pantomimed removing a mold. The imaginary H-28 rotated, with Brian following it, narrating every maneuver with increasing urgency and passion, still on his toes, gliding around and around, his hands a blur. He danced like Astaire.

TWO

The All-American Town

1947–1982

For generations, every school kid in Lancaster could tell you at least part of the story. Ebenezer Zane made a road called Zane's Trace. The road came through Lancaster. Settlers followed the road. They met some Indians called Wyandots. A girl named Forest Rose was kidnapped by the Indians, who took her to the top of Mount Pleasant, except it wasn't called Mount Pleasant back then: The Wyandots called it Standing Stone, because it's really a big stone, not an actual mountain. The Wyandots called the Hocking River HockHocking. Anyway, the girl was rescued. Then William Tecumseh Sherman was born. Thomas Ewing, too. And that's why the two junior high schools are named Ewing and Sherman. Sherman burned down Atlanta. And Richard Outcault, the guy who made the first comic strip, *Buster Brown*, and another one called *The Yellow Kid*, was born here, and Lancaster makes lots of glass, and those are just some of the reasons why Lancaster is special.

Until the 1990s, you couldn't spend more than a few days, even a few hours, in Lancaster without somebody trying to indoctrinate you as to why Lancaster was an exceptional town, and why living there was the same kind of lucky break as being born in America. Come to think of it, being born in Lancaster was sort of like being born in the innermost nesting doll of America, and if you thought that was prideful exaggeration, the proof was right there, in black and white, in the November 15, 1947, issue of *Forbes* magazine.

Forbes devoted most of its thirtieth-anniversary issue to making the argument that Lancaster, Ohio, of all places, was the epitome and apogee of the American free enterprise system. The cover showed the intersection of Main and Broad streets. A corner of the Anchor Hocking headquarters peeked from the right of the frame. Main Street bustled with people and cars. Small American flags flew from streetlight poles. "This Is America," *Forbes* declared.

Some *Forbes* readers may have wondered why the magazine would pick Lancaster as its model community to illustrate the brilliance of capitalism, but the choice wasn't a mystery to Lancastrians. The backstory was just one more justification for Lancaster's self-regard.

In 1941, *Forbes* founder and editor in chief B. C. Forbes set up the *Fairfield Times*, a weekly Lancaster newspaper, for his son Malcolm to run. Two days after graduating from Princeton, B. C.'s fledgling arrived in town. Months later, Malcolm founded another weekly, the *Lancaster Tribune*. Neither lasted long against the *Eagle-Gazette*, whose heritage dated back to 1809. Malcolm left Lancaster in 1942 to join the army (leaving, some locals still say, a few debts behind). But while his stay was short, Malcolm Forbes's Midwest sojourn became Lancaster lore. Then, when Malcolm and some reporters from the magazine returned after the war, the resulting issue validated for all the magazine's back-east big-shot readers what Lancastrians already believed: "Li'l ol' Lancaster" was no hick town.

The *Forbes* issue painted an especially flattering portrait in the service of propaganda. B. C. wanted to use it to tantalize readers with the American Promise while warning them of the danger of "Socialistic New Dealism."

The features opened with a sketch of Lancaster's geography and history, its placement at the transition from the last western foothills exhaled from the Appalachians to the beginning of the plains, the road—more of a path through the woods—Zane and his brothers started in 1796, and the pioneer German-Dutch Protestants from Lancaster County, Pennsylvania, who named their settlement New Lancaster. The favorite sons received a mention: U.S. senator and secretary of the treasury Thomas Ewing and the Sherman brothers, William T. and John (U.S. senator, author of the Sherman Antitrust Act, secretary of the treasury under Rutherford B. Hayes, secretary of state under William McKinley). So did the canal built to carry Fairfield County's agricultural products to New York.

Forbes was mainly interested in the story of Lancaster's industry, which started when Civil War veteran Albert Getz opened a downtown shoe factory that employed a hundred people. Getz sold out to a bigger Columbus maker named Henry Godman in 1890. H. C. Godman Shoe eventually opened four factories in Lancaster.

But Lancaster did not become an industrial town until the late 1880s, when the city discovered that it sat atop a sea of natural gas. Once drillers started looking for it, they found so much gas that the county fair board sunk a well on the fairgrounds, on the northeast edge of the city, and the racetrack became the first in the world to hold nighttime harness races illuminated by gaslight. Gas was even piped into the water of a pond in the infield, then ignited to create an attraction called the "Lake of Fire." Along with Forest Rose and Sherman, horse racing by gaslight became part of the Lancaster story. People still mention it today.

The city pioneered the public ownership of an energy utility by forming a municipal gas company to exploit the find. A bond issue to raise $50,000 passed by a wide margin. (The municipal gas company still exists, serving about fifteen thousand customers, though the gas now arrives via pipelines from other states.) As of 1906, Lancaster charged ten cents per month, half the rate for gas in surrounding cities and towns.

B. C. Forbes believed public ownership of utilities would be a disastrous step toward socialism, so *Forbes* clucked over the natural gas story. The resource "was channelized in a rather unusual fashion, for they decided that this new power was to be exploited for the good, and at the risk, of the whole community: the entire gasworks was therefore organized under municipal ownership." Because of low prices, *Forbes* sniffed, the "gas field had been wasted extravagantly."

Maybe, but the cheap, plentiful, publicly owned gas proved a powerful lure to glassmakers, for whom energy and labor were the biggest expenses. Glassmaking towns like Clarksburg, West Virginia, and western Pennsylvania cities like Pittsburgh, Jeannette, and Monaca were close enough to draw migrating glassmen in search of lower costs to Lancaster. By 1890, a company called Highland Manufacturing was making window glass and lenses in Lancaster. Highland was followed by C.P. Cole, Columbus Plate

Glass, Fairfield Sheet Glass, Lancaster Lens, and Ohio Flint Glass Company. (Though "flint glass" now refers to clear glass, it originally referred to glass that used a calcined flint in its production.) The Hocking Glass Company, the forerunner of Anchor Hocking, was founded in 1905.

In a series of articles dissecting the three pillars of the U.S. economy—Main Street shops, agriculture, and big business, as exemplified by Anchor Hocking—*Forbes* left readers with the belief that Lancaster was the purest distillation of America. Lancastrians were plain and plainspoken, and community-spirited. They didn't believe in ostentation. Even the rich lived in relative modesty. Class distinctions were present, but fuzzy. Those with a little more money hosted cocktail parties in their homes and golfed, swam, and danced at the country club. But a factory worker might live three blocks from a factory owner. The store clerk might be chief honcho of the Moose lodge where the bank president was also a brother. No matter how much money you had, your children attended the public schools or the small Catholic one and made friends across the economic spectrum.

Lancastrians were patriotic. *Forbes* profiled a "big brawny man" named Jack Fisher—an ex-GI who'd fought his way through France, Germany, Austria, and Italy during the war, only to return to Lancaster and work at Anchor Hocking "in areas where the temperature reaches 204 degrees." In fact, Lancaster's glassworkers and shoemakers walked out of the factories and into the military just as young lawyers, businessmen, and Malcolm Forbes did. Over three thousand Anchor Hocking employees joined up; sixty-three of them were killed in action. Once the war was over, 80 percent of those veterans walked right back into the furnace rooms and offices of Anchor Hocking. They loved their town. As *Forbes* wrote of Fisher, "He has returned to his roots, to stick."

The Lancaster in the *Forbes* imagination was orderly, convivial, and upright. There was little of the "roughneck element." What crime there was seemed to be of the most petty, almost prankish, sort. Pretty much everyone lived in a home they owned.

A semi-pro baseball team entertained in the summer. There were bowling alleys, parks, the country club, plenty of taverns, and about thirty churches. A couple of locally owned department stores brought in fashions from New York, and regional retail chains like S. S. Kresge displayed their faith by establishing outlets. Two movie theaters showed the latest films.

In the *Forbes* image, Lancaster was governed by a set of long-held rules and customs. People possessed, and used, good common sense. They were a little stodgy, even stolid, but—and *Forbes* considered this a boon— homogenous to a degree that was unusual even then. "Though there are a number of rather exotic southeast European names in town," one article stated with a nearly audible Princetonian accent, "there is no distinctly 'foreign element.'"

There were no communists, socialists, and not even any "left-wingers." There were, however, unions. *Forbes* considered these an unfortunate intrusion of the mean outside world upon Lancaster's bubble of harmony, but it approved of the way Anchor Hocking had tamed them.

> While rigorously quelling any union agitation during the '20s and early '30s, they had at the same time distributed their subsidiary factories in separate townships throughout the county to forestall concentrated organization, had used company picnics and other more or less paternalistic measures to foster employee goodwill, and had encouraged their people to buy their own homes and, often, to settle outside the city in small farms, thus preventing the growth of any inflammable proletariat. Their foresight enabled them in 1937 to have the city police bar the approach of a CIO organizer without raising much local protest, and to arrive at a comfortable understanding with the AFL.

Lancaster was not a company town in the strictest sense of the term. Though the other glass companies had come and gone by 1947, Lancaster Lens was still an important national producer. In 1934, a handblown Lancaster Lens was placed in the Statue of Liberty's torch. Lancaster Lens made many of the taillight and headlight covers for American automobiles, and it was gearing up to supply the glass cases for the new television picture tubes. Godman sold out to the Irving Drew Shoe Company in 1937; ten years later, Drew was still making shoes. Essex Wire, Alten's Foundry, the Stuck Mold Works, and other, smaller firms were all employing people and making money. But *Forbes* was correct when it wrote that the two glass companies, especially Anchor Hocking, were the economic skeleton on which Lancaster's society hung.

"They sometimes wonder what would happen if the glass factories moved away," *Forbes* wrote, "but there is no reason for thinking that they will, and as long as they remain and continue to manufacture low-cost glass tableware Lancaster can look forward to a relatively even economy that will not be unduly disturbed by either war or depression."

A lmost two years after the *Forbes* issue, two young newlyweds, Nancy and Herb George, stepped into their '46 Plymouth convertible to search for their future. It was springtime, when green shafts of daffodils knife through thawed ground and pink and white blooms fluff dogwood branches.

Nancy (her last name is now Frick) was recovering from an attack of polio that had frozen most of her body. But she was up and walking now, and she'd earned a business degree at Ohio State. Herb, who'd delayed college due to military service, would graduate soon. World War II had been over for four years. Rationing was a memory. Businesses all over Ohio were hiring. They both had jobs already; Herb worked at the Columbus water department, and Nancy had an office position at the Sherwin-Williams paint company. But these were just jobs, not careers. Now they were ready to dive into the postwar economy and begin their adult lives.

Though they were definite about all of this, they weren't sure exactly where they wanted to stake their claim. Both of them wanted to stay in Ohio—to be away from their families, but not too far away. That meant leaving Columbus for a smaller town in which they could buy a home and raise children. So, as Herb finished up at Ohio State, the couple spent Sundays that spring driving around Ohio.

One day, they pointed the Plymouth southeast down U.S. 33—then a two-lane stretch of blacktop—and toward Lancaster. There wasn't much of anything between Columbus and Lancaster, just tiny farm villages that briefly interrupted the newly planted fields. As the Georges rolled into Lancaster, 33 became Memorial Drive, a road built along the bank of the old canal. They took a left at Main Street—U.S. 22—and drove through the three blocks of thriving downtown businesses, past the tremendous golden-hued sandstone city hall, then up Main Hill, with its antebellum Federal-style homes.

Nancy thought the city looked like a painting. "It was a really beautiful town. I mean, it was picture perfect, just like a Norman Rockwell."

They traveled east beyond High Street, at the crest of Main Hill, and down the other side, where they crossed Cherry Street, then Ewing Street by the hospital, and headed out toward the eastern boundary of the city. They passed a few small manufacturing plants, and then the buildings gave way to fields. They stopped at an A&W Root Beer stand for lunch to compare notes.

After lunch, they retraced their path back through town. They were Episcopalians, so they wanted to look at the local Episcopal church. They parked the Plymouth near the corner of Broad and Wheeling streets in front of St. John's, a beautiful redbrick structure built in English Gothic style. The still-new Hotel Lancaster rose up right across Broad Street. An antebellum mansion with Greek columns, the Georgian, stood on the opposite corner across Wheeling. Other grand houses stairstepped up Wheeling Hill, behind the church. The Georges had been there less than a day, but they already hoped Lancaster would be their town.

As soon as they returned to Columbus, Herb researched Lancaster's businesses. For a town its size, Lancaster had many of them. But Anchor Hocking, with its two big plants—one on the west side, on Pierce Avenue, and one on the east side, on Ewing Street—and the downtown corporate headquarters that occupied a three-story brick building on the corner of Main and Broad, was by far the biggest: the rare *Fortune* 500 giant based in a small town.

Nancy used an old typewriter to clack out a letter on Herb's behalf. She wrote of his pending graduation. She mentioned that he was a cheerleader for Ohio State. That carried weight then, as it would now. She asked for information and an interview. They didn't have to wait long for a reply. All across the country, ex-GIs were graduating from college or landing jobs that paid union wages in factories. They were marrying, setting up house, and having babies. And they needed glass: glass dishes, glass tumblers, glass cookware, glass jars. They drank beer out of Anchor Hocking bottles. Anchor Hocking was ramping up its production and sales. After two interviews, Herb George signed on as the company's newest salesman, starting at $50 a week.

Herb and Nancy rented a tidy little house on the west side, within walking distance of Plant 1. They paid $45 a month.

Nancy lived by an old motto: "You grow your seed where you are planted." Lancaster proved to be rich soil. Unlike Sinclair Lewis's fictitious Zenith—a larger city, more like Toledo—Lancaster didn't have Babbitts. She found it to be an intimate, democratic place, where everyone knew one another, and people made judgments based not on class and material goods, but on time. A Lancaster saying held that if your grandfather wasn't born there, you weren't a local.

In the very next year, 1950, another major employer, Diamond Power, a maker of soot blowers for industrial boilers, opened a plant out east on Route 22. Diamond Power was not welcomed by Anchor Hocking. Cheap labor was part of Anchor Hocking's business model, and Diamond Power represented competition for that labor. Anchor controlled—officially and unofficially—the newspaper, along with a good part of the city government, and it used that power to stall approvals. Diamond countered by siting its plant just outside the city limits. It brought in, or hired locally, hundreds of employees, including a new crop of executives that brought wives and children. Sixteen years later, Lancaster gained another significant employer when General Mills opened a plant near Diamond Power to make snacks like Bugles and Whistles.

At first, all the new hires bumped up against Lancaster's clannishness. Even Nancy felt the chill of a cold shoulder, but she shrugged it off. She immersed herself in St. John's and made new friends there. She got to know some of the other "Anchor wives." Then, a member of an old Lancaster family stepped up to invite some of the newcomers to a tea—a mixer, really, for the new and the established. From then on, Lancaster became home. She embraced it, and felt embraced in return.

After a year or so, the Georges moved into another rental, by the fair-grounds. Herb's career advanced, and children arrived. They bought a house, then another one in an even nicer neighborhood, near "Pill Hill," where a lot of the doctors—more of them had come to town, too—had moved into modern homes close to the city's hospital.

Through it all, Nancy threw herself into civic life. She was invited to join Twig 1 (of several Twigs), a women's group with a mission to raise funds for the hospital. She volunteered as a "gray lady" in the hospital, working in a gray uniform at the reception desk, distributing newspapers to rooms, selling snacks.

She campaigned for school levies. When Nancy came to town, there were four main elementary schools, dating from the 1920s and 1930s and prosaically named West, North, East, and South. They were the result of a series of levies and bond issues passed by a previous generation. In 1938, despite the Great Depression and the possibility of a new world war, Lancaster's voters passed a $268,000 school bond issue by 80 percent. Now, with more children and new neighborhoods, the city needed new grade schools. "And within not many years, we built all these new schools," Nancy recalled. "We passed one bond levy after another, and we all didn't have a lot of money, either, but we voted for them."

She was a Cub Scout leader and a Girl Scout leader. In 1962, seven women formed the Fairfield Heritage Association to begin preserving Lancaster's old buildings. Nancy joined. "We all worked on the Heritage," Nancy said. The Sherman House, the Georgian, and other old buildings were rejuvenated. The association held a tour every year that attracted people from all around Ohio.

Nancy was not unique. She was one of scores of young women—the "Anchor wives," but also the wives of men who worked at Diamond Power or Lancaster Glass (the renamed Lancaster Lens), doctors' wives, lawyers' wives—who poured effort into bettering the town.

"We were busy girls. Our husbands were gone all the time, so we didn't have to have a big, fancy dinner every night. We had dinner, but the kids wanted applesauce and fish sticks or hamburgers, you know. So you just kept dinner warm in the oven, and the kids rode their bikes to [sports] practice; you didn't take them. So there was time to be a mom, because there wasn't as much expected, or we didn't expect as much—I don't know which."

When the polio vaccine came out, the women ran inoculation drives. They agitated for improved sidewalks. They formed Parent League, an organization that attempted (and largely failed) to civilize children by teaching them how to play bridge and dance a waltz. The wives made Lancaster work.

Nancy enjoyed this life. She didn't feel the nagging disquiet or disappointment described in 1963 by Betty Friedan in *The Feminine Mystique*. She was using her talents every day to build a community.

"I was happy with what I was doing," she told me. "I loved being a mom.

I didn't mind keeping house and doing all the other things. And we did a lot of fun things."

Parents left children with babysitters to attend house parties. They'd go out to dinner at the one good restaurant in town, Shaw's, a steakhouse. Or they gathered at the country club. Far from the image of a country club in, say, Greenwich, Connecticut, the Lancaster Country Club was pretty middle-class, and not restricted to WASPs. (Jews joined, but there were no African American members, a reflection, perhaps, of both unspoken policy and the fact that there were so few blacks in Lancaster.) You could join for $500 and small monthly dues. Many did: The country club soon developed a long waiting list for entry. The Georges joined in 1960.

"We'd be out at the [country club] pool and I'd say, 'Well, I've got all these hot dogs and stuff; why don't you come over?' And the other mothers would bring chips and baked beans and whatever they had, and we'd have an impromptu party with all the kids on a Sunday night. You," Nancy said, looking at me, "were probably one of them." (I was. I spent more than one sleepover at Kevin George's house not sleeping in his backyard.)

If you weren't part of the country club set, or even if you were, you'd go over to Old Bill Bailey's—Benny Smith's place on the west side—a couple of blocks from Plant 1, where Smith banged away on an out-of-tune upright piano and Anchor Hocking vice presidents and factory workers sang equally out of tune between gulps of Pabst Blue Ribbon or Stroh's. If you weren't at Old Bill Bailey's, it was Charlie's (later Leo's Bier Haus) or the Fairview or the Pink Cricket or one of the lodges: the Elks, the Moose, the Eagles, the Knights of Columbus, the Veterans of Foreign Wars.

When school was out, children went feral. Parents often had no idea exactly where their offspring were for hours at a time. Nobody worried unless a kid failed to show up for dinner.

When America passed through its tiki bar phase, a developer built Tiki Lanes off of Sheridan Drive, a South Seas–themed bowling alley decorated with palm trees and coconuts. The owner of Tiki Lanes built the biggest swimming pool in town, even bigger than old Miller Pool, in Miller Park on the west side. An Olympic-size job, it was next door to the bowling alley. You could spend the day there for fifty cents. On sunny summer days, the pools were packed with adolescents, their ears filled with AM radio, their loins filled with longing. On the Fourth of July, you'd climb Mount Pleasant to *ooh* and *aah* at the fireworks shot into the sky from the fairgrounds below. In the winter, if you were a kid, you'd ice-skate on Rising Park's ponds, then warm yourself by the big log fire, your stomach filled with hot chocolate, your loins still filled with longing.

Almost every child attended the public schools or the tiny Catholic ones and still made friends across the wage spectrum, just as they had in 1947. They played pickup baseball games in parks, shot hoops on garage courts, swam on swim teams, played school sports.

Kids could stroll into Beiter and Flege Drug Store, in the middle of downtown, order a cherry Coke at the lunch counter, grab a pack of gum, and ask Mr. Flege to put the charges on their parents' accounts.

All this, too, had become part of the Lancaster story, and Lancaster clung to this chapter with even greater ferocity than it had to Sherman. Brian Gossett heard it the whole time he was growing up. His mother, Melinda, was one of those teens who roasted and flirted on hot days at the Tiki pool. His father, Greg, grew up working-class but played and partied with friends like Bruce Barber, whose father, George, became CEO of Anchor Hocking in 1977.

This was Lancaster's version of the American Promise, the ideal of today's powerful nostalgia. Residents believed their town was the way America was supposed to be, the fulfillment of two hundred years of American struggle and progress, as embodied in Weber barbecue grills, Sea & Ski suntan lotion, good schools and a hospital, and children on Sting-Ray bikes in a friendly, civic-minded community of right-thinking people who were either moderate union Democrats or moderate business Republicans.

People worked hard, but most believed they'd made a fair deal. You could walk off the high school graduation stage on Saturday and walk into a plant on Monday, where you could stay for the next forty years. The company would make you a mechanic, a millwright, an electrician, a machine operator, a mold maker, a salesman. You'd do bone-wearying work, but there were the perks, too, like the company softball, baseball, golf, and bowling teams; the company choir and drama clubs; the insurance and pension.

You'd never get rich, and you'd bitch about management and fat cats, but you could buy a little house on the west side, then maybe over on the east side or out in the country, and maybe a boat to fish from on Buckeye Lake. You could get married. You could pay for your kids to attend decent state universities. Best of all, you could stay in the town where your kid's fourth-grade teacher had taught you, too. If you bought in, obeyed the rules—spoken and unspoken—paid your taxes, loved your town and your country, that was the bargain on offer.

A lot of people made it. A 1982 Anchor Hocking employee newsletter noted retirements: Carlos Wolfe, furnace-room operator, forty-five years; Francis Danner, machine attendant, forty years; Roy Gwin, burn-off operator, forty-one years; Helen Savage, selector, forty-two years. Similar listings were published in 1972, 1962, 1952.

Lancaster wasn't paradise. It had vices and scandals like any other small town. People drank hard—all those taverns weren't there for nothing. Though it wasn't talked about much, alcohol sometimes led to family abuse, dissolution, poverty.

Even after Diamond Power came to town, many workers were still paid less than they could make elsewhere. *Forbes* noted the low pay back in 1947 before dismissing the wages as a problem by mentioning the low cost of living in Lancaster.

For generations people called Lancaster "the whitest town in America." That title may have been quite dubious, but people believed it, and many hoped it was true. Despite its pride in Sherman and the Union cause, Lancaster was streaked with Copperheads during the Civil War. The sentiment never disappeared: the segregationist George Wallace attracted 1,574 votes in the 1968 presidential election.

Lancaster did have a few African Americans living within its borders, but from the time the first black person arrived, they were treated as barely tolerated guests. In the 1920s, Lancaster fell into the grip of a resurgent Ku Klux Klan preaching its nativist, racist philosophy. The mayor and sheriff were both Klan members, and the city gave Klan ideas the force of law. The few black children attended the public schools, but they were permitted to swim in the Miller Park pool only on Fridays. Every Friday evening, the parks department drained the pool, then refilled it so whites would have "pure" water on Saturday.

Cross burnings were routine. They occurred even when Malcolm Forbes lived there in 1941—sometimes on the top of Mount Pleasant, where the flames could be seen all over town.

The handful of black Lancastrians understood their place. Most worked as domestics or laborers and didn't try to take jobs normally filled by whites. So, with available jobs scarce, the resident blacks screened newcomers. If a black man wanted to move to Lancaster but didn't have a job, he was told to move on. Whites told themselves (and some still do to this day) that blacks policed themselves in this way because they had good lives in Lancaster.

The Klan, fearing papist conspiracies, expended much of its energy harassing Catholics and anybody who served Catholic customers. When a young dentist named Hubert Eyman came to town to open a practice, he moved into an office in what later became the Anchor Hocking headquarters. The two men who occupied the offices on either side of Eyman were Klan members. One, Eyman later recalled, "was the main Gazebo or something" of the local chapter.

"Every time I stopped in the hall, they jumped me to join. I kept refusing, and finally they said, 'We'll fix you. We've got a blacklist. Believe it or not, we can get you on the Catholic blacklist.' I said, 'Well, you are going to have to do it, because I am not going to join.' Well, apparently they did, because I had a few lean months. Then the truth came out, and I had quite an influx of Catholic patients. I still had some of them when I quit sixty years later."

Lancaster could also be stifling, staid, and conformist in its sameness. It was no place to be different. Teenagers constantly whined that it was boring.

Even with its flaws, though, the Lancaster of *Forbes*, of Nancy, of Brian Gossett's parents, really was about as close to the clichéd image of the all-American town as you could get, outside of a Hollywood movie set. In fact, it *was* a Hollywood movie set when the 1948 film *Green Grass of Wyoming* came to town to shoot harness-racing scenes at the fairgrounds. But contrary to how the *Forbes* story had it, industrialists didn't create the community out of wise benevolence. In its zeal to defend the "American Way" against the New Deal, *Forbes* had ignored the fact that the

Lancaster it celebrated had been difficult to build. It was the product of battles—real and metaphorical ones—and no small amount of intervention from the federal government, from the very New Deal B. C. Forbes hated.

n 1903, a young glassworker named Isaac J. (I. J., or Ike) Collins left his job at the Phoenix Glass Company, in Monaca, to take a new position as an assistant superintendent in the decorating department of the Ohio Flint Glass Company. He rented a room in a Lancaster boardinghouse called the Kreider.

Born in Maryland in 1874, Collins appears to have dropped out of school around the eighth grade. He worked locally in Maryland before moving to Pittsburgh, where he became a barber.

At the time Collins would have been living in Pittsburgh, Andrew Carnegie was consolidating his control of America's steel industry. In 1892, goons from the Pinkerton National Detective Agency fought a pitched gun battle with striking union steelworkers at Carnegie's Homestead Steel Works, about six miles upriver from the city. Twelve people, Pinkertons and strikers alike, were killed. The Pinkertons retreated, but the victory proved Pyrrhic for the workers. Pennsylvania governor Robert Pattison sent the state militia to take over the works. Carnegie's company then brought in strikebreakers and crushed the union.

One of I. J. Collins's customers was a Pinkerton strikebreaker named Edward Good. The two became friendly.

Good later headed another Pittsburgh detective agency and became prominent in local politics. Drafts of a history written for Anchor Hocking's fiftieth anniversary state that Collins worked as a Good public relations man, but this may have been an attempt to give Collins a business background he didn't possess: In 1894 Collins went to work in the factory at the Phoenix Glass Company.

The glass business was booming at the start of the twentieth century, but it was also ruthlessly competitive, tenuous, even dangerous. Small companies popped up, served a local area for a few years, pocketed the profits, and shut down. Workers moved on. Some factories burned down. Others fell into receivership. By late 1905, it looked as though Ohio Flint, too, was beginning to fail.

Meanwhile, the Dickey-Sutton Carbon Company, which made the carbon rods used in early electric lights, was becoming enmeshed in Teddy Roosevelt's trust-busting movement. Its Lancaster plant, called the Black Cat because so much carbon dust clung to its exterior, had fallen under the control of a trust engineered by the National Carbon Company of Cleveland. National, in turn, was accused of price fixing through its control of the U.S. market. Caught in the fallout, the Black Cat closed. The dark hulk sat empty on the west side.

As Ohio Flint's prospects dimmed, Collins viewed the Black Cat as an opportunity. In late 1905, he and a group of partners that included Fred von Stein—Collins's immediate boss in the Ohio Flint decorating department and subsequently the mayor of Lancaster at the time of the 1947 *Forbes* issue—pooled their money and bought the Black Cat for about $8,000. They incorporated the Hocking Glass Company with about $30,000 worth of stock. The balance came from Edward Good.

Collins and about a dozen employees melted the first glass in February 1906, inside a "day tank," a glass furnace that was used only during the day. "The Hockin'," as the company soon became known, made a profit in the first year, even as Ohio Flint Glass folded.

Collins approached Ohio Flint's treasurer and receiver, a young man named Thomas Fulton, to negotiate the sale of some of the defunct company's equipment, including a continuous tank. Fulton squeezed dimes out of Collins, who, figuring he could use a tough negotiator like Fulton, asked him to invest in the Hockin' and join the company. When Fulton successfully tapped a relative for $5,000, he became one-quarter owner as well as secretary and treasurer. Collins owned another quarter; Good owned half.

After World War I, Collins hired a young military engineer named William Fisher, a native of Wapakoneta, Ohio, to help run the plant and design machines and processes. Collins, Fulton, and Fisher formed a ruling triumvirate.

The glass business was a rough trade. That was true no matter where, but the Hockin' earned a reputation as an especially tough place to work. Though the company made a profit every year, Collins was a stingy paymaster. The men worked twelve-hour shifts. If they fainted, their coworkers dragged them outside to lie under the shade of a tree. Fresh air was

scarce inside the Black Cat. In the winter, anywhere other than the furnace room could be so cold that workers wore three or four layers of
clothing. All through the year they wore extra layers in the hot end to protect themselves from the flames and heat.

Ellsworth Boyer, employee number 87, "went in" in the early 1920s. (In
the same way coal miners talk of going into a mine, company workers still
say "went in" when they talk about starting their glassmaking jobs.) Boyer
started at 27.5 cents per hour, grinding stoppers for perfume bottles. Then
he sandblasted streetlight globes—until one of Collins's first employees,
John Behrens, approached him.

"He come out and said, 'You wanna work in the furnace room?' I said
I did, because furnace-room men made more money. It was a real hot day,
and I didn't know whether I could stand it or not, but, God willing, I stood
it right on through forty-three years."

W. Robert Taylor quit school and started working at the Hockin' in the
spring of 1924. He worked five nine-hour days and one half-day every week.
He once worked three days and nights with no sleep: "We just kept a-goin'."

Alice McAnespie's brother, Charles, worked at the Hockin' for decades.
She remembered an especially hot summer watching as "that ambulance
passed that door so many times, hauling them to the hospital. They just
dropped in their tracks."

Ollie Smith was hired on in the early 1930s, mainly because he was a
good baseball player. By then the Hocking Glass Company fielded a team
in an industrial league.

"Leon Miesse, my captain in [World War I], was head mechanic over
the repair shop there. I was working for him. I was out there about five or
six weeks, I guess, and I said, 'Cap,' I said, 'thirty cents an hour is not very
much money.' He said, 'Well, what would you get if you wasn't working,
Ollie?' I said, 'I wouldn't get anything.' He said, 'Thirty cents an hour's
pretty good wages.' Well, anyhow, Miesse said, 'Mr. Fisher's up there in
the plant someplace. He'll come down in a little bit.' I said okay. I come
down in the tool shop to get something to work with upstairs in the press
room, and so, just as I was going in the door, [Fisher] was comin' out, and
he says, 'Well, Ollie, when did you start to work here?' I says, 'Four or five
weeks ago.' He says, 'Oh, I'm so glad, and you're going to play ball with
us.' I says, 'Yes, I hope so, Mr. Fisher.' I said, 'By the way, I'm only getting

thirty cents an hour here. Could you see if I could get me more money?'
He said, 'Well, Ollie,' and he began to jerk at the lapels on his coat, and at
the bottom of his coat. And just there, Johnny Noice come along, and he
says, 'How do, Mr. Fisher?' 'Hi, Johnny.' 'Hi, Ollie.' 'Hi, John.' And when
he got by, Mr. Fisher says, 'Now, there's Johnny Noice. Now, he's been with
this company when it was down there along the railroad on Maple Street
under Mr. Collins.' He says, 'He's only makin' thirty-five cents an hour. I
said, 'What?' He says, 'That's all he gets is thirty-five cents an hour.' I says,
'Well, by that, then, old Smith's doomed; he won't get no more money.' He
says, 'No, I don't think you will, Ollie.' "

In 1918, the average manufacturing wage in the United States was fifty-
three cents per hour. By 1935 it was fifty-eight cents per hour.

Working conditions were safer at the Godman Shoe factories, but
the pay was low there, too. Employees, many of them women, worked from
6:30 a.m. to 5:30 p.m., Monday through Friday, as well as every Saturday
morning. Around 1918, an edge trimmer made about five or six cents per
dozen pairs.

Industrialists could get away with the low pay and lousy conditions
because the manual labor force in and around Lancaster had already been
leading hard lives. Many were from subsistence-farming families. Others
had been draymen, brickmakers, coal miners. They had little education.
They were poor.

Unions formed to protect workers like the ones in Lancaster. *Forbes*
traced unionism in the glass plants to the 1930s, but the American Flint
Glass Workers' Union (the "Flints") was in Lancaster as early as 1904, at the
Lancaster Glass Company plant, on the east side of town on Ewing Street,
by some railroad tracks.

Contrary to *Forbes* magazine's comforting assurance that Lancaster was
an island free of leftists, the early Flints were militantly socialist. As a Lancaster Flint wrote in the national union's magazine, "The question in my
mind is 'What must be done?' Has it come to a time when labor cannot
protect itself in a peaceable manner? Has it come to a time when the government will stand and see the capitalist of this country drive little children
into starvation in order to force the fathers to work for a wage which they
cannot exist under? I say 'Yes.' "

The Flints were inside the Hocking Glass Company within a year of its founding, but the union had little power. Collins could do most any-thing he wanted—and he did. When a dispute arose in 1911, Collins hired scab labor from out of town. The Hocking's abrasive relationship with the union was a topic of regular discussion at national conventions. Flints even coined a phrase for Hocking's reputation as a hard place to work. When a union brother would leave for some other company, they'd say he'd been "scratched by the Black Cat."

With the passage in 1933 of FDR's National Industrial Recovery Act, labor in Lancaster, as well as across the nation, seized its opportunity. The NRA's Section 7(a) forced company owners to recognize a right to join in-dependent unions, to bargain collectively, to receive a minimum wage. So many union locals organized that, by 1934, the *Lancaster Gazette* felt the need to print this advisory: "Due to the many unions being formed, and the frequency of meetings, it is impossible for the newspaper to send a re-porter to these meetings." Union leaders joined in a Central Labor Body to work collectively across industries. Collins still hated unions. But, forced by the new national law, Fisher met with Central Labor Body leaders work-ing on behalf of Hocking employees. Relations between union and man-agement improved.

Godman Shoe took the opposite approach. Godman's Lancaster chief, William Miller, the man who donated Miller Park and Miller Pool to the city, refused to yield.

The union struck, and struck again. During the unrest, a Godman supervisor was shot. A truck driver was roughed up. Six Lancaster shoe workers went to state prison for the assault. In 1937, frustrated and facing financial setbacks, Godman sold its factories to the Irving Drew Shoe Com-pany, which had moved from Portsmouth, Ohio, after that city suffered Ohio River floods.

The Supreme Court overturned the NRA in 1935, but that same year, Congress passed the National Labor Relations Act, better known as the Wagner Act. The law expanded upon the labor provisions of the NRA. Though still low by national standards, wages in Lancaster rose and work-ing conditions improved. Main Street stores *Forbes* had profiled were supported by those factory workers' wages. Fiery calls for socialist revolts ceased. The industries kept growing and kept making profits.

The same year Godman cashed out, the Hocking Glass Company

merged with a New York outfit called Anchor Cap and Closure, a container-making company. By 1946, the year before the *Forbes* issue, Anchor Hocking reported consolidated net sales of $64,399,742 ($837 million in 2016 dollars). The company had its own natural gas supply division, Gas Transport, Inc. It sponsored one of the nation's most popular radio shows, *Casey, Crime Photographer*, on CBS, and in 1950 invented late-night television with *Broadway Open House,* an NBC show hosted by Morey Amsterdam.

It had plants across the country, eventually including the old Phoenix Glass in Monaca, where I. J. Collins started in the glass business. Its container division supplied beer bottles, liquor bottles, peanut butter jars, baby food jars, coffee jars. The company's Jade-ite and Fire-King brands competed with Pyrex baking dishes. When you filled up at a Texaco station or opened a new bank account, you got a free tumbler made by Anchor Hocking—showing the company's little anchor at its bottom. Your electric meter was covered by an Anchor Hocking glass dome. Millions ate off of Anchor Hocking dishes and stubbed out their after-dinner cigarettes in Anchor Hocking ashtrays. "Li'l ol' Lancaster" was a national player.

Over the following decades, company and town developed a deep symbiosis. With the exception of the scattered plant managers and some sales chiefs, every executive resided in Lancaster—Collins and Fisher lived on Mulberry Hill, right in town. Especially in the case of Anchor Hocking, the people of Lancaster came to see themselves as owners as much as any big shareholder was.

On the night of March 6, 1924, the Black Cat was destroyed by fire. (One man, Merrill Deaver, was killed. A hundred robed and hooded Klansmen presided at his graveside funeral.) There was doubt that the Hockin' would ever reopen—the plant was insured, but the loss wasn't entirely covered. So the chamber of commerce offered free land and buildings and Lancaster residents dug into their own pockets to help raise funds—as if the Hocking were a charity and not a private company.

When it merged with Anchor Cap and Closure and went public, new board members felt the combined company should be headquartered in New York rather than in a small Ohio town. Collins, Fisher, and Fulton resisted. They loved Lancaster, too (and enjoyed their control there). The board reluctantly agreed to stay in Lancaster on the condition that the town build a hotel for visiting businessmen. So, in 1938, local townsmen, including Collins, created the Community Hotel Company of Lancaster. They sold stock at $100 per share. In fifteen days—in the midst of the Great Depression—the people of Lancaster raised $227,000. When the Hotel Lancaster opened in 1940, it was considered the best hotel of its size in the Midwest.

Heeding the campaign slogan "Good Will for the Ill," Lancaster voted in 1914 to tax itself so it could build a public hospital. But by midcentury a new facility was badly needed to serve Lancaster's growing population: New doctors were refusing to hang their shingles in town. One young doctor, Gordon Snider, turned to an Anchor Hocking executive named Roger Hetzel.

"He was very community-minded," Snider told me, "so I said, 'You know, you, Anchor, if you're going to recruit anybody, you're going to need good schools, you're gonna need a good hospital." In 1970, Hetzel and Snider organized a meeting in the hotel's Jadite Room. Anchor executives, a couple of doctors, and Boo Miller, a prominent local attorney who'd long represented Anchor Hocking, agreed to mount a bond-issue campaign with Anchor Hocking's full support. The bond issue passed, and the hospital was rebuilt.

In the 1970s, when the company was hit by a national shortage of cullet—scrap glass that is critical to making new ware—Anchor Hocking put out a call. Families loaded their cars with every bottle, jar, and tumbler they could spare. Lines of cars stretched across Pierce Avenue at Plant 1, and down Ewing Street at Plant 2.

When the Flints struck—and there were a couple of angry strikes—Lancaster rooted for both sides at once. Residents knew what working in a glass plant could be like, because they'd done it, or their fathers, mothers, or children had. On the other hand, they knew how important Anchor, Anchor executives, and Anchor wives were to the life of the town.

Anchor's leaders—and the leaders of Lancaster's other industries, too—usually reciprocated the devotion. They gave land or money or both to charities and civic organizations.

When William Fisher died in 1970, his widow gave $400,000 to build a new Catholic high school. I graduated from William V. Fisher Catholic. Today, the Lancaster High School football team plays on Fulton Field.

Some concluded that Collins was a hard man—true—and that Lancaster hadn't gotten into his bones the way it had so many others. He had interests elsewhere. He owned race horses and spent much of his later years in Florida, where he was a regular at the tracks.

But still, he never really left. Even as a very old man, Collins liked to sit at a back table of the country club bar, where he was a somewhat imposing presence. (I met him there. When I was introduced, he shook my hand and said, "Hello, young man." I was about eight years old.) He did give some land to the community, though the donation wasn't publicized. Once, as he was being driven down 33, he looked out the car window at the passing farmland and sighed, "It sure is fair fields." The skinflint reputation persisted, though, stoked by a well-known Lancaster tale: Not long before his death, in 1975, just before turning 101, his Lancaster attorney pointed out to Collins that, unlike other top executives around town, he'd left no provision for the city in his will. Collins brushed off the suggestion. "I gave them all those jobs," he countered.

THREE

Triggering Events

July 1987

N obody imagined it would end. In the 1970s, Lancaster watched steel mills in Youngstown, the NCR (National Cash Register) Corporation in Dayton, and the GM plant in Lordstown lay off thousands. But just as *Forbes* predicted, the furnaces continued to blaze at Anchor Hocking and Lancaster Glass. Stuck made molds. Drew made shoes. Diamond Power made soot blowers, and Ralston made snacks.

Collins semi-retired in the late 1950s. Fisher more or less ran the company—the Anchor Hocking board was notoriously weak—but soon decided to bring in an outsider, John Gushman, a Toledo lawyer who'd long worked for glass clients; he'd been involved in the 1937 merger between the Hocking and Anchor Cap. Under Gushman, Anchor Hocking kept growing. Profits rose. The company expanded to include more than forty plants, distribution centers, office locations, and research and engineering labs.

For all its impressive size, the company was managed like a giant family enterprise, not with the new scientific, business school techniques that had come into vogue. Gushman did turn Anchor into a modern corporation, but without "a killer atmosphere," said Peter Roane, a longtime container division official. "It sounds trite, but it was one big family. I didn't like all of them, and not all of them liked me, but there was no corporate brutality. We fired some people, but usually people could find their level of competence in Lancaster."

The family ethos sometimes went deep. When Herb and Nancy George faced marital trouble that led to a divorce, Herb's boss called Nancy and asked if she'd like him to transfer Herb out of town.

When corporate decisions were made, spouses felt free to opine. In 1978, a man named J. Ray Topper was promoted to president. Topper was not a glassman, nor was he a Lancaster man. Cursed with the hypercompetitiveness of the insecure, he soon gained a reputation around town as a man who would cheat at cards or kick his ball out of the rough on the golf course—venial sins in most places, but not in Lancaster, where people could tell you what John Gushman ate for breakfast. Still, Topper was promoted—first to vice president in charge of the tableware division, then to company president. Days after that promotion, Jim Miller—the son of Boo and also an attorney—and his wife, Sarah, celebrated their twenty-fifth wedding anniversary by hosting a party in their backyard. The wife of another executive cornered George Barber, who was CEO at the time. "Eve Burns pushed that George Barber up against the fence, and she said, 'You'll bring this company down! You are making wrong choices!'" Miller told me. "Boy, she was tough."

But while life went on within Lancaster and Anchor Hocking, American business and finance changed. Big-box stores like Walmart, with their intense pressure on suppliers to reduce wholesale prices, nibbled away at Anchor's margins. When Sam Walton realized that Anchor shipped its ware in its own fleet of Anchor Hocking trucks, from its own Anchor Hocking distribution center, thus saving freight costs, he demanded those savings be passed on to Walmart, rather than to Anchor's bottom line.

Cheap gasoline evaporated into Saudi riyals and Venezuelan bolívars. Customers waited in lines to buy gas; stations no longer had to entice them to the pumps with a free tumbler. Brewers and food producers poured more of their product into cans, and soda companies turned to plastic for their bottles.

Anchor Hocking had long been a large exporter of glass. From Africa to Germany to Brazil, tables were set with Anchor ware. But by 1980, imports were beginning to attack Anchor Hocking at home. The French company Durand Glass (now part of Arc International) and smaller outfits in Poland and Turkey were sending cheap glass into the United States.

Anchor had also developed middle-aged corporate spread. Managers had become infamous for boozy hotel bar lunches that could stretch to dinnertime. Whereas executives had previously held meetings and retreats at the hotel, or at the lowly Holiday Inn just north of town on Route 33, they now started taking a corporate jet to Florida.

A big blow was self-inflicted by Topper. When he took over the tableware division, salesmen were paid on commission. The most productive made six-figure incomes that approached, and sometimes might have exceeded, Topper's own. Personally galled, Topper approved a decision to turn the sales force into salaried employees—effectively mandating a severe pay cut. Many of the best left the company.

Anchor Hocking was slow to respond to these challenges, but eventually it did. In 1975, in an effort to improve margins in the container division, Gushman hired Boston Consulting to map out a strategy to help Anchor compete against container giant Owens-Illinois. One of the consultants was a freshly minted Harvard M.B.A. named Mitt Romney.

"It was probably my first project," Romney told me. "The overall objective of the study, as I recall, was to say, 'What can the company do to be more successful, to grow sales, to be profitable?' I think people recognized that the industry was seeing decline in demand, number one; and number two, Owens-Illinois was such a strong, if not dominant, player. The question was: How does a smaller company like Anchor Hocking compete successfully and survive and thrive?"

There's an old saying about consultants: They're like seagulls. They fly in from the coast, shit on your company, and fly back. The smart boys from Harvard were not welcomed. On a tour of Plant 1, Romney was hazed when his guides paused the walk-through just as they stood between two furnaces.

"Now, we're maybe four or five feet from a furnace on each side," Romney recalled. "It's got to be well over 120, maybe 150 degrees where we're standing. I was thinking to myself that they were saying, 'Okay, which of us is going to blink first?' They were used to the heat, and, of course, we didn't want to act like we were total newbies, so we stood there, acted innocent, asked questions about the process. We stood between these two furnaces for what seemed quite a long time, as the perspiration was beading down our foreheads and down our shirts." The point was made. This was the life the workers led, and they did it willingly. But they didn't appreciate tassel-loafered Ivy Leaguers teaching them about the glass business.

Change was grudging, but the company adopted at least part of Boston Consulting's plan for the container division. Anchor sold a bottle plant in Northern California and installed new, more efficient machines in other plants.

Anchor also innovated. It had its own research, design, and engineering facility on the western edge of town near the distribution center, and engineers there were put to work developing new mold materials and glass formulations. The company raced Durand to engineer new machines with more mold stations so more ware could be made in the same amount of time, lowering the per-unit cost. A new generation of promotional outlets replaced gas stations: In 1980, sixteen million Anchor-made commemorative *Empire Strikes Back* glasses were distributed through Burger King franchises.

The company gained market share, thanks to the demise of smaller companies like Jeannette Glass, in Jeannette, Pennsylvania, Federal Glass, in Columbus, and the Brockway Glass Company's tableware factory in Clarksburg, West Virginia, which closed in 1979.

These were tactics Anchor Hocking understood: Make better products, make them more cheaply, and sell more of them. In 1981, sales rose 11 percent for the year, to $953 million (about $2.5 billion in 2016 dollars). Margins and net profit continued to fall, but the company had low debt—and no short-term debt—and was able to raise its stock dividend to shareholders. (It had paid dividends for sixty-eight years without interruption.) The company employed over seventeen thousand people, about five thousand of whom were in Lancaster. It had the financial firepower to invest in the face of a changing market.

But in the dawning world of 1980s finance, none of that mattered. "They would have turned it around," said Ben Martin, former head of the company's international division. "But with Carl Icahn trying to buy them—well, they didn't. You couldn't talk about that then, but we would have been . . ." Martin paused and looked at a catalog of Anchor ware he held in his lap. "We would have made it."

n the spring of 1982, a sharp-eyed employee in the company's finance department noticed that Anchor Hocking stock—long a boring widows-and-orphans investment—was unusually active. She reported her observation. When officials investigated, they found that Icahn Capital Corporation was buying up Anchor shares.

Nobody had to tell them what that meant. Armed with borrowed money and marching under the flag of reform, Carl Icahn had recently begun his assault on corporate America. He argued that corporations had become too flabby, too clubby, too inefficient. The free market demanded profit for shareholders, but management was not making all the profit it could. Icahn would buy up enough shares to demand one or more seats on the board from which, he claimed, he could agitate for change. He was doing it all for America—and for fellow shareholders. Naturally, corporate leaders wished Icahn would go away, and he sometimes did, for handsome payoffs that came to be known as "greenmail."

Icahn didn't specialize in any industry. He went after Chicago's great department store, Marshall Field's. He attacked a textile company and a can company, and now he was onto Anchor Hocking. By late summer he owned 6.1 percent of Anchor's shares. (He bought Owens-Illinois shares at around the same time, as part of an attack on the glass container business.) Anchor Hocking was one of the first victims of what became a wave of corporate raiding.

Ray Topper had been elevated to the CEO slot just a few weeks before Icahn began buying shares. He was precisely the wrong man in the wrong place at the wrong time: George Barber would later say his endorsement of Topper was the worst mistake of his life.

Topper called Icahn and asked for a meeting. Topper and several other company officers met with him in the boardroom in Lancaster. Icahn criticized the container division as inefficient and demanded a board seat. Instead, Anchor offered to buy him off.

On August 17, 1982, Anchor repurchased Icahn's shares at a premium of $3.75 per share—about $3 million of profit for Icahn. "It was like taking candy from a baby," Icahn's deal analyst Alfred Kingsley told author Mark Stevens for his biography *King Icahn*.

Icahn's raid passed quickly—and $3 million wasn't going to bankrupt the company—but the episode ultimately changed Lancaster forever by inducing panic at Anchor headquarters and by putting Anchor Hocking "in play" by turning the old-time manufacturer to chum in shark-infested financial waters.

I n 1962, distinguished University of Chicago economist Milton Friedman published the book *Capitalism and Freedom*. It was reviewed in economics journals—but almost nowhere else. Friedman himself acknowledged that the views he expressed in it were, at the time, far removed from the mainstream.

President Franklin Roosevelt, father of the New Deal, had died in office only seventeen years before, and John F. Kennedy, an heir to Roosevelt's political legacy, now occupied the office. Both had won their elections against small-government conservatives; Friedman was a small-government conservative. But despite the slow gains among lay readers, Friedman's book ended up as a founding document of what became the resurgent conservative philosophy that finally flowered in the 1980 election of Ronald Reagan.

Had he lived long enough, B. C. Forbes would have endorsed Friedman's philosophy. As a young government economist in the 1930s Friedman endorsed some parts of the New Deal. But by 1962 he viewed it as a disaster because, he believed, it substituted government for individual self-interest. He preached an almost absolute faith in the wisdom, rationality, and rectitude of business, and a trust in the unfettered market to automatically improve the welfare of all. The free market—and Friedman, quoting British legal scholar A.V. Dicey, explicitly favored "a presumption or prejudice in favor of individual liberty, that is, laissez-faire"—was responsible for nearly all the progress the United States had made since the Great Depression. Yes, Americans were better fed, housed, clothed, transported, and educated. Class distinctions had narrowed. Minority groups were less oppressed. But all this, Friedman claimed, had occurred in spite of, not because of, labor unions, minimum wages, civil rights laws, or any government-imposed reforms. "We have been able to afford and surmount these [government] measures only because of the extraordinary fecundity of the market. The invisible hand has been more potent for progress than the invisible hand for retrogression."

Friedman wasn't just writing about economic well-being. He linked threats to the free market with existential threats to America itself. New Deal–like government interference in the market was of a piece with Soviet nuclear missiles. The implication was clear: To oppose his strain of thinking wasn't just wrongheaded, it was unpatriotic.

Friedman framed some of his theories in less academic language for an influential *New York Times Magazine* article published in September 1970. He laid down a "Friedman doctrine," arguing that business had only one social responsibility: delivering profits to shareholders. Businessmen who concerned themselves with "employment, eliminating discrimination, avoiding pollution and whatever else may be the catchwords of the contemporary crop of reformers" were "preaching pure and unadulterated socialism."

"Businessmen who talk this way," Friedman wrote, "are unwitting puppets of the intellectual forces that have been undermining the basis of a free society these past decades."

In a fit of willful blindness to America's own industrial and social histories—as if he had never read Ida Tarbell's *The History of the Standard Oil Company*, which exposed John D. Rockefeller's oil trust, or Upton Sinclair's *The Jungle*, the harrowing novel about the American meatpacking industry that led to the passage of the Pure Food and Drug Act—Friedman believed that a market free of government regulation "forces people to be responsible for their own actions and makes it difficult for them to 'exploit' other people for either selfish or unselfish purposes. They can do good— but only at their own expense."

Friedman would have disdained Lancaster's symbiotic relationship with its businesses. "It may well be in the long-run interest of a corporation that is a major employer in a small community to devote resources to providing amenities to that community or to improving its government. That may make it easier to attract desirable employees, it may reduce the wage bill or lessen losses from pilferage and sabotage or have other worthwhile effects."

But such motives made social responsibility mere "hypocritical window dressing." "I can express admiration for those individual proprietors or owners of closely held corporations or stockholders of more broadly held corporations who disdain such tactics as approaching fraud."

The Friedman doctrine told every executive, financier, and shareholder not only that it was okay to make a profit, but that making as much profit as possible, without regard to some broader social responsibility, was a duty. The regulators, the unions, the environmentalists—people many executives already loathed—weren't just thorns in the side of a company. They were un-American.

Milton Friedman was awarded the Nobel Prize in economics in 1976, for his studies of money supply theory and consumption (not business and social responsibility). Four years later, he became an economic adviser to then–presidential candidate Ronald Reagan. After Reagan's successful 1980 campaign, Friedman served as the most prominent member of the new president's Economic Policy Advisory Board. Eighteen years after *Capitalism and Freedom* was first published, the once-fringe Friedman doctrine had found its place at the center of government power.

A year after Icahn's run at Anchor, William Baxter, the man leading the antitrust division inside the Reagan administration's Department of Justice, threw the government's support behind tactics like Icahn's. There was no need for more regulation, he told a panel convened by the Securities and Exchange Commission. In the new Friedman universe, takeovers were "a very socially beneficial mechanism" for assuring that corporate assets would serve the highest value. Employment, community cohesion, and the general welfare of the country did not seem to figure into Baxter's calculation. Carl Icahn addressed the panel on the same day as Baxter. He agreed that no regulation was good regulation.

At the time of Icahn's raid on Anchor, Vincent Naimoli ran the container division. Naimoli was a Topper hire. He wasn't a glassman, either; he'd come from a Tampa, Florida, building products company just two years before. Naimoli didn't particularly like Anchor Hocking, and he didn't seem to particularly like Lancaster: It was too small-town, too insular, too old-fashioned. The loathing was mutual. Naimoli struck the few in Lancaster who encountered him during his short time there as a self-important blowhard, in a place where even the richest people didn't put on airs. More important, Naimoli wanted to be a wheeler-dealer like Icahn.

Icahn had focused his critique of the company on the low-margin container division, so Naimoli offered to spin it off from Anchor Hocking. Topper—who never liked the container division and perhaps reckoned that disposing of it would satisfy any other Icahns in the wings—agreed. There was just one problem: Naimoli didn't have any money. He was a well-paid salaryman, not a multimillionaire. But this was the 1980s, the era of junk bonds, and as Icahn was proving, you didn't have to have money to make money.

In early 1983, a Kidder, Peabody banker introduced Naimoli to Bill Simon, who had been treasury secretary under both Richard Nixon and Gerald Ford. Simon had formed Wesray Capital Corporation, an early leveraged-buyout shop—what is now called private equity. Simon agreed to back Naimoli to the tune of $76 million, only about $1 million of which was Wesray's. In March, Topper took the deal. With the stroke of a pen, Ray Topper halved the size of Anchor Hocking at a Filene's Basement price.

When Dale Lamb, then a full-time official with the American Flint Glass Workers' Union, received the phone call from a Lancaster "Flint," he couldn't believe what he heard. " 'I just got the word,' " the man said to Lamb. " 'That sonofabitch Topper just sold all the container plants for $76 million. The goddamned ground costs more than that!' I said, 'If you think the ground costs more than that, the machines in Plant 1 alone are worth $40 million.' He said, 'That sonofabitch. It's gonna be havoc.' "

Naimoli ordered all the container division's plant and sales managers from Lancaster, as well as nationwide, to gather at the country club on Easter Sunday. He told them the container division was splitting off. The new company, to be called Anchor Glass Container Corporation, was moving to Tampa. He invited them to move, too. "I had the opinion people in Lancaster were set in their ways," Naimoli told me. "I told them they would work a lot harder in Tampa." He also said he was giving them a raise by moving them to Florida—not because he was actually giving them a raise, but because the state had no income tax.

The deal turned out to be an early example of modern financial engineering. The $75 million Simon borrowed wasn't Wesray's debt, nor Naimoli's. It was loaded onto the back of Anchor Glass Container. Anchor Glass then loaned part of this money to Wesray. Wesray used it to buy some of the company's real estate and equipment, even furnaces. Anchor Glass

then leased these assets back from Wesray. Whether the company suc-
ceeded or failed, Simon and Naimoli couldn't help but win.

Anchor Glass went public in 1986, and Simon cashed out. Three years
later, a Mexican container company, Vitro, mounted a successful hostile
takeover—the first hostile takeover of a U.S. company by a Mexican one.
Vitro paid $900 million, nearly twelve times what Topper had sold it for
just six years earlier. Naimoli took his windfall and bought a Major League
Baseball franchise, the expansion Tampa Bay Devil Rays. He became
a Tampa grandee, and self-published a hagiographic autobiography, *Business, Baseball & Beyond*.

The Anchor Glass Container story looked like an unqualified success.
But the old container division, which was never able to breathe under all
of its debts, spent years falling in and out of bankruptcy.

Selling the container division was just one of Topper's leaps into 1980s
finance. Supposedly as part of a poison-pill plan to fend off any future
Icahns, the board instituted a golden-parachute scheme for the executive
officers of the company. If anybody else tried to swallow Anchor, they'd
have to pay off Anchor's leaders.

For generations, through both periods of harmony and episodes of
friction, workers and management understood that their interests were
aligned. Now they weren't. Cartoons soon appeared on bulletin boards: a
man under a gold parachute descending onto Plant 1, his penis out, piss-
ing into the rooftop vents.

Anchor Hocking's fortunes continued to decline. Sales fell domestically
and overseas, hobbled by macroeconomics. After Reagan's 1981 tax cuts,
the federal budget deficit soared, boosting the value of the dollar and making Anchor Hocking's ware more expensive overseas while making ware
from foreign companies like Durand cheaper for American buyers. By 1984,
glass was stacking up in warehouses.

As it happened, Anchor owned a plant in Clarksburg, West Virginia:
the former Brockway plant. The Clarksburg plant first opened in 1885, but
in March 1979, Brockway shut it down. Local and state economic development officials provided $8.5 million in low-interest public-money loans
to Anchor so it could play savior. And because the Flints in Clarksburg
wanted work at almost any price, they agreed to a number of concessions.

Topper, then president under Barber, cackled over the terms, bragging that he'd bested a Rockefeller—West Virginia governor Jay Rockefeller.

Now, with sales slowing, Topper pitted Plant 2, over on Ewing Street, against Clarksburg. Plant 2 made Fire-King baking dishes, blender jars for small-appliance makers like Sunbeam, Crock-Pot covers, mixing bowls. The Ohio Environmental Protection Agency was pressuring Anchor to install new exhaust scrubber equipment on the Plant 2 stacks. West Virginia, on the other hand, had looser environmental laws.

In late November 1984, Lamb and another union official were in Clarksburg negotiating a new contract for the Flints there when he received a call from the Anchor Hocking general counsel.

"He said, 'We're comin' down tomorrow, and, out of due respect for you, we're gonna give you a proposal. There'll be no counterproposal.'" The proposal was in fact a demand: Clarksburg workers had to walk back even more on wages, benefits, and work rules. If they refused, Anchor would shutter the plant it had purchased just five years before with public money. If they accepted, Anchor would close Plant 2 in Lancaster and move its machines to Clarksburg.

"'Plant 2 is a goner. It's a goner!'" Lamb exclaimed to another union official, Roy. "I hung up the phone, and I said, 'Oh, shit, Roy.' I told Roy. He says, 'You're shittin' me.'"

Lamb phoned friends in Plant 2. They spoke to the plant manager. Nobody knew anything about a closure.

A management team arrived in Clarksburg and made the proposal. Lamb had hoped to negotiate, at least a little, but the local workers wouldn't hear of it. "They said, 'You get the hell back to Lancaster, 'cause you got all those friends in Lancaster. You're a Lancaster boy. You don't want those jobs comin' down here. You get the hell out of here.'" Lamb was angry at the locals in Clarksburg, but he understood. "They didn't want to lose their jobs."

The Clarksburg Flints' capitulation wasn't unusual. Unions were in full retreat all over the country. Ronald Reagan demolished PATCO, the air traffic controllers union, in 1981. Other industrial unions, like the United Steelworkers and United Auto Workers, had been weakened by plant closings and cutbacks. Strong anti-union sentiment was fed by instances of union corruption and by the conservative winds blowing through American politics.

On December 5, 1984, twenty days before Christmas, Topper announced that Anchor Hocking would shut down Plant 2—for good.

The shock in Lancaster was numbing. "Plant 2's closing is devastating. . . . It will set us back years," an *Eagle-Gazette* editorial grieved. The paper, and most people in Lancaster, accepted the story that the closing was a simple response to overcapacity. It couldn't be helped.

Even after the news broke, the Plant 2 workers, led by the plant manager, produced for five more months, right up to the moment they shut off the fuel to the furnaces. The plant manager told his bosses at headquarters, "You missed out. You misjudged these people. These guys are professionals."

Some Plant 2 production employees, like skilled machine operators, were offered jobs in Plant 1 on Pierce Avenue or in Clarksburg, but most were fired. Plant 2's equipment was trucked to West Virginia.

The year had already been a lousy one for Lancaster. In February, Hickle's department store, a mainstay since 1900, announced its closing—done in partly by the Reagan Recession and partly by local fear. Forty people worked there. It was the fourth downtown business to close in a year, including Kresge's. The worst, though, was still to come.

Not long after Anchor settled up with Carl Icahn, another CEO decided to get into the leveraged-buyout business. Daniel Ferguson, CEO of Newell Corporation, made a deal with an Arizona bank called Western Savings and Loan. Western loaned Newell $42 million for fifteen years and purchased 800,000 shares of Newell stock for $18.4 million. Western's chief, Gary Driggs, took a seat on Newell's board.

A relatively small Arizona savings and loan—as opposed to a New York investment bank, for example—would seem to have been an odd choice for such a package. But Driggs was a maverick gambler, a perfect match for Ferguson.

Ferguson's father, Leonard, had been CEO and chairman of Newell, a maker of drapery hardware, window shades, home hardware, and sewing notions. Ferguson took over in 1965. The company plodded along, making a healthy profit in an unglamorous industry. But by the 1980s Ferguson had caught the takeover bug. He used Western's money as dry powder for a spree. In 1983, Newell acquired the Mirro Aluminum Company, which made cookware, for about $42 million. Most of that purchase price was debt. In 1984, Newell bought another Wisconsin company, Foley-ASC, which made cooking tools, for $8 million by issuing preferred stock. In 1985, it bought 40 percent of American Tool Companies, makers of Vise-Grip pliers—again, mostly with debt—and gained control of William E. Wright & Sons, a Massachusetts textile firm that had been family-owned since 1897. In every case, Ferguson subjected the targeted firms to "Newellization," his own brand of what business schools called "operating efficiencies." He fired people, cut product lines, sold off bits of the companies. Thanks to Icahn, Anchor Hocking was now in play, too.

In May of 1986, Ferguson met with Ray Topper. To this day, nobody seems to know exactly what the two men discussed, but on June 11, Newell began buying Anchor Hocking's stock.

On July 3, Topper demanded that the unions at Plant 1 enter into early negotiations for a new contract. He wanted more cost cuts, more wage concessions. The unions were under no obligation to begin negotiations early. But if they refused, Topper said, he would gut Lancaster by closing both Plant 1 and the distribution center, moving production and distribution elsewhere.

On July 31, Anchor's board adopted a stockholder-rights plan, a second poison pill designed to sicken any potential acquirer by giving Anchor's leadership the right to buy shares at a deeply discounted rate. That would require the issuance of more shares, devaluing each share, and making it more difficult to execute a hostile takeover.

By late August, Newell owned 5 percent of Anchor Hocking, at which point it had to reveal its Anchor holdings to the Securities and Exchange Commission. In its SEC filing, it announced it might seek control.

Topper now demanded major concessions from the union: a minimum 15 percent pay cut, new work classifications that would allow the company to pay lower wages for certain jobs, retirement cuts, and—fifty years after the Wagner Act—the hiring of non-union contract workers. The Flints offered a 5 percent pay cut and other concessions. Both sides took out competing newspaper ads to explain their arguments to the town.

Talks between the Flints and Anchor Hocking broke down on the night of September 30. At midnight on October 1, the Flint leadership called a strike.

In the past, Dale Lamb had tried to be a conciliator who understood the company's side and that of his union brothers. He took heat for that approach.

"A lot of union guys didn't like me, but tough shit," Lamb recalled. "I'd tell 'em, 'Remember, you went to them and asked for a job. You're working for them; they're not working for you.'" He negotiated hard, and he wasn't afraid of strikes, but he knew that neither side could win when there was one. Likening the company to a woman, he told his men, "If she says no and crosses her legs, that's frickin' no. You don't wanna get rid of her, 'cause she's the one that doesn't have bad breath."

This time, though, things were different. Lamb and every other union member, along with a good number of Lancaster's residents, hated Topper.

The strike lasted three weeks. Topper placed armed guards around some Lancaster facilities and hired scabs to ship ware. Police were stationed at Topper's home. Union men attacked people they thought were scab workers coming in and out of the distribution center. They smashed windshields and placed nails in the roadway. They convinced some union truckers not to load or deliver product. Six picketers were arrested and jailed.

None of it did any good. The strike ended on October 22. (The mold makers held out a few days longer.) The unions gave up 15 percent on wages, bringing Plant 1 into near parity with Clarksburg. They agreed to cuts in vacation pay, bonuses, and incentives. Lancaster still had about two thousand people employed, but Anchor Hocking had a bitter workforce.

To Newell, though, Anchor Hocking was an even sweeter morsel, because Topper had fought a battle Newell wouldn't have to fight. Two weeks after the strike ended, Newell wrote a letter to the Anchor board of directors offering $34 per share to buy the company outright. Topper dismissed it as "a nonoffer."

Over the succeeding weeks, Newell and Anchor traded barbs, but the end was never in much doubt. On February 23, 1987, the board of directors of Anchor Hocking voted to approve Newell's offer. The deal, valued at $32 per share—about $338 million—represented a premium over the 1985 high for Anchor's stock, 27 5/8. The $338 million was mostly debt, as with other Newell acquisitions. A story went around that Topper cried. But some Anchor executives said Topper wanted to sell.

The five years since Carl Icahn made his run at Anchor Hocking had been dizzying ones for Lancaster, but the denouement of the Newell take-over was catastrophic. Six days after the July 1987 shareholder vote ratifying the board's decision, Newell fired 110 people from the downtown head-quarters. Anchor Hocking treasurer Sam Hurley was one. And because he was one, he was assigned the job of breaking the news. He asked the office workers to walk across the alley into the hotel I. J. Collins and the town had built. Everyone assembled in a back room. "You could see they were thinking, 'My God!'" Hurley recalled.

By the end of the year, the rest of the office employees were fired, too—about three hundred in all—and the headquarters closed up. A core group of Lancaster's leadership class, and their all-important spouses, were swept away, ripping a huge hole in the social fabric of the town. None of the executives Newell brought in to run Anchor Hocking moved to Lan-caster. To this day, locals insist that Newell ordered executives to live elsewhere—most moved into the Columbus area—so they wouldn't be troubled by requests for civic involvement or charitable contributions.

The headquarters building sat empty. Eventually a local law firm bought it. Gerry Stebelton was a partner in the firm. His mother spent thirty-five years working in the cold end, selecting and packing ware in the sluer. He grew up on Harrison Avenue—on the west side—eventually making it to law school, and then worked in New York, but he came back home, where he served on the city council. He was elected state representative. When he and his partners reopened the headquarters building, they held an open house. About three thousand people streamed through. Many of them wept.

There were tears in Clarksburg, too. A month after the takeover was ratified, Newell shut down the Clarksburg plant. Clarksburg workers, lo-cal politicians, and West Virginia governor Arch Moore were outraged by what they saw as obvious betrayal. Moore, citing the money the govern-ment had supplied to lure Anchor, called out state troopers to prevent New-ell from moving equipment back to Lancaster. Newell and Moore tossed competing court injunctions back and forth. Moore impounded the plant's machines and molds and filed a $614 million lawsuit. Newell accused the governor of holding it "hostage."

Then it secretly sent Anchor employees, crane rigs, and flatbed trucks to West Virginia. The people and the gear holed up at highway rest areas around Clarksburg. As soon as a court granted Newell permission to remove certain equipment, and before the state could reply, the small army dashed to the Clarksburg plant. They switched tags on some still-impounded machines and molds, replacing them with tags reflecting permitted items, to fool the troopers—who didn't know a mold from a press—guarding the plant's gates. Trucks used back roads to get across the Ohio state line before a new injunction, and West Virginia state police, could stop them.

In its annual report for 1987, Newell called the showdown over Clarksburg "a 'public' exposure type problem."

It kept selling off bits of Anchor Hocking—the natural gas transmission division, the packaging and closure plants, the trucks—until Anchor Hocking amounted to Plant 1 and the distribution center in Lancaster, as well as the Phoenix plant in Monaca.

Meanwhile, Western Savings and Loan collapsed during the S&L crisis of the 1980s. Driggs resigned as president and CEO in 1988—at just about the same time that Newell declared victory in Clarksburg. In 1989, the Federal Deposit Insurance Corporation took over the insolvent Western. Driggs was sued for fraud and conspiracy. He settled for $650,000. He also pleaded guilty to federal felonies and served probation in lieu of prison. Driggs resigned from Newell's board in 1989 but was soon back on it, serving as a member of Newell's audit committee.

D ale Lamb was far removed from people like Driggs and Simon. He'd lived the farm life, but he didn't see much romance in it. His parents owned a farm just outside Lancaster, and they also worked another one nearby, growing oats and corn and raising hogs and a few dairy cows. This meant that Lamb worked the farms, too, because that's what you do when you grow up in a farm family. The other kids in the "county" school he attended foretold their lives at forty by wearing the blue corduroy jackets of Future Farmers of America, but when Lamb projected that far ahead, he knew he didn't want to "ride a plow around and talk to Bessie." He wanted to be a teacher.

He started down that road by taking some college courses at the OU Lancaster campus. To make a little money along the way, he worked a part-time job filling in on a rural mail delivery route. But then he fell hard in love and decided the only way to salve that ache was to get married. He'd have to make a lot more money than he could working a couple of days a week carting mail across the countryside, but that wouldn't be too tough a nut to crack. He'd just apply at Anchor. Lamb started in June 1962, packing ware at Plant 1. After a few months, he put his name on the bid sheet to go into the hot end.

The hot end had its pecking orders and traditions, some of them codified by the union, some of them lore passed down from one generation to the next. Like everybody else, Lamb had to step on the rungs of the ladder in the proper order. He was a floor boy. He cleaned ware. He worked in the batch house, where raw materials were fed into the furnaces. He became a lehr attendant, watching the glass enter the long annealing tunnels, making sure the temperature was controlled. Finally, he was formally inducted into the apprenticeship program, and his union membership changed from an industrial local to a skilled local.

He bought a little house on the west side and walked to work. As the weeks passed, he began to change, or the job changed, or both. Something. He wasn't sure. He'd come to Anchor Hocking to make a living so he could get married, but he found that life in the plant wasn't just a matter of doing your work and collecting a check.

As a rookie, Lamb relied on the older, more experienced men. To them, the plant was a heaving being, its innards strung with cables and plumbing and wires, its machines sighing and churning, with silica and other minerals flowing in and glassware flowing out. The old boys had a feel for the place. They could diagnose a bad mold ring just by looking at a tumbler, mix batch by feel, gauge temperature without looking at a dial. By tapping that wisdom, Lamb could shorten his climb up the learning curve and pocket more money, too. The fewer rejected pieces a man made, the more bonus money he could collect. Always, it seemed, somebody was willing to lend a hand.

The Flints looked out for one another. Layoffs came around not long after Lamb started, but layoffs didn't necessarily mean any Flint was going to be laid off.

"If we was working six days, you had to go down to five. Instead of the youngest guy, who needed the most, for family and stuff, getting laid off, we divided it. And that was good for the company and good for us. Our hours went on for vacations, our insurance kept tickin'."

As a newcomer, Lamb didn't know the names of many of his coworkers, so, country boy that he was, he called everybody Laddy-Buck, as in "Hey, Laddy-Buck, can you help me with this mold?" Word got around, and then one day, Lamb walked into the break room, and everybody in there shouted, "Hey, Laddy-Buck!"

The tears in his eyes when he told that story got him thinking about another one. Bill Nutter, a good ol' boy who'd been working in Plant 1 since the 1930s, when it was still the Hockin', was a west-side neighbor and a mentor who was smart as hell about making glass. Back when Nutter started, the company gave each man his own metal toolbox. He could have it custom-fabricated in the tool department at the plant. Nutter carried his pretty near every day of his working life. One day, he held it up to Lamb and said, "I want you to have this, Lambie."

"There's a lot of guys that were nice to you and would help you," Lamb said. "You gotta believe in empathy and reciprocity, you know? You should have that in life in general."

That Dick Ellwood would become a friend of Dale Lamb's might seem unlikely if you knew nothing about Lancaster. Ellwood ended his career at Anchor Hocking as one of the four executive officers with a golden parachute and all that stock. Because of that, he became a controversial figure in town.

But that was not how he started. Ellwood grew up swimming in the Tuscarawas River, because, unlike Lancaster, with its Miller Pool, the little town of Dover, Ohio, northeast of Columbus, didn't have swimming pools. Ellwood's father was a bricklayer. The family was so poor that, sixty years later, Ellwood could remember all the details of the day they moved from a four-dollar-a-month cottage to an eight-dollar-a-month cottage that had honest-to-God running water piped right into the house. To help fund the family, Ellwood became a bricklayer. He joined the bricklayers' union. Hoisting bricks was hard work, but it helped build a body. Ellwood's was squat and thick, a solid mass, his head a block with the defined angles of a mason's square.

Ellwood moved that strong body with scary speed across the high school football fields of Ohio, including Lancaster's, where his Dover squad was always an unwelcome sight. Ellwood parlayed a star high school career into a starting spot for Ohio State, where he played in the 1950 Rose Bowl, an OSU victory over Cal, and the following season's "Snow Bowl," a game famous for its arctic conditions.

After graduation, Ellwood served in the navy during the Korean War. He married and, after he mustered out of the navy, spent a few weeks enjoying civilian life back in Dover with his wife, Barbara. She let about thirty days go by before suggesting that, perhaps, he might like to look for a job. She reminded him of Lancaster.

"She said, 'What about that town down there, Lancaster?' " Ellwood told me one afternoon as we sat in the bar of the Lancaster Country Club. " 'They have that beautiful swimming pool, beautiful parks. You oughta go down there. Remember? They have a dish plant down there.' "

Ellwood drove to Lancaster, parked by the Anchor Hocking headquarters at Broad and Main, and walked into the offices. A man who happened to work in personnel was on a ladder behind a secretary. Ellwood asked the secretary if they were hiring, not caring all that much whether they were or weren't; he wanted to satisfy his wife.

The man on the ladder turned around and said, "Hey! Are you Dick Ellwood?" Ellwood was easy to recognize. He still looked exactly like a central-casting football player, with his rugged, slightly flattened face, dark slashes for eyebrows, and that forward-leaning physique, as if he were still charging a quarterback—something the personnel guy had seen Ellwood do in Lancaster, in Ohio Stadium, and on the Rose Bowl TV broadcast.

"What are you doing?" the man asked.

"Looking for a job," Ellwood answered.

"Come with me," the man replied. Ellwood never worked for another company.

Throughout all the new job titles and pay raises, Ellwood remained Ellwood. He moved into a big house—practically an estate—out on BIS Road, with a horse stable, even, and people talked because it was a little showy and extravagant, a former poor boy's dreamland. But he also spent a lot of evenings inside Old Bill Bailey's with glassworkers. More than one person landed a job by drinking beer with Ellwood.

He walked the plant floors. "I loved going to work at six in the morning and leaving at six at night, rolling through the plant every day, seeing all those people. Those people were amazing. Nice people."

The union and Ellwood had fist-pounding fights at contract time, but they spoke each other's languages. "Dale Lamb, hell, we were friends. We had some problems, you know. He knew his job and I knew my job. Those other guys who were tough, tough labor guys? Shit, I got along with 'em."

After Icahn, though, he stopped understanding what it was Anchor Hocking was doing. It seemed to him that getting a mention in the *Wall Street Journal* had become more important than making and selling glass. He claimed Topper controlled the board and kept decisions within a tight circle with a couple of others, neither of whom was Ellwood.

Some believed Ellwood sold out the workers—and the town—by closing Plant 2 and taking the pillowy payday at the Newell sale. He insisted that the Clarksburg plant, the Ohio EPA, the lower labor costs in West Virginia had nothing to do with Plant 2 coming down. The decision to shutter it, he told me, was the hardest day of his life. "The eight or nine hundred people working out there? Their kids went to school with my kids. We knew everybody. Everybody." As for the Newell sale, Ellwood claimed he wasn't consulted, had little say, and so kept his mouth shut.

After the Newell sale was approved, Ferguson asked Ellwood to lunch. They sat at the same table where we sat. Ferguson asked Ellwood to stay. "I wanted no part of it," Ellwood told me. Ferguson, he said, was "a jerk-ass."

Topper left town for Florida. Ellwood stayed.

Though he had been retired for nearly thirty years, he remained haunted by an elegiac shadow. Some evenings he'd wander into the Pink Cricket, order a beer, and talk to an old waitress who, like many in Lancaster, worked two jobs, her other one in the Anchor sluer. She'd been there for decades. She'd fill Ellwood in on what tanks were down and how many feeders were running inside Plant 1. Good news was rare. Everybody who still worked at Anchor, like Brian Gossett, was on edge.

The day after our conversation, Ellwood went to a funeral. He attended a lot of funerals—every funeral of every Anchor Hocking employee who worked for the company during the years he did. "I go to all of them," he said. "I just feel like these people represented Anchor Hocking, and I am the last representative they've got that they know. I'm the last."

During the 1980s storm of deal making, critics like Felix Rohatyn, an investment banker with Lazard Frères & Company (and, later, U.S. ambassador to France), Harvard University business and social policy professor Robert Reich (secretary of labor in Bill Clinton's administration), Yale economics professor and Nobelist James Tobin, and others warned against the long-term effects of the frenzy of financial engineering, executive self-interest, and greenmail, but they were screaming into a Friedmanesque typhoon.

A. Bartlett Giamatti, then president of Yale and later the commissioner of baseball, worried about something more ineffable than what was good or bad for a company's future. People, he said, might become disillusioned about "the idea of institutional loyalty." An institution, whether it's a political body, a corporation, a school, or a club, is a "means for translating private impulse to the public good." Without a sense of that purpose, people might feel cut adrift until "the impulse to private gain has nothing to connect itself to except itself."

FOUR

Newellization

March 2004

S ome civic leaders argued that the Newell takeover benefited Lancaster. The paper editorialized that the town should welcome the newcomer with open arms and make the arriving team feel like Lancaster was their home, too. Even the unions said at first that they were pleased with Newell. But the enthusiasm felt forced, based more on relief than on real optimism. Coming after the intense uncertainty and resentment that had haunted the company and the town since Icahn, Lancaster clung to any island of stability.

And there was optimism within the company itself. "Newellization" introduced a few needed modern efficiencies and systems that Anchor Hocking had neglected—like data and accounting techniques, order tracking, customer service methods. Profit as a percentage of revenue rose. Newell also tried smoothing relations with the unions that had been left embittered by Topper. It held regular "burgers on the bricks" events, during which salaried staff cooked hamburgers at the plant for the hourly workers.

On the other hand, Newell infused Anchor Hocking with some of the "brutality" that Peter Roane said had been missing in the old management. It eliminated the apprenticeship program, in which raw talent from the community would be turned into skilled, specialist experts. Newell was laser-focused on bottom-line performance. Nobody got hired at Old Bill

Bailey's anymore, and if you failed to hit targets, nobody hunted for a position in which you could find "your level of competence." You were fired.

"They told us that, going forward, we'd never be any more responsible or any more accountable for what we did and our actions than from this day," recalled Mike Shook, who led a product design and development team. Shook liked that.

But not everybody did. Newell fired a lot of people throughout the operation, not just in the headquarters building.

"Newell was bad people," Dale Lamb said. "Bad people."

This was certainly the view of Vermont American. At the same time Daniel Ferguson was pursuing Anchor Hocking, he was also chasing Vermont American, a Louisville, Kentucky–based tool company. Vermont American was public, but closely held by members of two families. It had always been run very much like a family business, with a conservative, long-term view. It grew by investing profits in new products, marketing, and quality, not by making acquisitions. Lee Thomas, the chairman of the board, preferred decision-making by the Quaker principles of "consensus and compromise." The strategy worked. Vermont American had a long record of profitable growth.

Using tactics Thomas and other officers of Vermont American found deceptive, Newell began acquiring stock, just as it had with Anchor. And just as he had at Anchor, Ferguson at first denied having any desire to take over the company. But Vermont American had learned a lesson from Anchor's experience.

"At times Newell had acquired public corporations at bargain prices through 'creeping acquisitions' and two-tier tender offers," Vermont American told a Delaware court. "This was true, for example, in Newell's acquisition of Anchor Hocking Corporation in 1986. There Newell accumulated the company's stock and eventually acquired complete equity control of Anchor Hocking. In order to generate increased profitability Newell at times would follow its acquisitions by asset-stripping, plant closures and layoffs."

After a long battle, Vermont American escaped Ferguson's uninvited embrace by selling itself to a consortium of Emerson Electric and the German company Bosch. Newell walked away with a $26 million profit on the sale of its Vermont American shares.

Lamb's opinion hardened in 1992, when Newell tried to increase the amount those who had already retired would have to pay for health insurance premiums. "They was gonna triple it or quadruple it," he recalled.

The Flint rank and file seemed reluctant to invite conflict over the issue. According to Lamb, that was because Newell "was in bed with some of the union guys." Newell, Lamb charged, would co-opt a union officer by having him appointed as a shop lead, which paid more per hour. The officer, in turn, wouldn't challenge the company or rouse his members to action, for fear of losing his new position and extra pay. So Lamb mounted a campaign.

First, he put some old retirees on a picket line and had them walk in front of the distribution center and Plant 1. Then, as contract negotiations dragged on at the old Holiday Inn on 33, Lamb hired a ragtime piano player to beat out militant march songs and called workers to come over to the motel's lounge.

"They started comin' in, and she's pounding that baby like, man! The place was packed. Standing room. The old guys was all there; we had four policemen just in case. They knew what might happen."

Lamb explained the issue, saying the union had the right to strike to protect the benefits of the retirees. Some younger workers resisted: "'Why do you care about them? They're gone.'"

Lamb couldn't believe his ears. This wasn't the union he thought he knew. Perhaps the Flints had been beaten down since the 1980s. Maybe they considered themselves so lucky to have a job at all, when the news was filled with disappearing union work, that they preferred not to endanger the status quo. Lamb's theory was that too many of them had bought boats and motorcycles, lived a little high—often on credit—with no stomach for sacrifice.

"'Well, they made it what we are!'" he exclaimed of the old retirees who had fought for better pay and working conditions, suffering through a long strike in the 1960s, for example. "'If we do it to them, what [is the company] gonna do to us? That's not the way life is! You know that's not the way it is! He died for us on the cross!'"

His tactics worked. The union issued an ultimatum to management: Roll back the retiree premium hikes and slightly boost current-worker retiree benefits or the Flints would walk. In response, Newell preemptively shut the plant down, bringing in security guards dressed like storm troopers.

Joe Boyer walked a picket line, even though he'd been in Plant 1 for only two years. Boyer had worked at an auto parts store and as an auto mechanic before that, but when he realized working on cars was never going to get him out of his parents' house on Mulberry Street, just a few blocks from where I. J. Collins and Bill Fisher had lived, he talked to a neighbor who worked in the furnace room at Anchor. Boyer's father had worked at Anchor, making a decent living there, and now Boyer thought maybe he should, too.

Like the generations before him, Boyer started in the sluer, put in a bid for the hot end, became a floor boy, and worked his way up. He operated a press, making pressed-glass casserole dishes and other bakeware, mainly. He preferred presses over the H-28s—their rotations, and walking around them to service the molds, made him feel a little queasy, almost dizzy.

"Standing right next to it gives you a funny feeling, and I had some bad experiences. I got caught in one: It ripped my glove off, it ripped my watch off. I just didn't like operating those. I liked the press 'cause they will move, and then stop, and you've got time to work on it. You could lose a hand in a press, too, but it's different."

Joe was a gearhead who was good with his hands—and took pride in his work. But he didn't feel especially attached to the company. Guys would tell him about how it used to be in the plant and the company, back before Newell, but it wasn't like that anymore. There were no more baseball or bowling leagues, no more softball games, golf outings, company clubs. The company didn't love him. He didn't love it. It was strictly business. He put in his time, took his check, went home. He even avoided union meetings. Though he walked the line, he wasn't sure what the strike was all about. Most of the younger guys were like Boyer: They didn't care who signed their checks, as long as somebody signed them.

The strike lasted a month. Salaried employees tried to work the machines. They packed ware and loaded trucks. For some of them, it was the first time they lived the life of a factory worker. "We had nurses there, and when we'd come into work, they'd tape up our fingers and hands, put elbow braces, knee braces on some of us," Shook recalled with a laugh. In the end, Newell decided not to raise retiree premiums as it had planned, but the company gave current workers only a token increase in retirement benefits for the future.

Lamb didn't want to settle on those terms. Newell was spending millions upon millions of dollars on acquisitions—it could spare a few bucks for workers' pensions. In fact, even as Newell was trying to cut Anchor retiree benefits, Ferguson was mounting yet another hostile-takeover fight, this time over the Stanley Works of New Britain, Connecticut. (It lost when a court approved a settlement that maintained Stanley's independence and forced Newell to desist.) Who knew what the future would bring? Lamb told his Flint brothers, "Be prepared." You might think life with Newell was okay now, but it wasn't like the old days, when Anchor was just Anchor, and your kids went to school with Gushman's kids and Barber's kids and Ellwood's kids. Now it was just one of many Newell divisions. The real power was in Illinois, inside Newell's offices. Just five years after the takeover, there were already signs that Anchor wasn't Newell's favored child anymore. Someday, Anchor could be tossed aside.

The members instructed him to settle. "I lost a couple of friends on that one," he said. The strike didn't dent Anchor's profits. The glass operations made money for their new parent, contributing significantly to Newell's return on equity, a measure Newell liked to parade for investors.

Anchor Hocking's success in satisfying Newell's management put to rest the myth that Anchor Hocking—and the glass business in the United States in general—could never compete against imports and that offshoring American glass manufacturing was the only way American glass companies could stay in business.

Shocked as it was over the events since Carl Icahn first put Anchor Hocking in play, the town tried to tell itself that everything would be okay. And on the surface it seemed to be, at first. People got used to the absence of the headquarters. There were still about twelve hundred people working at Plant 1 and the DC. Not all the former executives and spouses and families left—not right away, anyway. At the insistence, and through the persistence, of an Anchor attorney, extra weeks of service were added to the tenures of some office employees during the negotiations with Newell, so some were able to take an early retirement and remain in town rather than having to find a new job elsewhere. Lancaster Glass remained in business, and though Diamond Power was losing orders for its soot blowers, thanks to a move away from coal-fired power generation, it remained, too. Drew Shoe had nearly a hundred people making footwear.

The county fair still arrived every October, kids still showed their prized heifers and rabbits and lambs, and people still tossed Ping-Pong balls into little goldfish bowls to win a fish in a baggie. The festival—thank goodness for the festival, many said—still animated the town every July. Well over a hundred people still volunteered, Andy Rooney–like, to put on the show. Those who could still donate money did so. Attendance climbed every year. Membership at the country club declined, but kids still swam in the club pool. Tiki and Miller weren't as crowded in the summers as they once were, but they were still popular.

But the bond between Anchor and Lancaster had been as much emotional as financial, and that bond was irredeemably broken. Newell had no emotional investment in the town. On the contrary, it seemed determined to avoid it.

Anchor Hocking donations to the local United Way dropped to just a few thousand dollars, from $50,000 the year before the takeover. Despite the *Eagle-Gazette*'s entreaties to make the new team welcome, there wasn't anyone to welcome. Newell executives rotated in and out of Anchor Hocking, a way station to what they hoped would be higher-ranking jobs within the Newell galaxy. From 1987 to 2004, Anchor Hocking had six CEOs, none of whom lived in Lancaster. The company had five CEOs in the eighty-two years before the takeover, all of whom lived there. To Newell's executives, Lancaster looked like an old hick town. They didn't know the Lancaster story, and didn't care to know it. That was what hurt the most, maybe. Nobody came out and said, "You're not good enough for me," and I could find no evidence that Newell ordered executives not to live there, no matter how many people told me otherwise, but the humiliating insult of their absence was real enough all the same.

Whether because of the conservative small-government tide ushered in by Reagan, or because many internalized its diminished status and lost confidence in the future—and any willingness to invest in it—or both, Lancaster stopped spending on itself. In 1988, the year Brian Gossett was born, a vote to increase Lancaster property taxes to support the schools failed. The next year, the year Mark Kraft was born, the city's school district tried to pass a small income tax, with the proceeds allocated for operating expenses. That failed, too. Voters soundly defeated road improvement taxes and bond issues.

The trend continued into the 1990s. A 1996 school-funding ballot measure lost by a thousand votes. Out of 18,521 registered voters, only 6,939 participated.

In the late 1990s, Lancaster's schools, once a source of town pride, cratered. According to a state "report card" of school districts, Lancaster's passed only ten of twenty-seven standards. Most fourth graders couldn't pass a reading test. By 2000, fourth and sixth graders failed nine out of ten proficiency standards.

In 1991, the fire department employed seventy-four firefighters. By 2016, it employed sixty-nine, even though the number of calls had more than doubled and the population had increased, thanks to Columbus commuters buying up tract housing on the city's newly annexed north side.

Old rules and common restraints eroded. Lancaster suffered embarrassing scandals that made people from all around Ohio wonder just what kind of hillbilly town it was. In 2000, Gary DeMastry, the Fairfield County sheriff, was indicted for misspending the public's money, roughly $300,000. He was convicted and sentenced to state prison in 2002. Also in 2002, Municipal Court judge Don McAuliffe torched his own house to collect the insurance money. He was indicted in 2003, convicted in 2004, and sentenced to prison.

In the mid-1970s, every teenager with even a few social skills knew where to find some anemic marijuana. (My first joint was shared with the sons of a local attorney and an insurance man. We survived.) But the poorer Lancaster became, the more drugs clung to the web of its life. In June 2001, county law enforcement agencies applied for—and were given—a state and federal grant to start a new task force called the Major Crimes Unit (MCU). When they applied for the grant, they cited methamphetamine and crack as their number-one concerns. But they'd also begun to see a new drug: Oxy-Contin pills. The mere existence of something called a Major Crimes Unit appalled the longtime Lancastrians who remembered when a "major crime" was a kid stealing a case of beer from the basement of a grocery store.

Some in Lancaster, led by the old core of post–World War II residents, refused to go prostrate. They responded the way they always had. The west side, around Plant 1, suffered the most from the breakdown of Lancaster's education system. As Anchor Hocking declined, more and more west-siders fell into poverty and family dysfunction. Too many children were failing to learn. So in 1998, Rosemary Hajost, MCU chief Eric Brown's mother-in-law, along with the director of a west-side food bank, the principal of West School, and a west-side minister, formed a committee to address the problem. They created the West After School Program.

Hajost rounded up now-elderly friends like Nancy Frick (the former Nancy George) for another tour of volunteerism. They brought paper, pencils, and their children's old books to the basement of the United Methodist Church, by the Anchor Hocking parking lot. One day each week, the volunteers tutored children in reading, math, and general behavior.

By 1990, the Lancaster YMCA had fallen into disrepair. A capital campaign raised $840,000 to rejuvenate the building. Then, in 1998, Robert K. Fox, the retired president of Lancaster Glass, donated $1.5 million—almost half the cost of a $3.5 million expansion.

With the sale of Anchor Hocking, there was a pool of well-to-do retirees who were migrating out of town, but no mechanism to capture money they might wish to leave to Lancaster. So, at the urging of a local probate judge—who had seen too many estates leave the city, as I. J. Collins's had—forty people, most of them older, met and formed the Fairfield County Foundation in 1989. Nancy Frick volunteered to serve as the first executive director.

As the town felt diminished, so did Anchor Hocking. When it was purchased, Anchor ware was considered a "core" product line for Newell, though Newell continued to sell off bits of it, like a perfume bottle maker. Dan Ferguson retired as CEO in 1992, the year of the Anchor strike, but Newell kept acquiring: WearEver cookware, which it combined with Mirro; an office products company; pencil and pen makers Faber-Castell and Sharpie; Levolor window treatments; hair and beauty accessories. In 1990, it even made a run at Lancaster Glass. But after financier James Goldsmith made an Icahn-like charge for the Akron-based Goodyear Tire and Rubber Company, Ohio passed anti-takeover laws, joining a parade of other states responding to the leveraged-buyout wave with a bipartisan counterattack meant to protect their industries. So Lancaster's parent company, Columbus-based Lancaster Colony Corporation, moved the corporate registration from Delaware to Ohio. Lancaster Colony found shelter back home.

Newell was relentless. The American Promise had changed from the time of *Forbes*'s elevation of the Lancaster way. Modesty was out, acquisitiveness was in. America became a big-box nation—cheap goods for a people newly addicted to cheap stuff—and Newell wanted to be the big-box wholesaler to the big-box retailers, the place where Walmart, Target, Kmart, Home Depot, Staples, and Lowe's could go to find all kinds of products for their shelves. Every new annual report contained a list of companies Newell had absorbed. And as the list of Newell companies grew longer, Anchor's relative importance grew smaller.

In 1997, Newell acquired Rolodex, and, in 1998, cookware maker Calphalon. Then, in October of that year, it decided to swallow a whale: Rubbermaid, a company that included not only the famous Rubbermaid storage containers, but Graco baby strollers and Little Tikes toys. Newell, already carrying about $900 million in long-term debt, agreed to pay $5.8 billion. Newell changed its name to Newell Rubbermaid.

The merger, completed in 1999, nearly killed the company. Rubbermaid was more troubled than Newell had suspected. Newell's enormous debt was suffocating. And Newell had grown so many tentacles, each with its own operations, that its famously strict control over each tentacle eroded. Return on equity fell, and Newell, once Wall Street's darling, was cast off. On April 21, 1999, Newell closed at $52 per share. By the fall of 2000, it was trading at $19, even as the stock market was on the biggest bull run in history.

G lass plants run on money as much as on heat, sand, and labor. The best furnace can't hold up forever under the strain of 2,400-degree molten glass. Furnaces need overhauls, and then—when overhauls won't do—to be rebuilt. Machines require maintenance.

The factories themselves need to run. Unlike, say, when a company makes strollers, pens, or hair clips, you can't just stop a glass factory. Back in 1905, when Collins ran day tanks, he could make glass until he emptied the tank. He could shut off the lights and go home. But you can't easily idle a glass plant like Anchor Hocking, where huge continuous tanks contain tons of molten glass. Glassmen understand this. For much of its history, when the slow spring-to-early-summer sales season rolled around, Anchor made ashtrays and other items from which it expected to make little or no profit, just to keep the plant operating. The items were put into inventory to be used as loss leaders. But the business school boys Newell sent through Anchor never seemed to grasp the concept. That lack of understanding didn't matter so much when both Anchor and Newell were running full steam and Anchor was meeting its financial goals for the parent. But now that Newell was tripping over itself, the goals changed. Newell needed—or wanted—better margins, and Anchor came to be viewed as an expensive stepchild. As a result, Newell began skimping on maintenance and upgrades.

"We ran by the seat of our pants," Chris Nagle recalled. "If baling wire would go out of business, Anchor wouldn't have been running, 'cause we used wire to keep stuff. You wanted a piece of equipment up, you'd wire this section up."

Newell shuffled CEOs. On January 1, 2001, the board hired forty-two-year-old Joseph Galli. Galli had started his career at Black & Decker, then, in 1999, joined Amazon as president. He made a generally bad impression on the employees. Thirteen months after he was hired, Galli left Amazon for another Internet company called VerticalNet. Five months after being hired there, he took over Newell Rubbermaid.

Galli restructured the company into four brand segments: Rubbermaid, Sharpie, Irwin Tools, and Calphalon Home. Anchor was shunted into Calphalon. Most office operations in Lancaster, like marketing, moved to Calphalon's offices in Toledo. More Lancastrians lost their jobs.

"They took the business away from us," Shook recalled. "I started attending product development meetings, but would have to drive to Toledo. I just sat around, waiting for the other shoe to drop, waiting for them to tell me to go pound sand: 'We don't need you.' Well, that all went to hell in a handbasket in pretty short order." Calphalon wanted no part of trying to market a product it knew nothing about; it soon sent the work back down to Lancaster.

Shook kept his job, but it was obvious to everyone that, fourteen years after fighting like hell to take it over, Newell no longer wanted Anchor Hocking. It was now a "non-core" business.

"They did everything under the sun to ruin us," another Anchor veteran recalled. Anchor was not alone in feeling the pain. Other towns with a Newell presence had it worse, crushed by global politics and Friedman-esque corporate profit seeking.

The North American Free Trade Agreement (NAFTA) went into effect on January 1, 1994, removing tariffs from goods traded between the three signatory nations. Republicans and many Democrats swore NAFTA would be a boon for American business and workers. That same year, Bill Clinton renewed China's most-favored-nation trading status, despite having criticized the same move by his predecessor, George H. W. Bush. Clinton had cited China's repression of human rights as the reason for his initial opposition, but lobbying by U.S. manufacturing executives apparently changed his mind. China quickly joined the World Trade Organization.

Most CEOs, corporate boards, and large shareholders loved the trade agreements. But factory workers and the unions that represented them paid the price.

Galli shut down Mirro's offices and factories in Manitowoc, Wisconsin, where the company was first established in 1897, and sent the manufacturing to Mexico. Mirro's corporate functions were sent to Calphalon in Toledo. About nine hundred people were thrown out of work.

Galli was increasingly desperate to dump Anchor, too. In May 2001, he laid off three thousand employees from several Newell companies. Rumors spread around town that Anchor was about to close. Company officials refused to comment.

Lancaster had already lost jobs that year. The heirs of the longtime owners of Drew Shoe sold the company in 1997 to BCAM, an outfit trying to commercialize ergonomic pump bladders like the ones once built into athletic shoes. BCAM hoped to use such bladders in the medical shoes Drew made for diabetics, the elderly, the arthritic. The hope proved illusory, and BCAM never made a penny. A year later, it sold control of Drew to Wexford Management, a New York investment company founded by an alumni of Alvarez & Marsal, the same fix-it firm Sam Solomon would encounter on his first day in the Anchor offices. On March 30, 2001,

Wexford announced it would close the Drew factory in Lancaster and move production to China. Ninety-four shoemakers received pink slips. A century of shoemaking in Lancaster came to an end. Drew Shoe's presence in Lancaster narrowed to a few office workers and a warehouse that received shipments from China and sent shoes to retailers and dealers.

A s it turned out, the rumors of an Anchor sale were true. Negotiations were already under way to sell Anchor to Libbey, its longtime Toledo rival. On June 17, Newell and Libbey signed the deal. Libbey would pay $332 million for Plant 1, Monaca, and the DC.

Lancaster celebrated. Now, at last, glass people would resume control of Anchor Hocking. Ohio glass people. Yes, Libbey and Anchor had been fierce competitors for nearly a hundred years, but suddenly all that history was recast as two brothers who fought constantly but who both had glass in their veins.

There was, however, a problem that few considered: Libbey led the market for food service glassware—the glasses used by restaurants, hotels, cruise lines, institutions. The little cursive "L" on the bottoms of bar glasses was as ubiquitous as the little anchor was on glass measuring cups, pie plates, and tumblers in homes all across America. Anchor also sold to the food service segment. The Libbey-Anchor combination could result in overwhelming domination.

The Federal Trade Commission thought so. In December, it registered its opposition to the sale. Local officials were outraged. Mayor Art Wallace, a retired Anchor employee, argued that the FTC shouldn't be worried about Libbey and Anchor taking over the market; it should be worried about the Mexicans and the Chinese. Wallace and others tried to enlist their state and federal representatives in a lobbying effort to turn back the FTC's objections but were met with either silence or token letters. Wallace was dismayed by the anemic response, but he shouldn't have been. It was the harvest of what had been sown by the Ohio state Republican party.

Clarence Miller served as Lancaster's congressman for decades. Miller was a former municipal gas company employee, city councilman, and mayor. Since being elected to Congress from what was then Ohio's Tenth District, he'd been an unexciting but diligent and well-respected Republican in

Washington. Though conservative, Miller was no dogmatist. He advocated for coal miners in the southern part of his district, as well as for the area's businesses. But by the 1990s, Miller was viewed as old-school. He didn't fit with the red-tie-wearing, well-coiffed, Young Americans for Freedom Newt Gingrich ideologues who ascended to power in the wake of Reagan. So, in another blow to Lancaster's prestige, Republicans in the legislature gerrymandered Miller out of his own district. Lancaster's new congressman lived in Springfield, a small city between Dayton and Columbus on the I-70 corridor. He didn't know Lancaster, certainly didn't care about it like Miller did, and lacked the D.C. firepower to make any sort of difference. Mayor Wallace and his local colleagues were on their own.

Newell tried to appease the FTC by carving Anchor's food service business out of the deal and lowering the price to $277 million, but the agency remained adamant. The FTC insisted that Anchor Hocking was healthy, with a strong balance sheet. And it was, despite the backlog of deferred maintenance. But Lancaster had witnessed the closing of one major manufacturing plant and the world headquarters of a *Fortune* 500 company, had suffered the loss of thousands of jobs and much of the city's civic leadership, and had stood by while Newell whittled what was left of Anchor Hocking down to a matchstick. Drew Shoe had sent its workers to the unemployment line that very year. None of that looked like health.

In April 2002, a U.S. district court judge ruled in favor of the FTC. Negotiations to find a way to satisfy the agency and the court resumed, but were quickly shut down when the FTC filed a complaint in May arguing that even if Newell retained certain molds and accounts related to the food service market, there was still a substantial risk that Libbey would wind up with a monopoly. On June 10, almost exactly one year after it first offered to buy Anchor, Libbey gave up.

A few people did stop to think that Lancaster's enthusiasm for Libbey might have been misplaced. Perhaps the FTC's opposition was a blessing in disguise. Most just assumed Libbey would still operate Plant 1 as it was, or even expand it. But Nagle, for one, knew a little about what was happening inside Libbey's Toledo factory. "They got thirty-some feeders up there," he said to himself, thinking of the lines delivering molten glass from the tanks to forming machines. "They're wantin' machines underneath them. They'll just move Anchor up there."

"They woulda gutted us," Nagle told me. Galli promised Lancaster that the factory would stay open. "If we can't sell it, we're going to do a good job running that business," he said. Analysts agreed that Anchor Hocking would still make profits for whoever owned it.

Three weeks later, Newell cut forty-five salaried and clerical jobs at Anchor Hocking. Eventually, in the Newell annual report, Anchor was no longer accounted for under "Calphalon Home." It fell into a category labeled "Other."

Galli still wanted out of the glass business. But he couldn't simply walk away from Anchor Hocking. For one thing, glass had been made on the site of the old Black Cat for a hundred years. During much of that time, the Hocking, and then Anchor Hocking, used toxic ingredients, as did all glassmakers. A 1916 recipe for ruby (red) glass from the old Lancaster Lens included arsenic, selenium, and cadmium, among other materials (like "bone ashes," which was exactly what it sounded like). Newell owned not only Plant 1 but whatever had accumulated in the buildings, soil, and groundwater around it.

His only option was to sell. But the FTC had made it clear that selling to another large glassmaker would likely bring scrutiny. He could, however, sell it off to an investment group. To do that, Newell would have to make Anchor as appealing as possible.

New rumors circulated that layoffs were coming, but Newell refused to tell anyone what it was about to do. It rebuffed inquiries from the mayor, the unions, the paper, the local branch of the state's Department of Job and Family Services. Finally, under pressure from the unions, which pleaded that workers needed to know their fate before Christmas, Newell acted. On December 3, 2002, five months after Galli reassured Lancaster, Newell fired 175 factory workers and shut down one of the plant's three tanks and all the shops that tank supplied.

Lancaster reacted like a desperate lover. It was both furious and appeasing, wanting to mend the relationship any way it could, hoping that if it just kept appearing at the door with flowers, it would all be different next time.

On February 27, 2003, the Lancaster Board of Education voted to approve a deal brokered by the Lancaster City Council and the Fairfield County Commissioners to take money from the city schools and give it to

Newell. The deal granted Newell a 100 percent tax abatement—a loss of $50,000 per year to the schools—on $30 million of new investment Newell promised to make in Anchor Hocking. Newell also promised to maintain at least nine hundred jobs there. The city and the county also lost tax dollars in the deal.

Lancaster's schools, and the rest of the town's finances, were already suffering. Just one year earlier, the city council president had told Lancaster that the streets weren't being maintained, that fire protection was inadequate, that city employees would be laid off. The city was in a financial "crisis," he said. In fiscal year 2003, Ohio's Republican governor, Bob Taft, cut school funding after the Republican-dominated legislature refused to increase cigarette taxes. In May 2003, Lancaster's schools cut $2.2 million. In February 2004, the district cut another $1 million out of its budget and fired twenty-one people.

A month after the schools agreed to the deal with Newell, Newell issued its annual report for 2002: net sales of $7.5 billion. In his letter to shareholders, Galli was ecstatic over the results. "These are exciting times at Newell Rubbermaid," he said.

They were not exciting for Anchor. As he unwrapped a generous gift from the schools, the city, and Fairfield County, Galli successfully lowered Anchor's employee count and cut its production by one-third.

Joe Boyer moved into the operators' local in 1998. Despite his lack of enthusiasm for the union, the local made him a committeeman for his shift. Committee members who failed to show for union meetings were fined. So Boyer showed. Somebody at one of those meetings nominated him to be a vice president of the local. "I thought: Well, I'll do that . . . just 'cause I don't know anything about unions. I'll just see what's going on, how a union works from the inside."

Not everything was rosy, but, like Lamb, Boyer "enjoyed being part of the Flints. It was kind of like a big family then with the Flints. They were really nice."

Because Newell was both a hard employer and never really understood glass—its Anchor CEOs were never there long enough to pick up the nuances—the Flints became more important to each worker than the union had been in fifty years. The Flints knew everything there was to know about making glass and operating a glass factory. An experienced operator could tell when a nut with more threads, good threads, holding up the spring cage of a press might be coming loose, because he could hear a change each time the press descended onto a mold. But even experienced workers couldn't hear that same noise if the threads on the nuts were old and worn. If one of those old, worn nuts gave way and a spring cage let loose and fell, it could wreck a machine. The worker would take the blame. He wasn't paying attention, management would say. But with the Flints, when the local filed a grievance on behalf of the worker in such a situation, the president of the union, usually a glassman himself, would often come down from Toledo; he wouldn't just send a rep. Boyer watched his union save jobs.

His good opinion of the Flints was shared by the president of Lancaster Glass, where the union also represented workers. Back in 1987, as Newell was taking over Anchor, the Lancaster Glass Flints talked strike because the company was asking for wage concessions. After negotiations, the Flints agreed to a 5 percent reduction for one year, followed by increases the following two years, for a net increase of 2 percent by the third year. They gave a little and got a little.

Company president Joe Ehnot praised them. "For the nearly forty years I have been associated with the many glassworkers throughout the country and the leadership provided by the American Flint Glass Workers' Union, my respect for the employees and the union leadership has never wavered. They are responsible people trying to make a respectable living."

But by 2003, so few Flints remained, thanks to plant closings and cutbacks across the industry like the ones at Anchor, the union was forced to seek safety within a bigger tribe. It voted to join the United Steelworkers. There was no joy in the decision.

The local Flint leadership barely had time to learn the way to Pittsburgh, where the Steelworkers were headquartered, before Galli's seduction paid off. On March 12, 2004, one year after the school board's vote to give up some of its own budget, Newell signed a purchase agreement to sell Anchor Hocking, Mirro, and a picture frame operation called Burnes of Boston to Cerberus Capital Management for $310 million. Anchor Hocking and Lancaster were about to enter the world of private equity.

Joseph Galli was fired from Newell the next year. In 2016, Newell Rubbermaid merged with Jarden, a collection of old brands and products that been taken down by the same kinds of financial maneuvers that took down Anchor Hocking: Ball Corporation (the old canning jar company), Rival Crock-Pots, First Alert smoke detectors, Sunbeam. Jarden was one of Sam Solomon's former employers. The $15 billion deal created Newell Brands, now based in Hoboken, New Jersey. As of May 2016, Newell's stock price still hadn't reached its 1999 high.

FIVE

Hook, Line, and Sinker

April 2007

A t first, Lancaster believed it was an answer to its prayers: Finally, twenty years after the Newell buyout and a subsequent aching decline, Cerberus's purchase of Anchor Hocking seemed to foretell a renaissance.

Lancaster was a place of strong belief. The System had made some mistakes, had not done right by Anchor Hocking. The company took it on the chin, and the town was knocked to the mat as a consequence. But if everybody just worked harder, The System would come through in the end—and now it had. Life would return to normal.

There wasn't much choice but to believe. Nobody clamored to situate a big manufacturing business in Lancaster—or in just about any place in the United States, for that matter. In 2002, Ohio's own economic development guru made a swing through the region and told everybody that manufacturing was dead in that part of Ohio—and was going to stay dead—which didn't do a hell of a lot for morale. After all, people in that part of Ohio had spent the past two hundred years either growing food or making things. If they couldn't make things anymore, what were they going to do?

Many on both coasts, and Ohio politicians, too, seemed very excited about the bright future of the "knowledge economy," but they didn't seem to have the slightest idea just what the term meant for a place like

Lancaster, or to care much about the knowledge residing there. Glass-workers were not about to be transformed into Razor-riding keyboard whizzes in tech incubators.

If you had the right education, you could get in your car every morning at 6:30 and trek to Columbus to work at a bank or an insurance company, then arrive home at night too wrung out from work and the commute and too busy with kids' soccer practices to know what the city council was doing or to volunteer to administer CPR to the city's downtown. More and more people were doing just that. As far as private industry in Lancaster was concerned, Anchor Hocking and Lancaster Glass were about it.

Diamond Power's parking lot was less than half full. Drew Shoe was now a warehouse and a few offices. Stuck Mold folded after the Newell sale. The Essex Wire building sat empty. Alten's Foundry was gone. The hospital was the town's biggest employer.

And so, though nobody knew exactly who or what Cerberus was, Lancaster believed. It did know that Cerberus was New York guys. Smart guys who turned distressed companies around. Anchor Hocking wasn't distressed; it was profitable. But still, if the Cerberus guys could save distressed companies, they had to know what they were doing. Good times were coming again for Anchor, and, with any luck at all, for the whole town.

As always, the *Eagle-Gazette*'s editors advised the city to uphold its long pro-business tradition and forge an alliance with Cerberus. "We hope the city, state and county elected officials and civic and business leaders begin to take proactive steps to help the new owners succeed and to ensure the jobs stay in the community. Intervention is necessary on the front end, although the buyer has a reputation for turning around distressed companies. Local leaders, especially city officials, should not take a wait-and-see approach to this pending change."

Citizens of Lancaster fantasized about ways Cerberus could help the town. "Maybe they could sponsor one of the area schools, giving incentives to kids who have good grades and attendance," one man told the paper.

Newell failed to partner with the community, the city council president pointed out, implying that now, maybe, Lancaster would have an Anchor owner like in the old days. Mayor Dave Smith, whose mother, "Petey" Smith, served as Malcolm Forbes's factotum when he lived in Lancaster, and who was himself a former Anchor Hocking employee, said the Cerberus purchase was "exciting." "Anchor will be in more control of its future than it has been in the past," Smith said. "It should be a strong benefit to the community."

Anchor employees said they were delighted, too. "We were super-excited," a longtime Anchor Hocking manager recalled. "We had gone through some pretty tough times with the Galli stuff, the Toledo thing, the Libbey thing."

"There was an expectation of some renewal, some better outcome," Mike Shook recalled. "A better tomorrow. 'Wow,' you know? 'Somebody wants us.' "

To buy the three businesses from Newell, Cerberus formed a company called Global Home Products Investors, LLC—Cerberus in another guise. Global Home Products Investors, in turn, created seventeen companies, all of which amounted to Global Home Products (GHP), a company it head-quartered in the Columbus suburb of Westerville. Even labor was happy when Cerberus showed up, explaining how this new entity, Global Home Products, consisting of Anchor, Mirro/WearEver, and Burnes, would be bigger and stronger than any one of the businesses alone.

" 'We got WearEver. We got this framing company. We got all these companies. We're gonna make a corporation that's unreal,' " union leader Chris Nagle said, recalling Cerberus's pitch. "And we took it hook, line, and sinker."

Cerberus, named for the three-headed dog that guards the gates of Hades in Greek mythology, was founded by Stephen Feinberg as a hybrid hedge fund/private equity manager. A Princeton grad, Feinberg, forty-four years old at the time he bought Anchor, had been weaned in the nursery of Drexel Burnham Lambert. Drexel achieved infamy as the Wall Street junk bond giant that helped finance much of the 1980s leveraged-buyout mania, sometimes using unethical—even illegal—means. Its biggest junk bond rainmaker, Michael Milken, wound up in federal prison. Drexel pleaded guilty to six felony counts, paying $650 million, then the largest-ever fine levied by the federal government for such crimes. The company later collapsed.

Feinberg founded Cerberus in 1992. At first, the firm focused on distressed debt. There's a lot of money to be made in poverty, whether you operate a payday-and-car-title-loan storefront in Lancaster, Ohio, or a multi-billion-dollar fund in New York. By buying the high-risk debt of a foundering company, Cerberus could collect high interest. If the company survived, Cerberus could sell its stake for much more than it had paid for it. If the company failed, Cerberus would duke it out with other creditors in the dogfighting pit of bankruptcy court in order to walk away with the best terms. Cerberus wasn't named Cerberus for nothing.

Cerberus had its own affiliate banking operation, called Madeleine. Madeleine would throw a lifesaving loan to a company. In return, the company would pay fees for that loan, and Madeleine would wind up owning a piece, or all, of the company. Should the company go bankrupt after all, Madeleine, as a senior lender, would be a front-of-the-line creditor.

Feinberg subsequently swerved into a more standard private equity business by buying up companies, just as he did with Global Home. These deals were aided by the presence of well-connected VIPs on the Cerberus roster. Dan Quayle, George H. W. Bush's vice president, joined the shop in 1999. Former Canadian prime minister Brian Mulroney signed on in 2003. Donald Rumsfeld invested between $1 million and $5 million, a stake he was forced to sell when he became George W. Bush's secretary of defense. George W. Bush's treasury secretary, John Snow, is now the chairman of Cerberus Capital Management.

Cerberus had already shown an interest in the glass industry before it formed GHP. In April 2002, it bought Anchor Glass Container Corporation, the old container division Bill Simon and Vince Naimoli had spun off from Anchor Hocking. Vitro had acquired it for $900 million. It went bankrupt. Cerberus took it out of bankruptcy for $80 million.

As Cerberus transitioned into standard PE deals, it shopped hard. In 2003 it took control of the Alamo and National rental car companies and a Japanese bank. The following year, Cerberus and two other PE firms bought the Mervyn's department store chain from Target for $1.2 billion; Guilford Mills, a North Carolina textile company; and a building products distribution business from Georgia-Pacific—along with Anchor Hocking and the other Newell businesses that made up GHP.

By the time it bought Anchor Hocking, Cerberus had an estimated $12 billion under management, a lot of it in Cerberus Institutional Partners II, a pool of cash handed over to Cerberus by institutions and wealthy individuals in the hopes that Cerberus would turn the pool into a lake. Some of this money was used to buy Global Home Products.

Just how much of the $310 million was pulled from the fund remained unclear, but most of the money to buy and form GHP was borrowed by GHP. When Cerberus, as Global Home Products Investors, bought the companies from Newell, it, on behalf of Global Home Products, opened a $200 million revolving loan with Wachovia, a bank based in Charlotte, North Carolina. GHP also took out a term loan and a revolving credit line for $210 million from Madeleine. In other words, Cerberus (Madeleine) loaned itself (GHP) up to $210 million.

The three companies bought from Newell booked $695 million in sales in 2003. Anchor was the largest contributor to that figure by far. But from the moment Cerberus took control, Global Home Products owed hundreds of millions of dollars and had to service all that debt. In addition to the interest payments, Global Home Products was supposed to pay preferred dividends to Global Home Products Investors (Cerberus). These dividends appeared to have amounted to about $841,000 per month. GHP would not last long enough to pay them.

Cerberus appointed George Hamilton, a former Newell executive who was already working for Cerberus, CEO of Global Home Products. Hamilton hired another Newell alumnus, Mark Eichhorn, to run Anchor Hocking.

Though Hamilton had served a rotation at Anchor under Newell and was sitting on the board of the Cerberus-controlled Anchor Glass Container, he was no glassman. Anchor employees were used to that by now, but Hamilton's management alarmed them right away.

"Their idea was not to put money in anything," Joe Boyer said. "Just let it break down, then work on it. Fix it then don't do maintenance. It's cheaper to do it that way. That's the way the place was run."

Lax maintenance led to breakdowns. Breakdowns led to equipment being pulled. The tanks hadn't been maintained well during the last days of Newell, and now they were ignored by Cerberus.

Both the cookware and frame companies proved to be immediate drains on GHP. Both bought their products from low-cost sources in Mexico and China. Quality suffered. "It was garbage," one employee told me. Anchor's cash flow wound up supporting the structure of Global Home Products, and because of that it starved.

In an effort to cut expenses, Hamilton ordered an IT change. When Global Home Products was formed, it paid Newell for the right to continue using Newell's enterprise resource planning (ERP) system for orders, pricing, inventory, and shipping. The expense made sense, since all three companies within Global Home had been Newell's, and all had used the same system. Everybody understood it, and the infrastructure was in place. But in October 2004, GHP signed a deal with Perot Systems for an entirely new ERP at less cost.

Hamilton demanded an immediate switch. "We had to do it in eight months," recalled Sue Powers, Anchor Hocking's customer service manager, "because he didn't want to spend the money [for the Newell system]. I said, 'We can't be ready. It's not gonna happen.' He said, 'I don't care; we're doing it.' We couldn't ship; pricing was a mess. We fell to our knees. He was only seeing the short term, not the long term."

Invoicing stalled. Shipments were delayed. Ware sat in warehouses. Cash stopped flowing. Bills to suppliers went unpaid, and customers screamed that their products weren't arriving.

With all the debt interest GHP had to pay, and now with a cash-flow backup, GHP found itself in a liquidity crisis. In January 2005, only seven months after Cerberus bought the company, Eichhorn announced that the workforce in the Monaca, Pennsylvania, plant would be cut in half. About 250 workers there would lose their jobs by spring. Eichhorn blamed foreign competition, health care and energy costs, and overcapacity. Some of the work done at Monaca would be shifted to Plant 1, on Pierce Avenue.

Union members in Plant 1 had mixed feelings about the news. More work for them was good news for the plant and for Lancaster, but they felt for the workers in Monaca. They also realized that everybody's jobs looked shakier than they had just a few months before. The hope for a new beginning faded away.

The news also worried Lancaster and state-level officialdom. Both the city and the state reflexively resorted to what had become a standard response across the country: They tried to figure out a way to give Cerberus, an outfit managing $12 billion, more public money.

As if to ratchet up the pressure to deliver incentives, Eichhorn shut down Plant 1 for eleven days in April 2005. There was too much inventory and no place to put the ware coming off the lines. The shutdown seemed odd to Nagle. Just weeks before, Plant 1 had been ordered to speed up production to make more ware. A conspiracy-minded person (and workers had learned to be conspiracy-minded) might think management had been stocking up in preparation for a shutdown.

The next month, the state of Ohio, Fairfield County economic development director David Zak, and the city of Lancaster announced a deal to give Global Home Products a 55 percent tax credit and $100,000 to train fifty new glassworkers by 2008. Global Home Products was also still benefiting from the tax giveaway the schools gifted to Newell, but in June the city council anted up another 100 percent tax abatement on any new machinery the company installed in Plant 1.

"Anchor is like any business and we need to offer them incentives to stay and expand here," Zak told the *Eagle-Gazette*. "They are committed to this city."

The most charitable interpretation of this statement was that Zak suffered from willful blindness. Anchor Hocking leadership hadn't been committed to Lancaster for nearly twenty years, and now it was impossible for Anchor to be committed to the city, because it *wasn't* Anchor—it was Cerberus. Commitment to anything other than Cerberus was not part of its business model. Cerberus closed the factories and stores of its portfolio companies all the time and laid off workers by the thousands, as they had in Monaca. Six months before Zak said those words, Cerberus shut— without notice—an Anchor Glass Container bottle plant in Connellsville, Pennsylvania.

Unbeknownst to Zak, Global Home Products likely knew it couldn't fulfill its obligations to hire fifty workers by 2008. It was already imploding. GHP sought the first in a series of forbearances from its creditors to avoid default.

GHP had even stopped paying into its employees' pensions, though it didn't tell anybody that. Before Newell bought Anchor Hocking, the company ran a traditional defined pension plan for its workers. After Newell took over, it switched to a 401(k) matching plan—cheaper for the company. When Newell sold the businesses to Cerberus, Newell transferred

$43,885,449 in 401(k) savings plan funds to Global Home Products. The plan had been adequately funded, but under Cerberus GHP's wasn't.

"I was settin' on the [labor management] council 'cause I was [union] vice president at the time," Nagle recalled of a conversation he had with plant manager Dan Taylor. "I said, 'We see you're in trouble. You're not payin' your bills, 'cause the vendors are sayin' you're not even payin' *them*.' 'No,'" Taylor said, "'we're okay. We're okay.' I set there, and I was heading the 401(k) at the time, and I said, 'Hey, you haven't put in our 401(k) for two months,'" Nagle said of the company's contracted contributions. "'Our money's comin' out of our checks.' And old Dan says, 'Yeah, we are. That's our 401(k), too.' He checked into it. They weren't puttin' in 401(k). They was using money, our 401(k) money, to pay bills, 'cause they was so far behind, and he didn't know anything about it."

Between April 2004, when it formed Global Home Products, and April 2007, Cerberus shorted the 401(k) account by an estimated $5,749,809. The gap between the fund's assets and the benefits it had promised employees amounted to $8,754,578. The plan had only $1.3 million to fund benefits of $10.1 million.

Cerberus was not alone in stiffing workers out of their pensions. In June 2005, after Nagle said he spoke to Taylor, the Pension Benefit Guaranty Corporation (PBGC), an insurance company created by the 1974 Employee Retirement Income Security Act (ERISA) and funded by premiums paid by companies that sponsor pension plans, testified before the U.S. Senate that 1,108 company pension plans were each at least $50 million underfunded as of 2004.

The same month Ohio gave its gift to Global Home Products, Cerberus paid $2.3 billion to buy papermaker MeadWestvaco. (Mead had a large paper plant in Chillicothe, about thirty miles from Lancaster.) That was just one of a number of 2005 deals engineered by Feinberg, who, the *New York Times* reported, was thought to have paid himself about $75 million in 2004.

Global Home Products became a snowball rolling down a mountain of debt, with nothing but bad news left in its wake. For years, Anchor had shut down for a couple of weeks—in July and in December—to clean and maintain the plant, but two months after the unscheduled April shutdown, it decided to extend the July shutdown. Altogether, workers would lose at least four weeks of work and a month's pay that year.

By fall, GHP had stopped paying the offshore companies making its picture frames and cookware. The Chinese issued stop orders on goods making their way across the Pacific Ocean. They also instructed the shipping company not to release any frames that had already landed in the United States.

Cerberus, however, wasn't slowed down at all by GHP's troubles. It began discussions to buy the Albertsons grocery store chain. At that point, some Global Home Products managers began looking for new jobs. "We didn't have any money, and Cerberus wasn't going to put any more money into it," one said. "Once they bought Albertsons, that was their entire focus."

The cash crisis paralyzed Global Home Products. By January 2006, GHP wasn't even paying the rental fees on forklifts used in Plant 1, or on the air compressors that powered the machines. Looking for options, it called in a consulting firm.

Mirro/WearEver and Burnes had to go. That was obvious. But Cerberus apparently wanted to keep Anchor Hocking, the only profitable part of the company. Because it wanted to keep Anchor, Cerberus plotted to avoid bankruptcy court. As good as its lawyers were, the proceedings could be unpredictable, and it might lose Anchor. So it explored a recapitalization of GHP as a way to stay out of court. But by March, with creditors pounding on the doors, there wasn't much choice but to declare Chapter 11. GHP filed for bankruptcy on April 10, just twenty-four months from the day Cerberus formed it.

In those twenty-four months, Global Home Products had accumulated nearly $400 million in debt. It owed Madeleine about $200 million and Wachovia $115 million. Debts to other creditors added another $66 million or so.

When Cerberus bought GHP, Lancaster's leaders voiced enthusiasm. When those leaders offered enticements from the public coffers, they thought they were assuring Anchor Hocking's long-term future. Now, after a century, Anchor Hocking found itself in a bankruptcy court.

A few tried to muster some optimism for the outcome of the proceedings, but much of Lancaster had ceased caring. They tried to rally around Newell, but then they were betrayed. Their hopes for Libbey rose, then were sunk by the FTC and the impotence of their political leaders. Some let themselves be talked into the benevolence of Cerberus, but that faith became grist for absurdist slapstick. Nobody wanted the glassworkers or the shippers and customer service reps in the DC, or the people in Monaca, to lose their jobs, but the saga of Anchor wore everyone out.

The bankruptcy proceedings were long, messy, and contentious. Burnes and Mirro/WearEver were sold off—Burnes for $33.5 million in May and WearEver for $35.7 million in August. But Cerberus didn't give up on Anchor Hocking. Global Home Products continued to make glass in Plant 1 and in Monaca as court-supervised "debtors-in-possession."

Nothing improved for the employees, though. In December, Cerberus announced it wanted to scratch the health care plan for all future retirees and to stop workers from accruing service time used to calculate pensions and benefits. Pensions and benefits would be based on the years worked until then, but no more. Health insurance would be cut back for current employees. Even those who'd already retired would lose much of their health care security—just what Dale Lamb had fought to prevent in 1992. There'd be no more holiday pay for Thanksgiving or the Sunday before Labor Day for Plant 1, no more extra pay for the day after Christmas and the Saturday before Labor Day for the DC. The judge sitting on the U.S. Bankruptcy Court for the District of Delaware, a district with a long reputation for being debtor-friendly, approved it all.

GHP worker Brenda Stone despaired. "I was a very dedicated employee from 1982 until March 2, 2006, always giving 100 percent," she told the judge in a letter. Brenda worked in quality control. She retired before the bankruptcy, fully expecting the benefits of the retiree health plan that had been agreed to by the company. She had diabetes, high blood pressure, acid reflux, and arthritis. She might as well have tried to buy the Hope Diamond as pay for her medical costs. "Now, without insurance, there is no way of surviving."

As 2006 turned into 2007, creditors accused Cerberus of delaying the proceedings. Cerberus, meanwhile, was trying to figure out a way to buy Anchor Hocking back out of bankruptcy without spending another penny.

Section 363 of the bankruptcy code was written to provide for the quick sale of a bankrupt company when delay would critically wound its chances of emerging from Chapter 11. Under 363, a judge can allow a company's creditors to bid for it at auction. The bid can consist of the debt the company already owes to a creditor, a so-called credit bid. Cerberus planned to make a credit bid for Anchor Hocking based on the $200 million owed to Madeleine (essentially $200 million owed by Cerberus to Cerberus). If the credit bid was successful—and it would be, because nobody was going to top $200 million for Anchor Hocking—Cerberus would own Anchor free of bankruptcy, and largely free of creditors like vendors and the pension plan.

The Pension Benefit Guaranty Corporation pointed out the obvious self-dealing. "Under the Amended Bid Procedures, Madeline [sic] may submit a credit bid for the Subject Anchor Hocking Assets," it told the Delaware court. (Like roughly half of all U.S. corporations, GHP was legally domiciled in Delaware, a tax haven that allows companies to move revenues to Delaware tax-free as a way to avoid state taxes in the state where they're headquartered or do business.) "If Madeline is the Successful Bidder, closing of the Anchor Hocking Sale is conditioned on confirmation of a plan of reorganization that releases Cerberus, Partners, Madeline and the members of the Debtors' Board of Directors 'from any and all claims which may be asserted against them by the [Committee], the Debtors, or any other creditor.' "

Cerberus should not be allowed to walk away from its obligations to the workers, the PBGC argued. Though GHP, which now amounted to just Anchor Hocking, was technically separate from Cerberus, the distinction was a fantasy of law. GHP was a "controlled group." Global Home Products Investors, LLC, owned 97.7 percent of the company, and Global Home Products Investors was controlled by Stephen Feinberg.

The back-and-forth continued until April 2, 2007, when Wachovia refused to extend the debtor-in-possession financing that was keeping Global Home Products afloat. Without that financing, Cerberus was forced to hold a quick 363 auction, at which it did not offer a credit bid. The sole bidder was a much smaller private equity outfit: Monomoy Capital Partners.

Wachovia was repaid in full, but other creditors, including the pension, lost most of what they were owed.

The Pension Benefit Guaranty Corporation negotiated a settlement. Cerberus agreed to provide $912,347 for "administrative costs" to the PBGC. In return, the PBGC assumed control of the Global Home Products pension plan; agreed to release Cerberus, and anybody who worked for Cerberus, from any debts, damages, claims, or causes of action; and agreed to pretend, for the sake of the deal, that, based on a declaration by Cerberus, "there is no 'controlled group' under applicable provisions of ERISA that would support a potential claim against the Cerberus Affiliates for liabilities under the Pension Plan." In other words, to make the compromise work, the PBGC had to say that Cerberus did not control GHP after all, letting Cerberus off the hook for any future pension-related claims.

Some Anchor Hocking executives who had lived through the two years of Cerberus ownership remained convinced that Cerberus walked away with a profit. That seemed doubtful. After paying Wachovia, there was little left for Madeleine to collect. Still, as we'll see, private equity outfits have ways of making money even when they appear to only be losing it. And since Global Home Products was a private company, the total payouts to Cerberus over the course of its ownership were opaque.

But whether it lost money on this particular deal, broke even, or made a profit, its ownership of Lancaster's largest private employer was just one of many transactions in which bankruptcy was part of doing business. Lancaster didn't understand that. Under the capitalism it knew, bankruptcy was failure, perhaps even evidence of one's flaws as a professional, if not as a person.

Sue Powers later ran into George Hamilton, Cerberus's handpicked GHP CEO, at a housewares show. "He said, 'How's things going?'" Powers recalled. "I said, 'You know, I could have done without that bankruptcy thing,' and he said, 'Oh, everybody's gotta go through that once in their life.' I'm like, 'Really? Do you know what that did to me?' Sometimes that is what you had in those leadership people. They didn't understand what it was doing to the city of Lancaster, Ohio, when they made those stupid, short-term decisions, you know?"

Brenda Stone wound up trying to pay $1,183 per month for a health insurance plan with high deductibles. She had to drop it. She wanted the bankruptcy judge to know that, and to ask him—and really Cerberus, too—a question.

How could it be, she wanted to know, "that the law and the government allows companies to go back and take our insurance and other benefits? If you can only imagine how hard and impossible you make it for us! I guess none of you really care just as long as your bank accounts get larger." Brenda spent twenty-five years doing what she thought she was supposed to do. She earned a living through hard work. She received excellent performance reviews. "I am sure sorry this is how you decided to repay us."

Brenda had a lot of company. Cerberus businesses had a habit of going bankrupt: Mervyn's department stores; OnePage, the papermaker once called MeadWestvaco, with its plant in Chillicothe; and Chrysler (which was then bailed out by American taxpayers) among them.

Anchor Glass Container was in that huddle, too. In September 2003, Cerberus took the old container division public with an IPO. It'd be a terrific investment, Cerberus told would-be buyers—not only because it was selling bottles and jars to Snapple, Kraft, and Anheuser-Busch, but also because of the "execution of an agreement with the Pension Benefit Guaranty Corporation, or PBGC, which we refer to as the PBGC Agreement, which eliminated all of our past-service pension liabilities." Also, Cerberus had been able to arrange the "reduction of our retiree medical obligations by approximately $24.4 million."

Cerberus made a sizable profit off the Anchor Glass Container IPO. Within a year, though, Anchor Container was in deep trouble. It closed the bottle plant in Connellsville, leaving more than 250 workers suddenly unemployed. Overburdened with debt and facing investor lawsuits, Anchor Glass Container went bankrupt in 2005.

Chrysler's bankruptcy made news because it was Chrysler and too big to ignore. But the failures of other Cerberus-owned companies, and the complicated financial reasons for their failure, went largely unreported, or were noted in a paragraph embedded in business news roundups. Plant closings in small towns had become part of the national noise, easily blamed on foreign competition or unions or anti-business liberals. Meanwhile, Cerberus continued to thrive. As of mid-2016, Cerberus was one of the largest private equity firms in the world, with more than $30 billion under management, and Stephen Feinberg was named as one of Donald Trump's key economic advisers.

The embarrassment was almost worse than the money and the bankruptcy. Lancaster had spent many years believing itself to be a much more sophisticated place than outsiders realized—and, for a long time, it was. But people in Lancaster (and people from Lancaster) could still be prone to self-consciousness about their origins in a small Ohio working town. More than anything, they hated being seen as rubes. "Li'l ol' Lancaster" was supposed to be ironic. Cerberus left them feeling like a slicker in a checked suit had shown up and sold them imaginary band instruments. There was no reason why they should have understood a joint like Cerberus—nobody teaches the Cerberus role in The System. Americans are taught to celebrate the builder-capitalists like I. J. Collins and Bill Gates. But Lancaster was infected with hurt just the same. Over time that hurt festered into bitterness.

Mike Shook, for example, knew a hell of a lot about glassmaking. He could tell you why a stainless-steel mold was cheaper in the long run than a cast-iron mold, how to design a product with the latest technology, why the chemical composition of one piece of ware was better than another's. He was a west-side boy, born and raised, but he left Anchor for a time to take his skills to other companies. He and his wife had lived in New Jersey and California. He had contacts around the world. He was a smart guy.

Libbey called him to come work for them. He and his wife even drove up to Toledo to look at some land. "I couldn't bring myself to do it. I've worked for almost every glass company in the United States except Libbey, and I couldn't bring myself to do it." Libbey was Anchor's archrival, and signing up there would have been a betrayal of both Lancaster and Anchor Hocking, like rooting for Michigan against Ohio State.

Despite his experience and savvy, Cerberus left Shook feeling as if he'd never set foot out of the west side. When he, his wife, and I sat down in his living room, he said, "Here again, I'll plead my naïveté of high finance, the Wall Street world. It was certainly foreign to me back in those days, not understanding the role that it played in the world of business and how these kinds of things happen, why they happen. I guess, again, I was more of your average Joe that said, 'This has got to be good.' Now, looking back, it was probably an odd understanding of what it meant, or not understanding at all."

Next time, Anchor Hocking employees told themselves, they'd be smarter. They understood that their new owner, Monomoy Capital Partners, was another private equity firm. They crossed their fingers and wished for it to be different, but they'd learned their lesson. As Monomoy took control, they were wary and skeptical.

Lancaster Glass died just three months after Monomoy bought Anchor Hocking. Like every other American glass company, Lancaster Glass lost sales to imports starting in the late 1980s. General Electric decided to buy its TV picture tubes, the picture tubes Lancaster manufactured, from Taiwanese makers. At the time, about a thousand people worked for Lancaster Glass; within a few years, that number was down to about four hundred. But Lancaster Glass still ran specialty glass and some tableware out of its plant on the corner of Main and Memorial Drive, at the entrance to downtown. Lancaster Colony also owned a glass plant in Sapulpa, Oklahoma, that made ware like flower vases for the floral industry—the Sapulpa plant was part of Indiana Glass Company of Dunkirk, Indiana, a company Lancaster Colony purchased in 1957.

Though Lancaster Glass was a fraction of the size of Anchor Hocking, it was still an important American glass company. For example, after Newell shut down Clarksburg, the Sunbeam blender jar business—the same blender jars that had been moved from Plant 2 to Clarksburg when Topper shut down Plant 2—came to Lancaster Glass. The specialty ware, like cathode ray tubes and the tubes used in medical monitors, required exacting handwork by Flint craftsmen. Because it did, it was, for a time, almost free of import competition and yielded a high margin.

By the mid-1990s, Lancaster Glass was among the highest-margin performers in the Lancaster Colony family of companies, a group that came to include truck-bed liners, candles, and some food products, like bottled salad dressing. Yet it worked out of a plant that was more than a hundred years old and wasn't even built to be a glass factory; it may have started life as a canal warehouse.

A man named Dave Gallimore was running Lancaster Glass in 2007. He'd come to town decades before to manage a small factory for another company. Like so many transplants before him, he grew to love the place. One day, out at the country club, Gallimore had a casual conversation with a member of the Gerlach family, which had founded, and still largely controlled, Lancaster Colony. Joe Ehnot, the man then in charge of Lancaster Glass, was about to retire. Would Gallimore think about taking it over?

"I fumbled around with it for weeks trying to decide," Gallimore recalled. "I mean, is this even possible? What I saw was a real old plant here and real old equipment and real old employees. And I didn't realize the extent of the relationships with people, the families that worked here. But I knew something about the Anchor Hocking guys: Their fathers worked there, their brothers worked there."

Gallimore liked that. He'd spent time working for big companies in other towns, saw how those companies were operated, and thought the stable town and the stable workforce, even the stable union—the Flints— were all positive signs. "They were willing to work," Gallimore said of the Flints. "Glasswork is harder than hell. I mean, those swing shifts, that fluctuation of temperatures, the potential dangers . . ."

By the early 2000s, though, Lancaster Colony stood at a crossroads. Its glass plants were old. The foreign competition had invested in new, better equipment. If Lancaster was going to stay in the market, it would have to spend for new machines and improved facilities. Lancaster Colony could afford to invest in the future of Lancaster Glass. It could have competed against the imports. But it chose not to.

That choice was not entirely its own. In the spring of 2006, just as Cerberus was taking Anchor Hocking into bankruptcy, an activist hedge fund in the mold of Icahn began a campaign to force Lancaster Colony to rid itself of glass. Barington Capital Group of New York was cofounded in 1991 by James Mitarotonda. Its business model was based on the notion that it knew how to run companies better than the people who were running them. "Better," in Mitarotonda's dictionary, meant the Friedman doctrine: maximum return for shareholders, free of other considerations. So Barington would buy a stake in a target company, then agitate for board seats and changes in corporate strategies in an effort to spike the share price, thus enriching Barington.

Mitarotonda had two demands: Shut down the glass plants, and borrow $300 million in order to buy back shares of Lancaster Colony. Buying back shares used to be forbidden by Securities and Exchange Commission rules. If a company—which, naturally, had inside information—went into the public markets and bought a lot of its own shares, thus increasing the share price, that would be stock manipulation. But in 1982, the Reagan administration SEC created Rule 10b-18, which allowed public companies to buy back almost unlimited amounts of their own shares—as long as they publicly announced it.

This was wonderful news for the Carl Icahns and James Mitarotondas of the world. In their new capitalism, a balance sheet free of debt was a waste. It meant you could afford to buy your own stock, thus increasing the share price, thus making James Mitarotonda (along with CEOs, who began taking a lot more of their pay in the form of their own stock) a lot richer a lot faster. By the early 2000s, share buybacks were sweeping through corporate America. From 2003 to 2012, the companies making up the Standard & Poor's 500 spent 54 percent of their earnings buying back their own shares.

Lancaster Colony carried no debt on its balance sheet. Most old-time businessmen—like the Gerlachs, I. J. Collins, William Fisher, and Thomas Fulton—regarded zero debt as a good policy. In the 1960s, Anchor's CEO, John Gushman, bragged about Anchor Hocking's lack of debt. That freedom meant they could use earnings to invest in plants, equipment, workers, research and development—all the things Lancaster Glass needed to compete.

In mid-March 2007, Barington filed a disclosure showing it owned 5.2 percent of Lancaster Colony. Two days later, CEO John Gerlach, Jr., announced that Lancaster Colony would shut down Lancaster Glass and the Indiana Glass plant in Oklahoma. In October, Lancaster Colony said it would buy back at least two million of its own shares by June 2008—at the top of a bull market just before the biggest stock crash since the Great Depression. In return, Barington promised to back off.

Lancaster Colony fired the 140 workers in Lancaster. Most of the equipment was sold for scrap. The factory that made the reflector for the Statue of Liberty's torch, lenses for battleship searchlights, millions of automobile headlight and taillight covers, millions of TV picture tubes, was torn

down. The lot at the entrance to Lancaster's downtown sat empty, surrounded by a chain-link fence.

The day he had to tell his employees was the hardest day of Gallimore's
working life. "I grew up in the era where the idea was to make product,"
he said. "Working for the community, for the United States, maybe for the
world." Then America decided none of that was so important. Jobs went
overseas. The knowledge of craftsmen was lost, in order "to make a product for a little bit cheaper and not worry about what happens to the guy
that used to make it for you." Gallimore had been in town for about thirty
years. His wife worked at the hospital. "I knew most of the people. I couldn't
walk down the street, go to the grocery store, go to the doctor's office. I
mean, people would just . . . I mean, 'What? You're gonna close? I don't
believe it. It can't be.'" Those people were not experts on the global economy, NAFTA and free trade, or activist hedge funds and share buybacks.
"All they knew was that place had been there for a hundred years, and the
flames coming out the tubes, and their mothers and brothers, and all that."

I was one of those people. As a boy, I'd go to see a Saturday afternoon
matinee at the Lyric Theatre, which used to sit in the middle of the block
on Main Street. After *The Love Bug* or *The Computer Wore Tennis Shoes*,
I'd walk around downtown, visit the stores, and wind up outside the greenish, corrugated plant gate at the rear of Lancaster Glass, where my father
once worked. A small mountain of cullet, the scree of past production—
shiny black, emerald green, opalescent blue boulders—glimmered in the
sunshine. Some days—especially in summer, when they opened the big
plant wall as wide as it would go to let out the heat—I could see inside. I
was a Catholic boy. Nuns had spent years engraving images of hell on my
imagination. The flames shooting out of the squat stack on the roof, the
white-red glow of the furnace inside, the gray shadows of the men hoisting their gatherers to collect glass from the inferno sure looked like hell.
But it wasn't, because these men could step outside. They were dirty and
sweaty, but sometimes they'd smile and wave at me in my boyish short pants
and sneakers. And I'd think to myself that it was manly business going on
in there, done by serious men.

"It was a tough thing," Gallimore said. "But when it came down to having to make that announcement, I mean . . ." He didn't finish.

Instead, he echoed Dick Ellwood. "My kids knew their kids, and my wife knew their wives and worked at the hospital. People came in there and had their babies there. They came in there sick. And the next day, they're not working. It was a really tough deal."

Lancaster Colony did invest a little bit in itself, though, to meet the changing America. It became a convenience food company, making salad dressings and breads. Instead of glass, it announced it would spend $23 million to build a factory in Kentucky to manufacture frozen dinner rolls: Sister Schubert's "homemade" rolls, a name seemingly designed to prove that corporate America had no sense of satire.

The new American economy had come to town like an unwelcome stranger, leaving Lancaster broken. Later, some Lancastrians, mainly those over fifty, would identify 2007 as the town's nadir. Younger people like Brian and Mark Kraft didn't. The Lancaster of their parents' youth was just a bunch of stories. They came of age around 2007. Their Lancaster hadn't ever been different.

As for Anchor Hocking, an executive who'd worked for the company since she was a teenager reported that after Cerberus, "People told me that now I knew what the devil was like."

Then she worked for Monomoy.

SIX

The Cheese, the CEO, and
Lancaster's Year

January 2015

P eggy Cummins smiled down upon Carly Bowman like an American madonna. Cummins had starred in *Green Grass of Wyoming*, the 1948 20th Century Fox release filmed at the fairgrounds. The movie poster on the flaking wall of Mark Kraft's crumbling living room was an artifact from a trove of Lancaster ephemera collected by his family. It was a memento of the filming and the world premiere, held not at Grauman's Chinese, nor Radio City Music Hall, but in Lancaster, Ohio, just one year after *Forbes* crowned it America's town. Now Cummins—blond, pretty, wholesome as fresh air—watched as Carly melted her dope, filled her syringe, and slid the needle into her leg.

The house was dissolving around Carly. The risers of the staircase to Mark's second-floor bedroom and the bathroom where he shot up had rotted to the verge of collapse. Patches of the plaster ceilings had decayed until cavities lay open to the lath underneath. The plumbing had corroded. Bits of dog shit dried where they dropped.

Carly had made a resolution to quit smoking. So far, she'd stuck to it. "7 days down, no cigarettes," she wrote on her Facebook page on January 8. The self-congratulation appeared along with other upbeat tokens from the life of a twenty-five-year-old Ohio girl: the selfies, the cute clichés about friendship, the canned empowerment mottoes.

She didn't post anything about heroin. Heroin was a need-to-know part of her life. She wasn't trying to quit heroin.

The day after her triumphal Facebook post, a customer knocked at Mark's door. Before, this customer had bought small amounts of dope, less than a gram. Now it was a little more than a gram, Carly's upper limit. She was strict about selling within a set range: between .40 and a full gram. Her connect up in Columbus had given her a scale so she could be sure of the weights. She sold this gram for about $100, or $10 a point—a profit of 50 bucks.

Carly sold dope most every day. Though business was good, she had no savings, no checking account, no credit cards. She lived an all-cash life. Money flowed by her in a stream of fleeting euphoria.

Aside from dealing heroin, Carly wasn't much different from any of her friends. She went to the same bars, ate the same pizzas, listened to the same music. Like most everybody else, she was a Buckeyes football fan. On January 12, the day of the national championship game against Oregon, Carly showed her support by posting "Sleepy today, but GO BUCKS!" on her Facebook page.

Lancaster had spent eight years skittering through the mucky cellar of its misfortune. Many of its older residents had come to feel exiled in place. It was a confusing sort of exile. The town looked like an inept imitation of the one they'd loved. Every day delivered another painful, frustrating discordance.

About three out of every five pregnant women who came to the hospital for prenatal care screened positive for cocaine, opiates, meth, Xanax. And those were just the women who came for prenatal care—a lot of young women didn't even bother. Many babies were born addicted. When they were, they often wound up in foster care or with relatives.

"What was I going to do, let the state take them?" one unmarried woman on the west side—herself only marginally employed at a social service agency—said to me as a way of explaining how she had come to be raising a relative's children in addition to her own.

About half of Lancaster City School District students, and three-quarters of children on the west side, were eligible for free or reduced-cost lunches, though many didn't accept them because they didn't want to be seen taking free food. Almost half—44 percent—of Lancaster households led by a single woman lived in poverty. Of those single female households, 57 percent with one or more related children were living in poverty; the figure was 80 percent for single mothers living with a child under five. The overall poverty rate of all families—married, single, cohabitating—with children under five was over 38 percent. The median household income was $37,494. The median household income in Ohio was about $45,700. In the United States, it was $51,849.

The hospital may have been the largest employer, but many of the jobs there, like housekeeping and assistant, were low-paying. Linda had worked there for twenty-three years, she told me, and made $17.25 an hour. After health insurance and other deductions, she figured she took home $28,000 a year, give or take. She paid $550 a month to rent a small apartment in an area known for drug traffic. Really, she said, she was doing fine, because she'd managed to save $53,000 in her 401(k) plan. She was fifty-eight years old.

Another woman, Tina, served me a drink at a bar. Later that week, I ran into her in another bar, where she pulled a draft beer for me. When I asked if she worked two jobs—commonplace in Lancaster—she said, "No, three. I'm full-time at the hospital."

Doctors, some of the best-paid hospital employees, stopped wanting to live in Lancaster. They and their families moved to Granville, a college town up the road that's home to Denison University. Or they lived in upscale Columbus-area developments and commuted in the opposite direction from their patients. They often cited the school system to justify their reasoning, but it wasn't just the school system.

The streets sagged, the houses sagged, people sagged. The country club went bankrupt. Three prominent men, including a longtime Lancaster doctor, Henry Hood, the husband of Lancaster Festival cofounder Eleanor, bought it as a way to save it from becoming a commuter tract-housing development.

Vape shops, tattoo studios—Lancaster was heavily inked—mattress stores, car-title-loan offices, Dollar General, Family Dollar, and other retailers to the impoverished peppered the town. Hickle's department store had turned into Lev's Pawn Shop.

One day, I walked into an appliance store to find the childhood friend who'd taught me how to shoot BBs into plastic soldiers. His forefathers started in Lancaster retail a hundred years back. His father ran the place. His son worked there, too. He'd lived in Chicago for a while but had returned to Lancaster because his family was there, the store was there—all that tradition. After a hug and a moment or two of reminiscing, he looked down at the floor, sighed, and said, "It's like everybody is just so discouraged."

The mayor's wife, Deb Smith, referred to the Lancaster story, the story *Forbes* told and the story kids used to learn, and said, "The mythology is so persistent and so deep in the culture, in families here, that the reality of this community—more people in poverty, away from opportunities that are the core of that mythology—creates immense fear and distress in those who have not fled. And when you are fearful, you become extremely defensive."

Defensiveness manifested itself in denial or in a chasm of wrathful division mirroring the country's own. When a developer named Leonard Gorsuch announced a plan to build Pearl House, a downtown residential facility for recovering addicts and their children, his daughter, Jennifer Walters, who spearheaded the project, received death threats.

Walters understood the vitriol. She'd opened a wound many wished would stay closed. Several years before, Lancaster's medical, law enforcement, and judicial leadership produced a publicity campaign to alert the town and the rest of the state about the creeping opiate addiction. Since then, many, including some of those same leaders, had concluded that the effort had backfired by turning Lancaster into the easy exemplar of the problem. Now, once again, Lancaster wanted to avoid eye contact with its Carlys and Marks. Some, echoing the way many felt about Anchor Hocking, said they wanted heroin addicts to just die already and get it over with so Lancaster would be free of them.

It wasn't just addicts. Though Lancaster retained a reservoir of goodwill for the disadvantaged, the unwell, the physically and mentally challenged, many others tried to ignore the town's poor and ill-educated.

Lancaster still had a couple of nice neighborhoods, and if you lived in one, you never had to confront the erosion. Walters didn't see it until she served on a federal jury in Columbus. It was a drug case. Afterwards, she traveled with a friend, a local judge named Patrick Harris. She told him about her jury duty, and what she'd learned about how the system of drug distribution operated in the region, including Lancaster.

"And he looked at me and goes, 'Has your head been in the sand?' But if you focus on your own career, your own home, you don't have to see things if you don't want to. He said, 'Come to my court one Wednesday.' So I show up, and I'm like, 'Holy Crap! Where did all these people come from?' "

Many refused to believe Lancaster natives—multigenerational families— could be part of the trouble. Surely, outsiders must have discovered that Lancaster was an easy touch for free food, Housing and Urban Development–subsidized apartments, welfare. The theory relied on the improbable notion that ne'er-do-wells in Dayton, Cleveland, Columbus, and points east into West Virginia and Pennsylvania looked at a map of the United States and—instead of California, Florida, or any of a hundred other towns in Ohio—decided that Lancaster was the freeloader Shangri-la they'd been looking for.

A significant faction within Lancaster lost its moderate conservatism. Stoked by cable news, Internet videos, and right-wing politicians, they insisted that most of Lancaster's problems had to be the natural product of an over-generous social service system that coddled lazy, irresponsible people.

How else to explain all the "Obama phones" those supposedly poor people carried around? they asked, referring to Lifeline, the subsidized telephone program that was created not by Obama's administration but by Reagan's. The program was expanded by George W. Bush to include cell phones so the poor could have phone service.

Back in the 1980s, Community Action, a social service agency based at the far eastern edge of town on Route 22, in what used to be the old county children's home for orphans, received about two hundred requests for food packages per month. The number was now over two thousand per month. The agency also offered a limited number of supportive housing units. There was a waiting list.

Kellie Ailes, the Community Action executive director, often heard the narrative about lazy, irresponsible outsiders who could somehow afford lots of tattoos and cell phones. When I repeated it to her, she shook her head.

"The people who come to us do not want public assistance," she said. "They feel shame when they come." When she was asked by a city councilman if the people to be helped by a planned subsidized housing project were locals, she researched the question and found that "virtually all" were from Fairfield County zip codes, mostly from the city of Lancaster.

"From the time Plant 2 closed, people lost jobs, lost homes, lost families, lost everything," she told me. "And we worked with a bunch of guys from Stuck Mold" when it closed after the Newell takeover. She recalled a man she helped who'd lost his house. Then his wife left him. He could work but had some cognitive limitations. In the past, she said, he could have found a place at Anchor Hocking, but no more.

Ailes's grandfather had been a foreman in the Anchor Hocking furnace room. He also served as president of the Lancaster Board of Education. Her father was a machinist in Plant 1. She was as Lancaster as it was possible to be. But when the Pearl House debate raged, she had to put her job on the line to support it. Some around town hadn't yet forgotten. She'd made enemies.

Lancaster's water was still not fluoridated, she pointed out, because a few die-hard anti-government conspiracy theorists remained convinced that fluoridation was a nefarious plot.

"They vote against their own self-interest!" Rosemary Hajost exclaimed to me one afternoon. Many with money preferred the low-tax mantra and conservative social-issue stances of the Republicans. Many union and working-class Democrats didn't vote, and some who did viewed the modern party's social-issues agenda—such as gay and transgender rights—as an attempt to impose an exotic order. Joe Boyer pasted a John Kerry sticker around a pole in his garage and an NRA sticker on his truck. He leaned Democrat but sometimes voted Republican because he worried that Democrats wanted his guns.

"I was on the school board," Hajost continued. "And except for the first year, we were cutting and cutting and cutting. Over a hundred teachers out." She worried that one day the wealthy would wake up to find a rabble in the streets. "People say that could never happen, but people thought we would never lose Anchor Hocking." She said that, among her friends, "I don't talk about the fact I voted for Obama."

Even as many condemned both federal and state government programs and government spending, they ignored the fact that their town owed many of the jobs it had to both. Medicaid and Medicare supplied over 60 percent of the hospital's income. The public schools were the second-largest employer in town. Anchor Hocking was third.

The absence of the critical mass of sophisticated leaders and their spouses that Lancaster once enjoyed left local politics to well-meaning but amateurish dogmatists. Once sedate city council meetings turned angry. In addition to the building of Pearl House, other issues, such as where to place a new, larger county jail, split the council into bungling, combative, factions. Endless arguments over seemingly minor issues—downtown parking dominated meeting agendas—sidetracked members from the city's bigger problems. The majority remained captured by an ultra-conservative, anti-tax philosophy that prevented them from raising funds to repair the crumbling streets or challenging the ridiculous ban on fluoridated water, even as their pro-business bias blinded them to how Newell and Cerberus picked their pockets.

Some, supported by gadfly citizens, were convinced that Gorsuch secretly orchestrated a cabal that ran the town and foisted low-income Section 8 housing on Lancaster. Nobody ever presented any evidence ("I'm not sure I can trust you," one citizen told me after swearing he had proof, then reneging on his offer to show it), but they were convinced the low-income housing, not the economy, was responsible for the undesirable "outsiders."

There was real corruption, though. In September 2014, the county clerk of courts, Deborah Smalley, a Republican, was sentenced to eighteen months in prison for misusing nearly $40,000 of public money and for intimidating employees to campaign for her election. Her conviction, coming after former sheriff DeMastry's in 2002 and former judge McAuliffe's in 2004, was yet another black mark on Lancaster's reputation.

Others blamed a generalized immorality, a breakdown of old restrictions and codes: all those young single mothers and "baby daddies." All that drug use. An aversion to hard work. But they attributed these trends to "the media" or liberalism, not the decades of lousy education, economic collapse, and the minimum-wage and barely-above-minimum-wage dead-end jobs that replaced factory work.

Some responded by retreating into the comforting certainty of fundamentalist Christianity. As membership at Nancy Frick's beloved St. John's Episcopal declined, along with that at other mainline Protestant—and Catholic—churches, membership boomed at Fairfield Christian. (Brian Gossett referred to the big, modern campus on Lancaster's northwest edge as "Fort God.") Its affiliated school, Fairfield Christian Academy, founded in 1998, enrolled about five hundred students, making it by far the largest private school in the county. Every Sunday, another ministry, Crossroads .TV, packed a couple hundred worshippers into a big space in the River Valley Mall vacated by an out-of-business store and broadcast its rock-'n'-roll-and-tattoos brand of evangelism on cable TV.

The town had approved that small shopping center, located by the banks of the Hocking, north up Memorial Drive, in the wake of the Plant 2 closing, hoping it would bring in some taxes. When it opened in 1987, just as Newell took over Anchor Hocking and closed the downtown head-quarters, the mall gut-punched the downtown merchants for the second time. Almost twenty years later, there were days you could shoot a cannon down the mall's main artery from Dick's Sporting Goods to the Sears and be pretty sure you wouldn't hit anybody.

Like Carly, who trumpeted her will to stop smoking while pumping heroin into her veins, many in Lancaster, at least many over fifty, concluded that negativity, not reality, was the enemy. People were discouraged, but they were sick of being discouraged, sick of talking about drugs, sick of fretting over jobs, sick of bad news. The new year, 2015, was going to be the year it all turned around.

The mayor, the few remaining service clubs, and an organization pro-moting a rejuvenated downtown, called Destination Downtown Lancaster, stressed the truth, though it was obvious: "We're no worse off than a lot of other places." Some—likely many—towns were indeed worse off than Lancaster, but setting such a low bar had never been the Lancaster way. Lancaster had always thought of itself as exceptionally wonderful.

Though the optimism seemed forced, it wasn't entirely unjustified. After pointing out the addition of a couple of new restaurants and the two down-town buildings being restored—the Mithoff and the Columbian, which was being turned into a court building—most talked up the new schools. After years of starving them, Lancaster had narrowly passed a convoluted tax levy engineered to convince voters that Lancaster's upper class would be squeezed the hardest. The new money would have been nowhere near enough, but the state government kicked in funds—nobody seemed to object to that government spending—and now five new elementary schools were either on the drawing board or under construction.

When the Buckeyes romped over Oregon, 42–20, on Monday, January 12, Lancaster celebrated. Once again, the title would return to where everyone knew it rightfully belonged. For a moment, echoes from the era of legendary coach Woody Hayes bounced around town. Many still remembered when Lancaster sent quarterback Rex Kern to Hayes. Kern was the son and the nephew of barbers; Uncle Bud ran the shop in the basement of the hotel. When Hayes and Kern beat O. J. Simpson and those other flashy Californians from USC in the 1969 Rose Bowl, "li'l ol' Lancaster" claimed the victory as its own.

This win wasn't quite as sweet, but it seemed to be a portent. The day after the game, the board of the Lancaster Festival announced more good news. Joe Piccolo, a northern Ohio native who'd been working at the Aspen Music Festival, in Colorado, was hired as executive director. Aspen was big-time, yet Piccolo talked about how excited he was to come to Lancaster.

The town and the festival's board felt lucky to get him. There had been anger over the firing of the previous director, Lou Ross. Nobody used the word "fired"—everyone thanked everyone else for years of service, expressing mutual best wishes—but Ross had been fired and he was sore about it.

The festival was nearly broke; the whole enterprise seemed a little stale. The blame fell on Ross, and for him that was the worst part. He'd worked like a mule, year after year, coordinating the volunteers, helping set up stages, paying bills, and booking talent. In the weeks before each festival, he lived on junk food and little sleep.

The whole point of the festival was to showcase the Lancaster Festival Orchestra by having it play with whatever musical group or singer agreed to headline. That was what made the Lancaster Festival different from a dozen other summertime music and arts fests around the region. The orchestra was Lancaster's own. The first two festivals featured the Columbus Symphony, but every year since, for two weeks in July, the festival had formed an ad hoc orchestra made up of musicians from Chicago, Columbus, Cleveland, New York, Portland, St. Louis—even Taipei—under maestro

Gary Sheldon, now the principal conductor of the Miami City Ballet or-chestra. Some musicians had been coming for more than twenty years. They stayed with families and ate at the Pink Cricket. They performed chamber concerts around town. And on the two Saturday nights, on a stage set up by a creek fronted by a hill that formed a natural grassy amphithe-ater behind the Ohio University branch, they joined the likes of the Beach Boys, Ben Vereen, and Aretha Franklin in what amounted to Lancaster's backyard party.

Seeing the famous-but-faded was fine back in the 1980s and '90s, but the novelty had worn off. Young people wanted music that was very dif-ferent from that favored by the old guard left over from Lancaster's glory days. But the old guard were the only people who could afford to make donations and pay for catered tables up by the stage, instead of bringing picnic baskets and a blanket to spread out on the hillside. Most people loved the festival, and many said it was the best thing about Lancaster. But there were gripes that Ross never booked Taylor Swift or that guy on the show—what's his name—Blake Shelton. He tried his best to book acts people wanted to see (and would pay to see), but it was never easy. He explained over and over that the festival's budget couldn't come close to paying Taylor Swift's fees.

Worse, during the two weeks of the festival, the art shows, piano concerts, and kids' puppet theater didn't make a profit, ran at a loss, or were free of charge. Nearly the entire operating budget depended on free labor from platoons of volunteers, on donations, and on drawing big crowds to the two Saturday nights. But it rains in Ohio in July—sometimes with vio-lent electricity arcing through the sky and tree-bending winds. Storms had hit the previous two years, smack-dab on those Saturday nights, and walk-up ticket buyers, having seen the forecast, didn't show. What the hell was Ross supposed to do about the goddamn weather?

That was the past, though, and Lancaster was now looking forward with all the determination it could muster. Piccolo was to be the man who would take the Lancaster Festival into a new, splashier era. He didn't know it yet, but Lancaster was counting on him to help save the town.

Much of the grim optimism was invested in a vision of Lancaster as a tourist magnet. Lancaster could be hip. It could be an artist colony. Those hopes partly depended on the success of the festival.

A group of Ohio State University urban-planning students had come to Lancaster and suggested as much. Spruce up downtown, it instructed. Showcase the old buildings and Sherman's house—the assets saved by Nancy Frick's generation. Put a modernist glass sculpture on the empty block where Lancaster Glass used to stand. Maybe open up a few cool coffeehouses. Use the festival to promote Lancaster as an arts destination, get some artists to live there, and—voilà—you'd have a midwestern Brooklyn.

"It is okay for Lancaster to embrace its old industrial ways, but the economy is demanding a more leisure-oriented and cultural base." The group did not say who would pay for the leisure, or who would serve the leisure class. And even if "the economy" were demanding such a thing, Lancaster never had. Lancaster worked for a living—or at least it used to. But those days were over. Industry had died of natural causes—everybody knew that. Lancaster should become a postindustrial amusement park. The future was an artisanal-scone-based economy.

As tenuous as that future may have been, many cast their eyes toward it. They wanted to ignore Anchor Hocking the same way they wanted to ignore Carly and Mark. Like it or not, though, Lancaster still needed Anchor more than it wanted to admit.

"Oh my gosh, we would really, really be in bad shape" if Anchor Hocking closed, city council president Cathy Bitler told me. "Do we need those thousand jobs? You bet we do!"

Sam Solomon, EveryWare Global's—and so Anchor Hocking's—new CEO, was loath to say it out loud. Every time he thought about doing so, he pictured himself sitting in a courtroom witness chair. But it was clear that he'd concluded that the only way to save EveryWare Global—and therefore Anchor Hocking—was to scrape Monomoy off its back. Anchor Hocking wasn't dying a natural death; it was being killed.

Pinpointing exactly when he began to despise his bosses at Monomoy Capital Partners was a little like trying to decide exactly when a marriage curdled: you could never blame the sour taste on one incident at one moment in time. But by January, his contempt was obvious. Nothing had gone the way he'd hoped when he first walked through the doors on Pierce Avenue the year before.

Since leaving his first post-M.B.A. job, at Procter & Gamble, Solomon had fielded calls from headhunters. Depending on the match between his current job and his ultimate ambitions, he'd listen, or not. In November 2013, he received a call about the EveryWare Global CEO job.

At the time, Solomon was working at Sears Holdings. He ran the Craftsman brands—tools and paint. The majority owner of Sears was a hedge funder named Eddie Lampert. Lampert made a name for himself in the early 2000s by avoiding Internet companies and investing instead in unglamorous businesses like AutoZone, a chain of auto parts stores. After the dot-com bubble popped and he became a multibillionaire, fawning media profiles followed. So when Lampert merged Sears with Kmart and made lots of claims about how profitable the new Sears Holdings would be, the stock ran up. But by the time Solomon joined it in 2011, Sears was faltering.

Solomon thought he would be able to spin Craftsman out of Sears and run it as a stand-alone company. He believed Lampert would go along with the idea, but Lampert, Solomon said, decided he didn't want to lose a revenue driver for the Sears stores. Also, and perhaps not coincidentally, at about the same time that Solomon got the call from the headhunter, Sears stock was falling like a sack of potatoes. On November 25, 2013, it was a hair above $50. Two months later, it hung at just over $29. So Solomon listened.

By January 2014, conversations with Monomoy had turned serious. Solomon flew to New York to interview at Monomoy's offices, in the Metropolitan Tower on Fifty-seventh Street, next door to the Russian Tea Room and just down the block from Carnegie Hall. The reception lobby of the seventeenth-floor suite was decorated with totems of American industry. To the left, a silvery piece of cast metal, about eighteen inches high, sat on a display pedestal like a piece of brutalist art. On the wall to the right, a large photograph depicted an industrial landscape with a man walking across a bridge, a factory in the background. The red-tinged light in the picture made it hard to tell whether the man was walking to or away from work.

Solomon understood the basics of private equity's business model, as well as both sides of private equity's reputation. PE's general partners—the firm and its principals—formed one or more funds. The funds were pools of cash, obtained from investors, such as pensions, endowments, other investment houses, and very wealthy individuals. These investors were the limited partners. The PE firm made money by charging the limited partners 2 percent management fees on the money the investors deposited into the fund, and 20 percent of any profit after the fund vaulted a rate-of-return hurdle. Monomoy set an 8 percent hurdle, standard for the industry. Legally speaking, the 20 percent was not salary; it was "carried interest," a term with roots dating to the era when cargo was shipped—carried—by sailing vessels on risky voyages, and the captain of a vessel took a percentage of the cargo as part of his compensation. As carried interest, PE's income wasn't taxed as regular wages subject to the tax brackets that bound most people. It was considered capital gains and taxed at 20 percent. The top bracket most PE principals would occupy if they weren't in private equity but earned the same amount of money would require them to pay double that—39.6 percent. PE firms also charged a variety of fees. For example, they billed the companies they bought "advisory fees" for providing business wisdom.

PE enthusiasts tended to view private equity investment outfits as saviors who could buy a company, boost efficiencies, create strengths that had faded under previous owners, and then sell the company at a profit, thus enriching both the general partners and the limited partners. The target company emerged better positioned to compete in capitalism's grand marketplace. Everybody won.

PE critics, on the other hand, viewed the buyout shops as chain-saw cowboys who slashed employment, cut investment, and shut down marketing and research—all in order to goose the bottom line just long enough to foist a shiny, but hollowed-out and highly indebted, company onto new buyers and then count their money on the helicopter flight from Manhattan to their summer houses in the Hamptons.

Solomon regarded private equity as a matter of perspective. If you were a PE general partner, he told himself, "strip-and-sell is a great freaking return" on your money. If you were a target company employee, or a small town where that company was located, you might prefer to add value through investment in people, machines, and research and development, for a long-term benefit. Business finance isn't religion: Nobody—at least nobody whose voice mattered much—was going to condemn you for making money either way.

Solomon's dispassion hadn't come naturally. He had to learn it.

He liked to say that he was bred with a blue-collar work ethic. No matter how successful he became, Solomon always carried thoughts of his father and the rest of his people in the tobacco fields of Warren County, North Carolina. They shopped in the usurious landowner stores, went into debt, made up the debt by sweating through backbreaking days, then fell back into debt the next year laboring for "Mr. Charlie." In between harvesting and planting tobacco, they worked odd jobs like stacking wood and got shortchanged for their labor. But they didn't do much about being cheated, because arguing with a white landowner was never going to get you anything but trouble. His father joined the air force to escape that life, and because of his dad's decision, Solomon had been educated in good, integrated military-base schools in Panama and along the East Coast.

He was a smart kid, and though his school counselors had their doubts—because Solomon was black—he applied to Duke University, a temple of the white South named for tobacco barons. He was accepted, with a scholarship.

Then he messed up. He was still dating his high school girlfriend that first year. By the end of it, she was pregnant. He started his sophomore year as a married man, then became a father. With his scholarship, continuing at Duke might have been possible, but then the child was diagnosed with leukemia. His scholarship wasn't going to pay medical bills, but the military would. So Solomon dropped out and joined the army. When the boy died less than a year later, the marriage seemed to lose its purpose, as did Solomon's military career. Solomon and his wife divorced, but the military refused to let him divorce it. For the next three years, he worked in computers, telecommunications, and intelligence for the army while his former Duke frat brothers went on to medical school or good jobs.

When his hitch was up, Solomon pulled out of Fort Sill, Oklahoma, and drove toward Houston, where his parents were living at the time. Normally, that's a six-and-a-half-hour trip, but Solomon took six days. He saw some sights, he partied, and he called Duke. The university told him he was welcome to come back. The scholarship, though, was gone.

At his reunion dinner in Houston, he announced the good news about resuming his college education at Duke, fully expecting his father to offer financial as well as moral support. There were toasts and huzzahs, and then his father took him into the backyard for cigars and brandy to express his pride in his son for accepting his responsibilities like a man. He had made a big-boy mistake but had done the right thing. But because he had blown his first shot at a paid-for education, he should keep right on being a man and pay his own way.

Solomon moved to New Jersey, where he studied marketing at Rider University while supporting himself with his army-gained computer skills by working at tech companies. After graduating, he applied to Duke's M.B.A. program. This time, his parents agreed to help.

When he was accepted into Duke's grad school, his mother, swelled with pride, couldn't help bragging to Solomon's aunt that her boy was getting an M.B.A. at Duke University. M.B.A.s could make real money, maybe $60,000, $80,000 per year *right away*, she said.

"That boy is gonna drain you of every penny you have," his aunt snapped. "No black person ever makes that kind of money."

Solomon did make that kind of money, and a lot more. But his tour around America's corporate landscape taught him that the career he chose did not mirror the life he had left behind. His family's history—and the military, too—instilled in Solomon "a huge sense of fair play, that there's a right way to do things, a right way to treat people." As a junior executive in modern business, though, "you pretty quickly learn that these people that you are supporting aren't exactly playing the game the way you thought it was gonna be played."

Solomon became a pragmatist, not an idealist. The game existed, and he wanted to win, but to do so he'd have to play the game he found. If PE was part of the game, an instrument he could use to further his ambition, then so be it.

Still, he was a build-value guy, not an extract-value one. So he was cautious going into his meetings with Monomoy. As he walked back out onto Fifty-seventh Street, though, he felt encouraged.

"This was also articulated, and I believed to be true: [EveryWare] was the jewel of [Monomoy's] crown. It was their largest investment at the time, the only public entity that they had at the time. And they were now professing a desire to move to the next level of private equity."

Monomoy was a small shop, compared with giants like Cerberus, the Carlyle Group, Kohlberg Kravis Roberts (KKR), the Blackstone Group, and Apollo Global Management. After his interviews, Solomon believed Monomoy saw EveryWare as a ticket to PE's big time. EveryWare had potential to grow, to maybe become a billion-dollar enterprise. Monomoy had already extracted enough cash to make back its investment and more, but Solomon was fine with that as long as it was willing to pivot to growth and to hire him to lead the way.

That's what he'd always wanted but—as with the near miss at Sears—had not yet found. He had come to believe nobody was going to hand him the reins of a big, stand-alone company. Maybe his race had something to do with that, maybe not, but if he was ever going to be the man in control, he was going to have to build a billion-dollar company beneath himself. He was fifty-five years old. EveryWare looked like his shot.

But Pierce Avenue in Lancaster, Ohio, proved to be a world away from Fifty-seventh Street in Manhattan, and not just geographically. Too much had gone on within EveryWare since he'd come to town in February, most of it hidden from view, buried by nondisclosure clauses in contracts: silence bought with money paid to departing executives.

The month before, he'd sat down at a table in his office, scribbled a series of numbers on a piece of scratch paper, shoved it across the table, and stared at me as if the meaning of the numbers were so obvious, so incriminating, that there was no need to dissect them. He walked into a low-rent circus when he entered his new office that first day. The situation was worse now. EveryWare, and therefore Anchor Hocking, was near death, though nobody in Lancaster knew what Solomon knew.

The day after the national championship game, around noon, at almost exactly the moment the Lancaster Festival Board announced the hiring of Joe Piccolo, Carly heard another knock on Mark's door—this time so thunderous and angry it rattled the house. Men in bulletproof vests smashed through the door and charged into the living room.

Eric Brown was one of them. His Major Crimes Unit had been buying heroin from Carly for over a month, a little more each time. The January 9 buy of a gram, and the fact that Mark's house was within one thousand feet of East School, jacked up the possible charges against Carly to a felony, mandating a "presumption for a prison term," according to the Ohio Revised Code. The MCU had been biding its time so it could make that charge. Now it could hold prison over Carly's head and hope she would drop a dime on everybody she knew in Lancaster's parallel society of dope.

Brown took a few minutes to look around the house: the dog shit, the staircase, the trashed bedrooms upstairs, the falling-down plaster, the beat-up walls, a vintage Lancaster High School class photo, Peggy Cummins. None of it really surprised him. Unlike most people in Lancaster, he spent a fair amount of time in the homes of addicts.

Brown was tired. The MCU had been formed in 2001, when meth was the drug everybody worried about. It was fourteen years later, and what had been accomplished? Different drug, same story. He told himself that the situation would be far worse without his work and that of his fellow officers—which was probably true—but they were treading water, and he knew it.

He'd once attended a National Narcotic Officers' Associations' Coalition conference in San Diego, during which he trooped down to the Mexican border as part of a field trip. "Here I am, hometown America, and I just couldn't believe it. It was like a whole other world. I walked around down there with my jaw dragging on the ground." Thousands of cars, and many thousands of people, crossed the border hour after hour. In his mind, he saw dope in the cars, and imagined that dope finding its way into Lancaster, to a dilapidated house on King Street.

While some of it would come from poppies grown in Mexico, the war in Afghanistan unleashed tons—8,600 tons in 2014—of opium onto the world market, depressing prices no matter where it originated. Brown believed the war in Afghanistan was a lot more complex than most Americans realized. The way he figured it, behind-the-scenes deals between the Americans, the poppy farmers, and the Afghan government had been made to keep the place from blowing apart.

A detective pulled Carly out of the house and sat her down in the backseat of his car while his colleagues searched Mark's place. They'd find over ten grams of heroin and $103; Carly had just brought down a fresh supply.

Using the gentle tones of a priest preparing to hear a confession, the detective recited her Miranda rights. Carly sniffled a little, but recovered quickly. And then she talked. She named every customer she could remember and her Columbus connect, too. Once they were sitting in a cop's car, Lancaster junkies always talked. The junkies all knew they always talked.

Carly also knew what else to say. "I do want help," she told the detective. "I would prefer to have rehab and get help, because obviously I'm not a bad person. I have a problem, and I would love to be clean." Every arrested junkie said this, too, or some version of it. Who wouldn't prefer rehab to jail? Most of the time, they meant it—at least when they said it.

Mark wasn't home. He'd just left work on his lunch hour to make a run to the ATM. He had cell phone and car insurance bills to pay. On the way back to work from the bank, his phone buzzed. An MCU officer told Mark that Carly was in trouble, but he wasn't. Mark should come home, though, to retrieve his dog.

Mark wasn't too worried. He'd skated by so many close calls with cops, it was downright weird. Besides, he stashed his dope elsewhere. Anything the MCU found would be Carly's.

He almost laughed when he pulled up to the house. King Street was blocked off with those big $50,000 SUVs, like they were busting a terrorist cell or something. The front door was damaged, like they just had to crash it. He stepped inside, and right away thought the house felt like a big show—cops all suited up to take down a girl drug addict—but before his thought about how bogus it was had completely formed, somebody threw him on the floor, searched him, took the $360 he'd just taken out of the bank, and said the cash sure looked like proceeds from his criminal behavior. They took his phone and said he was now under arrest for permitting the use and sale of drugs from his home.

Brown called Carly's father. He hated making those calls. They ate away at him. At least the bust might help Carly and Mark. Addicts sometimes told him that being hauled into jail, and then diverted into rehab, saved their lives, but you could never tell. Arresting a couple of kids—which was what they were, really—was not guaranteed to change them or to nick Lancaster's heroin trade.

A s a matter of fact, Brown was unaware that, at the moment of Carly's arrest, a man named Jason Roach was appointing himself Lancaster's new dope king. Jason had just met this guy, the Cheese, in the same place lots of people in Lancaster met a connect: the Fairfield County Jail, on Main Street. What Jason was doing in the Fairfield County Jail for a day or so made for a long story, but anyway, the Cheese seemed like a good dude. Jason had met him before, you know, around, and when he heard Jason was at loose ends—just out of a South Carolina prison as of January 1, no job, no money, living on a little SSI (Supplemental Security Income)—the Cheese said, "Dude, I can totally fix you up."

That sounded good to Jason. He was a family man, in love with Jessica Cantrell, though they were kind of broken up at the moment, seeing as how Jason had spent the past two years in prison.

Jessica, who looked a little like Ava Gardner if Ava Gardner had played in *The Grapes of Wrath*, arrived in Lancaster in 2005 after Hurricane Katrina. She and her mother and brothers had lived in Louisiana. They weren't doing all that well, and the storm only made everything worse, so when Jessica's mother called a friend who lived in Lancaster, and the friend suggested they come north, they did.

Jason and Jessica had a child together, and she had kids of her own with a couple of other dudes, though Jason considered himself their father, too. The hitch, though, was that Jason was sick of scrambling around for minimum wages and government checks. He'd watched his own mother live on SSI and never have anything, and there was no way in hell he was going to raise his little brood that way.

Jason had a soft face, with gentle eyes framed by short brown hair. A tattoo of a single tear under one eye looked like actor's makeup for a prison picture, not the genuine tat of a guy who'd served time in prison, though Jason had done two stretches already—the first for a felony assault; he'd served five years for it. Really it was his brother's rap; Jason just happened to be there.

He married shortly after that first time in prison, and lived for a little while with his new wife in the Columbus suburb of Upper Arlington. (Jason always stressed "Upper Arlington." He'd grown up around Columbus and knew that rich people lived in Upper Arlington.) Life wasn't working out as well as he'd hoped, so the couple moved to South Carolina to be near Jason's father-in-law.

His wife went to work for her father while he got a job with a moving company. Moving's brutal on a fellow's back. Jason blew a disc. During the operation, the doctors gave him fentanyl, and then, after the surgery, Perc 30s—or was it Oxy? Jason never told a story exactly the same way twice—and Xanax, all of which Jason enjoyed very much, which explained how he morphed from a casual drug user into an addict, and why he used his father-in-law's credit cards.

When he heard that a warrant for misusing them had been issued, Jason ran back to Ohio. His mother had since moved down to Lancaster. So, in 2009, Jason landed there, too. He worked a little landscaping here and there, and for a small catering business, but the pay was bullshit. He wasn't ever going to get anywhere that way.

When he met Jessica, they fell in love pretty quickly. The relationship was messy and volatile, with a domestic violence charge against Jason and a trip to court over support, and both of those cases were complicated by Jessica's arrest for heroin trafficking. She served a stretch in prison during 2013, right about the time Jason's South Carolina warrant finally caught up to him. He was extradited and served a couple of years, but now he was out, back in Lancaster, and clutching a phone number provided by the Cheese.

The Cheese was a man of his word. He really did have a big-time con-nect: Mexicans up in Columbus.

Jessica was almost twenty-six; Jason was nearing thirty-eight. If he and Jessica were ever going to have anything, the time had come to go big and go hard.

The Cheese told him the Mexicans might front him dope—serious weight: ounces, not grams. Jason could bring it down to Lancaster, divvy it up among a few trusted junkie sellers, collect the proceeds, make an-other trip to Columbus, pay back the Mexicans, keep the profit, and load up again. Jason wanted to go into the wholesale pharmaceutical business.

Though he knew where he wanted to end up, he was vague on how to get there. Jason was not a management guy; he was an eighth-grade drop-out who had never been able to manage himself. But then Lloyd Romine hit him up on Facebook.

Lloyd barely knew Jason. They'd met in the county jail annex out by the Southeastern Correctional Institution, on BIS Road, a couple of years before and hadn't spoken since, but when Lloyd heard Jason was back in town, he wanted to say hello. No particular reason. When Jason saw Lloyd's message, he said to himself, " 'He has a reputation in this town for beating people up and shit,' and I was like, 'Well, shit, I'm gonna put him on my team.' "

SEVEN

The Shutdown

February 2015

Mark Kraft's family holidays had been so loving and peaceful, and the first few days of the new year so positive, that his mother, used to a stream of doom in Lancaster, wondered, "What the heck's going on here?" She even allowed herself to share in the general optimism slowly making its way through town. Then the MCU bashed in Mark's front door.

He spent thirty hours in the jail on Main Street. Each hour dragged more slowly than the one before, until Mark wasn't sure what to fear most: the hour that was scraping by, or the next one to come. He'd been a little dope-sick before, but nothing like this. He didn't sleep and didn't eat much. What he did eat, he threw up.

He pleaded not guilty to drug-related charges in Municipal Court and posted $1,000—10 percent of his $10,000 bail—and the $25 cost for his jail time, and when he was finally released, he wobbled east down Main Street, blowing chunks into the curb.

The only way he'd managed those thirty hours was by telling himself that as soon as he got out, he would find his stash in its secret spot and get high. Then the pain would go away. The pain was temporary. He wouldn't feel this way forever. He could see it in his mind, how it would go: his arm, the syringe, the needle, the warm, cozy feeling of safety and contentment. He made for it as soon as he could. But the dope was gone. It had been discovered.

His father went back with him to the house on King Street to look over the damage and get a few things for his stay back with his parents. Mark opened a drawer in his bedroom. A gram the cops had missed shone up into his face like a bright sun through dark clouds of T-shirt. His father was right there and saw Mark palm it. Mark knew his father had seen. That was the bad part, his father's knowing. Mark pulled the dope from a pocket, in front of his father, walked over to the toilet, dropped it in, and flushed. It was the first time in the two-plus years he'd been shooting heroin that he'd made a choice not to use it, and his dad had seen him do that. He thought, "We did it together."

The sweetness of the moment didn't last long. The sickness overwhelmed it.

By early February, he wasn't throwing up anymore, but he'd never felt worse. He ached. Anxiety infested his mind like a thousand buzzing bees, making it impossible to sleep. He lay in bed for hours, feeling like he could crawl out of his skin. To get some sleep, he picked up some Xanax—Mark always knew where to get whatever drug he wanted—though he knew he'd be tested for drugs. The Xanax helped a little, but what he really wanted more than anything was dope. Any dope, from anybody. A Perc 30 would do.

A t first, when his buddy Aaron Shonk, who sat in a cubicle out at Drew Shoe making phone calls to China, told Brian there was a warehouse job opening up, Brian dismissed the idea of applying. He couldn't afford to make that move. The Drew job started at $10 an hour, $4.50 less than he made at Anchor.

Then he thought about it some more, weighed the goods of his job in Plant 1 against the bads. The heat was bad, the machines were dangerous. The longer he worked his H-28, the more he feared losing a body part or getting burned. Really, though, it wasn't the heat or the machines. They were in lousy shape, for sure, but in his more honest moments, he'd admit there was a small kernel of attraction to them. He had to pay attention. The job focused his mind.

The attitude of the place bugged him more than the condition of the machines. His supervisors, the men who were supposed to be training him, weren't interested in training him—not anymore. Brant, his floor operator, still stepped in when Brian needed a hand and tried to teach him, but the rest of his bosses seemed to have given up.

The whole place seemed to have given up. He counted five other guys on his shift alone who'd left. They were all about his age. A couple of them already had journeyman cards, but they left anyway. Guys like Brant, though, were stuck. They'd been there too long and were too old to quit. But they hadn't been there long enough—and were too young anyway—to retire. Despite Plant 1's long slide, it still offered the best-paying jobs in town— in the whole county, for that matter—to guys like Brant, who'd grown up poor, out in the country. They had no choice but to hold out and hope the place kept running until they could earn their release.

Brian didn't want to wake up one day and be forty-five years old and working in a run-down glass factory or, even worse, be out of a job at forty-five because it had closed. Then what would he do? He might really have to move out to Hilltop and live like a hillbilly.

His own friends sometimes wondered why he worked there in the first place. Young people around town thought you had to be some sort of sucker to work at Anchor, even if you did make more money than you would emptying bedpans at the hospital or deep-frying chicken at Buffalo Wild Wings. Plant 1 had a reputation for hiring dope-sick addicts off the street to work in the sluer. People clocked in high. Some stepped out of prison and into the factory the way workers used to step into work right out of high school. Brian got the whole "second chance" thing, but he didn't think EveryWare Global was hiring ex-cons to be noble; he thought the company took advantage of them because Plant 1 was their last resort.

There wasn't any prestige in working at Anchor. The place possessed zero integrity, from top to bottom.

He weighed the shift work. By going to Drew—and just working normal hours during the day, not rotating days and late nights with a day off in between, which he spent sleeping or feeling groggy, fucking up his body clock—maybe he'd have more time for art, for cutting brush at Hilltop.

At Drew he'd ride a cherry picker to pull big boxes of shoes off shelves and unload the trucks that delivered them from China. It sounded pretty mindless to him—not like making something. The job would be a new start, though. Maybe he could work his way up into a more fulfilling position at Drew.

Brian teeter-tottered up and down, one moment deciding to quit, the next deciding to stay. His mind kept coming back to the shutdown. His calculations would be very different if not for that. Those two months squeezed the last drops of spirit out of Plant 1.

At about the time Solomon was hired, in February 2014, EveryWare Global hauled the weight of $290 million in loans up its profit-and-loss chart. Its total liabilities were in the realm of $400 million. The combined Anchor Hocking and Oneida owed that money to the likes of Deutsche Bank, Western Asset Management Company (WAMCO), Voya Investment Management Company, Nationwide Life Insurance, Nation-wide Defined Benefit Master Trust, Nationwide Mutual Fire Insurance Company, CIFC Asset Management, and Wells Fargo. The agreements ratifying those loans were trussed by a variety of covenants, the conditions set by lenders. For example, EveryWare was forbidden from exceeding a certain ratio of debt to earnings. Breaching any of these covenants allowed the lenders to call the loans, which EveryWare would be unable to repay. In that event, the lenders could take the keys, shut down the business, and sell it off for parts if they chose to.

Just a few weeks into his new job, Solomon realized EveryWare was about to breach its covenants. Having become aware of the prospective breach, EveryWare would have to include notice of the danger in the 2013 annual report that was just about to be issued—the company's first since going public—and in the earnings call to follow. Solomon didn't want to communicate this, because it could trigger panic among investors, suppliers, and employees. So, in a bid to buy time, he and the board of Every-Ware decided to delay the earnings release.

He used the time to fly to New York and ask the lenders for covenant relief. Solomon still thought Anchor Hocking—and EveryWare—had the bones to become a much larger, more profitable company—but first he'd have to convince the lenders to give him time.

Solomon entered the fifty-story Deutsche Bank headquarters at 60 Wall

Street unsure of the reaction he'd face. By the time he sat down at a large table inside an upper-floor conference room looking out at the glass sides of other Financial District towers with other conference rooms containing large tables, he had no doubt. An employee of Deutsche—which had played the role of administrative agent to create the loan package for EveryWare—lenders' representatives, and lawyers all sat on the other side of the table, facing him and not smiling.

The lenders had read the same public filings Solomon had before he took the job. They knew EveryWare could be a risky bet, but they specialized in risky bets. Like Cerberus, with its Madeleine arm, they made more money charging high interest rates to outfits like EveryWare. On the other hand, they weren't in the business of financing lost causes. The risk was a calculated one, based on the numbers EveryWare, its executives, and its owners had provided.

When Solomon was looking at EveryWare back in December 2013, he saw the huge debt, but he also saw that, in April of that year, during its initial public-offering road show, the company told prospective investors it expected over $60 million in 2013 EBITDA (earnings before interest, taxes, depreciation, and amortization), a proxy measure of how well the company operated. With good management and marketing—Solomon's wheelhouse—you could keep a company going and slowly pay down that debt with $60 million in EBITDA. That amount was comfortably within the margin demanded by the loan covenants.

As it turned out, the results Solomon saw in March didn't show $60 million in EBITDA, but more like $50 million. Where the $10 million went was a little mysterious. Also, the company was about to report that revenue was up in 2013, to $439.8 million, but it still lost money. Interest payments absorbed profits. Even so, Solomon believed he could salvage EveryWare on $50 million, though not if he couldn't convince the lenders to forbear a covenant breach.

Solomon looked across the conference room table and announced to the people on the other side that EveryWare was nearly out of cash and would have to borrow more money from a revolving line of credit provided by Wells Fargo; was not paying its own vendors; and still had a warehouse full of inventory.

"We shocked the shit out of them," he recalled. " 'How the fuck do we go from here to a breach, and nobody say anything?!' There was a lot of venom in the room." The bankers thought they'd been spoofed. Some accused EveryWare of manipulating the numbers. Some wanted to call the loans. Nobody blamed Solomon directly, since he'd been at the company for less than a month, but they wanted to know how the picture they had in their minds after reading the public filings and talking to EveryWare executives could be at such variance with the crisis they now faced.

As Solomon would later discover, the real EBITDA was not only less than $60 million, it was nothing like $50 million, either. EBITDA is a non-GAAP number, meaning it's not computed using generally accepted accounting principles. Independent auditors don't opine on EBITDA, making it susceptible to fudging. EveryWare's real EBITDA, Solomon would later argue, was closer to $28 million.

After a series of meetings, the lenders decided not to take the keys, but they didn't agree to covenant relief, either. By doing so, they handed responsibility squarely back to EveryWare's majority shareholder, Monomoy Capital Partners. Meanwhile, analysts and investors were still waiting for an earnings announcement.

On March 31, Monomoy sent a credit agreement to Pierce Avenue committing Monomoy to buy $12 million worth of stock, debt, or other security should the company actually breach a covenant. If needed, the $12 million would be applied to equity to bring EveryWare back into covenant compliance. That same day, EveryWare issued a press release highlighting its earnings. It claimed the company made $51.5 million of EBITDA. There was a net loss of $17.4 million. The loss reflected all kinds of one-time and special items.

Solomon faced a dilemma about what to say on the earnings call. He had a choice between two truths. He could say he believed in the company, was excited about its prospects, and saw lots of potential. For all the neglect and decades of humiliation, Anchor Hocking was still one of the most important players in the American glassware industry. No other company made glass using as many different processes, or had as many different products sold to retailers, the food service industry, candlemakers, florists, winemakers, and distillers. Anchor was still the largest domestic maker of glass bakeware, not only under its own brand, but also Pyrex, which it made for a company called World Kitchen. Or he could say

EveryWare Global was in the emergency room with a defibrillator pasted to its chest.

He didn't have full control over his decision, or over his script. He'd made a mistake by agreeing to come into the company as "interim" CEO. His authority was clipped, his offices crowded by Monomoy's John Stewart—to whom he had to report—and the consultants from Alvarez & Marsal who had Stewart's ear. He couldn't fire or hire on his own initiative. Yet he was now the face of the company, a public company with Securities and Exchange Commission oversight.

Erica Bartsch, an agent with Sloane and Company, Monomoy's New York public relations firm, began the earnings call with the kind of straining, upbeat "Good morning, everyone!" that was designed to make listeners think the morning was fantastically good. She read some boiler-plate disclaimers about forward-looking statements, then introduced Solomon.

He spoke in the tongues of business: "While getting to know the team, I met with key customers and suppliers. We also prioritized the initiatives that we believe will drive free-cash-flow generation, free cash that can be used to invest in the business and pay down debt. This, of course, is all underscored by iconic brands: Oneida and Anchor Hocking."

He admitted that the team wasn't satisfied with 2013's full-year results. He provided the required warning about the possible breach of loan covenants but quickly softened the news with the cure. "Our largest share-holder provided the company with an equity commitment letter, which demonstrates their dedication and enthusiasm for the business. Their com-mitment also provides us the operational flexibility we need to maximize free cash flow and de-lever the business." He used terms like "customer value," "accelerate," and "laser-sharp focus." Then he introduced Bernard Peters, EveryWare's CFO.

The analysts didn't ask many questions about the numbers, but when they did, Peters replied with vague answers, refusing to provide specifics. Joseph Altobello, of Oppenheimer & Company, teed Solomon up to deliver an optimistic soliloquy by asking what drew the new interim CEO to the company.

"What drew me to EveryWare is this is a fantastic brand with a com-bination of manufacturing, sourcing capabilities, as well as deep, long-standing customer relationships. If you look at my prior experience, that's exactly the kind of business that I successfully transformed at Coleman, a division of Jarden. And also the kind of experience I used to reinvigorate the Craftsman tool business at Sears Holdings. I see all of the right foundational elements for this to be a very successful company going forward. We simply, in the near term, have to focus on the blocking and tackling necessary to build a solid foundation for growth."

This may have been puffery—and Solomon knew the legal line between permissible puffery and lying—but none of these sentences, on their own, were untrue. They just didn't add up to anything. They were air. In the press release of the day before, the one people in Lancaster saw, he was quoted as saying, "I'm excited about the company's prospects."

The $12 million commitment from Monomoy wasn't used. Unfortunately for Anchor Hocking, its workers, and Lancaster, it wasn't used because it didn't come close to filling the financial chasm. Sam Solomon's more immediate problem turned out to be not the breach, but cash: EveryWare ran out.

Solomon was told that, despite its debts, EveryWare had plenty of liquidity, thanks mainly to the Wells revolving loan. But Wells Fargo was under no obligation to keep lending money out of the revolver. When EveryWare asked for $20 million more, the bank turned off the spigot. Of all the problems he faced, Solomon said, "I didn't expect that we would run into the big aha! of 'What do you mean you don't have any more money?' Nothing shuts down a party like running out of alcohol."

On Thursday, May 15, 2014, six weeks after the earnings call, Chris Cruit worked the early shift. He was a burn-off specialist. Burn-off men weren't the highest-paid employees in the plant, but they weren't the lowest, either. Cruit liked his job, but what he really wanted to do was show-biz wrestle. The wrestling he'd done on a small-time circuit was written on his face. It was a dark, handsome face, but his nose had been rearranged, a tooth had gone missing, and his ears showed the early blooms of cauliflower. A guy could knock around the Midwest for a few years and scratch out a living getting slammed into wrestling mats, but Cruit knew he was never going to be Hulk Hogan. Attitude wasn't the problem: He was a naturally sweet guy, but he'd been a bouncer once and had learned to fake badassery. He couldn't fake his size, though, or his age.

Cruit was a born-and-raised west-sider. He lived right around the corner from Plant 1. He enjoyed giving wrestling lessons to some kids in the neighborhood, so he began to think about starting his own wrestling school and about maybe getting into the wrestling-show-promotion racket by bringing some touring wrestlers into the fairgrounds. He needed money for that, though, plus he had a wife and son to support. Cruit tried selling cars, "but you gotta be a special kind of person to sell cars, and I didn't do so good," especially once the Great Recession hit. Cruit estimated he'd walked by Plant 1 "eight billion times," but had never thought of working there. Then, in September 2008, he applied and was hired, and had worked there steadily ever since.

His shift ended at 2:30, and he left the plant. Cruit had been home a couple of hours when his phone started to ring. "They were going, 'Hey! Anchor Hocking's gonna shut down.' And I was like, 'Whaddya mean Anchor Hocking's gonna shut down?' 'They shut down. They're closed, and they don't know if they're gonna reopen.'"

While Cruit was on the phone, Joe Boyer stood in a small space by the guard shack at the main Plant 1 entrance. He and some other union leaders had been called off the floor for a special meeting. By now Boyer had worked under three different ownerships. Not much of anything surprised him anymore. But when the plant bosses started handing confidentiality agreements to the assembled union leaders, Boyer knew something surprising was about to happen and that it wasn't going to be good. He didn't want to sign the agreement, but the bosses said that he and anyone else who refused would have to leave. Until everybody signed, they couldn't even know what it was they were supposed to keep secret. Boyer thought that was ass-backwards, but he signed it.

Unbeknownst to Boyer and the other union men, as they were signing their names to confidentiality agreements, operations executives were walking through the plant, telling workers like Brant, Swink, and Brian to go home. The plant was shutting down. Rank-and-file workers thought the union officers, now separated from them in a secret meeting, must have been warned. But the union officers had no idea what was happening, either.

The agreements Boyer was forced to sign said the reps "weren't allowed to discuss any specifics with any of our people," he recalled. "They were giving us facts and figures on some of the money, what was going on. We were not allowed to discuss any of that with anybody. While they are telling us all that, what was going on, they are shutting the place down!"

A "big-time" lawyer came in and started talking numbers. Boyer and the other union reps were skeptical. They'd long murmured among themselves, not always joking, that management kept two sets of books—one they showed the union and the real one. Whatever the real numbers were, they knew Anchor Hocking had been mismanaged for years, and now the big-time lawyer was telling them EveryWare Global had run out of money. And there was another message: If the plant was ever going to reopen, "they were gonna want concessions from us, and all this, and we were gonna have to make up our mind what was gonna happen."

With the exception of the Cerberus furloughs, Anchor Hocking had gone 109 years without a long-term unplanned shutdown. It remained open through every economic, political, and war crisis. During the Great Depression of the 1930s, Anchor Hocking cushioned Lancaster. In 1933, its payroll of 2,565 employees amounted to $1.8 million. Now it was closing, maybe for good. More than nine hundred people suddenly lost paychecks.

When Solomon issued a release saying the shutdown might last four weeks, Lancaster clung to that figure as if it were gospel. A councilman estimated that if the shutdown lasted a month, the city would lose $75,000 in income tax revenue—a significant enough dent in a small town's budget to require cutbacks in the police, fire, and streets departments. Thank goodness, though, it would only be for four weeks. Four weeks was bad, but manageable. What would happen beyond that was anybody's guess.

Anchor's workers, salaried and hourly alike, felt ignored by the residents of the city that used to celebrate them. Now, some in Lancaster shrugged as if to say, "Well, finally."

Others exhumed the old Lancaster civic initiative and tried to buck up the workers. Stores offered discounts. Restaurants donated a free lunch to people with Anchor Hocking ID cards. The local office of Ohio's Job and Family Services set up a dedicated phone line to teach workers how to file for unemployment. It gave résumé tips and helped with job searches.

Jeff Couch, a firefighter, started a group called Save Anchor Hocking.

His dad had worked for Anchor twenty-five years before but had been fired in one of the layoffs, plunging the family into poverty. So Couch knew what the workers faced.

"I started the group because this is not just about Anchor Hocking," he told me. "I am tired of watching the country go downhill, and nobody ever takes the time to stop and say, 'Hey! No! What is going on is unacceptable.' I decided maybe we could try to do something."

Thirty-four people joined his group. Couch and a few others decided the only way to save the company was to buy it. Lancaster had built its own hotel, its own hospital, its own gas company, and its own schools—and Couch didn't see any insurmountable obstacle barring it from taking over its biggest private employer, not if everybody banded together and pooled their money. He wasn't sure how much money a buyout would require, but somebody had to do something. He turned to online crowdfunding. Save Anchor Hocking raised pledges for a few thousand dollars.

Mayor Dave Smith offered to let the company extend utility payments, but there wasn't much more the town could do. The city didn't have $20 million. May turned into June. There was still no word on when the plant might fire up. Wall Street analysts predicted doom.

On June 6, three weeks after the shutdown, EveryWare sent a WARN (Worker Adjustment and Retraining Notification Act) letter to Mayor Smith, the Fairfield County Commissioners, and Ohio Job and Family Services stating that while some lender relief had been extended to June 30, there was no savior in sight.

Federal law requires WARN letters be sent to labor and government officials sixty days before a plant closing or layoff, not three weeks into one. (Cerberus was forced to pay workers $480,000 for not providing a WARN notice when it closed that Connellsville, Pennsylvania, bottle plant.) There are exceptions to the WARN requirements, including "unforeseeable business circumstances."

Anyone who knew what Solomon and Monomoy knew would have a rough time arguing that EveryWare's situation was unforeseeable, but Monomoy had a history of flouting the WARN Act. In July 2008, Monomoy bought Kurdziel Industries, an iron foundry located in the village of Rothbury, Michigan, that manufactured cast parts for construction equipment makers like John Deere. Monomoy changed the name of the business to Carlton Creek Ironworks and swept up state and local tax breaks and funds to train employees.

When it announced the purchase, Monomoy partner Justin Hillenbrand said, "This is a great deal for us. Carlton Creek is a market leader for iron castings that will continue to be essential to infrastructure repair and expansion in North America over the next 10 years. After planned improvements in manufacturing and sourcing, Carlton Creek will be better positioned to continue providing its global customers with a high-quality, cost-effective product and should grow substantially over the next few years as it re-acquires volume from Chinese foundries. This transaction is a great win for the company's customers and employees, for the state of Michigan, and for North American manufacturing."

Five months later, in December, Monomoy began mass layoffs, leading to a complete closure. More than two hundred employees lost their jobs, crippling Rothbury. In September 2009, Carlton Creek workers sued Monomoy for violating the WARN Act. As is typical of PE firms, Monomoy argued that it was not the employer, though it owned the company. Carlton Creek was the employer.

John Philo, an attorney with the Maurice and Jane Sugar Law Center for Economic and Social Justice, who represented the workers, argued that Monomoy was indeed the employer. "The PE folks are making the decisions," Philo told me.

Monomoy settled the case out of court. It later settled another one of Philo's WARN cases, this one involving Hess Industries of Niles, Michigan. "My impression is that they make that decision because they do not want to be bogged down in litigation for two or three years," Philo said. "One thing with the WARN Act is that it's fairly clear: You've either given the notice or you did not. Each time they were offering the fig leaf of 'unexpected business circumstances,' but if we got into trial, that would require them to show all the business stuff in the background, and they don't want that public discussion."

EveryWare's board met three days later, on June 9. First it had to figure out what to do about Sam Solomon. He'd been "interim" for six months and had found the uncertainty damaging. The board offered Solomon a

new employment agreement, making him CEO and president of Every-
Ware Global, with a base salary of $600,000, stock options, bonuses, and
$100,000 in moving expenses.

Perhaps because the incongruity between that decision and the alarm
around Lancaster was so jarring, the board also announced that a few
workers would be called back to Plant 1. That wasn't much to celebrate,
though. There was no mention of how long those few people would have
jobs. EveryWare also announced that it would "complete a reduction
in force at its Lancaster, Ohio, facility over the next few weeks and will
seek additional ways to conserve cash and reduce expenses through continued cost cutting measures."

The people of Lancaster, largely in the dark about the goings-on inside
Anchor and EveryWare—even middle management wasn't aware of many
details—developed theories about how the situation had become so dire.
Some blamed China, Mexico, and cheap imports. Some suggested that Anchor Hocking was just old and tired, ready for the fossil beds. Maybe it
was the housing bubble and the recession, or the unions, or Obama. It was
complicated, that was for sure.

On June 12, local ministers and other volunteers held a rally for the
workers on the West School playground, one block from Anchor
Hocking's front gate. There was food—hot dogs, popcorn—and a bounce
house for the kids. Police chief Dave Bailey, Mayor Smith, the fire chief,
and the sheriff all attended. Service groups set up stations to explain how
workers could find help to pay bills, secure health insurance, and qualify
for food assistance.

Michele Ritchlin, executive director of the West After School Program,
loaded up a little cart with a canopy and some pamphlets on the program's
free summer lunches and wheeled it across Garfield Street and onto the
playground.

The tutoring program started by Rosemary Hajost and the other volunteers had grown to meet an ever-increasing need. Children on the west
side didn't just require tutoring; they had to be fed. They needed a safe
place to be after school. They needed attention—and not just for a day,
but for all five days of the school week. The program expanded all across

the city, too, because the problems of the west-side children had spread outward to all compass points.

Now headquartered in a converted house on Garfield Street, just across from the West School playground, it survived on government grants, donations, and income from after-school childcare services. Finding money to operate was a constant struggle that required all the doggedness Ritchlin, a thirty-nine-year-old body builder and a brash blond whirl of energy, possessed. Now the Anchor shutdown threatened to stress her little agency more than ever.

Ritchlin's grandfather, father, and uncle had worked at Anchor Hocking. But that was then. When she first heard about the closing, she thought, "Oh my God, things are just going to get worse." Already too many of the children she served had one or both parents in jail, out of work, addicted. They went home when her center closed at six o'clock to not much of anything, including food. Or they were being raised by an aunt, or a grandparent, who was doing the best she could but who was probably poor herself. Fairfield County had one of the highest rates of children in foster care in the state of Ohio.

She handed out flyers to the employees at the playground rally. A free lunch for the kids wasn't going to solve anything; she knew that. But it was something. "Those people were devastated," she thought. "What are they going to do? They live paycheck to paycheck anyway."

The sheriff and the police chief picked up a microphone and said a few words of encouragement. Then a minister took the mic. He asked the crowd to pray for the workers, for Anchor Hocking, for the owners of EveryWare Global. The attendees on the playground bowed their heads.

Brian wasn't there. He spent his forced time off skating, listening to music, making art in the studio, and out at Hilltop, where he began gathering rocks for a cabin's foundation.

In July, EveryWare and Monomoy presented the union with an ultimatum. Monomoy would provide liquidity by investing $20 million in EveryWare, in return for preferred shares and transaction fees, but only if the unions in both Lancaster and Monaca agreed to roll back wages, to give up the company contribution to their 401(k) plans, and to pay increased health insurance premiums. If the unions didn't agree, Monomoy would shutter Anchor Hocking.

Some workers thought Monomoy was bluffing and wanted to call it. (Solomon himself wasn't sure if it was a bluff or not.) Others were just angry and wanted to use their vote as a middle finger to management. "All or nothing," Chris Nagle recalled of the terms. "Presser called me up on the phone," he continued, referring to Monomoy cofounder Stephen Presser. " 'Nagle,' he says, 'if you can get the concessions in Lancaster, I will help you out.' " Nagle phoned Steelworker union reps. A couple of them "was sayin', 'Fuck them. We're gonna put 'em down. [Any concessions] are just a Band-Aid anyway. We're gonna put 'em down.' And I said, 'Oh, fine. I wanna job at Anchor Hocking. You have to get your ass out of bed and start talkin' to Presser or we will find us another international member now.' "

Negotiations continued until "Presser called me on the phone and said, 'Nagle, you know, by the end of the day, if I don't have concessions in my hand, I will not give them twenty million dollars.' " Presser told Nagle he would "lock the door Tuesday at noon and liquidate the assets of the whole plant."

Lancaster approved the cuts. The union at Monaca rejected them. EveryWare reneged on its word and reopened both plants anyway, leaving the Lancaster workers feeling like fools and Nagle and the rest of the Plant 1 union leadership discredited among the rank and file.

The deal was finalized on Wednesday, July 30. The four-week shutdown had lasted two and a half months. Both Anchor Hocking and Lancaster had their reprieve, but the union was angry, and EveryWare had alienated its own customers. Winemakers and distillers lacked bottles from Monaca, fouling up their production lines. Candlemakers didn't have glass holders, so they couldn't ship. Retailers wondered if they should start buying overseas. Maybe China or Mexico would be more reliable.

Lancaster's state and federal representatives, both Republican and Democrat, had been mostly absent during the shutdown, leaving workers feeling abandoned. But the next day, Ohio's Democratic U.S. senator, Sherrod Brown, issued a platitude-filled press release applauding "both management and members of the United Steelworkers for finding common ground and working toward shared success." Brown tried to take a little of the credit, highlighting a letter he'd written to Monomoy back in June. The union guys in Plant 1 laughed when they read it.

CFO Bernard Peters resigned on September 17, effective October 3. On its face, his resignation was an odd move. The employment agreement he'd signed stipulated that, unless he was terminated for cause or resigned before his contract was up—which he'd just done—he would be entitled to a generous severance payment. By resigning, he'd forfeited the severance. He'd worked at EveryWare for less than two years. In 2013, his first year, Peters made $1,128,998, most of it in stock awards and performance bonuses linked to achieving EBITDA numbers.

To replace Peters, EveryWare contracted with Alvarez & Marsal to provide a new CFO. The company agreed to pay A&M $31,680 per week, more than Brian Gossett would make in all of 2014. In 1985, before the sale to Newell, the average Anchor Hocking hourly employee made about $9.33 per hour, almost $21 in 2016 dollars. Even before the concessions, the current generation of Anchor factory workers made less than the previous one had. Now they made less still—Brian earned $14.55—and had no retirement plan.

When the shutdown was first announced, the *Eagle-Gazette* published an editorial insisting that "Anchor Hocking Owes Lancaster Explanation." "We were shocked and disturbed at just how little the company seemed to care about its employees or the city." Community spirit, the paper argued, "at least from the corporate level, seems to have dried up in recent years." Lancaster still wanted its company's love.

Solomon smiled at the naïveté of such thinking, but he understood it. Most Americans held old ideas about how The System really worked.

The shutdown was six months in the past, but the sting of it lingered and festered until it metastasized to the point that some Plant 1 employees were ready to walk out on any pretext. They no longer believed Sam Solomon. "He's just a cheerleader for the company," some said. Some of them didn't believe their own local president, Nagle, or the rest of the Steelworkers union. The old Flints would never have stood for the raw deal; the Flints were just a tiny speck to the Steelworkers. The Steelworkers didn't give a crap about them. It seemed they were always the ones giving back. A few wanted to take down the company out of spite, just to be able to tell themselves they walked out like men. Being jobless afterwards would just about be worth it. Most, though, reacted with learned helplessness, keep-ing their heads down and going to work. They had families to think about.

Brian did not have a family, and the more he thought about it, the more he started to think that whether he could afford it or not, he wanted to quit Anchor and go to Drew. He still worried about earning less money, but he figured the company always moved backwards anyway, forcing its workers to march backwards with it. Brian did the math and realized that, after the previous summer's concessions, the forced furloughs, and the big-ger health insurance bite, he wouldn't be making that much less money at Drew anyway.

Telling Brant was the worst part. Brant had invested time in Brian, and Brian considered him a friend and mentor. They'd gone deer hunting to-gether out at Hilltop. They were both standing on the platform around the H-28, working on the machine, when he said it. "He comes up to me and is like, 'Did you get that job?' And I was like, 'Yeah,' and he was like, 'Good.' I could tell he was disappointed, but he couldn't hold it against me."

Leaving Anchor wasn't quite as hard as the breakup with Renee, but he already missed Plant 1. Why did it have to happen? He couldn't figure it out. They had to be making money. The company was always saying it was losing money, but Brian saw through that bullshit. He didn't claim to understand the politics of the place—he had only the vaguest idea that something called Monomoy controlled it—but it was open, wasn't it? It wouldn't be open if they weren't making money. Why'd they reopen it after the shutdown if they weren't? "Somebody's making money," Brian con-cluded, "and it's off the sweat of other people."

EIGHT

The Bankruptcy

March 2015

t's not about making the product," Sam Solomon said. "It's about making money appear, and the 99 percent doesn't understand that."

The American economy had come a long way from the days when
I. J. Collins could lasso some people he knew to kick in a few thousand
dollars each and start the Hocking Glass Company. It had come a long way
since 1938, when the first annual report of the combined Anchor Hocking
featured a short note from Collins, four pages of financial tables that a
seventh-grader could understand, and some comments about the numbers.
Since those days, the American economy had advanced under the wise
tutelage of financial experts trained in the subtle art of the acronym and
the esoteric word, the secret codes that imbued the finely engineered
tables and reports and footnotes—the pages and pages of footnotes and
subfootnotes—with the sheen of brilliant scientific inevitability, the words
flexing with the muscular bona fides of graduate school brains to justify
the thousand-bucks-an-hour legal advice and the multi-million-dollar-deal
percentages.

Those brains had been trained for years. Imagine the resources poured
into them, the hours and days and months of molding. How could anybody working an H-28, or packing ware, or selling it be expected to know
where the money went? They'd been trained to make a tangible thing,
and to sell the thing for a little more than the thing cost to make, and then

to use that profit to pay people, make better things, and slide a little dividend into the pockets of those who'd risked their money to invest in the creation. The idea was pretty simple. But America had come a long way—and had decided the idea was *too* simple. So, of course, Brian wasn't the only Anchor Hocking employee to wonder.

The people who wrote shipping orders in the DC wondered, too. They could see goods being purchased.

The sales guys were selling. In the company's New York City showroom, at 41 Madison Avenue, where major manufacturers of tableware that included Libbey, Lenox, Orrefors, Ralph Lauren Home, Spode, Arc, and many others leased space, buyers seemed enthusiastic. And why not? The showroom evoked a land of perpetual summer-friendly entertaining, with backyard grills and gingham-tableclothed picnic tables set with glassware and Oneida place settings. You could almost smell the rib eyes sizzling over the coals and hear the giggles of rambunctious kids and their tolerant parents sipping gin and tonics out of Anchor tumblers and Budweiser out of Anchor bottles: the Lancaster, Ohio, of Nancy Frick's memory preserved inside a Manhattan skyscraper like a museum exhibit.

The glass business had struggled for a generation, and imports gnawed away at both volume and margin, but as far as the employees could tell, Anchor seemed to be doing okay. Anchor was making tons of OEM (original equipment manufacturer) Pyrex-branded bakeware for World Kitchen, right alongside its own branded glass. And EveryWare Global—mainly Anchor—secreted enormous potential in the substrata of its ancient geology. Foreign glassmakers may have paid their workers much less and ignored already lax environmental regulations, but they suffered from two important disadvantages: Glass breaks, and some of it, especially bakeware, is heavy, so shipping it across oceans can be expensive. And though tariffs had dropped on imported glassware, the United States still gave domestic makers a little protection against the low wages and subsidized manufacturing in China, though no longer in Mexico.

How could Anchor, or EveryWare, or whatever the hell the company was being called these days, not be making money? Yet they'd been forced to submit to wage cuts. They watched the plant disintegrate. They lost their retirement contribution from the company.

And now, on March 11—as Brian settled into his new job as a Drew warehouseman, Lloyd Romine settled into his rental house across the street from Plant 1, Mark Kraft tried to wrestle the monkey off his back, and Joe Piccolo narrowed the list of possible festival headliners—the situation at Anchor Hocking once again turned dire.

Nobody outside the company's C-suite had any hint, and certainly not anyone in Lancaster did. As far as the town knew, EveryWare's problem had been solved during the shutdown crisis of the previous summer. But it wasn't, and it never would be. It never could be, wearing the cement shoes of all that debt. The latest trauma arrived at the hands of EveryWare's independent auditor. It was about to issue a "going-concern" qualification as part of the upcoming earnings report. The auditor doubted EveryWare could stay in business.

So, exactly one year after he faced their venom in New York, Solomon had no choice but to inform the lenders. He placed a conference call to an ad hoc committee of them and once again aggravated the people who held a firm grip on the corporate testicles by telling them the auditor believed the company was at risk of collapse.

The shutdown of 2014, and now the going-concern crisis, were not the kinds of events that gestated overnight. Understanding how they were birthed required hacking through private equity's Enigma machine.

Stephen Presser, Daniel Collin, Justin Hillenbrand, and Philip Von Burg founded Monomoy Capital Partners in 2005, two years before buying Anchor Hocking out of bankruptcy. All three Wall Street veterans had worked at another PE firm, KPS Special Situations Funds (now KPS Capital Partners), before breaking away to open their own shop. Their first fund, Monomoy Capital Partners, LP, raised $280 million from limited partners like the IBM Personal Pension Plan, Travelers Casualty and Surety Company of America, and "funds of funds"—investments made by other money management outfits like Morgan Creek Capital Management and Swiss Re Private Equity Advisors.

Armed with this dry powder, Presser visited Lancaster in 2007, as the Cerberus/Global Home Products bankruptcy case wound down. Before committing to make an offer for Anchor Hocking, he met with labor officials. Monomoy would not buy, he told them, if the unions didn't agree to lower pay.

"He said he couldn't run the place paying us what we got," Joe Boyer recalled. Boyer and the rest of the workers thought Plant 1 faced closure. So the union gave away the production bonus—extra dollars a worker could make for boosting the percentage of good ware. Presser also insisted on tiered wages, with new hires forever earning less than existing employees.

Chris Nagle told Presser about the tanks. "When they was in the process of buyin' us, I said, 'Our tanks are in bad shape. Our one tank needs rebuilt.' Tank 2 was one of the oldest tanks. He says, 'We already know the tanks are in bad shape. We don't care. We're only gonna keep ya for two, three years. We're sellin' ya.'" According to Nagle, Presser told him, "'If I can't get you sold in three years, I'll shut ya down. I don't care. I'm just in it to make money.'"

Both Boyer and Nagle were a little surprised, but they'd been through the Cerberus buyout and bankruptcy. That had been Cerberus's plan all along, too, they figured. At least Monomoy was up-front about its intentions.

(I wanted to ask Presser—and others at Monomoy—about such statements and many other issues. Repeated attempts by phone over a period of eight months, to both Monomoy's offices and to its public relations firm, were rebuffed. In a final effort, I flew to New York to visit Monomoy's offices. I was told they were in a meeting, but that I could wait. A few minutes later, the receptionist told me that she'd been advised that the meeting would be "very, very long" and that I shouldn't wait. I handed her my card with my contact information and asked her to convey the message.)

To purchase Anchor Hocking, Monomoy invested $6.5 million from Monomoy Capital Partners, LP—the $280 million pool of money it had raised from investors—and borrowed $68.5 million. As had become standard practice in PE deals since the days of Wesray, that $68.5 million was not Monomoy's debt or Monomoy Capital Partners' debt. It became Anchor Hocking's debt.

When a PE firm buys a company with a view to selling it, it needs to increase the company's profits so it can resell it at a premium. You can increase profits by building value through research and development, creating new products, investing in plants and equipment. But that takes time—usually far longer than the two or three years Monomoy had in mind. Instead, you can also increase company profit by making the same products with the same sales volumes, but cutting expenses.

The cuts came quickly. First, Anchor Hocking fired all the temporary workers who'd been part of the labor pool at the distribution center. Then, on Friday, September 28, the company fired seventy union workers without warning.

The chairman of the union council, Dennis Harvey, told the *Eagle-Gazette* that Monomoy had promised that any layoffs would occur through attrition. Few retired, though, because Monomoy took away retirement insurance. He felt deceived. "We gave some concessions when Monomoy bought it and we were told they would hire more people. I hope things come out right, but for the working person it never does," he told the paper.

Twenty-three days later, Monomoy sold off the DC. Anchor had built it in 1969 on land I. J. Collins once owned. Lancaster's congressman, Clarence Miller, and the state governor, James Rhodes, cut the ribbon at the DC's opening celebration. From then on, property taxes and upkeep were the only expenses Anchor paid for it. The deal to sell it, as many such deals are, was convoluted.

The buyer was an entity called NL Ventures VI West Fair, LLC. (The DC was located on West Fair Avenue.) It paid $23 million. NL Ventures VI West Fair, LLC, was created just for the purpose of buying the DC. The real buyer was NL Ventures VI, LP, an investment pool of $111 million. NL Ventures VI, LP, in turn, had been created by AIC Ventures, a real estate equity-fund manager—private equity for real estate. Such funds were often described as "vulture" funds that catered to investors like high-net-worth individuals.

Anchor Hocking immediately signed a deal to lease back its own distribution center for twenty years. Anchor agreed to pay $2.3 million per year, with a 2 percent annual increase during years two through ten, then a 1.5 percent increase every year through year twenty. (As of 2015, the Fairfield County Assessor's Office appraised the DC at $12,381,930.) In August 2011, NL Ventures resold the DC for $25.8 million.

The $23 million Monomoy received for the DC could be applied to Anchor Hocking's bottom line, another shortcut to make the company look profitable, though at the price of a twenty-year lease. Monomoy likely gained money for itself, too, because it charged fees for the transactions of its portfolio companies. If the fee was 1 percent, a percentage Monomoy was known to charge, then Monomoy earned $230,000 on the deal, to be paid by Anchor Hocking to Monomoy. But it may have reaped more than that.

Sale-leasebacks are common for PE-owned companies. PE firms often call it "unlocking equity." As the equity owner, Monomoy Capital Partners, LP, could have pocketed some or most of the $23 million as a special dividend. Because it was a private company, Anchor Hocking didn't have to publicly report any such dividend. Monomoy did announce that some of the proceeds from the DC sale were used to pay down Anchor Hocking's debt, though it didn't say how much.

It also may have used some of the money to buy another glass company. In November 2007, a month after the DC sale-leaseback, Monomoy arranged for Anchor Hocking to buy Lancaster Colony's Indiana Glass plant in Sapulpa, Oklahoma, for $21.5 million. Once again, Monomoy may have charged Anchor Hocking its 1 percent transaction fee. How this deal was financed—how much, if any, debt was required—remained opaque.

In early 2008, Anchor Hocking closed the Sapulpa plant, which had been in the city since 1914. About 425 employees lost their jobs.

Mark Eichhorn, who had retained his Anchor CEO job after Monomoy bought the company, released a statement, in which he said, "We know this presents a hardship for employees, their families, and the people of [Sapulpa]. We want to assure everyone affected that this decision-making process was not an easy one."

By several accounts, that was a lie. All along, the plan had been to buy the Sapulpa plant to obtain its machinery, then bring that equipment to Lancaster so Anchor Hocking could enter the flower vase market. That could have been good news for Lancaster—and, in some ways, it was. But the deal proved a lot less lucrative than advertised.

Monomoy especially prized a machine developed by the Italian company Olivotto to make large flower vases. "But the vase business is a whore's market," a longtime sales executive insisted, using slang for a saturated, low-margin market with no barriers to entry. "The price fluctuates as the [delivery] truck goes down the road. And this Olivotto machine they brought to us from Oklahoma, we never got it to work."

EveryWare management, working under the advice of Monomoy, hadn't bothered to consult with veteran operators in the plant. "They brought all these machines," Chris Nagle recalled. "They were in junk shape. They said, 'Oh, we did this. It's a great machine.' It was a pile of junk." The Olivotto machine sat in the parking lot for the next two years.

Anchor Hocking didn't just bring machines from Oklahoma. The company also bused Mexican families into Lancaster and put them up in the Hampton Inn on Route 33. While fathers went to work in Plant 1, children enrolled in the city schools.

"We all knew they was illegal," Chris Nagle charged, "because they all had the same Social Security number." Nagle knew this because they told him so. Anchor Hocking's human resources department, he said, also knew their immigration status, but the company wanted them because they earned less money and worked as if Plant 1 were a non-union shop.

"They did what the company told 'em to do. I had to keep pullin' 'em back. 'You can't do that—that's someone else's job. It's a union shop. We gotta work as a union.' "

Some of the Mexican workers were supposed to have been trained operators, but many were not. And they didn't know Plant 1's equipment. Nagle insisted they start as apprentices, angering the company, which wanted them working as low-wage operators right away. The training proved to be a waste, thanks to U.S. immigration authorities.

Being as far north as it was, and not having as much of the kind of industry—meatpacking, large-scale vegetable and fruit agriculture—known to use immigrant labor, Ohio was not a high-priority state for immigration enforcement. In 2008, federal authorities arrested only sixty-nine people on immigration charges. So it took a while for authorities to show up at Plant 1. Company salaried and hourly employees alike recalled the day with near-exact language. Immigration agents entered the plant "and got two of them right away," Nagle said. Panicked phone calls zipped across Lancaster.

"My son was in high school," another veteran executive told me. "And this Mexican kid's phone rings. He stands up right in the middle of class and walks out the door."

Old cars and beat-up minivans showed up at the plant's gates to meet workers who, in some instances, sprinted out of the plant. "They ran out any door they could. In one day, everybody was just gone."

Meanwhile, machines continued to run. The production line moved ware through the plant. But with too few workers to handle the ware, a lot of it crashed to the shop floor, with broken shards piling up under machines and conveyer lines.

"I remember old Constantine," Nagle told me. "He came up to me and he sat there, and I said, 'Hey, sorry about you gotta leave and all this,' and when he was leaving, he said, 'Chris, you got a right to know. My name is Juan. My name's not Constantine. That's the name they gave me.'"

When it bought Indiana Glass, Monomoy issued a press release. "Since acquiring the Company in April of this year, Monomoy has instituted a series of business improvement programs at Anchor that have substantially reduced operating expenses and increased profitability throughout the Company.

"'We are pleased with Anchor's progress following its emergence from bankruptcy,' said Stephen Presser, a Monomoy principal and chairman of The Anchor Hocking Company Board of Directors. 'We have challenged nearly every aspect of the Anchor business model over the past seven months, and the entire employee group has stepped forward to make Anchor a much stronger, much better company.'"

"We got no return on what we did," the sales executive told me, referring to the Indiana Glass purchase. "None."

In December 2007, a month after buying Indiana Glass, Anchor Hocking was approved for two business incentive loans from the state of Ohio, amounting to over $10 million, at 3 percent interest. Anchor said it would use the state's money for tank repairs. The commitment to use the public money, and the purchase of Indiana Glass, Presser told the *Eagle-Gazette*, "are evidence we're in this for the long run and to build something special and viable. We're not just in this to see if we can make a quick buck."

Monomoy had already made a buck. So far, just about everything Monomoy had done to Anchor Hocking followed the standard private equity playbook: jawbone the unions, cut costs even at the price of damaging longer-term success, do a sale-leaseback of real property assets, take whatever public money you can get from communities eager to save their industries, and do an "add-on"—the Indiana Glass buy. And collect fees.

Monomoy charged "monitoring and consulting fees" to Anchor Hocking—the price of its business expertise. How much Anchor paid to the firm in 2007 remained hidden, but in 2008 Anchor paid Monomoy $1.2 million in fees and expenses. The fees increased year after year: $1.3 million in 2009, $1.6 million in 2010. Monomoy employees also were paid directors' fees for sitting on the board of the company their fund owned. The firm charged similar fees to the other twenty-five companies in the first fund's portfolio. As for Monomoy Capital Partners, LP, it may have already recouped its $6.5 million investment from any dividend it may have taken from the $23 million disposal of the DC.

That's not the magnitude of payoff PE outfits or their investors seek, though—they'd earn better returns investing in a stock market index fund. The goal is to reap many multiples of the invested cash. To do that usually requires an "exit," the sale of the company to another buyer, just as Presser told Nagle he planned to do. But even as Monomoy bought Anchor Hocking in 2007, the most powerful seismic upheaval of the world economy since 1929 rumbled through credit markets.

Subprime home mortgages began to explode lenders' balance sheets. By June 2007, Wall Street giant Bear Stearns was forced to pledge $3.2 billion to save one of its own hedge funds from collapse. (Bear Stearns itself would fail in March 2008 and be absorbed by J.P. Morgan.) Credit dried up all across the economy, making leveraged buyouts like the one Monomoy had executed for Anchor Hocking increasingly difficult, and then nearly impossible. Monomoy found itself stuck with a glass company it didn't want and couldn't unload.

Monomoy waited, while business at Anchor Hocking continued. Sales were dented by the recession, and the Mexican workers had to be replaced, but the company managed to chip away at the debt handed to it by its owner. The country, too, dug itself out of the economic trenches, but emerged damaged and skittish. Deals of the kind Monomoy needed for an exit remained scarce. By 2011, Monomoy had owned Anchor for nearly four years—at least a year longer than Presser had predicted to Nagle. Still unable to unload it, in late summer 2011, Monomoy decided to use Anchor Hocking as a cash machine by executing a PE magic trick called the dividend recapitalization, or recap.

Monomoy had Anchor Hocking borrow $45 million. Anchor then paid Monomoy Capital Partners, LP, $30.5 million as a dividend. But Monomoy had an even bigger play in mind.

The following month, November 2011, Monomoy Capital Partners II (MCP II), the firm's second investment fund, went looking for its first purchase. Monomoy had more ammunition this time, $420 million, supplied by the California Public Employees' Retirement System, the Municipal Fire and Police Retirement System of Iowa, the Ford Motor Company Master Trust Fund, the Standard Fire Insurance Company, RCP Advisors, 747 Capital, and, most ironically, the School Employees Retirement System of Ohio, among the MCP II limited partners.

MCP II bought Oneida, the iconic flatware brand based in Sherrill, New York, for what sources told the *New York Times* amounted to $100 million. Another source calculated the price at closer to $85 million. MCP II kicked in $5.8 million. The rest was borrowed (or assumed existing Oneida debt) and placed on Oneida's books. That was a lot of money to pay for what amounted to a name. Oneida no longer manufactured anything.

Its flatware business was so damaged by cheap Asian imports that it stopped making its own products in 2005. It shut down the famed manufacturing facilities in upstate New York, fired about two thousand people, and contracted with Chinese manufacturers to make Oneida-branded products. The company Monomoy bought consisted of a logo, office staff, and distribution centers where goods arrived from overseas and were then shipped to customers.

In announcing the Oneida buy, Monomoy declared that Oneida and Anchor Hocking would work closely together to market their products to food service businesses like hotels, bars, and restaurants. (Oneida had already licensed the brand name for consumer retail sales to another company.) But in March 2012, Monomoy decided to not just have their two portfolio companies cooperate, but to merge and become EveryWare Global. Monomoy hoped the combination would attract a buyer, or that it could exit by taking the company public.

Anchor CEO Mark Eichhorn resigned. He was replaced by John Sheppard, who was thought to be better equipped to prepare EveryWare for an IPO. In connection with the merger, the new EveryWare refinanced its debt once again, this time with a $150 million loan. But by now, Anchor and Oneida were so deep in hock that, to attract investors to buy the debt, Monomoy had to sweeten the deal, offering to pay a high interest rate, shorten the term of the loan to five and a half years, and include other investor-friendly terms like selling the loan at ninety-eight cents on the dollar—all signs of junk debt.

Monomoy planned to take another $15 million dividend for itself. Instead, it was forced to accept a more modest $10 million.

Monomoy foisted a new advisory agreement onto EveryWare. Now EveryWare—a company owned by Monomoy—was required to pay Monomoy $625,000 every three months for "advisory" services, plus a daily fee "for the services of operating professionals of the Advisor" (meaning Monomoy). EveryWare would also pay 1 percent of the value of any transaction—say, a recap, acquisition, divestment, like the sale of the DC, or refinancing, like the new $150 million loan package.

Anchor/EveryWare paid Monomoy $3.6 million in advisory fees in 2011 and $3.2 million in transaction fees. The advisory fees and expenses in 2012 amounted to $2.6 million. (If you're counting, that's $54 million in known dividends and fees, compared with a combined $12.3 million Monomoy invested from the funds to buy the two companies.)

Monomoy colonized EveryWare like a nineteenth-century imperialist. It obligated EveryWare to use Monomoy's services, whether EveryWare wanted them or not: "The fees and other compensation specified in this Agreement will be payable by the Companies regardless of the extent of services requested by the Companies pursuant to this Agreement, and regardless of whether or not the Companies request the Advisor to provide any such services."

Yet it also denied any obligation to serve EveryWare's interests. It exempted itself from any liability and gave itself permission to work for competing companies and do business with EveryWare's own customers; to withhold knowledge of possible business opportunities; and to exempt itself from any liability "for breach of any duty (contractual or otherwise)" if Monomoy acted on such knowledge for its own profit, even at the exclusion of EveryWare. EveryWare had to indemnify, hold harmless, and defend Monomoy, at the former's expense, against any lawsuit—"just or unjust."

Even as Anchor Hocking was paying Monomoy tens of millions of dollars, it wasn't funding the employees' retirement plans, just as it hadn't under Cerberus. As of December 31, 2012, the plan was underfunded by $8,758,000. Between the October dividend recap and the merger with Oneida to form EveryWare, all the debt reduction Anchor achieved in the preceding few years turned into more debt—about $181 million—than it had since being bought by Monomoy in 2007.

"We were within months—and I don't mean a year or even six months, but a couple of months—of being debt-free," an Anchor insider recalled. "And the decision is made that we're going to be EveryWare, and we acquire this bankrupt, broken-down company nobody wanted. And now, all of a sudden, we have this chain around our neck, and we are starting to sink." He stopped, but the aggravation he felt didn't. "We were *that* close!" he shouted, holding up his thumb and index finger in the universal sign for *damn close.* Another executive, hearing the comment, defended not the deal but the Oneida employees: "Those people at Oneida were fighting and clawing just like we were. It wasn't their fault."

Not only did it now have much more debt to service; EveryWare Global also had a sword hanging over its head—the $150 million loan—that would drop in five and a half years. Monomoy tried to make a company some-body wanted to buy before that five-and-a-half-year deadline by giving EveryWare a compelling story. The EveryWare story became "the tabletop." EveryWare would supply everything you could want for your tabletop— the glasses, the flatware, the casserole dishes, the pie plates. You could eat "synergy" for breakfast, lunch, and dinner.

If Presser or Collin had walked into the Pink Cricket and asked Ell-wood, as he drank his beer, or Ben Martin, as he sat at the bar having his Monday evening glass of wine, they'd have heard a true story about how Anchor Hocking tried to execute almost the same strategy in the 1980s. Anchor did a little shopping of its own back then, acquiring small, loosely related outfits like a pottery company and a silver-plate company. The plan didn't work. With the benefit of hindsight, they conceded that losing its focus on glass weakened Anchor.

But some people who tout themselves as business geniuses will always fall for a story—sometimes because they want, or need, to believe in it. For-tunately for Monomoy, a hedge fund called Clinton Group needed to believe.

On September 19, 2011, at just about the same time Monomoy awarded itself that $30.5 million dividend, Clinton Group formed a special purpose acquisition company—a SPAC—called ROI, a finance pun re-

ferring to "return on investment," or, in the Clinton case, the name of a
horse.

ROI was an empty suit, a "blank-check company," sent in search of a
body to fill it. The suit was stitched together by a public offering of ROI
stock on February 24, 2012, that raised $75 million to buy a company. But
Clinton didn't have any particular company in mind.

Clinton, a collection of funds, some domiciled in the Cayman Islands,
was founded in 1992 by a man named George E. Hall, who was fifty-one
at the time of ROI's creation. Financial engineering had made Hall rich.
In addition to an estate in New Jersey, he owned a 385-acre thoroughbred
farm outside Versailles, Kentucky, called Annestes Farm. He and his wife,
Lori, liked to jet in from New Jersey to spend long weekends there. A few
months before ROI was created, one of his horses, Ruler on Ice (ROI), won
the 2011 Belmont Stakes.

Clinton had its fingers in a number of businesses in a number of different ways. Sometimes it behaved like an activist out of the Icahn and Barington mold. It teamed up with Barington on occasion to target companies
like the Dillard's department stores and Griffon Corporation, a defense
electronics firm that had turned into a conglomerate. Clinton also went
after Steve Madden shoes. In most cases, the goal was to win board seats
and recapitalizations that threw cash into Clinton's hands, much like the
strategy Barington used to pressure Lancaster Colony to buy back shares.

Sometimes Clinton acted more like private equity, buying controlling
interests in companies. Clinton had recently bought up chains like Red
Robin and California Pizza Kitchen. ROI's initial purpose was to find another dining chain to take over. That's why ROI's most famous director,
former NBA star Jamal Mashburn, served on its board. Mashburn owned
thirty-eight Outback Steakhouse restaurants, thirty-two Papa John's Pizza
restaurants, and three Dunkin' Donuts stores.

But ROI had trouble finding a chain to purchase. As the months ticked
by, with no target acquired, Clinton became anxious: ROI had a deadline,
too: A provision of its SPAC charter required it either to buy into a company
by November 29, 2013, or to dissolve ROI and return its investors' money.

On November 13, 2012, with one year to go to complete an acquisition,
ROI president and Clinton portfolio manager Joseph A. De Perio received
a call from Lampert Debt Advisors, a firm hired by Monomoy to shop

EveryWare to potential buyers. EveryWare wasn't a restaurant chain, but it was related, sort of, because it sold ware to restaurants. Libbey was a much bigger seller of products to the food service industry—food service was still a smaller part of Anchor's business—but Monomoy told the story of how it had turned EveryWare into a big food service player. Whether De Perio bought into the EveryWare story, was motivated by ROI's deadline, or both, he was interested enough to open negotiations.

Monomoy did have other chances to sell EveryWare, or parts of Every-Ware. ROI reported that at least one other SPAC had expressed interest. According to two EveryWare insiders, a man described as "a Canadian billionaire" was alarmed at some of the numbers Monomoy had offered up, specifically its EBITDA. He thought they looked suspicious. A second possible buyer brought in by new CEO John Sheppard balked when Monomoy tried to "get that last penny" for the sale.

The reasons why those other deals fell through may have been contained in the initial terms sent to Clinton by Monomoy. Monomoy wanted too much. In return for a minority stake in EveryWare Global, Monomoy demanded $100 million in cash, a $7.5 million promissory note, 12.44 million shares of common stock, preferred stock that could be converted to common stock saleable if the stock price reached certain levels, and six board seats, to Clinton's two. The other board seat would go to Sheppard, who'd been hired by Monomoy.

As negotiations over terms continued, De Perio and others from Clinton traveled to Lancaster and toured Plant 1 on December 13, 2012. Workers like Joe Boyer and Chris Nagle were used to seeing guys in suits walking around, curious and dumb. They always took it as a sign there was about to be news. The first couple of times it happened, back when Libbey's people toured the plant, they'd get the jitters. They barely looked up from their work now.

Clinton noticed the off-kilter EBITDA numbers, too. But after more negotiation, and a lowered price, Monomoy and Clinton signed an agreement on January 31, 2013, to merge ROI and EveryWare Global and take the combined company public.

At the deal's closing date, Monomoy received $246.9 million, $90 million of it in cash and the rest in stock. Monomoy retained almost two-thirds of EveryWare. Clinton paid the $75.1 million held in ROI and $16 million of its own money. The rest came from loans totaling more than $265 million. As always, that debt would be EveryWare's.

Both Monomoy and Clinton stood to gain more by selling the stock, but there was a hitch. Most of the stock was handcuffed by a so-called lockup: Neither Monomoy nor Clinton could sell their shares for 180 days following the closing of the merger.

Such lockup agreements are meant to reassure investors that a stock's sponsor will share risk rather than quickly bailing out of a company with little chance of success. But this lockup agreement was worthless. Under the terms, Monomoy and Clinton could sell earlier if the stock sold for at least $12.50 per share on at least twenty trading days during any thirty-day period after August 19 (ninety days after the closing date). This could provide an incentive to manipulate the share price during that period. Even if the price provisions weren't met, they had yet another out: Monomoy and Clinton could sell earlier if the audit committee of the board of directors—made up of Clinton and Monomoy personnel—approved an earlier date.

Sheppard, Monomoy's Dan Collin, and members of Clinton all hit the road to sell the new company to investors. They showed PowerPoint slides. They held conference calls. On one such call, Collin promised that "we believe in the business, we believe in its people and we believe in the future growth of the organization. We also believe that the structure of the transaction we are discussing today aligns the interests of all parties involved as we will work together tirelessly to drive go-forward performance and shareholder value in the years to come."

All of them trumpeted words like "world" and "global" over and over, to hammer home the idea that EveryWare was going to compete worldwide. Sheppard took a moment to praise his CFO, Bernard Peters: "I'm proud to have a strong partnership with my CFO Bernard Peters who has a strong, very ethical financial background with unique global experience."

Despite the hard sell, the stock strolled languidly out of the gate at $10 per share. It barely moved over the next several weeks. But by mid-June 2013, the price began to perk up as Oppenheimer, hired by Every-Ware to prepare a secondary offering of stock in anticipation of qualifying for the shorter, ninety-day lockup term, talked up the shares to potential investors.

On July 8, it closed at $12.96. On August 1, EveryWare released earnings results for its first quarter as a public company and for the first six months of the year. They looked good. Revenue was up. EBITDA was way up—32 percent—and if you excluded one-time expenses like merger costs, earnings came in at twenty-seven cents per share for the quarter.

On August 19, ninety days after the closing date, the stock closed at $12.75. On September 3, it closed at $12.95 per share. On September 13, Monomoy and Oppenheimer entered into an underwriting agreement to sell four million shares. The stock price, however, had not met the ninety-day lockup terms set forth in the public filings. The audit committee waived them.

The market for EveryWare's shares was fragile, and the price of the stock was already dropping before Monomoy could get to market. Monomoy had to settle for a sale of 1.75 million shares (90 percent of which were Monomoy's shares) at $11.50 per share, yielding another $18.5 million.

Two weeks later, on October 30, EveryWare released another earnings statement. Sheppard sounded the upbeat notes CEOs always sound in such calls, but he also announced that EveryWare might pull back from some of its earlier, more optimistic predictions. He further said that, to save money, the company was not going to rebuild one of the Lancaster furnaces, as promised. Instead it would "reposition" the capacity.

The stock lost more than 10 percent of its value that day. On October 28, EveryWare shares opened at $10.50 per share. On November 11, they closed at $7.49. The price would never hit $10 again. By March 9, 2015, two days before Solomon called the lenders to break the news about the going-concern qualification from the auditor, it closed at eighty-nine cents.

The question that puzzled Brian Gossett and so many other Anchor employees—Who was making money?—wasn't so hard to answer once you chopped away the acronyms and footnotes and jargon. EveryWare Global was drowning in over $400 million in liabilities. It possessed just over $100 million in total assets. Sales were respectable, but the company had to pay high interest on all that debt. It had to lease a distribution center it used to own. It paid generous salaries and stock options to Sheppard and Peters—Sheppard was paid $2,281,966 in 2012. Most of all, it paid Monomoy, and

Monomoy's funds, many millions of dollars while Brian Gossett, Swink, Joe Boyer, Chris Nagle, Chris Cruit, and hundreds of other Anchor Hocking workers gave up wages and benefits.

A fter the summer shutdown of 2014, EveryWare's board became increasingly desperate to find a way out of the debt prison it had constructed. Monomoy had used $20 million to buy preferred shares as a bridge over the covenant breach during the shutdown, and it was still the majority owner of the company. It wanted that money back. And Clinton hadn't begun to recoup its investment. So the board formed a mergers-and-acquisitions committee.

"The concept is very simple," Solomon explained. "I combine *that* company with no debt with *this* company with too much debt, and the combined company has about the right amount of debt. It's basically: they'll make beautiful kids together. That's all you are lookin' at. Clean balance sheet, ugly balance sheet—it's an average kid."

At one point, Clinton's De Perio tried to bluster his way into a merger with CSS Industries, a maker of stationery, greeting cards, ribbons, bows, baby books, and photo albums under the brand names C. R. Gibson, Paper Magic, and Berwick Offray. On November 17, 2014, De Perio wrote to the CSS board of directors and issued an implied threat to mount a hostile campaign to win over CSS shareholders.

> I write on behalf of Clinton Group, Inc., the investment manager to various funds and partnerships ("Clinton Group") that invest in public equity securities of companies such as CSS Industries, Inc. ("CSS" or the "Company").
>
> We have monitored the Company from afar for the last few years and have owned its common stock in the past. We are ambivalent to owning stock of the Company if it continues to operate as an independent entity in a declining industry niche. . . . The liquidity in the stock is what keeps us on the sidelines today, and *I imagine current shareholders wonder how they will eventually monetize their positions.* [emphasis added]
>
> I believe Clinton Group can set forth an alternative path to equity value creation. Clinton Group is also the owner of a significant stake in

EveryWare Global, Inc. ("EveryWare") (NASDAQ: EVRY), and I sit on
both the Board of Directors and the Acquisition Committee of the Board.
Assuming both parties can come to an agreement on a contribution
analysis and an exchange ratio and based on our detailed review of
the Company's publicly available information and our substantial knowledge of the industry, I believe EveryWare Global can offer as much as
$34.00 per share in an exchange offer to CSS shareholders.

"The rest of the story plays out, unfortunately, like much of my early
dating exploits when I tried to date models," Solomon laughed. "You can
easily envision a model saying, 'I understand why you wanna date me. Tell
me why I wanna date you.'"

CSS, which had very little debt and a healthy share price, laughed off
the threat from the crippled EveryWare. The idea sputtered out. Solomon
did not tell me so directly, but by December 2014 it seemed clear to me
that he believed bankruptcy was the most likely outcome for EveryWare.

Bob Ginnan knew as early as October 2014, just after the shutdown,
that the company would probably collapse. A headhunter had called him
to talk about replacing the Alvarez & Marsal–supplied interim CFO, who
was costing EveryWare more than $31,000 per week. Ginnan was CFO of
an Ohio printing company that had navigated rocky financial shoals, so
he wasn't intimidated by EveryWare's basic finances. But when he looked
up the filings, he was alarmed by the nuances. "I could start to see there
were some things going on here that probably weren't right," he recalled.
"The way I saw some of the earnings and the words flow and the cash flow
and the investments, it looked to me like this thing was headed towards a
problem."

Besides, there'd been a lot of turmoil inside the executive offices on
Pierce Avenue, with executives like Sheppard, Peters, and Kerri Cardenas
Love, the general counsel, suddenly departing. Ginnan decided he wasn't
interested.

Solomon later called Ginnan and asked him to rethink his position.
Monomoy and Clinton were probably not going to be around forever. He
convinced Ginnan that the Anchor Hocking and Oneida brand names,
freed of the PE shops, had value. Ginnan liked the fact that Anchor made
its glass in the U.S.A.—and, more specifically, in Ohio. He was a born-and-

bred Buckeye with an affinity for manufacturing who would rather be on the shop floor than the New York Stock Exchange floor.

"I like dealing in things that have value and use beyond the intellectual value," he said. "It's just something about the craftsmanship of people, and seeing that, and these guys out there on the forming process. They're craftsmen. They really are." He changed his mind and took the job.

In early March 2015, on the Thursday before Ginnan was scheduled to be in Lancaster, Solomon called him. Referring to a bankruptcy filing, Solomon said, "Oh, by the way, we've got this little project we need to start on Monday."

The board, however, refused to go quietly. On March 12, the day after the going-concern call to the lenders, it appointed Solomon to a seat so he could explore another junk-financing scheme involving the issuance of high-interest securities in return for a cash infusion.

But when the plan was presented to the lenders, they rejected it. The board asked the investment banking firm Jefferies to draft other possible out-of-court restructurings. Jefferies offered advice on at least five occasions between March 19 and the end of the month. The lenders rejected them all.

EveryWare had been servicing the debt at the sacrifice of the plants and the workers. The payments arrived on time. No skin would be shaved off the lenders' backs if they let EveryWare try to figure a way out of the going-concern qualification. If a new financing plan failed, or proved inadequate down the road, the lenders could take the keys at that time. Meanwhile, why not wait and keep collecting the interest payments? The lenders could have done just that, Solomon said. "Or they could say, 'I don't like you.'"

By now, most of the lenders were disgusted. Had there not been the shock of the previous year, and had Monomoy not left them with a soured relationship, the lenders might have been willing to explore such alternative financing schemes. But they insisted they would only settle for bankruptcy.

As much as he seemed to favor it, Solomon had mixed feelings about heading for court. On the one hand, he thought of Monomoy as abusive parents and longed for "a forever home." But he was the CEO, and not interim anymore. And now he had a board seat. From the outside, EveryWare looked like his ship. He didn't relish the idea of being the CEO of a corporate *Titanic*. He worried about the patina of failure, especially if he decided to look for another job. That reluctance, however, was outweighed by his desire to rid the company, and himself, of Monomoy and most of the debt. Freed of both, he might finally be able to do what he'd come to do: build that billion-dollar company beneath himself.

NINE

Pump It and Dump It

April 2015

They turned off the lights at Foundation Dinners, the little charity on West Fifth Avenue that fed all comers at outdoor picnic tables, the food prepared in its overworked kitchen. Fifteen yards across Fifth and half a block down, Lloyd Romine, his girlfriend, and whoever happened to have dropped in watched TV and got high. One block behind Lloyd's house and halfway down Garfield, Michele Ritchlin and her teaching staff of one closed up the West After School Center after the last parent/guardian picked up the last child. Directly through the West School playground and across Pierce Avenue, Sam Solomon, Bob Ginnan, Every-Ware general counsel Erika Schoenberger, vice president of sales and marketing Colin Walker, and new vice president of operations Anthony Reisig pored over numbers.

They were only partway through a fourteen-hour day preparing the bankruptcy filing of EveryWare Global. Coordinating with the partners at Monomoy, with two law firms—Kirkland & Ellis, and Pachulski Stang Ziehl & Jones—and with Jefferies, the investment bankers, they planned to blitz the Delaware federal bankruptcy court with a prepackaged plan they hoped would sail through with no delays and not many questions.

The filings hit the court on April 7. On the afternoon of April 9, Ross M. Kwasteniet, from Kirkland & Ellis, rose to address Judge Laurie Selber Silverstein.

So, Your Honor, I'll spend a few minutes on how we got here. In 2013, the company engaged in an aggressive strategy of international expansion that, frankly, fell flat. We built inventories that we expected to sell overseas and that simply didn't sell. We also embarked on a supply chain consolidation effort that went poorly and that resulted in key outages of key products and the company started losing customers. This led to a financial and liquidity crisis and led to potential covenant violations. The company simply had a situation where we had a lot of unsold inventory and we were running low on cash. This resulted in the board deciding to make a change in management. We brought in a new CEO [Solomon], and we also brought in the Alvarez & Marsal firm to help turn things around at the business level.

At the very least, Kwasteniet was admitting to the court that the combined brains of John Sheppard, as CEO, and the Monomoy partners—to whom EveryWare had been paying millions for advice—were lousy business operators.

A former EveryWare executive agreed with that assessment. "These guys were financial engineers, not operators," he told me. "They don't know how to run businesses. They think they do, but they don't." Monomoy, he argued, was too interested in "foisting financial engineering" on the two companies to operate them.

As embarrassing as poor management may have been, though, it was a far better excuse than the alternative theory: EveryWare's debt was so deep by design—allowing Monomoy to strip the company of cash—that EveryWare couldn't move.

In order to reward itself with all that money, Monomoy was forced to engage in stomach-churning corporate maneuvering. In the space of just a few months, Monomoy bought Oneida, rid itself of Anchor CEO Eichhorn, merged two companies—Anchor and Oneida—executed a merger with the Clinton SPAC, and took the company public.

"That's too much change very rapidly," the former executive said. "We would all think to ourselves, 'We need to tap the brake pedal here.' But Monomoy always had the pedal to the metal."

As damning as these interpretations of the events leading to the bankruptcy may have been, they were innocent when compared with the one suggested by other EveryWare insiders. "There was communication between Kerri and Peters about what Peters knew about the numbers and the real state of the company and filing fake information," a source recalled, referring to EveryWare general counsel Kerri Cardenas Love and CFO Bernard Peters. Cardenas Love, the source alleged, believed that Peters, under pressure from Monomoy, knowingly released phony results and estimates in order to make EveryWare seem healthier than it was before the September 2013 secondary stock offering that allowed Monomoy to begin cashing in its shares. Alarmed, Cardenas Love purportedly confronted Peters. "Kerri said, 'You guys figure this out, or I'm going to the SEC.'" Peters asserted that "he could make the numbers say anything he wanted them to say," the source alleged.

Cardenas Love was fired in October 2013, three weeks after the secondary offering. She wrote a whistleblower letter to the SEC and followed up with a lawsuit of her own. On April 1, 2014, EveryWare settled out of court by paying her almost $1 million in damages, back salary, and legal expenses.

The International Brotherhood of Electrical Workers bought stock at the time of the secondary offering. When the stock price collapsed shortly afterwards, the IBEW mounted a class action lawsuit that accused CEO Sheppard, CFO Peters, Monomoy, Clinton Group, and the stock sale underwriters of an illegal stock "pump-and-dump" scheme, "in which the Monomoy Defendants refinanced, merged and took their privately owned and thinly capitalized company public, while stripping it of the cash necessary for it to operate." The IBEW further alleged that

> Monomoy accomplished this by developing a wholly baseless set of 2013 operating projections—revenues of $457 million and [EBITDA] of $61.1 million—which it continued to tout and reaffirm until the weeks following the Secondary Offering, while EveryWare's operations sharply deteriorated as a result of the Company's inadequate capital and its inability or unwillingness to pay its suppliers. To convince EveryWare's creditors, ROI, and the merged company's public shareholders to fund this scheme, the Monomoy Defendants, Sheppard and Peters made a number of material false and misleading statements and misleading omissions.

According to the suit, "when an information technology manager tasked with investigating Ms. Love retrieved incriminating electronic files—which he was required to report to CFO Peters, the subject of Ms. Love's charges—the technology manager, too, was fired."

The suit further alleged that, "by July 2013, the Company was unable to pay its vendors and was on track to run out of money by the end of the year." At that point, EveryWare "engaged in accounting manipulations that misstated EveryWare's inventories. Even after taking out all of EveryWare's capital, causing the Company to become deeply insolvent and threatening the livelihood of thousands of EveryWare employees, the Monomoy Defendants had additional plans for extracting wealth from EveryWare," the suit charged. "Specifically, the Monomoy Defendants retained over 15 million shares of EveryWare which they needed to sell before investors realized that the Company was essentially worthless."

Based on statements from confidential witnesses (CW), the plaintiffs also alleged that Monomoy's cost cuts damaged the ability of the company to function: "CW3 observed that, in May 2013, EveryWare cut back on the bonuses it paid her staff and also radically reduced her staff from 8 to 2. CW3 explained that Monomoy tried to 'squeez[e] every nickel' out of the Company and was not making any investment in the Company's future success."

Solomon was named as a defendant when the suit was first filed, but he was later dropped when it was amended because he hadn't been there for most of the time in question. He couldn't be sure if "there was real fire with all that smoke" or if the suspicious series of events were the consequences of a stressed company that was poorly run.

"All I can tell you is the great sense I take away, from talking to some who were around at the time, was that because you're trying to pump the stock and sell shares, and Monomoy is trying to figure out their secondary offering, you just don't want any noise." Bad news makes noise. He compared the secondary offering to selling a house. People caulk leaks in the upstairs bathroom rather than repairing them because they've got a showing in the morning.

"If you just look at the facts, you're trying to move the stock, and you can see from the quarterly forecast and earnings reports there's pressure on the top line. Ultimately, you reported 51 [million dollars of EBITDA in the October 2013 announcement]. That's a far cry from the 60 that you've guided." The reality that, as Solomon believed, the truer figure was actually $28 million "is a pretty shitty story. So that's not a great story to be selling stock on. So the question is, 'Who knows what when?' "

He believed Monomoy played "a game" in the second half of 2013 by running "the shit out of the factories" to put the production in inventories and account for the inventory as working capital that would goose EBITDA. In other words, the inventories were not what the company "expected to sell overseas and that simply didn't sell," as Kwasteniet described to the judge. They were a gimmick to caulk the upstairs bathroom so investors couldn't see the leaks.

As of June 2016, the question of whether any of these moves were illegal remained unsettled. After months of filings and counterfilings, the IBEW suit was eventually dismissed on the grounds that some charges were too vague, confidential informants may not have had complete knowledge of the company's true financial picture, the defendants' state of mind may not have been to commit a deliberate fraud, and, as Solomon suggested, there were other possible interpretations of events and actions that could excuse the defendants. The International Brotherhood of Electrical Workers appealed the dismissal.

The SEC confirmed that "a law enforcement proceeding is pending or prospective," citing it as a basis to deny my appeal for information about the EveryWare Global investigation under the Freedom of Information Act. While cautioning that any such proceeding did not imply violations of law, the SEC wrote that "the documents you seek come within categories whose disclosure would generally interfere with enforcement proceedings."

Whatever tricks had been played in the past didn't concern Solomon as much as what he could do about the future. He was confident bankruptcy would release EveryWare from its chains, and it mostly did. The prepackaged plan wiped out nearly $250 million in debt. In return, the lenders acquired 96 percent of the company. Monomoy and Clinton were left with about 4 percent. Monomoy, of course, was still far ahead on its investment. The $20 million it reinvested in EveryWare during the 2014 shutdown was a small price to pay to be able to walk away with its other millions. Clinton, on the other hand, took a beating. (I also tried, again over a period of months, to interview Clinton and De Perio. When I finally reached De Perio, he said, "I don't get what's in it for us. What's the upside for talking about a deal that didn't go so well?")

Though it was "prepackaged"—meaning that the creditors and debtors agreed to a plan in advance of filing, making the proceedings streamlined—the proceedings themselves were costly. Kwasteniet, for example, billed $1,030 per hour for his time. He was one of twelve Kirkland & Ellis partners to work on the case; the top rate was $1,235 per hour. The rate at the second law firm representing EveryWare, Pachulski Stang, topped out at $1,025, for Laura Davis Jones. (It was Jones's second turn at bat for Anchor Hocking in an eight-year period. She'd led the Global Home Products bankruptcy case.) Jefferies, the investment bank, and Alvarez & Marsal, the consultants, also billed out enormous sums. Jefferies's fees were capped at $2.5 million. In the ninety days *before* the company filed for bankruptcy, EveryWare paid A&M $1,129,070. Before it was over, the bankruptcy would cost roughly $21 million, all the profit EveryWare expected to make in 2015.

Solomon, who'd never led a company going into bankruptcy, was amazed at how the superstructure of the American bankruptcy process operated—and how much money there was to be made from it.

"I think it's an egregious expense, and it's ridiculous," he said. "But that's the magic." If you wanted to make a quarter of a billion dollars in debt disappear, you had to pay The System. "And not only the amount of money, but the rate at which it went out! Unimaginable. I remember saying to one of the consultants, 'Hey, listen. You guys seem to know what you're doing. This is clearly not your first rodeo. Why do I have to buy a new saddle? Can't you use the saddle from the last rodeo?'"

As it happened, the U.S. trustee for the case, charged with protecting the rights of the creditors, strongly objected to parts of the prepackaged plan, arguing that it amounted to a hit-and-run over smaller creditors, allotted too much money to pay the professionals, and let Monomoy and Clinton off the hook for any part they played in wrecking the company. In return for its cooperation, Monomoy had demanded the same kind of release from responsibility that it imposed on Anchor Hocking for Monomoy's advice and services.

The exculpation and release provisions in the original prepackaged plan released Monomoy, Clinton, and the lenders "conclusively, absolutely, unconditionally, irrevocably, and forever" from any claim arising out of the dividend recaps, the sale of assets like the DC, or any other action the parties took, even if such actions included "fraudulent or preferential transfer or conveyance, tort, contract, breach of fiduciary duty, violation of state or federal laws, including securities laws, negligence, gross negligence." The plan did allow a cause of action for willful misconduct, but then gave the parties an out by allowing them to say they had taken such actions on advice of their attorneys and so were not at fault. "All someone has to say is, 'My attorney told me to do it,' " the trustee argued.

Monomoy hoped to further inoculate itself by having the court find, in its acceptance of the prepackaged plan, that the exculpation was made "in exchange for the good and valuable consideration provided by the Released Parties" (i.e., Monomoy and the others), was "a good faith settlement and compromise of the Claims released by the Third-Party Release," was "in the best interests of the Debtors and all holders of Claims and Interests," and, finally, was "fair, equitable, and reasonable."

In the end, some compromises were made in the plan to accommodate the trustee's objections regarding smaller creditors, but the Monomoy partners got most of the free pass they wanted for their past actions.

Solomon, Schoenberger, Reisig, and Walker received something, too. As an inducement to stay on and run the business under the direction of a new board appointed by the lenders, they were promised, in addition to their salaries, 10 percent of the company when the time came for the lenders to sell. If, for example, EveryWare were to be purchased for $300 million—a figure mentioned several times as a fair estimate once it was back on its feet—they'd split $30 million, $7.5 million apiece.

In its confidential "pitchbook," the sales document PE firms use to convince potential limited partners to hand over millions of dollars to establish new funds, Monomoy bragged about its high return rate—"3.1x"—on Anchor/Oneida/EveryWare, declaring the investment a big success, evidence of its business acumen. From the standpoint of a private equity firm, it *was* a success. Like a lucky old lady hitting a slot in Reno, Monomoy put a little money in and pulled a wagonload of money out. The MCP funds got rich, and so did the Monomoy partners. In 2014, for example, even as

EveryWare imploded, Daniel Collin took $250,000 in board director compensation for his few days of meetings. It was deals like the Every-Ware episode that enabled Presser to own a multi-million-dollar co-op apartment in the Kenilworth building, touted as "the best location on Central Park West."

The ultimate fates of Anchor Hocking, Oneida, the people who worked for them, and the communities in which they lived were irrelevant. It wasn't about making the product; it was about making money appear, the logical conclusion of the Friedman doctrine.

Monomoy sent what was left of Lancaster's once-grand, 110-year-old employer into bankruptcy court while it made off with millions and the employees walked their wages and benefits backwards in time. Lancaster's social contract had been smashed into mean little shards by the slow-motion terrorism of pirate capitalism.

While the bankruptcy was being finalized, Lloyd went shopping. Shopping had become one of Lloyd's favorite pastimes, as though he'd made it his mission to keep River Valley Mall open. He almost never walked out of the mall without purchasing something, whether he needed it or not. "I ain't never had nice things," he explained to me.

The Kentucky Fried Chicken Christmas Dinner was Lloyd Romine's Rosebud. He was ten, maybe, in 1987. His mother had remarried, to a fellow who sometimes worked construction during the day and always drank at night. She was employed at a small auto parts fabrication plant on the outskirts of Lancaster and didn't make much money. The family survived okay, though—until she broke one of her legs in a work accident. It was a bad break; she couldn't return to her job. What money there was dried up or trickled down his stepfather's throat.

She tried. She wanted her Lloyd and his older half-brother to have the kind of life other kids in Lancaster had, and Lloyd loved her for that intention, but somehow she just couldn't manage to fulfill it. On the Christmas when she picked up a bucket of Kentucky Fried Chicken, Lloyd wanted to cry.

Lloyd attended East School, near Mark Kraft's house, during most of his boyhood. But then his mother and stepfather moved out to the country, and he started high school in one of the county schools, Fairfield Union. He dropped out in his sophomore year.

Lloyd and his older half-brother fought a lot—with Lloyd on the receiving end. One day, he and his half-brother got into another fight. Lloyd picked up a two-by-four with a nail sticking out of it and shouted, "If you don't stop beatin' on me, I'm gonna hit you with this!" The threat didn't work, so Lloyd smacked the nail into his half-brother's thigh and ran as fast as he could over to his uncle's house, with his stepfather following close behind. The uncle confronted the stepfather. There was a lot of yelling, and a fist or two. Lloyd didn't stick around to see the rest. He started running again.

Lloyd ran and walked and jogged for miles through woods and fields, all the way into town. He never lived full-time at home again. He fended for himself mostly. He slept on the floors of friends. He broke into cars to sleep in them and steal the loose change out of the ashtrays. About the third car he broke into happened to belong to Sheriff Jim Peck—an unfortunate choice that proved to be a pretty accurate early indicator of the course of Lloyd's criminal career.

When younger men on Lancaster's streets ran into Lloyd, they'd shout, "Hey, Unc!"—partly out of deference to Lloyd's age and partly out of respect for his jail experience. Uncle Lloyd had an awful lot of experience.

Drugs were never a discrete part of Lloyd's life; they blended in as naturally as stealing, working at Lancaster Glass, beating up a guy who tried to cheat him, applying for a job at Anchor Hocking, falling in love, selling vacuum cleaners, fathering a child. His gig as the door thug of a trap house wasn't really any different from any other line of work for him.

The job involved standing just inside the front door and looking through the peephole at who might be coming up the steps to buy some dope or weed or meth. Lloyd would slide a mask down over his face, open the door, pat down the customer, and maybe ask a few questions. If the customer turned out to be a cop, and Lloyd couldn't run fast enough, he would have to become the sacrificial lamb to protect whoever worked in back. If the customer was there to steal drugs or money, Lloyd would have to be the enforcer.

So Lloyd didn't hesitate back in January when Jason called him and suggested working together. He saw an opportunity to become a partner and finally make some real money.

When Jason dialed the number the Cheese supplied and arranged to drive north up 33, he was skittish, because he wasn't sure how the deal would go down or who he'd find at the address. They could be cartel dudes, crazy fuckers who might cut off people's heads or break your arms or some shit. Having Lloyd with him eased his mind. Lloyd never seemed afraid of anything.

In the Columbus suburb of Whitehall, they found a street called Country Club and pulled up to a house. The neighborhood was part of a 1950s subdivision of once-tidy ranch-style homes that had frayed over the past two decades. The greenish house where Jason and Lloyd parked had been foreclosed on during the housing collapse. Now it was a rental.

While stalling for a few moments, they watched a guy walk out. Then they walked in.

The encounter was nothing like a cartel meet-up in a movie—there were no scowling faces, no scary dudes with dark shades. A friendly-seeming Mexican woman greeted Jason, and the conversation turned cordial right away, as if Lloyd and Jason had popped over from next door to borrow a cup of sugar. They didn't have to leave any money or anything. Just as the Cheese promised, the Mexicans were happy to front the dope, and just as the Cheese said, the Mexicans were willing to give them serious weight— about ten ounces, maybe fifteen. Lloyd wasn't sure, but anyway it was a shit ton of dope—283 grams if it was ten ounces, or, put another way, 566 doses at a hefty half a gram per hit, which was enough to supply an addict like Carly for almost five months. All Jason had to do was promise to bring back $1,000 per ounce, a price so cheap it left lots of room for them to impose the Lancaster tax and keep the margin. They'd discovered the Sam's Club of heroin connects.

They walked out of the house, returned to the car, and looked back at the front door just in time to watch another guy walk in. That place was like a fuckin' drive-through beer store.

Jason supplied a couple of other people in Lancaster, too, who would sell, keep a little for themselves—both cash and dope—and pay off Jason, who, in turn, paid off the Mexicans what he owed, then picked up another load: ten ounces, sometimes five. Jason drove the round-trip once a week.

Lloyd joined him only one more time. On that trip, the Mexican woman asked Jason if he could get rid of some ice—the pure crystal form of meth.

She had so much ice, she was offering clearance sale prices, $700 per ounce. An ounce used to cost about two grand, but she was overloaded with ice. She was practically giving the shit away, begging Jason to take some. Jason didn't know much about ice, so he asked Lloyd if he could sell it. "Hell, yeah," Lloyd said.

Jason gave Lloyd half of it. Some confusion arose about how much money Lloyd was supposed to return to Jason after selling the ice. Jason thought Lloyd fucked up the deal.

Incidents like that cooled the partnership a little. Jessica didn't help, either. She and Jason had resumed their relationship, and by April she seemed to have taken over the operation. That was how Lloyd saw it. He could feel himself being nudged out, and was a little resentful, but he didn't see much point in making a big deal out of his diminished role. Besides, he'd already supplemented the dope he was getting from Jason with moon rocks from his own Columbus connect, some white dude.

Moon rocks were supposed to be almost pure MDMA, or Molly. They were manufactured on an industrial scale, often in Mexican or Chinese labs, another blessing of globalization. But some moon rocks were cut with meth. Some moon rocks seemed to be *only* meth. Lloyd didn't really know what the hell they were. The white guy in Columbus described them as "like meth on steroids or some shit." When Lloyd took them, he'd stay awake for two days, so spun out his forty-year-old body would feel "real tore up."

Lloyd and Jason still called each other "brother," but their trust was conditional. Jason thought Lloyd might screw up at any time, and Lloyd regarded Jason as slippery: He'd say one thing, then another, so you could never tell what was true.

Lloyd lived by a motto of his own creation: "You can trust your enemies more than your friends, because your enemies need to do what they say they'll do." By that he meant that he didn't beat up his friends, so they lost their fear of him. His enemies, though, understood Lloyd had no reason at all to restrain himself for their sake. Bashing a guy was a form of public relations, a powerful message meant to influence concentric circles of others. Lloyd didn't have to be particularly angry to do it—it was business—though once his blood was up, he could be so implacable that he thanked God he never carried a gun.

Between the moon rocks and Jason's dope, Lloyd made more money than he'd ever earned in his life: more than four grand a month, an amount he'd never imagined. So two or three days every week, he'd drive out to River Valley and buy new sneakers—the good kind, like Nikes, not the off-brand ones—or new shirts, pants, and dress-up shoes. He bought for himself. He bought for his girlfriend. He bought for the improvised family of eight or nine people who wandered in and out of the gray-box house across the street from Plant 1.

Lloyd barely knew most of them. Some were homeless, some used the house to crash. There was a guy who often brought a kid with him (Lloyd wasn't sure of that guy's name, and the guy used a nickname for the kid), and a couple of girls, and his girlfriend's brother, and people who knew people who knew Lloyd. He was accommodating. Lloyd used at least a gram of dope a day, but even so, he tried to stay only one-fourth as high as everybody else, because he had to be the responsible provider. He supplied most of the food for the household. He paid the rent and the cable bill. He gave away drugs, and when he did, his facsimile family professed their love for him, which gave him a contact high even better than dope. But he never got one without the other.

Joe Strummer's choked voice shouted "Know your rights!" against the walls of the studio above the garage. Brian, his buddy Bayat, Bayat's girlfriend, Victoria, and I were listening to the Clash's *Combat Rock*. It was cold outside, and so it was cold in the studio—more like a late November night, not a late April one. Brian wore a blue hoodie over his T-shirt and a stocking cap with USAF embroidered across the front, a token from Renee. He could talk about her with more ease now. The cap didn't have any significant meaning; it was just a cap. Wearing the cap, and with his round face and blond hair and horn-rims, he looked a bit like Ralphie, the boy from the nostalgic *A Christmas Story* movie, though he got steamed when anybody said so.

Maybe it was just Strummer, but I started to wonder if Brian was an unlikely-looking revolutionary, part of a vanguard camouflaged by a pattern that appeared as laziness, slackerdom, or fecklessness but that just might be the bravery of refusal—refusal to pretend, any more than was absolutely necessary to survive, that the country in which he lived was anything like the country he saw advertised. If he was a revolutionary, he was a semiconscious and conflicted one. Brian had worked since he graduated from high school. He resented people who didn't work. But working made him part of The System he hated.

He'd slept late that day, Sunday, because he'd spent Saturday night partying down in Athens with Mike and some of their friends—something he could do more of now that he wasn't working shifts at Anchor. He still missed Plant 1, though. Summer was coming, he pointed out: the time when the hot end broils. Maybe summer would help him miss it a little less.

Brian liked going down to Athens, because the cops there were a little more tolerant than Lancaster's. You had to totally wreck a bar to get yourself arrested in Athens. Lancaster cops spent their time hassling skaters, prospecting for weed smokers, and handing out traffic tickets to young people—just to feel their authority—while the town was being hollowed out by much bigger problems. "I hate cops," Brian said.

This was not an opinion unique to Brian or erstwhile skate punks. Other people under thirty used exactly the same words. Older people tended to revere the police. Dave Bailey, the chief, announced his retirement at the beginning of the month after serving as a Lancaster cop for thirty-three years, seven of them as chief. Many in Lancaster's establishment told me how much they respected and admired Bailey, and when he and I spoke, I could understand why. He loved the place. But he was worn out, he said, and had decided to take a job as an investigator with the Ohio State Board of Optometry. That sounded so sedate, I wondered how long he'd keep it.

By the end of the month, Lancaster would have a new police chief, Don McDaniel. McDaniel, a former marine, and a cop for twenty-seven years, was a native Lancastrian. He was named acting chief, but nobody doubted he'd be appointed permanently as soon as the city had made a show of scouting out all possible candidates.

Brian Kuhn, a CPA who also worked as the city's safety director, had his eye on another job. He wanted to be mayor. Major Crimes Unit chief Eric Brown, meanwhile, was thinking hard about a move of his own. Nobody in town except his wife knew that, since about the time the MCU busted Mark Kraft and Carly Bowman, he'd been considering, and was being considered for, a state-level post coordinating units like the one he led in Lancaster. The new job would be a promotion—more money, more prestige—but that wasn't why he was interested. Though younger than Bailey, Brown was worn out, too.

Just a week and a half before, he and the MCU had raided another meth house, a few dozen yards from John and Wendy Oatney's place on the south side. Four adults and three toddlers were inside at the time. Another child had left for school. Brown found five small meth pots and a few grams of finished drug. Longtime neighbors stood outside their houses and watched. Some of them thanked Brown. The neighbors all used to know one another, they said, but that had changed in recent years.

Brown hoped he'd never have to walk into another ruin of a house to find small children with dirty mouths and saggy diapers sitting on a filthy floor as their parents cooked meth, or any more Carly Bowmans. If he did, at least they probably wouldn't be in the town where he grew up and played football and married his wife. They'd be in some other town, one of those towns that had it worse than Lancaster. There were plenty of them.

I'd been away for a little while, so I asked Brian what news I'd missed. Somebody shot up a house the other night, he said. Just drove by, down south of Main Street, in a poor section not far from the old Elmwood Cemetery, where gravestones dating from the 1800s sit cockeyed in the ground, and fired at a house on Walnut. In Lancaster, dude.

He nodded at the window of the studio to indicate Main Street. There sat Workingman's Friend. Workingman's Friend! Ha! How fucked up is that? An abandoned gas station with peeling paint and weeds growing up out of the concrete islands and broken windows—some of them broken by Brian long ago, back when he was a "professional vandal," which he wasn't, much. He just thought that was a funny way to describe being a lost-boy skate punk in Lancaster. Anyway, nobody in the city had done anything about the derelict station. The powers that be just let it corrode on the town's main street.

Shit like that was why he didn't even consider the notion that city leaders—formal and de facto—had a clue. They were corrupt, all of them. This was supposed to be a good year for Lancaster? Bullshit.

Oh, and by the way, if he felt like it, he could stand on the platform at the top of the stairs by the studio's door and watch heroin change hands over by Leo's Bier Haus.

"Everything changes," Bayat said. They'd been friends since childhood, though Bayat lived in Akron now, where he worked as a physical trainer.

Victoria said, "When I come here, it's like I'm going into the middle of nowhere." She was born in Mexico and raised in Brazil, the daughter of a pharmaceutical company executive. She was a cosmopolitan who, despite living in Akron, where she worked as a teacher, and despite wearing the same uniform of jeans as Bayat and Brian, retained the schooled, elegant bearing of a cosmopolitan. Bayat and Brian were not cosmopolitans. They were Lancastrians, and though they didn't disagree with Victoria, they defensively raised their chins. It was one thing for them to trash-talk the town, but another for an outsider to do so.

We'd just been talking about art. Brian showed off a new work, a graphic of the word CONSUME. He'd buried a little phrase in the picture: TROLL JUSTIN BIEBER.

The piece reminded me of Jenny Holzer, who became famous by making art out of phrases like "Alienation produces eccentrics or revolutionaries." To back up Brian's and Bayat's residual town pride, I told them how her little brother Fritz and I used to pull crayfish out of creeks, and how her father owned a Ford dealership on Broad Street, where the library now stands. Victoria googled Holzer on her phone, to verify that I wasn't making up such a fantastic story, and said, "Wow, it's such a small world."

Brian and Bayat had been talking about a possible summer trip to Lake Erie, where they'd do some fishing for walleye. Brian said maybe he could live up there. He wouldn't necessarily have to hunt deer—he could fish and grow his own apples.

Just the other day, another guy in the Drew warehouse told him he must be depressed. Brian couldn't be sure if he was or wasn't, but having someplace to go, even if only in his head, provided a refuge and a defense against accepting the status quo. He hated the status quo. A lot of kids had been defeated by the status quo.

"You got these kids who don't know how to identify who they want to be, or could be, or should be," he said, with obvious empathy born of personal experience. Brian had struggled his whole life with that question. He said he'd been a naughty boy right from the first grade. "I was like, 'I need permission to go the bathroom?'" he said, his voice dripping with incredulity. At lunchtime, he'd skate and lose track of the hour and wind up far away from where he was supposed to be. "I was a bad kid," he said, overstating the case. Brian wasn't a bad kid. He was a different kid, who couldn't pay attention and kept asking questions nobody seemed able to answer about why the real world he saw in the early 2000s was so different from the one school tried to impose on him. He'd concluded that "school's not for smart kids," a kernel of truth inside an excuse wrapped up as a brag: comfort for a refusenik.

"It's like they fall through the cracks, right?" he continued. "Maybe they never even got into trouble. And I feel like they look at media and stuff that makes you look cool." The world ran on marketing, he said. "I'm gonna have Beats headphones, and I'm gonna love 'em!" Brian shouted. Bayat laughed because it was so true.

"Like these same kids in Lancaster, they get in this mind-set . . ." Brian interrupted himself to give advice to imaginary kids: " 'Like, man, you could do so much better, even if you weren't, like, rich. You don't have to be a bad person, you know?' But they walk around with their head down and I feel like you get all these other people—horrible people—we idolize, and that bugs the shit out of me. Like when people are praising athletes, or politicians. And they're probably bad people, people that have these privileges. Man, it's like the fucked-up thing is other kids don't think they have them. They think, 'Oh, I do drugs, that's how it is. I'm a drug addict.' They got that attitude, man. People I know die of drug overdoses. They don't even recognize me on the street."

When Brian drove by Community Action on his way to Drew Shoe, he'd see people walking along the berm of the road to and from the offices and temporary housing units. They all looked the same: poor, demoralized, aimless. Part of him resented their presence. He'd bought into the idea that "they ain't even from around here," but part of him recognized himself. "I'm almost in the same shoes as those people."

Was that what engendered his escape fantasies? Maybe it was lots of things. For sure, something had to be rotten somewhere, and nobody in power at any level seemed willing to root out whatever that rotten thing was. They were as cynical as it was possible to be about Lancaster's forced optimism. "Small business?" he said. "We don't need small businesses. We need fuckin' billionaires" to open a big factory.

Another small business had just closed. In 1954, Sherb Johnson opened Johnson's Shoes on Main Street, across from the old Mithoff Building that Brad Hutchinson was trying to revive. Until the 1970s, there were six shoe stores on one downtown block. The mall killed off those that were left in the 1980s, except for Johnson's. Now Sherb's son, who had worked in the store since the 1960s, had announced the closing.

Anyway, whatever had happened to Lancaster had happened everywhere else, too. They just noticed it more in town because Brian and Bayat had grown up there, and it was still Brian's home. Victoria pointed out that Akron was messed up, too. Every day, she taught kids who suffered from starved schools in starved communities.

Brian was moving, but not far. He'd begun packing up a few things in the studio to transport them out to Colfax, a country crossroads east of Lancaster on Route 22. Aaron Shonk had found a small rental out there, next door to a gas station and pizza shop, and they'd decided to be roomies. Even splitting the rent, it was going to be a financial stretch for Brian, given his lower pay at Drew, but he looked forward to getting out of his folks' house. They were good about trying to treat him like a grown man, but living with his mom and dad felt weird at his age. The little house—more like a shack, really—didn't have a refrigerator or a stove, but Brian had mini versions of both in storage in the old garage under the studio, so they'd use those. There was a little upstairs alcove where Brian could set up his drums.

Brian cued up a video on his GoPro. Fat, tall marijuana plants, happy under bright lights, filled the frame. Bayat said, "Looks like Meigs County Gold," referring to Meigs, a county southeast of Lancaster, down on the Ohio River, that was known for poor people and white rural gangsters who grew weed in the woods. This grow belonged to an old pal of Brian's over on the west side. Brian had distanced himself from the guy, not because he grew weed—Brian was cool with that—but because the dude sold a bunch of other kinds of drugs, too, and to kids. What an asshole. Nothing annoyed Brian more than irresponsible adults.

Brian was pretty libertarian about drugs. He and Mike thought heroin "was fucking retarded," but when Brian was younger he'd tried most everything washing through Lancaster, including Oxys, back when they were cheap. When he began to see some of his friends get sucked up into the life—and especially when he felt himself craving a drug—he backed away. He wanted to be his own man, not to belong to drugs. Extricating himself was hard, because he had to leave some friends behind. So he felt qualified to say that drugs weren't really Lancaster's problem. That was one of the questions nobody seemed able to answer for him, or was even interested in asking. "Everybody's all like, 'We gotta stop the drugs.' But why isn't anybody asking why a sixteen-year-old girl is sticking a fucking needle in her arm in the first place?"

TEN

Turn It Around, or Turn It Up?

May 2015

Joe Hoch looked up at the TV hanging over the Pink Cricket bar to watch a pundit on CNN. "Hell, I wanna be one of these people yakkin' on TV," he said. "Yak, yak, yak. Make a shitload of money for yakkin' on TV and not saying a damn thing."

Ben Martin sat on the stool next to Joe's, the beads of sweat rolling off his glass of white wine. Paul Hoch, a retired Anchor Hocking Plant 1 employee, stood behind the bar. Wide suspenders stretched over a white T-shirt, itself stretched over an enormous belly, to hold up a pair of jeans. They were three old men in one of Lancaster's oldest taverns.

Joe had just been reminiscing about working for Dr. Fox, a founder of Lancaster Glass. Hochs had painted homes in Lancaster for at least sixty years, and Joe himself had probably been in half the houses in town. He liked sitting at the kitchen table over a beer with a homeowner after a day's work, he said. They could be rich, but that never mattered much. Joe said he learned a lot around kitchen tables. Dr. Fox, for instance: Sometimes the multimillionaire gave Joe advice, like how to invest money. One of the things Dr. Fox always told him was to "stay involved in the community."

Ben Martin looked at Joe through his round tortoiseshell glasses and nodded his head. Back when he'd headed up the international division for Anchor Hocking, he lived in Europe, where he was able to indulge his passion for art. He owned scores, maybe hundreds—he wasn't sure—of

French and American paintings, from late-nineteenth-century Impression-
ism to twentieth-century abstraction. Small sculptures, books, and copies
of the *New York Times* crowded his living room. He was an aesthete and
a liberal, though he didn't broadcast his philosophy around Lancaster.

Joe finished off his Miller Lite and said he had to get going. He had a
couple of acres to mow. It had been a wet spring so far, and the grass was
growing so fast people couldn't keep up. Joe figured he had about another
two hours of daylight.

"Okay, buddy," Martin said, and he meant it.

Joe Boyer couldn't be sure if he first felt the heat or saw the fire on Shop
1-2, about three feet away, but by the time he'd turned around, an angry-
looking blaze had swarmed it. Rivulets of flame flowed upward on the
pipes and columns rising from the machinery. With plenty of fuel and a
clear path, the fire raced toward the roof of Plant 1. It was early evening.
Boyer had just reached into his press machine—Shop 1-1—to change a bolt.
So this particular fire took him by surprise, but he wasn't surprised there
was a fire in general.

During normal operation, a burst of acetylene gas combusted to deposit
a lubricating layer of fine carbon soot onto the interior of a mold. This allowed for the smooth removal of hot, newly formed ware, much like a fried
egg slides out of a Teflon skillet. There was always a little carbon overspray.
Over time, the machines became coated with flammable carbon, grease,
and dust—but they hadn't been shut down for a thorough cleaning in a long
time. So much goo clung to the machines that, with enough heat buildup
and any stray spark, they could ignite. Boyer knew a shop could go up at any
moment, and now one had.

As a floor operator, Boyer was assigned to open a series of valves to release water in case of a fire. He ran to the valve that controlled a sprinkler
above the Shop 1-2 machine—but by that time the flames had climbed
beyond the sprinkler and were on their way to the clamshell, the giant,
pincers-like structures on Plant 1's roof that provided exhaust and ventila-
tion. He rushed to another set of valves.

He managed to open some, extinguishing part of the fire, but others
wouldn't budge. "There was three of us on one of these valves, and we

couldn't turn it," he said. The fire raced horizontally, across the top of the clamshell high above his head. As he and his shift supervisor and a mechanic struggled with the valve, a high-pressure spray of water shot from the pipe joints: a bad leak that drenched him "like one of those submarine movies." Finally, they managed to twist the valve open, but it was too late. A finger of the fire had found refuge in a ventilator. Lancaster firefighters had to haul hoses up into the clamshell to extinguish the flames. It was about 8:30 before they declared the emergency over.

"The stuff's wore out," Boyer concluded, referring to the fire safety valves. "They don't do anything, maintenance or anything, that they're supposed to do over there." The plant had to be shut down most of the night.

They were still mopping up Plant 1 the next evening when Lancaster's elite pulled into the long driveway leading to Brad and Penny Hutchinson's restored and modernized 1835 redbrick farmhouse, close to the OU Lancaster campus. The Hutchinsons were hosting a festival benefit—though they seemed mysteriously absent.

Every spring, Cameo League, a volunteer group that supported the Lancaster Festival, organized a preview of the upcoming event. In return for a donation, the price of admission, attendees were served drinks, hors d'oeuvres, and a helping of festival PR, including a sneak peek at the attractions. At this year's party, most were also getting their first real look at Joe Piccolo, though some were even more interested in the Hutchinsons.

The party wasn't Piccolo's first public event. He'd held a Q&A and open-mic poetry reading the week before, but that had proved to be an awkward bust—one in a series of incidents that made him privately question his decision to come to Lancaster.

He hadn't been in town a week when a woman pulled him aside and said, "You know, your job's more important than the mayor's." She was partly joking, but he thought that was an odd thing to say. He'd since learned what she meant. So many people seemed to be counting on the festival—and on Piccolo—to elevate the entire town that he was starting to get twitchy with worry over what he'd walked into.

Piccolo had had several careers already: a classical musician, a logistics-and-staging manager in Aspen, a laborer in a northern Ohio foundry that made wheels for railroad cars. He had just interviewed for a sales manager job when he saw an ad for the Lancaster Festival position. He'd never run an entire two-week production, but he had hoped Lancaster might prove to be the start of a new career in arts management.

He had come to put on a small-town festival, only to find that he was expected to help save the place. People kept talking to him about economic impacts, and town promotion, and the development role the festival was expected to play, but that was a responsibility he didn't want, and one he didn't think the festival—or any festival anywhere—should have to bear. The pressure to piece together this first edition under his leadership, with its constrained budget and thirty years of set-in-stone tradition in a town where everybody seemed to know everybody else, was plenty enough for him.

He kept these concerns to himself. After all, he was new to Lancaster, and Lancaster was new to him. Maybe both sides just had the jitters.

The Q&A should have been easy. The setting was Art & Clay on Main, an interactive art studio where people, especially those with physical or intellectual challenges, could come and make clay mugs, or glass earrings, or paint. For decades, Len Hajost, Rosemary's husband, had operated the local office supply store out of the space—until there were no more offices to supply. Becky Hajost, Eric Brown's wife, then turned it into Art & Clay and had since allowed the Fairfield County Board of Developmental Disabilities to run it. A coffee shop, Square Seven, opened inside the studio. You could hear live acoustic music on some weekend evenings during the spring and summer. So the mise-en-scène was ideal for promoting both an arts fest and Lancaster's new identity as a leisure destination. And Piccolo didn't have to do much other than answer a few questions, then turn the stage over to Lancaster's literary set.

But Piccolo was nervous, and it showed. Portly before he came to town, he'd since packed on a few more pounds, thanks to an overworked bachelor's diet. The buttons of his shirt strained against his belly, and though the evening wasn't particularly warm, damp continents of perspiration migrated through it. His forehead glistened.

Perhaps if more people had showed, he would have been a little more relaxed. He'd pictured a crowd, vibrant poetry readings, lots of espresso drinking. But only eight of us sat on the wooden chairs that faced a small alcove at the front of the gallery. There wasn't going to be much poetry reading. Piccolo would have to carry the evening.

The master of ceremonies, a diminutive man somewhat challenged by a speech impediment, who sometimes submitted freebie reviews of local arts events to the paper, began by turning to Piccolo and, playing the role of Lancaster's Walter Winchell, saying, "I can make you in this town, or I can break you." He was joking, too, but the comment slotted easily into the pattern of wary judgment Piccolo had already experienced from many Lancastrians. He squeezed out a thin smile.

Piccolo took the mic—an unnecessary prop, given the small space and its small group—and hit most of his talking points. "My goal for the festival is to create excitement about the city." He talked up the headliner acts: Blues Traveler, Mo Pitney, Thompson Square. Anybody who followed the festival knew there were budget concerns—though few understood just how fragile the money situation was—so Piccolo promised that "this year, we have a good, solid budget." He stressed that the budget had been set before he was hired, but quickly transitioned to his dreams beyond 2015, for what might be possible in three years, maybe five. He had visions of building a bigger stage, of attracting Harry Connick, Jr., or Sheryl Crow— performers who could straddle a generational divide.

The festival had to grow, he said, and he had some exciting plans to make it grow: more gallery space for art shows, more opportunities to exploit the Lancaster Festival Orchestra, expanding free events like the Rising Park Day for the kids. He embraced his assigned mandate by saying the festival should advertise to bigger media markets like Cleveland and Cincinnati, to draw new people to town who just might look around and say to themselves, "Hey, maybe I should move my business to Lancaster." But residents had to show a little patience. Meanwhile, he said, pray for good weather.

The emcee then kicked off the poetry segment by reading a composition of his own. About halfway through, overexcited by his rhythm, he spit his upper denture plate out of his mouth. Everyone pretended not to notice.

Jeff Barron, a reporter for the *Eagle-Gazette*, took the next, and last, turn at the mic. He read some well-crafted verse, ostensibly about Asbury Park, New Jersey. Asbury Park was "a town that fell apart," Barron recited. "Surely those fools must know that a Lost Paradise is forever gone."

The party at the Hutchinsons' home was cheerier, despite a persistent sprinkle. (Every time I ran into festival cofounder Eleanor Hood, she looked

to the skies as if in prayer.) About a hundred people came. A local folk
singer entertained, the gin and tonics were plentiful. Gary Sheldon, the orchestra director, flew in from Miami, taking the spotlight off Piccolo. Joe
only had to introduce himself, express his excitement about Lancaster and
the program for the coming event, and turn the microphone over to Sheldon. Sheldon, revered in Lancaster, lent Piccolo a warm public endorsement. He made a pitch for Blues Traveler, assuring his listeners that he was
not at all offended by the band's refusal to play with the orchestra, and that
Piccolo was doing a fine job.

Whatever interest the festival news and Piccolo's brief debut may have
held for the partygoers, they were secondary to the warm-weather coming
out of Lancaster society. People stood, their hands gripping highball glasses,
napkins wrapped around the bases, and exchanged tales of winter trips to
Florida. They debated whether Donald Trump could be a savior after the
perfidy of Obama, and whether Ohio governor John Kasich, the presidential
preference of most, stood a chance against Jeb Bush, who seemed a sure
bet to win the nomination.

Pretty girls in yellow spring dresses, their hair curled so it wouldn't look
curled, their makeup applied so their faces wouldn't look made up, chatted easily with their mothers' friends, who asked polite questions about the
just-ended college semester back east, or out west, or down south, while
their fathers' friends tried to suppress the wistful sighs of late-middle-aged
men. It was a scene that could have taken place forty years before, down
to the dialogue.

The party also represented the coming out of the Hutchinsons, though
they were nowhere to be found. Their absence only made them seem more
exotic.

"Have you seen her yet?" one woman asked another, referring to Penny
Hutchinson as if Penny were Garbo.

"No, have you?" answered her friend.

"No, but I've heard she's nice."

"Well, the house sure is."

Lancaster's pooh-bahs had no idea what to make of the Hutchinsons.
They were discomfiting forty-one-year-old arrivistes whose own amplified
light illuminated how much the brightness of the old gentry had dimmed.
For two generations, young people who left town for school rarely returned

to live in Lancaster, and after Newell wiped away so many young executives who would have taken the place of the soon to retire, a gulf had opened. The elite around town consisted largely of the sixty-something sons and daughters of former high-ranking industrialists, a few doctors, some lawyers. Some of them didn't even live in Lancaster. They drove in from Granville or from Columbus suburbs.

Forty years before, the party would have been hosted by an Anchor wife or an executive with Diamond Power or Lancaster Glass. They would have had excellent university pedigrees and low handicaps. Brad Hutchinson, though, was a west-side boy whose mother had died of a drug overdose, whose father had served time, whose siblings were either dead from drug and alcohol abuse, in jail, or addicted. He spoke with the accent and grammar of Lancaster and rode his lawn tractor with a nine-millimeter semiautomatic strapped on his hip as if he were expecting a mower hijacking. His formal education had stopped after high school. That he happened to have built a company with revenues of about $80 million per year made him one of the richest people in town. But he was as uncomfortable with the status his bank account and grand house conferred on him as Lancaster's old guard was mystified as to what it should make of him. So the Hutchinsons stayed hidden, self-consciously and deliberately—because they "didn't fit" with the crowd they'd invited.

Brad had never seen the Lancaster Festival and had no desire to see it. "We don't go because we don't like to," he told me. "I don't like to be in big crowds of people, and, quite frankly, most of those people act like they're better than you are. They feel like they've reached some stature level. I just don't ever wanna be that guy who the people think, 'Well, he thinks he's better 'n everybody 'cause he's got a little bit of money.' I've told people, 'If I ever get to that point, I want someone to kick my ass.' "

Hutchinson had a chip on his shoulder, but he wasn't alone. The perception that the festival was "just for rich people"—a table in front of the stage cost $500—was common around town, though the founders created it specifically to bring the arts to the whole community.

Even if Hutchinson perceived more snobbery than there was, it was at least true that scenes like the one inside the Pink Cricket with Ben Martin, the well-to-do former international executive, and the Hochs, the retired glassworker and the painting contractor, had become the exception.

There were no more Ellwoods at Old Bill Bailey's, no more local executives walking through plants and asking working men and women about their families, very few lodges or other organizations where the banker and the glassworker served on a committee together and drank beer together. The rich even shopped out of town, because there were no more department stores carrying fashionable items. A high-end men's haberdashery that once drew customers from Columbus had closed. Now the moneyed drove to Columbus or Cincinnati, or shopped during trips to New York or Florida. Ironically, the festival Hutchinson avoided was one of the few environments in town where volunteers from the upper crust and the hoi polloi seemed to work together for a common goal.

Otherwise, many people on each side of the class divide retreated into their own lives and their own prejudices. Behind these invisible walls, they no longer learned from, or empathized with, the other. The Hutchinsons weren't sure just where they belonged. On one hand, Brad wanted to retain his self-made pride and to never be seen looking down on anybody by associating too closely with town society. On the other, he and Penny bemoaned the Lancaster "mentality" they found among the class they'd left behind.

"It's always been a rough town for me," Penny said. "The people are rough. The people have just a mentality that's just, like, a baser mentality." She was born and raised around Granville and Newark, on the north side of Route 40, the unofficial but long-standing border between the perceived jerkwater towns to the south and east and the progressive, educated burgs to the north. "You know, Gap couldn't make it here. Gap clothing store in the mall couldn't make it, 'cause it was a higher-end clothing. The Gap! The Gap was a higher-end clothing store." Her eyes widened. "That's the people's mind-set in Lancaster. The Gap! I go to visit other places, like Savannah, and Providence, Rhode Island, and think, 'Ah, civilization.'"

Brad was rooted in Lancaster, though, and he refused to budge, so Penny determined to make the best of it. After building their business, they both decided to start giving back to the town by planting their stake in civic life. For years, they'd lived in a country village outside Lancaster. Transforming the old farmhouse and moving in, taking on the Mithoff rebuilding project downtown, and hosting the Cameo League party were announcements that, however reluctant they were, they intended to play a part in Lancaster's future.

Penny had just become involved with the board of the Heritage Association, and it was her idea to host the Cameo League party. "Some of the people I've really embraced—there's a lot of people that are, like, down-to-earth, and they're real wholesome and conservative, and they love their country, they love their guns. I love that. But then there are other things that are just that attitude of me-first, and I'm gonna take care of me, and nobody else matters. And people around here are just oblivious to every-body else, just oblivious."

If nothing else, Lancaster's civic-minded upper class needed the Hutchinsons because there were so few with both the means and the drive to do what Nancy Frick's generation had done. But it was going to be an uncomfortable fit. Many were skeptical of the Mithoff project, for exam-ple. They didn't begrudge Brad Hutchinson the effort—it was his money, and he could do what he wanted—but some wondered why he wouldn't just mow the wreck down and start over, maybe make a federal-style build-ing, but with all the modern innards a business might want. After all, there wasn't anything special about the Mithoff, either architecturally or histori-cally. It had once been a whorehouse. But Hutchinson believed his back-ground was the bigger obstacle. "Most of 'em know that I come from a very rough family," Brad said. "My father worked for the city, at the water depart-ment, so most of them know of my history."

Brad Hutchinson's family lived on Van Buren Avenue, two blocks behind the northeast side of Plant 1. As a little boy, he liked the west side. Kids rode bikes for fun, and once in a while some boy would give another boy a bloody lip. That's what passed for "rough" in those days.

A lot changed in the 1980s. The Hutchinsons moved to a newer, low-income tract development built not far away from Van Buren by Leonard Gorsuch, Jennifer Walters's father. Carl Icahn made trouble, Plant 2 closed, the 1986 strike turned violent, Newell took over. Fewer west-side men worked.

His mother didn't start abusing diet pills because of any of those Lan-caster convulsions: She was swallowing them by the fistful when Brad was six or seven. But by the early 1990s, the tremors of those events had helped loosen the strings that tied a culture of sociable work and responsibility to future aspirations, creating in its place a subculture of immediate, if tem-porary, pleasure. Drug trafficking joined drinking. Hutchinson's mother succumbed, and his father supported his wife's habit by selling and buy-ing. More than once, Hutchinson watched police raid his home.

When the Oxy found its way into Lancaster, his mother turned to it, working her way up to eight or ten pills a day. She moved on to "cancer patches," fentanyl patches prescribed to cancer patients to dull their pain. His mother would cut them up for quicker release, placing the pieces under her tongue. Fentanyl is vastly more powerful than heroin. She overdosed, but quick action by his father saved her life. Then one night when his father was out playing cards, his mother used another patch under her tongue. She died on the kitchen floor. She was fifty-nine.

Drugs and the crime associated with them became an extended-family affair. In addition to his own siblings, his cousins had records. Yet Brad Hutchinson escaped. At first, he said he simply decided to avoid the mistakes of his family, taking their trauma as a life lesson on what not to do. That's why he couldn't understand what was wrong with so many younger people around town. They didn't want to work, at least not work hard, like he did. They smoked marijuana and injected dope. They got themselves tatted up, even on their faces, which was like saying, "I will always be unemployed." And the babies. All those young women pushing charity-store strollers around town, playing mix-and-match paternity. They had no discipline, no drive. They made bad choices. When he was little, west-side men "didn't mind doing an eight-or ten-hour day in a 150-degree factory. That was their life. That's what they done."

Hutchinson, on the other hand, had ambition. After his high school graduation, he became a carpenter. By nineteen he owned his own small contracting company. In 1999, he founded Company Wrench, now a heavy-equipment sales and rental business with ten locations east of the Mississippi.

"We have a great life at forty-one years old," he said. "I don't think anybody could have a better life than I have. For my age, to do what I've done, coming from where I've come from? To me, I'm like the biggest man in the world."

He wasn't boasting. He meant that in comparison with what he'd expected out of life, he felt like a king—inviting contrast to Lloyd Romine, who was just one year younger than Hutchinson. But as it happened, Hutchinson had one advantage Lloyd never did.

When he was about twelve, the parents of a friend, aware of Hutchinson's plight, took him into their home. "They essentially raised me all my teenage years. I give no credit to my mom and dad whatsoever. But as far as being able to do what I do, going to work every day and living like a normal human being? I give all that credit to Sean's parents, Rita and Russ Miller." Russ worked for Diamond Power as a millwright. He also taught plumbing classes at a county technical school. Russ showed Hutchinson, and his own son, how to work with their hands, how to demand excellence of oneself—the rewards of discipline. Hutchinson owed his success in no small part to the fact that Russ Miller had a good job.

Eric Brown was friendly with Brad Hutchinson, though it could be said that Brown was friendly with lots of people—his mother-in-law's generation of local do-gooders, old football pals, attorneys and judges, people he'd helped over the years, a longtime friend at Anchor Hocking who was convinced the company wouldn't last long. Over the preceding months, I'd watched him walk into the Ale House 1890, and the Cherry Street Pub, and every time, people shot their arms up in the air to greet him from across the room. They shook his hand. They slapped him on the back.

That experience wasn't unique to Brown—this was Lancaster, where you had to work to avoid people you knew. But a lot of Lancastrians watched Brown grow up, or they grew up with him. They watched him play on the high school offensive line, and they cheered when he made All-Ohio. When pummelings from the 350-pound linemen of Division I college ball, along with homesickness, drove him back to Lancaster, he pinned a badge to his chest, belted a gun around his waist, and became a nineteen-year-old county deputy. He'd worked in local law enforcement ever since, for thirty-two years. During that time he drove people home who were too drunk to drive themselves, sparing them a DUI. He rescued their cats and dogs. He caught burglars who tried to rob their businesses. Once in a while, he knocked their heads. He worked undercover drug investigations, sometimes by himself, with no backup, when local police were just beginning to figure out how to conduct them. Too often, he sat in their living rooms, looked them in the eyes, and laid the news out in black-and-white: "Your kid is gonna die if something doesn't change."

And he was married to a Hajost, so even if he'd wanted to avoid socializing beyond the duties of his job, he couldn't. That's why his announcement to Lancaster that he was leaving the Major Crimes Unit to become deputy director of Ohio's HIDTA—the High Intensity Drug Trafficking Area program—was so painful, for him and for the town.

The new job came with a big raise over his MCU salary, and he considered it an honor. His gut told him it was the right move at the right time. Maybe he should have left even earlier. For sure he was burned out. The MCU needed some new leadership with new ideas. But Lancaster was his town and his responsibility. The MCU's charge was to act within both Fairfield and Hocking counties, and all the cities and villages in them, but he always tried to pay more attention to Lancaster. Now he felt like he was abandoning it. "I feel a lot of guilt," he told me.

He believed he could do some good on a bigger stage by helping to coordinate squads like the MCU all over the state and by attracting federal funding. But he'd be out of the field now, and the old football star in him, the adrenaline addict, couldn't help but feel that he'd be watching the action from the sidelines.

He rehashed a number of arguments in his head to shoo away the guilt. For example, he told himself that even though his job wasn't finished in Lancaster, it never would be. That's why he hated the term "drug war."

"It's not a fucking war!" he told me on one of the few occasions when he seemed to lose his temper. "We protect each other. We protect our community, our kids, families. We gotta keep it at bay, we can't just let it roll." A war, he argued, had winners and losers. But there were no winners or losers in his world. The best you could do was try to control the rot.

Brown understood that much of what plagued Lancaster was far out of the town's control. Too much of the local leadership was incompetent, or just overmatched. The world beyond Lancaster was big and merciless, but local officials had spent so many years being snugged into Lancaster's cozy society, and trying to re-create the town of their youths, they'd blinded themselves.

They kept thinking the world was a place of goodwill, where people would do the right thing. But it was all about the money. There was money to be made by the CTC, the transition center old Sheriff Peck created that brought felons into John and Wendy Oatney's neighborhood. Peck knew where the money was—newly released convicts were a growth industry— so he went after it. But hadn't the city ever heard of zoning regulations?

Why hadn't the state done anything about the car-title-loan shops and payday lenders that prey on people down on their luck? "We should have statutes," he argued.

There was no mystery to why Lancaster was pocked with car-title and short-term loan storefronts. The industry spent heavily to finance the campaigns of favored politicians. Lancaster's congressman, Steve Stivers, received $80,700 during the 2013–14 election cycle, making him one of the top recipients of short-term-loan industry money in the U.S. Congress. The Ohio Consumer Lenders Association, the lobby group that represented the largest Ohio title-loan lenders, gave generously to John Kasich and the Ohio House Republican Organizational Committee Building Fund.

I spent two hours watching an Advance America storefront, an outlet of one of the largest such lenders in the country, now owned by the Mexican firm Grupo Elektra. The outlet was near the hospital. One person after another, often dressed in medical scrubs, filed into the store.

I decided to ask about a car-title loan on the used Buick I'd bought. A young woman named Sarah tried, with little clarity, to explain the terms.

"It's a sixty-day loan. Your first payment would be due within thirty days. And, um, we can refinance anytime. Once you refinance, it saves you on your CSO fees and your—"

"What's a CSO fee?"

"Your interest and stuff. Rates. Stuff that you save 5 percent each time that you refinance. It's not very much, but it's 5 percent, but it helps. After the sixty days, you—your big lump sum would be actually due, um, you know, but you can refinance and it would take it down to um, let's see . . . I gotta have that little cheat-sheet thing. . . . You'll be renewing your loan—you get charged the same, but your principal is going down 5 percent rather than—or 10 percent rather than 5 percent—in sixty days. That makes sense. It's really hard to explain."

In order to help clarify the terms, I asked Sarah what most people do. "I have some people that refinance three times a week or three times a month. I have some that refinance every thirty days, and I got some that refinance on sixty days." A lot of her customers, she said, took out smaller loans, under $500, because they didn't have checking accounts. They used the money to pay bills.

I asked her if she'd let me take the "little cheat-sheet thing," which listed the payment schedule and interest rates, with me. Sarah said company policy forbade it. But after a lot of confused back-and-forthing, I finally figured out that, on a $1,000 loan, I would owe service-fee payments of $255 per month. None of that amount would be applied to the $1,000 principal. But not to worry, Sarah said, because I could refinance for another fee, rolling over the balance (now $1,255). She encouraged me to keep rolling it over, providing the incentive of a 5 percent reduction in principal each time I did so. The interest rate worked out to be about 300 percent. If I'd wanted a simpler $107.50 payday loan, the interest would have been 636.99 percent—at a time when a thirty-year mortgage was going for about 3.8 percent, and banks could borrow money from the Federal Reserve almost for free.

This was the sort of loan that helped put Wendy Oatney in a deep hole of debt, the kind of loan Loving Lending was trying to combat—against the efforts of the very politicians for whom most people in Lancaster voted.

Private equity and mainstream American banks helped finance outfits like Advance America. According to a report by Reinvestment Partners, a North Carolina–based financial justice advocacy organization, before being purchased by Grupo Elektra, Advance America was supported by a credit line of $300 million provided by Wells Fargo, Bank of America, and U.S. Bank, among others. The money the banks lent, which cost the banks almost nothing, helped enable Advance America to charge poor people 300 percent interest.

Advance America did not supply the loan. It was what's called a credit service organization, or CSO. The actual loan would come from NCP Finance, based in Dayton. NCP described itself as "the premier CSO lender in the country." NCP helped make Ohio one of the biggest markets for predatory lending in the United States. A report by the Center for Responsible Lending documented that five states accounted for half of the loan fees—amounting to $3.95 billion—charged by American high-interest car-title and payday lenders. Ohio was one of the five, accounting for $318,256,497 in fees, an amount that does not include interest payments.

NCP and its founders were also generous contributors to Dave Yost, Ohio's auditor, Stivers, and Kasich.

Brown mentioned the pawnshop in the middle of downtown, where Hickle's department store used to be. "That really burns me," he said. The people who owned it didn't live there. Out-of-towners and self-interested locals like Peck had fed on the bones of Lancaster. All local officials could do was argue about parking on Main Street or where to build a new jail or applaud a restaurant opening while they prayed for the tourists who were never coming.

The drug dealers were the ones with vision. They knew they lived in a global, rootless, gadget-coveting, atomized, every-man-for-himself world in which money trumped all other considerations. Mexican and African American dealers "used to be like oil and water. They never mixed. But money solved that." There was a time when black dealers in the Midwest, like Carly's connect, never touched heroin. "But they knew there was money to be made, and the best way to make that money was to fix those bridges, so they did." The Mexicans lost money on dope. Between Afghanistan and Mexico, heroin was now so plentiful they used it as a loss leader while they sometimes forced small-timers like Jason to sell higher-margin ice, a drug that used to be exclusive to blacks and whites. And local whites—who called blacks "porch monkeys" and "niggers" when they were in Lancaster—were happy to drive up to Columbus to help them traffic drugs. The moon rocks Lloyd was using and selling, and a new tide of fentanyl the MCU was beginning to find around town, were often made (like Drew's shoes, from Guangdong Province) in China.

The social contract, whatever that once meant, "was gone," Brown said.

"What happened?" I asked.

"Corporate America is what happened," he answered.

The fire on Shop 1-2 represented bad news for Solomon, beyond the obvious. The good news was that the Delaware bankruptcy judge approved the prepackaged plan on May 22. The company would again turn private. Monomoy and Clinton would become insignificant shareholders. The lenders would appoint a board of directors. He believed the company would come out of bankruptcy as a restructured business. With the changes he'd implemented in the last half of 2014, and now without the massive debt, he could shift his focus. In the motto-speak he often used, he said, "We've turned it around, now let's turn it up."

But the fire was an untimely reminder of Plant 1's decrepit condition.

It was possible that a new board would be a "turnaround" board that would want to step back and rebuild incrementally, starting with safety. More expensive consultants might be hired. Solomon regarded safety as an "apple pie" issue—nobody ever said they were anti-safety. But safety could also be used as an excuse to avoid undertaking initiatives that could build the business. He wanted to sprint. Now that a fire had broken out, Solomon was concerned a new board might want to walk.

Swink didn't have the least idea that the company he worked for was coming out of bankruptcy. He said he'd never heard of Monomoy. He knew about fire, though. As he and Aaron Shonk sat on the floor of Brian's studio, killing time by playing an old-school video game, he held up his right hand so I could see the scar on the meat just behind the knuckles. He'd been branded by his machine. He'd also had a fire erupt.

Just the other day, he saw a guy break his pinkie finger on a press. In a moment of distraction, the victim stuck his finger under a plunger, and the hydraulic power crushed it.

Memorial Day weekend was coming up, so I'd invited Brian to drive over to the west side for chicken-wing night at Old Bill Bailey's. I expected a crowd: I'd been told Bailey's wings were the best in town. But when we arrived, only five other people sat at the bar. We ordered a couple of basketloads of wings, with sauce enough for us to bathe in. The beer cost $2, unless you asked for something fancy. There was no piano, and hadn't been, since Benny Smith sold the place. A jukebox blasted rock 'n' roll from the 1980s into the near-empty space. A woman who looked sixty, but was probably forty, stood in front of the jukebox. She wore too-big jeans and an old T-shirt. With the arms and legs of dried sassafras twigs and the hips of a skinny eight-year-boy, she swayed by herself to a slow beat only she could hear.

"Tweaker," Brian said.

Overhead, a flat-screen TV mounted on a wall displayed a constant stream of keno games beamed in from the Ohio Lottery. Patrons could gamble away what money they didn't drink. The state of Ohio took in $298 million from keno in 2014, most of it from the pockets of people downing two-buck beer in places like Old Bill Bailey's. The money supported the state's schools so taxes wouldn't have to. The state's politicians didn't regard gambling as a tax. Nobody forced you to gamble.

As we drove back through the east side, Brian lit a cigarette. He steered the F-150 through a Kroger parking lot, and I pointed out a dry cleaner that used to be a Burger Chef franchise where I so profoundly flunked lunch-hour French-frying that I was encouraged to surrender my fry basket. Brian didn't know it was once a fast food joint. He never ate fast food. He believed people in Ohio, by which he meant Lancaster, were so fat because they were addicted to it. He took a deep drag, blew the smoke from his lungs out the driver's-side window, and said, "That shit'll kill ya."

ELEVEN

Hope for a Forever Home

June 2015

Mark Kraft loaded the syringe and injected the heroin into his arm, feeling its warm safety wrap itself around him. The dope was ten times better than what he used to get before his January arrest. And cheaper, too. There was a lot of good shit floating around now, and the price had dropped by half. You could buy two grams for $100—the old Columbus price, but right there in town.

That was thanks, in part, to Jason and Lloyd. Mark had known Lloyd over the years, and Jessica Cantrell and Jason, but he didn't know how they'd helped saturate the market.

Other than the cravings, the nagging torment of the addict trying to quit, there wasn't any good reason why he shot up that Sunday. Mark knew he'd be drug-tested, and that he had a court date in two weeks. His lawyer was working on a deal, called "treatment in lieu of conviction" (ILC), that would keep him out of jail and prevent a felony from appearing on his record if Mark entered a treatment program, stayed sober, and obeyed restrictions like curfews. An ILC mattered, because a felony stayed with you. Every junkie knew that felonies yoked you to a head-down future in menial, last-chance jobs. Now he'd put the deal at risk.

This wasn't his first slip. He'd taken Perc 30s at least twice since being busted but, through either luck or skill, had managed to slide through the drug tests. Maybe that was because they were fake; he suspected so because they burned when they went up his nose.

This dope for sure wasn't fake. But the warmth was temporary. It was always temporary. Moments after injecting himself, he thought, "What the fuck am I doing?"

Over on the south side, John Oatney was still looking for a job. He hadn't had much luck. There was hope, though. He'd heard about another warehouse opening just outside of town. He planned to apply.

And he and Wendy had good news. They'd finally completed their Loving Lending program. Except for a refinanced mortgage, they were debt-free. Loving Lending had helped them roll the second mortgage John had taken out to pay bills into a new loan at a much lower interest rate. They now paid $270 per month. They'd erased their credit card debt, too, and John had cut up the cards. He swore he'd never have another one. It was a big relief, he said, to have those debts off his back.

Wendy had been granted some stock as part of her compensation back when she worked at Sonic making hamburgers. The stock was now worth about $4,000. John planned to use the money to pay a contractor to re-level the house. Part of it was sinking. Once the house repairs were made, he hoped to sell it for maybe $50,000. Then he and Wendy could move out into the country, where it was peaceful.

Loving Lending helped John qualify for free government health insurance, saving him about $90 per month. "As soon as I was able to quit paying for my health care and stuff, that freed up even more money," he told me. The insurance proved timely. John was seriously overweight, and he'd started having chest pains. He assumed he was about to have a heart attack, but doctors diagnosed him as having Barrett's esophagus, a potentially serious condition caused by acid reflux from the stomach, and often a consequence of obesity. John had to drive all the way up to a Columbus hospital to see a specialist. The expense would have put him right back into heavy debt had it not been for the new insurance. He'd also started to receive food stamps. The Oatneys didn't have a landline; they received a subsidized cell phone service, an "Obama phone."

June was state budget month in Ohio. John Kasich signed new legislation that cut $2 billion worth of income taxes. The top rate in Ohio fell to just below 5 percent. Businesses would pay no tax at all on the first $250,000 in profits. Taxes hadn't been that low since 1982, when Ronald Reagan was president.

The legislature boosted the tax on cigarettes, used disproportionally by the working class and the poor, by another thirty-five cents per pack to help offset the income tax cut. In other words, the legislature was counting on the working class to keep smoking to balance the state budget. According to analyses by Gannett newspapers, a one-pack-a-day smoker would pay $127.75 more each year. The income tax cuts would save a family of four earning $40,000 per year $30.89, so the new tax package would cost a family with a one-pack-a-day smoker about $100 per year.

A family of four with a household income of $1 million per year, on the other hand, would save $3,075.17. The legislature refused to raise taxes on the small army of oil and gas drillers who'd been exploiting Ohio's shale formations. Meanwhile, the state also continued to be generous with taxpayer-subsidized grants, loans, and incentives to Ohio businesses—just as it had been with Cerberus Capital Management and Monomoy when they'd owned Anchor Hocking.

The Delaware court finalized EveryWare's bankruptcy on June 2. On June 4, the new board met by telephone. As Solomon feared, the lenders appointed a turnaround board. Other than Solomon himself, "there's no one from the industry," he said. "You have a banker, a couple of turnaround guys from other industries. Nobody knows food service, and nobody who really does industrial. These are not operators."

David N. Weinstein was a business reorganization consultant and a kind of itinerant board chairman, holding seats at Pioneer Companies, York Research, and Horizon Lines. Now he could add EveryWare Global to his list of chairmanships. Before he'd become a professional board chairman, Weinstein worked as a junk finance specialist with Lehman Brothers and other banking firms.

Brian Kushner was a Dallas-based consultant with FTI, a large consulting firm with branches around the world. A specialist in restructuring telecommunications companies, Kushner had also served on numerous boards.

Christopher Jacobs worked for Western Asset Management—WAMCO—one of the EveryWare lenders. He was a portfolio manager.

Rick Heller was yet another gypsy turnaround guy. He'd once been a partner at Carl Marks, a restructuring advisory firm that specialized in middle-market companies. He was also a former CEO and a board member of Motor Coach Industries, the bus manufacturer.

On June 17, as rain poured down on Lancaster in thick sheets, most of the board convened at Pierce Avenue for two days of meetings. Reisig gave Weinstein and Jacobs a tour of Plant 1 and the DC. The following day, the board reconvened to discuss the SEC investigation that had started the month before, based on the whistle-blower letter to the agency from Kerri Cardenas Love. The good news was that the board agreed to spend $8 million to rebuild Tank 1. The bad news for Solomon was the board's fixation on the issue of plant safety.

Solomon came away from the meetings disappointed. The thinking of the lenders was clear to him, and he didn't like it. The board had been hired by the lenders. They were frustrated by the surprise EBITDA news of 2014 and the subsequent shutdown. Not much had happened since to soothe them—they didn't follow the internal workings of the company closely enough to know what Solomon and the others had been doing to weld the seams back together. The new board's brief, Solomon believed, was "It's all fucked up—go fix it." And the people who'd fucked it up, as far as the board understood, were still sitting in the C-suite. Monomoy and Clinton were gone, but Solomon was left standing, and he'd been hired by Monomoy.

Like a shoe salesman whose store was filled with brown shoes (so lots of brown shoes had to be sold), turnaround guys were paid to turn stuff around. That was their game. If a turnaround wasn't needed, then why were they there? Why were they being paid the very high fees? The mere fact of their being hired signified to them that the incumbent management team had screwed up a business. So no matter what the incumbents had done, by definition it had to be wrong, and new strategies had to be implemented.

Solomon foresaw a bias toward action on the part of the new board. His earlier fear that it might hire another batch of expensive consultants to flip over all the rocks and white-glove all the company's corners and crevices now looked more likely. The idea would be to appear busy, to be doing *something*, and then claim credit for any problems found and solved. Solomon believed that's what he'd been doing already, and that the situation was now stable and primed for acceleration. But, whether he liked it or not—and he didn't like it—the specter of Monomoy still hung over the place, shadowing him and the whole company.

If events played out the way Solomon worried they might, both hourly union workers and salaried staff might revolt. He insisted that morale at the company, including at Plant 1, was now "very high," because Every-Ware had shed so much debt and because of his pep talks. He'd told them all that they were like homeless people: They had no debt and were just beginning to move toward a safe place where they'd find profitable growth. Someday EveryWare was going to be a bigger, richer, happier place to work. Every bit of the company had to be focused on that journey. Any move away from that basic mission by way of actions from the board or any hypothetical consultants could ruin the new wave of good feeling he thought he'd instilled in the workforce.

Whether or not Solomon was right about his own strategy or his prognostications about the board, he was wrong about the current morale. Even though EveryWare was terrible at communicating with its employees, from what little they understood of the bankruptcy, workers were pleased to shake off all that debt. But both Plant 1 and the DC were still nursing bitterness over the concessions from the shutdown and the conditions of the facilities. Nobody in Lancaster had forgotten that Monaca survived the shutdown without concessions. Plant 1 employees told me over and over that they'd welcome any chance to leave Anchor Hocking—if only there were some other job that would pay as much.

"The workers feel underappreciated," Chris Cruit said. "Especially the guys who've been there thirty, forty years, because they say, 'Hey, this was a lot nicer back in the day,' you know? And they've been taken from and taken from, you know? They go out on strike, and they always come back for less money."

Anchor Hocking had a difficult time finding glassworkers. Once, that would have been like saying you couldn't find a lobsterman in Maine. But now no young person contemplating entering the job market wanted to start at Anchor if they could help it. It wasn't the possible danger, or even the reputedly tough working conditions, that dissuaded them. It was the instability. Though Plant 1 paid the highest hourly wages in the area for experienced workers, would-be newcomers were reluctant to invest their time learning the jobs when the place might close at any moment.

But Solomon's larger point was that he'd been straight with employees. They'd been lied to over and over during the past twenty years, and he was trying to rebuild some trust. He'd told them the company would scrape off the PE owners, and it had. He'd promised to lower the debt, and he did. After the shutdown, he tried to stabilize sales and customer service—and, through the hard work of the staff, there were signs that the self-inflicted wounds were healing. EveryWare was making progress, but any change in direction could undermine Solomon's credibility.

Solomon would try to help himself in the eyes of the board and the lenders by convincing them to forget about old numbers, especially the $51.1 million EBITDA reported just before the shutdown of 2014. Comparing the performance of Solomon's team with those old metrics wasn't just unfair but inaccurate. The benchmark ought to have been $28 million, because, among the many items tossed out by former CEO Sheppard and former CFO Peters, none of the fees paid to Monomoy for "management" or "advisory" services had been accounted for in EBITDA. Neither had any of the fees collected by the Monomoy principals who'd served as board directors. Most significantly, none of the "equity compensation"—recaps, dividends—taken by Monomoy or Clinton factored into EBITDA calculations. And money for a tank rebuild—about $10.4 million—had been applied to EBITDA to make the number look better, even though that money was still sitting there, waiting for the rebuild.

And Solomon faced yet another problem: Bankers were not in the business of owning glass and flatware companies. At some point, sooner or later, the lenders were going to sell their various stakes. Whether one or another lender wanted out now or at some indeterminate future time was immaterial to Solomon. But he wanted an owner—whoever that might be—to offer EveryWare its "forever home" and to believe Solomon and his team were the ones to deliver the company to the promised land of profit. He hoped to convince those owners that, by taking their stake off the table now, they'd be settling for the short money. EveryWare could be worth $300 million or more in just a few years if they would let him run the show his way. If the entire group were to sell now—say, for $75 million—the management team would have to split only $7.5 million.

But he was confident that wouldn't happen, if only because the lenders had much more than $75 million of their own money sunk into EveryWare. So he and his wife started house-shopping in the Columbus area. His daughter was about to enroll in an Ohio university. Solomon wasn't going anywhere.

The quarter ending in June proved to be a mixed bag of progress and stasis. During the last half of 2014, the team slashed the number of items Anchor Hocking produced in order to focus on more profitable SKUs (stock-keeping units). If stores like Kmart weren't willing to pay a little more for some of the low-margin SKUs, Plant 1 would stop making them. The sales staff had some difficult conversations with such customers, but by late June the strategy was beginning to pay off. Gross revenues were lower, but margins rose.

EveryWare was still bleeding, but it was showing signs of improvement. Ginnan would figure EBITDA at $6.6 million, as compared with negative $2.3 million during the same quarter in 2014, a period that included the shutdown. Total revenue for the quarter would drop to $85.6 million, $5.5 million less than the year before. Total assets by the end of June amounted to $237,589,000, with total liabilities at $172,445,000.

In addition to the SKU reductions, the company was massaging former customers who'd been blindsided during the past year's turmoil. Food service revenue was down, and the candle-jar, flower-vase, and booze-bottle businesses were hit hard, down 20 percent because those customers feared they couldn't count on Anchor Hocking to be a reliable supplier.

All the deferred maintenance of past years still plagued Plant 1. For instance, a sixty-year-old electrical transformer blew out, and while it was being fixed, some production had to cease. The incident cost the company close to $1 million.

For years, Anchor Hocking had been the old dinosaur that had been smashed by one meteor after another yet still refused to die. But if Solomon couldn't deliver results now, either because of his own failure or because of unwelcome direction from the board, it'd be hard to imagine a future.

F our days after the EveryWare board left town, Mark Kraft was psyching himself up to appear in the courtroom of Fairfield County Common Pleas judge Richard Berens. He'd admitted to shooting up two weeks before, and now he hoped the judge would understand how hard it was to stop using. Lots of people around Lancaster didn't understand. After Mark's arrest in January, a lady at the gas station where he bought his cigarettes lectured him on how all addicts ought to be in jail. She said he was "trash."

The craving wasn't the only demon: He'd face cravings if he lived on a desert island. But triggers jumped out at him wherever he went in Lancaster. Some days it seemed that he couldn't go a hundred yards in any direction without running into somebody he knew who was either using or had once been addicted. Almost all the people he'd formed his tightest bonds with were part of Lancaster's drug community. Since his arrest, he'd been obsessively checking MobilePatrol, a smartphone app that listed local people charged with crimes. Every time he looked, he could pick out a couple he knew.

After his parole, Mark met with a case manager at the Recovery Center downtown, an independent agency originally founded as an alcoholism program by the Fairfield Department of Health. He was under court order to seek treatment. He paid cash for his assessment, hoping that, by not waiting for a decision from his health insurance company, he could start right away. But he still hadn't found a place in a program. The Recovery Center was overbooked. Even his parole officer had called, but was told there'd be at least a 120-day wait. At best, Mark could attend some of the center's open meetings, but there'd be no one-on-one therapy. They suggested that Mark attend AA meetings while he waited.

Months of AA convinced Mark that, aside from the county jail, the sessions were the best place in town to meet junkies. During breaks, some attendees would go out to their cars, crush a Perc 30, and suck it up their noses to help them get through the second half. He sometimes went to AA meetings with Nick, one of his best friends. Nick said he was trying to get clean, but he was still using both crack and dope.

Mark considered leaving town. A lot of junkies hoping to stay clear of drugs had the same idea—and so did their families. They trudged through the courtrooms looking wrung out. And when Berens, or his fellow common pleas judge David Trimmer, would talk about the future and ask what was to be done, often the defendant's mother would say something like "I have to get her out of this town."

But where would Mark go? He'd bought his own dope in Columbus. And it wasn't as if Cleveland, Cincinnati, Louisville, Pittsburgh, Indianapolis, or a hundred other cities, large and small, were dope-free. He'd find it no matter where he went. His family, which loved and encouraged him, was in Lancaster—and so was all that Lancaster history he liked so much. He certainly wouldn't be any less lonely in a strange city.

In some ways, Mark had it easier than other addicts. Not only did his parents encourage him, but since he'd become an adult, he didn't have to steal, break into houses, forge checks.

A lot of others spent most of their time boosting from stores. You could drive up to the I-270 beltway that encircled Columbus—away from Lancaster, where you'd surely be recognized—take an exit leading to a mall or a big-box store, and shoplift. One addict, Aaron, born and raised in Lancaster like Mark, used his own "crack baby"—a baby-size doll swaddled in blankets—as a diversion.

"I'd push it through the store and fill it with baby formula, Zantac, batteries, any expensive items," Aaron told me. "I'd pack it full and pull the blanket over it, go through the [checkout] line, and buy a couple dollars' worth of something, you know, and the cashiers would say, 'Ooh, that's a baby, let me see the baby,' and I'd say, 'No, the baby is sick. You can't see the baby,' and push it on through.

"We had a chain of these A-rab stores," he continued, referring to Columbus-area discount stores run by immigrants from the Middle East. "They'd buy anything from, like, a laptop or an unopened bottle of aspirin. I mean, I used to take trash bags full of stuff to the A-rabs, and they'd give me a third or a quarter of what it was worth." The merchants would put the goods on the shelf to be sold at retail, and Aaron would use the cash to make a drug buy.

The hearing on June 22 didn't last long. Berens and Trimmer both worked calendars so full of cases like Mark's that the proceedings had long ago become boilerplate. The judges looked at reports submitted by the prosecutor and the therapists, heard arguments from the defense, listened to short statements.

Berens wanted to know if Mark thought drug usage was a factor in the commission of the crime to which Mark had pleaded guilty. Of course it was, but a simple yes wasn't all Berens expected to hear. Before deciding if he'd grant Mark an ILC, Berens wanted to hear Mark's version of the Aesop's fable, laced with shame and regret and finished with an easy moral, that every junkie told. There had to be the story. Everybody had to agree on the truth of the story. The story was everything.

"Yes, I do," Mark said. "It started after I got out of high school with pills. That was opiates. And it slowly progressed and, you know, there were times I would get clean and have a good, clean time, and then I would fall right back into it with the same kind of people, and it was like a revolving circle."

Berens seemed determined to settle on the boilerplate, and Mark wasn't about to go off the script. Mark, Berens said, could see how he'd derailed, couldn't he? He tried drinking at a young age. He smoked marijuana. Maybe he progressed to a couple of joints, then two or three bowls. The judge described an event arc shared by millions of young Americans over at least three generations (including me, several Lancaster law enforcement officers, and at least three presidents of the United States) who didn't become heroin addicts. He told Mark to look back on his life and see that he could have behaved differently. He should, of course, have sought some help long before Eric Brown and the MCU burst through his front door. "I totally agree with that," Mark said.

So it was the drugs. It was always the drugs. The drugs had come into Lancaster from the outside. And the weaknesses and moral failings of the drug takers led to their committing crimes. The story was neat, symmetrical, easily understood. There seemed to be an almost desperate need to preserve it as dogma. Believing in it was as necessary as believing in the rightness of America, because if you didn't adopt the story, you might be forced to consider the idea that something had gone rotten in the heart of the all-American town—and, just maybe, in America itself.

Figuring out what that something might be, and how it might be connected to Lancaster's drug epidemic, was a lot harder than blaming the drugs and the outsiders who brought them. So most people seemed to have settled on a tale about how the tide of drugs collided with a culture of personal irresponsibility and weakness.

Judge Trimmer spoke for many. In conversations with me, he pinned the root cause of both those pathologies on the government, by which he meant mostly the federal government. Pick any tributary that fed the river of trouble, follow it, and you'd find the government at the headwaters.

Government stoked irresponsibility. "Today, for example, if we walked around, we could probably find large numbers of individuals sitting on their couches—free housing, free food, transportation vouchers, free health care—and they have no purpose in life except for their next paycheck. That's how they live." The unaccountable takers birthed babies they couldn't provide for. They lived with "reckless abandon" and dived into drugs. And yet government seemed to be rewarding irresponsibility, so, naturally, "we have seen the wrong part of our society, so to speak, grow dramatically in population while the other side is having to pay for that."

Trimmer was sincere in his beliefs, and, based on lots of surface evidence, he wasn't wrong.

You could see his diagnosis play out a mile from his chambers, where I first met Ashley. There, down Main Street, and across Memorial Drive into the west side, in a little Dogpatch of rusty single-wide trailers, chunks of glass crunched under our feet. The remnants from what was once a window lay scattered over broken concrete like hundreds of pairs of tiny dice. An old beach towel fluttered in and out of the hole left by the shattered glass. A Big Wheel tricycle, repurposed as a wrecking ball that had crashed through the window the night before, rested on its side near the crumbly base of the trailer. In her defense, Ashley said she only heaved it through the window because the woman who lived in the now-windowless trailer stole her medicine—her Adderall and Xanax.

That wasn't all, Ashley said, enumerating the grievances that justified her rage against the neighbor, whose trailer sat about six feet from hers. She nodded to her own. A SpongeBob SquarePants beach towel served as a curtain for her still-intact window. Then she pointed to an old white Ford Expedition decorated with Hello Kitty license plate frames and Hello Kitty seat covers and a Hello Kitty steering wheel wrap. All four tires had pancaked onto the concrete. They'd been slashed, Ashley claimed, probably by the woman next door.

Children, aged about six to fifteen, rode bicycles of the wrong size or walked around the broken glass, circling to eavesdrop. "She's on drugs," one of them volunteered. Whether the kid was referring to Ashley or the neighbor seemed irrelevant.

"They were knocking on my door, come in, stole my medicine!" Ashley said, in a clittering, pleading voice, like a tired little girl lost in the woods. "I grabbed her by her bra 'cuz I heard it rattling in there." I asked her if she was shooting up. "I don't wanna wear no long-sleeved sweatshirt in the summer," she insisted. As if recognizing that I might still have doubts, she added, "But my best friend is an addict."

Ashley insisted she was clean. She hadn't used drugs since Halloween of 2014, about eight months before. She stayed clean the whole time she was pregnant, she said. Her baby was ten months old.

The baby lived most of the time with Josh, her ex-boyfriend. Ashley lifted her left hand to show her fingers, on which J-O-S-H had been tattooed by "some guy." Josh lived two trailers down with his girlfriend. "It's weird living next to your ex and his girlfriend, but at least he's my baby's dad," she said.

She regretted the tattoo. Covering the letters on her fingers would be more difficult than it had been on her ankle, where an elaborate floral design had turned Josh into vegetation. MOM had been inked into her shoulder.

Ashley lived on government checks. She was twenty-six, blond, short. Her ankles were swollen, her belly paunched, her back swayed. A couple of teeth had gone missing. She owed money to a high-interest furniture rental place, which was one reason why she never answered her door—bill collectors had started showing up. When she was using ten Perc 30s a day, she weighed ninety pounds and drank Ensure to keep herself alive. So you see, she said, "it didn't do no good at all" to take her away from her own mother back when she was fourteen years old, even if her mother was a meth addict. And it wouldn't do no good for authorities to take her other children—I couldn't be sure if there were one or two others—and turn them over to the supervision of Fairfield County Job and Family Services. They'd be better off with her. She was going to get them back, soon, she hoped.

A young girl, about fourteen, whom I'll call Amanda, strolled up to us with a sashay that showed off her too-small denim shorts. Amanda was pretty enough that the missing bottom half of her left arm was not necessarily the first thing most people noticed. She'd taken care to apply mascara, and a little pale, glossy lipstick. She glanced up at me with the eyes of a coquettish puppy. Ashley looked at Amanda, and then at me, and said, "She's growing up too fast."

Of course, in the most obvious sense, people like Ashley made a choice to take drugs. Of course, some people lived off the taxpayers. But the answers provided by the cult of "personal responsibility" were far too facile to explain those choices.

Some people had always abused drugs. "Miss Lulu Ryder, age 16 years, who lives with her brother William Ryder, a glassworker . . . narrowly escaped death from morphine poisoning Tuesday night," began a Lancaster newspaper story from 1904. There were no food vouchers in 1904, no free transportation, no SSI.

Alcohol ruined a few families even when Lancaster was at its peak of prosperity. "My dad was an alcoholic, and, growing up, it was bad," Wendy Oatney told me. "My brother didn't like our mom's rules, so he went to live with Dad. Well, when Daddy came home from work early in the morning from Anchor, you don't go wake him up with something stupid. He went and said, 'Will you take me to a friend's house?' This is six o'clock in the morning. Dad's like, 'No!' Well, he goes back in and asks him again. The next thing I know they are in a fistfight in the living room."

A few people had always made lousy choices. But how had a preexisting human propensity for self-destructive behavior exploded into a plague? As Mark's real, much more complete story—the one he didn't tell Berens— proved, it wasn't the increased availability of a drug like heroin, though that was gas on the flames. Lancaster's drug problem predated heroin, Oxy-Contin, Percs. The problem wasn't caused by drugs at all, or government handouts, or single-parent families. While addiction could be as individual as people, common themes included alienation and disconnection.

Ilene and Kevin Crabtree were the opposite of Ashley, just the sort of young couple Trimmer preferred to see in Lancaster. They were both in their thirties. They were responsible parents to four little children. And they lived just three blocks away from Trimmer's courtroom in Lancaster's historic section. In many ways, the Crabtrees were the 2015 mirror image of Herb and Nancy George in 1949. But the differences between 1949 and 2015 were profound.

Unlike Herb and Nancy, Ilene and Kevin did not choose Lancaster because of the schools, parks, or job opportunities. Ilene worked as a physical therapist in a Columbus hospital, Kevin as a nutritionist in another Columbus hospital. Both were part of the boom in health care, which by 2015 accounted for 17.5 percent of gross national product. Just as the hospital had become Lancaster's biggest employer, the American economy was increasingly driven by the money that citizens and their government spent on their bodies.

The Crabtrees lived in Lancaster and made the long commute every day because Ilene's parents lived in Lancaster, and Ilene and Kevin, and the four little ones, all lived with them. This was an economic and logistical choice. Even with both of them working, the Crabtrees didn't have the money to buy or rent a decent house in Columbus, close to work, and to pay for childcare, too. Ilene's father was a retired army officer who could play Mr. Mom during the day. So her parents enlarged their own Lancaster home and invited the Crabtrees to move in to save money.

When they first arrived, Ilene and Kevin, who had lived in other states, were greeted by a constant beat of bad news about the local economy and drugs. "I wondered," Ilene said, "what was this little town we've moved to?" The house was crowded and chaotic—at any moment, a giggling child could come careening around a corner, sliding on stocking feet, being chased by a sibling. Privacy in what amounted to an eight-person family commune was precious. Even so, the Crabtrees, the children, and Ilene's parents all seemed happy and loving. But the Crabtrees' lives were as much in Columbus as they were in Lancaster.

They'd made a few friends in town. Most of them commuted, too. A young college professor drove to Columbus, while her husband drove in the other direction to Athens. Lancaster just happened to be a spot between their jobs that was also suffering from depressed housing prices. So a young professional couple could buy a big old house on a leafy street and spend weekends playing do-it-yourselfers.

Some believed that was a trend that would save Lancaster, but other than helping at their children's Catholic elementary school and socializing with the few friends they'd made, the Crabtrees didn't have time for civic projects or clubs. Ilene did join a hospital Twig, but she missed about half the meetings. There were no big parties, no major fund-raising dinners, no campaigns for school levies on their calendar. Mostly, they were just exhausted.

Jon Hale would have understood. Hale was a city councilman who also commuted to a job in Columbus. Though he was born and raised in Lancaster, and worked at the local radio station for a while, he dropped out of the civic and social life of the town when he took the Columbus position for a better salary.

"I'd drive up in the morning, work all day, drive back, eat some dinner, and go to bed," he said over a beer after a city council meeting. "I felt I didn't have time for anything else."

When he realized he'd fallen into a commuter rut, and out of Lancaster life, he decided to make a special effort to reengage and wound up running for his city council seat. Partly, he said, he was motivated by a family member's addiction to crack cocaine.

The growing commuting culture further fractured Lancaster life. The commuters left the Ashleys and Lloyds, and the Plant 1 workers, behind every morning. When they returned home at night, tired and focused on their own family concerns, they could close their doors and leave the Ashleys and Lloyds outside, and the Plant 1 workers to the late shift.

They were not a drain on the society like those people Trimmer described. They were good people making their way in the twenty-first-century economy as best they could. But that economy didn't include Lancaster, as it had in Nancy's day. Even their payroll taxes went to Columbus, or wherever else they might drive to each morning. And with the narrowing of vision to themselves and their families, the vibrant little town Nancy loved so much became a more disconnected place.

The commuters were chasing an inchoate dream of security, or success, or career. Mark Kraft was chasing something, too, though he couldn't tell you what it was. He tried not to ask questions about life's meaning, about who he was, what he wanted and believed in. He wasn't abused, neglected, impoverished. His family—his two-parent family—loved him. To say he was dissatisfied would make him sound like a spoiled asshole, so he didn't say it. He could think of no good reason to be dissatisfied. And yet, he was crushed by ennui.

Mark wished his life had more substance, though he wasn't sure what he meant by that. Maybe "fulfillment" would be a better word, but he wasn't sure about that, either. When he tried to think of a form fulfillment might take, aside from drugs, he couldn't conjure an image in his mind. He knew that people sometimes claimed to be fulfilled, or said their lives were imbued with passion, but he was unable to step into the shoes of such people. They existed in a fantasy world. He could see them through the glass screens of his smartphone, his computer, his television. They were all far more glamorous and altogether happier than anybody he'd ever known. Mark's world was Lancaster, and America as seen from Lancaster— and in them, with the exception of his own family, there was nothing deserving of his faith. Nobody inspired him. He didn't think this situation was uniquely unfair to him: He imagined himself treading water, kicking his legs harder and faster to barely keep his head above it, but everybody he knew was stuck in the same water, treading just as furiously as he was. "The world's stacked against everybody," he said. That didn't make him feel any less lonely, though.

He didn't notice so much when he was high. Dope's warmth fulfilled him. Or it made him not worry so much about not being fulfilled. Either way, the loneliness vanished. He liked other addicts, too. Users looked out for each other when they weren't snitching on each other. They were a tribe. They understood what it was like to need the drug, to risk obtaining the drug, to shoot or snort or swallow the drug. That was something, at least.

The last time he felt that way about anything else was back when he used to ride his BMX bike at the Miller Skate Park, down by Miller Pool. On a BMX, you could fly up over the rim of the ramp, yank a 360, and, for an instant, exist suspended in air. Mark was pretty good on the bike. Not great, but pretty good. He liked it down there at the park. There were some cool dudes down there, kids like him who weren't ever going to be, and did not want to be, the high school hero. There were some really good skaters and BMXers who could pull off wild tricks—like Ryan, a kid who spent parts of summers in Lancaster visiting his dad. Mark and Ryan became pretty close; Mark would later live with Ryan for a time. Ryan was a fucking badass on a bike. Mark got to know Brian Gossett down there, too. Brian could skate. But that was a lifetime ago: 2003, 2004, back when he was thirteen or fourteen.

Mark started dealing at fifteen, after he burned his hand trying to re-lease a frozen bolt with thread-loosening fluid and a torch, and the doctor prescribed the Vicodins, and a friend said, "Dude, you can sell those Vike 10s." Mark had thought to himself, "Oh, I could sell drugs!" He'd always been an independent-minded-entrepreneur type, which sounded a little nuts, he knew—but that was about the only explanation he could offer. He sold every pill from the script, taking Tylenol for his hand.

That required discipline—his hand hurt like hell. But Mark figured the sacrifice would be worth it, and it was. He'd already been buying a little weed from a much older teenager, Drew. Now Drew gave Mark some scales and two ounces of weed, telling him to come back with a hundred bucks off each ounce. That was easy in Lancaster, and, once Mark began to really apply himself, he discovered he was a natural at sales and marketing. In a couple of months, he was selling twice as much weed as Drew was.

Being a teenager who could walk around a small town with a pocket-ful of money can make you feel almost as invincible as the people you saw through your screens. His parents rose early, went in to work, came home, and did it all again every day. They saved pennies and bought only what they had to, rarely splurging on anything except a trip now and then. Mark admired them for that, but he figured he'd found his own path in the drug business.

Eventually, Mark teamed up with Dyke, a lesbian; Fat-Em, a big, fat guy; and Jim, a black dude. They'd met a guy in Columbus who knew a guy in El Paso. The guy in Columbus said the guy in El Paso would sell them bundles of weed for far less than they were paying by the time the shit got to Ohio. Of course, they'd have to go down to El Paso to get it, but Mark and the others knew an opportunity when it presented itself, and they weren't about to let the distance stop them.

They pooled some capital and paid a guy in a machine shop to modify the gas tank on a used car with quarter-inch steel to make a partition—one half for gas and the other for a cargo of weed. They lined the cargo space with a Vaseline-like goo to keep any telltale odors from escaping. Once they got to El Paso, they'd jack up the car, release three drop bolts, stuff bundles of weed into the tank, reset the bolts, and be on their way home to Lancaster.

The plan worked just like they'd imagined it. Soon, as far as Mark could tell, there was only one other person in Lancaster—some older lady— moving as much weed as he and his friends were moving.

That older people were dealing surprised Mark at first, but he quickly got used to it. Some of his friends' mothers would party with them. Later, after heroin arrived, one mother somehow got a prescription for Suboxone, the drug used to wean addicts off heroin. She dealt her Suboxone through her daughter, a friend of Mark's.

Marijuana was their main product, but they'd sell anything: coke, Ecstasy, red rock opium (a substance that was supposedly crystalline opium but was usually found to be an herbal incense instead). There wasn't much heroin around then. By his senior prom, in 2007, Mark had moved out of his parents' house and into another one just a few doors away down Main Street. He had $40,000 in the bank, his own money from his own labor, and that didn't count all the money he burned up or snorted or swallowed or gave away. He figured he'd won the capitalist lottery.

He and a couple of friends splurged on $4,000 worth of drugs for prom night. A lot of it was Ecstasy. Even the kids who weren't stoners did Ecstasy. At a party, they treated anybody who asked, and a lot of kids asked. "I don't even know who the fuck they were. I just know we had a hundred rolls, like a hundred pills fucking right there, and we had fucking—every blunt we rolled had a half-gram of fucking—some good-assed coke in it, or whatever it was."

Of course, the crew would get busted. He could see that now, looking back on it. The dumbest cop in Texas couldn't fail to spot a black dude, an eighteen-year-old butch dyke, and a fat white man heading north in an old Chevy with Ohio plates, a gas tank full of weed, and a gun in the glove compartment. Nobody was sure why they had a gun or what they'd do with it: It just seemed like you were supposed to have a gun if you ran drugs.

Mark wasn't along for that final trip. So some asshole and a couple of his goons in Lancaster figured Mark must have ratted out the crew. They showed up at his rental on Main Street, "fucking screaming at me, and they flipped the chair over when they came in and were just fucking getting ready to tear the place up." So Mark stuck his hand into a recliner and pulled out a big fucking gawky gun, a .45 that looked all fancy and chrome-plated. He cocked it and put that fucking thing right up to the asshole's face, but one of those little shitfuckers pulled out a snub-nosed .38 that looked like it had been fished out of a fucking sewer, like it had bodies on it. That wicked little thing was ten times scarier than his fancy gun that was too big for him.

Anyway, there they were, in a Mexican standoff, when Mark's dad, having heard the commotion from several doors away, burst in and said he'd called the police, even though he hadn't. His dad managed to coax them out the door. Mark's hand was shaking so bad he couldn't control it, but he'd hoped nobody noticed how scared he was.

With the demise of the little band of drug runners, Mark went more or less on his own. Lots of his friends knew that if they wanted something, Mark was likely to have it, or he'd know where to get it. Girls—cute ones, some of them—would fuck him, sometimes two at a time, like he was a goddamn silk-robed sultan, not a skinny kid who'd once hung out at a skate park. Later, he and a friend would have girls come over to clean house. The girls—"ho cakes," Mark and his friend called them—would strip out of their jeans and tidy up naked in return for Percs. Mark was smart enough to know girls didn't fuck him because they loved him.

By the time he was twenty-one, Mark was a serious pillhead—he'd always hated the idea of sticking himself with a needle. The deeper his own addiction became, the more close calls he had with the police.

The time a cop beamed a spotlight into a car he was riding in on Kimberly Avenue up in Columbus didn't stop him. He and this black guy had an ounce of cocaine in the car, but, lucky for Mark, the black guy got out and ran, and naturally, when the black guy ran, the white cop chased him and left Mark alone. He just walked away. The time a Lancaster detective who'd been eyeing him followed Mark into Arthur Treacher's Fish and Chips on Memorial Drive didn't stop him. Mark was spun out as hell, but he managed to stay cool enough. The time a Crown Vic followed him into River Valley when he was high on cocaine and had weed and a gun in his car didn't stop him.

His parents tried. They weren't aware of all he was up to, but they knew he was meddling in drugs. His dad lectured him, told him he was over eighteen now, an adult, and would be charged as an adult. *Straighten up, Mark. This is serious. A felony could wreck your life.* His mom called the school system and tried to tell them that drugs were everywhere, even among the "nice" kids—but back then, nobody wanted to listen.

The dying stopped his dealing. As Percs and Oxy and, finally, heroin began displacing weed and cocaine and meth, more people started dying. Ray, for example. One day Ray was over at Mark's family's home, just sitting and talking to Mark's mom. The next, paramedics were hauling Ray's body out of a place up on Mulberry Street that every kid in town knew was a party house: older guys and younger girls and pretty much whatever drug you wanted.

The scene wasn't as fun as it once was. Ho cakes were no longer so enticing. Besides, once Mark got heavy into the Percs, he didn't want sex all that much anyway, because opiates kill your sex drive. Mark decided he'd just be an addict with a job.

Maybe he was getting older. Or maybe it was because he fell in love. I'll call her Rea. She'd dated Brian Gossett for a while. She was a nice girl. She wasn't nearly as into drugs as Mark was, and, for the first time, he could picture himself making a life with a woman. He and Rea moved in together and even talked about getting married.

But the stream of pills almost dried up, and what pills he could find became so expensive that by 2012 he was forced to overcome his fear of needles and turn to heroin, which was cheap and available. He was now a needle-using addict. Rea wasn't, and their relationship suffered.

There were some bad incidents. Mark once tried bath salts and got so spun out and crazy, he hit Rea. Rea stabbed him. It wasn't a bad wound, but they both wound up at the police station. Mark told the cops he'd stabbed himself, and the episode blew over. One time when Rea injected Mark with dope, his eyes closed, his breathing slowed, and he seemed to fall out—OD. She freaked, thinking she'd killed him, but it was just that the dope was so much better than what he was used to. That was the thing about dope: It just kept getting purer. He finally broke it off. "I'm toxic," he told her. "You can't be around me."

He hated being an addict and hated to lose his love, but even the breakup wasn't enough to drive him into treatment. Neither was the time he found a neighbor who'd overdosed and was turning blue. "Maybe half a dozen people I know have OD'd, and I still kept going," he told me. Recently, some of Mark's dope had been cut with fentanyl. He wound up passed out in his car for most of a day.

No matter what he did, he couldn't hold on to the warmth of those first minutes after a hit. He'd spent many thousands of dollars, and ten years of his life, chasing the sweet safety of it.

Lancaster had a couple of cheap motels out on 33: the Baymont Inn, and a frayed dump called the Relax Inn. Mark called that one Relapse Inn because so many junkies checked in there. The pocked blacktop parking slots in front of the motel's paint-peeled doors were filled with rusty Fords and Chevys and beater pickups whose bumpers were wired in place. The rooms were so cave-dark, people squinted like Morlocks whenever they stepped into the light outside. He'd checked into both places at one time or another, figuring that if he could just go hard enough, he might catch and hold the warmth, and the warmth would pull him out of the water. He shot speedballs of coke and heroin—Mark hadn't been born yet when comedian and actor John Belushi died from a speedball OD. During one binge at the Baymont, he snorted fat lines of coke off a mirror while standing in the swimming pool. It was the middle of the day. When he checked into those motels, he figured he'd see just how far he could go. But he never got far enough. For days he full-metal partied until his heart was about ready to explode and he started talking to himself, yet he still couldn't break through and capture the warmth.

Lora Manon, the assistant prosecuting attorney, represented the state. Manon was a career prosecutor who'd seen hundreds of Marks. She appeared, at first impression, to be a steely stickler, a middle-aged, pants-wearing schoolmarm. On the contrary, she was pleasant, with the dark sense of humor prosecutors, cops, and reporters sometimes cultivate. She knew defendants like Mark weren't Pablo Escobar or John Gotti. She was sympathetic, and sometimes seemed more interested in helping them than in putting them in jail. The question, in Mark's case, was whether or not jail would help him most. She didn't know the full story about his past—nobody did. All she knew was that Mark was a young addict like a hundred other ones.

She'd read the report and had seen that Mark confessed to his lapse earlier that month. She'd prosecuted Carly. One month before, Trimmer (who had created the local drug court as a municipal judge) had sentenced Carly to "community control"—probation—instead of the three years in prison called for under the state code. Carly was "doing well," Manon told Berens. Mark, though, was having difficulty.

"I appreciate the fact the defendant has been candid with the court about the fact that he knows he needs to change, and I think that is the situation," Manon told Berens. There was no doubt now that Berens would go along with the ILC, but he wanted to throw Mark a last scare. "Time will tell how motivated you are," he told Mark. "How much you care about your future. I can tell you that county jails and state prisons are full of people who don't care about their future."

Berens misunderstood. Mark cared about his future. He just didn't have any idea what that future was supposed to be, and if it was worth living. An intelligent, funny young man, he coped by trying not to examine it at all, afraid of what he might find.

At least Mark was going home. If he managed to stay sober and pass his drug tests, in three years he'd have no record. It would be as if his January arrest, and the past ten years of his life, had never happened. All he would have left to remind himself of those times would be the black-and-blue stepping-stones on his forearms, the path he'd tried to take out of the water. Mark could not have guessed that his new path would lead him to Jason Roach.

O n June 28, six days after Berens granted Mark the ILC, a few friends and family members gathered in Rising Park for the wedding of Jason Roach and Jessica Cantrell. Jason wore a tuxedo, which surprised Jessica. She wanted to know where he'd gotten it. When she asked, he lied to her. They were on a tight budget, after all. They'd saved up about $1,000 for the day. Most of it went for the reception in the backyard of the house where they lived on Sixth Avenue, half a block from the old Baskin-Robbins where I used to scoop ice cream for the Glassco League softball players who walked over from Miller Park on hot summer evenings. That storefront became a Christian "university."

The wedding was nice. Jason had always liked Mount Pleasant. He thought both it and the park were beautiful. He imagined raising his family amid that beauty.

After the ceremony, everybody drove over to the house on Sixth. Jason had rented a little dance floor to spread out over the grass, along with tables, chairs, and a boom box. The newlyweds and their guests had a nice time.

Jessica thought she might be pregnant again. The marriage and the possibility they'd be raising four children made them think about stopping— using, dealing, everything. Jason had been shooting half a gram every time he got high, and Jessica had been using since she was a teenager, but they both had begun to regret the way drugs had grabbed hold of them. So about two weeks before the wedding, they vowed to quit, cold turkey, all at once, just like that. They vowed to make their family their focus.

Jessica hid a tiny stash of dope in her jewelry box, where Jason couldn't find it. Jason kept a side stash of his own. They used behind each other's backs. When they were together, they took only Perc 30s, which sorta didn't count somehow. But they were trying.

They also talked about stopping their runs to Columbus to visit the Mexicans. The money was good, but the arrangement was getting old. Lloyd had screwed up again, a matter of $1,700, leaving Jason short in paying what he owed the Mexicans. He and the Mexican lady were friendly and all—Jason's kids even rode the family's four-wheeler on his visits—but not *that* friendly.

"He said somethin' about April, his girl, fuckin' did this, did that, he fuckin' fronted some shit out and got all fucked up," Jason said of Lloyd. "And he was like, 'Well, see if you can get me, like, a quarter; I can make money up off that.' So I went and explained to her what happened and shit, and she was like, 'All right.' So I ended up bein' like sixteen hundred behind." Jason and Lloyd still called each other "brother," and swore fealty, but the partnership was sputtering out.

Maybe Jason and Jessica could leave all that behind and use what they'd made to start a little cleaning business. Jessica's brother was involved in landscaping work; they could open a landscaping business. Jessica laughed a little when they talked like that. It was weird, she said, how people she knew, once they started talking about quitting, always seemed to get busted.

TWELVE

Putting the Baby Back Together

July 2015

S am Solomon reached the finish line of his morning commute from Columbus, pulled his black BMW with Illinois plates into his parking space, stepped out of the car, and noticed the handful of police vehicles, lights still flashing, idling seventy-five feet down the street. "They here for me?" he joked to himself.

They were not. They were there for Lloyd, who sat in the back of one of those police cars. Early that morning, Lloyd had been standing in his bathroom in the gray-box house across the street from Plant 1—or he sat in a recliner in the living room; it depended on who you wanted to believe—when SWAT and the MCU crashed through the front door.

About five other people were there with Lloyd. He didn't know any of them well, except April, his girlfriend. They'd been awake all night, so most of them were a little strung out.

When the police ran through the house, they found moon rocks on the floor of the hallway leading to the bathroom. Diamond rings rested at the bottom of the toilet bowl, and the toilet was running. Lloyd said he'd been standing in the bathroom for the usual reason; he hadn't jumped up out of the recliner to try to flush any evidence.

If he *had* jumped out of that recliner, he might have been spurred to action more by instinct than by any deep will to avoid arrest. Lloyd was tired, and not just from staying up all night. Life, and a prodigious menu of drug use, had exhausted him. Now he just sounded relieved.

"I don't know what the hell it is. Something in my head, man," he said, referring to, well, everything.

"You said you are forty years old. Look what it's doing to you," the cop said. The two men on opposite sides of the law chatted like a couple of middle-aged women in a Saks Fifth Avenue dressing room. "You look a lot older than that. You should realize that," the officer said.

"Do I?" Lloyd asked.

"You do look a lot older than forty. Do I look forty-nine? You'll probably say yes, because everybody says I'm fucking old." The cop and Lloyd laughed.

Lloyd reassured him. "No, you're not there. Do I look older than forty-nine?"

"You do."

"Damn."

"Get out," the cop said. "You got to get out of this town."

That afternoon, Jason Roach, Jessica Cantrell, and the three small children they cared for—Jessica's two children with other men and the child they'd made together—drove south on 33 in their Mustang. It was raining. Again. The baby sat in the front seat so Jessica could calm it. The trip up to see the Mexicans on Country Club Road in Whitehall had transpired as it usually did. Jason dropped off the cash he owed from the last payload and picked up another five ounces. That dope, shaped like a baseball, was now sitting in a diaper bag in the backseat.

As they neared Lancaster, Jason received a text message on his phone telling him that Lloyd had been arrested. Moments after they crossed the city line on Memorial Drive, flashing red lights strobed off the rearview mirror. "Fuck, we're getting pulled over," Jason said.

Lloyd hadn't snitched. He didn't have to. The MCU had been tracking both of them for months. A GPS device on Jason's Ford Expedition reported his last few Whitehall visits. (He didn't take the Expedition on this day because his grandmother was using it.) Whitehall police had watched Jason go into the house on Country Club Road, then coordinated with the MCU.

Five ounces was the biggest single dope haul the MCU would capture all year. Detectives were excited about it. They saw it as an opportunity to get closer to the Mexicans in Whitehall—to "cut off the head of the snake," as they said. There was no such thing as one snake or one head. Busting a single Mexican family wouldn't have much impact on Lancaster's heroin supply—the market was a powerful force that abhorred a vacuum. But five ounces was enough to interest the Drug Enforcement Administration in mounting a cooperative investigation.

Jason sat in a detective's car and ricocheted from wheedling to weeping to bargaining. He was just a courier, he insisted.

He appealed to the cop as a family man. "I got a family to take care of." He began to cry, just a little at first. "I got a little baby and two other kids. I'm tryin' to take care of my family, man! I'm fuckin' strugglin' in life just like everybody else, man."

When his mother, sister, and brother-in-law pulled up to the scene to take the children, his shoulders shook with sobs. He shouted, "Oh, my God! My poor baby! I love you!" out the window.

The detective's cell phone rang. His wife was on the other end, wanting to discuss the transportation of a son to summer football camp and a ride to a sports tryout for another child. "Sorry," he said to his wife. "I didn't expect to be tied up tonight, but some shit broke loose. Yep. Love you. Bye."

Jason's mother stepped out into the rain and approached the car. "Mom, I love you," Jason said. "Love you, too," she answered. "I's ready to take care of things."

Jason offered to wear a wire. He promised to rat out everybody he knew. He called Lloyd "a piece of shit." He looked out the window again. "I just got married. I'm sittin' here lookin' at my kids, man!" He convulsed with weeping.

"I'll shut this whole fuckin' town down, man!" Jason shouted. "Like, I know every fuckin' drug dealer. I know every fuckin' connect. I know everything." He could do it, he said, because "anything that's coming in through here is comin' in through me. Like, I got the connect. I'm going up gettin' the shit. Like, anybody's fuckin' with weight is goin' through me."

Jason had been carrying a lot of weight into Lancaster, but his connect was only one of many. Lancaster addicts typically drove themselves up to Columbus—as Carly, Mark, and Aaron had done—or bought small amounts from one another. Jason even had family members who obtained their own drugs from other sources; they'd been using and selling, too. The collective weight of all those small-time heroin users—not to mention pills, crack, meth, moon rocks like Lloyd's connect was providing—likely dwarfed Jason's weekly ounces.

Even so, the Mexicans did trust him to pick up "OZs"—ounces—not just grams, and return with money. The local cops figured they could use that trust. To do so, they'd have to know a lot more about the woman and her family inside the house on Country Club Road in Whitehall.

Jason sensed that his best chance to cut a deal was to make the Mexicans sound as major league as he was trying to make himself, and to promise he could take them down. "It ain't no little shit!" he said of the Mexicans. "They fuck with dope, they fuck with ice. Those people I fuck with, they're not little shit."

And he knew them well. Not only did his son ride their four-wheeler, but he shared dinner with the woman, her parents, other members of the family. "She sees me, she hugs—fuckin' hugs—my kids. My wife. When I go over to her house, we either, like, eat, get something to drink, sit around, and talk." He refused to say the woman's first name, because he wanted to preserve his bargaining power, though he later mentioned it accidentally: Sola. He just called the males "Juan" or "Julio," and he never could pronounce their last name. "It's like Guatemaly or some shit," he said, making the cop laugh. As close as he said he was with the family, however, "I don't care about them people, you know what I mean? And, I mean, I've never been one to fucking, like, rat on somebody or nuttin', but, like, dude, I don't care about them people. Those fuckin' people don't mean a fuckin' thing to me."

Both Jason and Jessica were taken to county jail. Jessica tried to smuggle some dope into jail inside a body cavity, so she was slapped with a conveyance charge.

The detective told Jason that if he really could help, he might get only two years in prison and rehab. He'd probably lose the Mustang, and the cash police found inside his house, but he could keep the SUV—but only if the police successfully dismantled a significant dope-sales operation.

They'd already been frustrated the day Jason was arrested. They found nothing but $8,000 in cash inside the Country Club Road house. "I'm saying when I do the lick [arrest], I better get keys," Jason's would-be handler told him, meaning kilos.

If Jason wanted an easy ride, he'd have to perform. "If you can help yourself, then that's what's gonna happen," a detective told Jason. "It's just like a business."

Anchor Hocking was in the middle of an eleven-day shutdown when Jason was busted. This time, though, the shutdown was good news. The annual July 4 washout, when the factory closed for a cleaning, had been extended to allow for the most comprehensive cleanse and maintenance schedule in nearly fifteen years. Big projects would go unrepaired— there wasn't enough cash or time—but a list of nearly four hundred smaller projects had been compiled.

Equipment would be steam-washed, the plant floor cleaned, mechanical systems checked for worn parts. Anchor Hocking was "trying to put the baby back together," Solomon said. No doubt there would be unforeseen glitches when the process was complete and Plant 1 started back up. That was to be expected. But after those were worked out, Solomon looked forward to a long period of smooth operations and high efficiency—something he'd not experienced in the eighteen months since he arrived.

One hope was that the work inside the plant might improve quality. Both longtime workers and operations managers had been complaining about quality for a while. Line operators blamed the old machinery.

"I see it firsthand," Mike Shook said. "They pull product out of inventory to bring it into the decorating department to have it silk-screened" with images for customers, such as a brewer's logo. "You should see some of the crap that supposedly is classified as good product, that they can't even decorate. It's supposed to be round, and they look like eggs. It's sad."

Solomon knew there had been quality problems in the past, but he didn't seem to be aware of the depth of the issue, nor that it remained. He insisted the ware placed in inventory was good, though he was disappointed that only about 70 percent of what came off the lines passed inspection. The rest was tossed for cullet. Shook said he brought such problems to the attention of the next level of management, the plant manager. "I said, 'Hey, help me out here, man. These guys are dying down there. They have a standard. We quoted this thing with a cost of so much to screen-print, but we're throwing 20 percent away because it won't even fit on the machine.' "

The rest of the glass industry was not waiting for Anchor Hocking to clean up its house. Libbey announced a $30 million investment in a new "plant within a plant" in Shreveport, Louisiana. The new equipment would produce ware like wineglasses with long stems and a flat base. The "Perfect Signature" ware would be made using a proprietary glass formula created by Libbey's R&D.

Anchor Hocking couldn't compete in stemware, because Plant 1 had been so abused over the years. Anchor had once made it—Anchor Hocking once made scores of items it no longer made—but now wineglasses were simply too delicate for Lancaster, and EveryWare didn't have the money to make an investment like Libbey had. Instead, EveryWare distributed imported stemware made by Stölzle, a German company.

Solomon argued that Libbey's financial results proved that his strategy of focusing on what Anchor was good at making—"heavy" glass like bakeware—was the right one. Libbey's sales had risen during the Anchor Hocking shutdown of the previous summer, with some of Anchor's customers migrating to Libbey. But since then, Anchor was showing signs of winning a few of them back, and Libbey's sales were being hit. Second-quarter net sales at Libbey fell by more than 4 percent. Solomon was convinced that the decline was at least partly attributable to Anchor's halting rejuvenation.

But Anchor remained vulnerable because of its reliance on manufacturing ware for World Kitchen. World Kitchen–branded items like Pyrex constituted such a large percentage of Anchor Hocking's overall production that Plant 1 earned more money producing World Kitchen ware than it did by making its own. But World Kitchen was not necessarily any more stable than EveryWare had been, because it, too, was a product of private equity financial engineering.

World Kitchen had gestated under Kohlberg Kravis Roberts (KKR). In 1989, KKR led the leveraged buyout of RJR Nabisco, the tobacco/snack food giant, in a $25 billion boondoggle immortalized in the book *Barbarians at the Gate*. The deal proved disastrous. KKR was soon forced to begin dismantling RJR to pay the interest on the debts. Thousands of employees lost their jobs. The episode so tainted the leveraged-buyout landscape—already plagued by spectacular failures and economic havoc—that it supposedly signaled the end of the era. But LBO shops simply rebranded themselves under the "private equity" moniker.

In 1994, KKR used RJR Nabisco stock to buy Columbus-based Borden, a food company that included dairy products and Cracker Jack, for about $2 billion. Then, in 1998, KKR and Borden bought Corning's consumer products division, which included Pyrex, in a $603 million leveraged buyout, followed by yet another purchase, of Ekco Housewares and General Housewares (Chicago Cutlery), in 1999. KKR combined all these to create World Kitchen, much as Cerberus would later do to form Global Home Products.

Such names were no coincidence. The business gurus who dreamed up these combinations preferred words like "world" and "global" to names that were attached to any real place, person, history: Rootless and meaningless, their labels floated on vapor. It was all about a "platform" to "leverage brands"—though, increasingly, the brands stood for nothing. A lot of World Kitchen's product, after all, wasn't made by World Kitchen but by Anchor Hocking.

Like Global Home Products, World Kitchen, saddled with $812 million of debt, quickly declared bankruptcy, in 2002. By the mid-2000s, Oaktree Capital Management and W Capital Partners owned it. Suffering from declining sales, they'd been looking for a buyer since at least 2013. World Kitchen could pull the OEM work from Anchor Hocking at any time.

For now, Solomon was banking on keeping the World Kitchen OEM business, with the improvements he foresaw coming with the cleanup. As the washout began, both were being factored into bottom-line projections. All month, he and the other top executives would pore over computer screens, nag underlings for data, and add up numbers to prepare for the first formal, comprehensive board meeting since the bankruptcy. The meeting, scheduled for early August, could well determine the future of both the company and its management.

There was no rain on the Fourth of July. Normally that wouldn't be news, but it was this year because the spring and early summer seemed like one long storm. The morning parade passed under a blue sky. The Soap

Box Derby queen rode behind a Ford SUV that towed the champion derby car. A troupe of little girls in pink danced their way east on Main Street toward Broad Street. The Lancaster High School Golden Gales marching band played Sousa. People lined the sidewalks, waving tiny American flags.

Yet despite the good weather and the holiday, Lancaster remained eerily quiet all day. Miller Pool was nearly empty. Fewer than twenty children swam at Tiki.

Better-off Lancastrians weren't any more visible. The country club had tried to hold a July 4 pool-deck party, with barbecue and music and drinks. Until the Great Recession, such holiday parties were well attended—during the 1990s, they were packed with families—but only six reservations had been made, so the club canceled. At about 6:00 p.m., Eleanor and Henry Hood sat alone on the patio overlooking an empty swimming pool, eating hamburgers with a couple of young relatives. Only one group sat inside the clubhouse bar: four or five middle-aged people, who spent the early evening talking about Bruce (now Caitlyn) Jenner, who, they decided, had turned transsexual just for the money.

The bartender blamed demographics for the low turnout. The older generation had mostly died off, she said, and people with families "are pretty into organized sports with their kids." On the occasion of America's birthday party, the all-American town's quietude seemed symptomatic of the slow-motion, but disturbing, change.

Two weeks before the Fourth, the United Way of Fairfield County held a Day of Action in front of Fountain Square, across the street from the old Anchor headquarters. The purpose of the Saturday event was to teach children how to play outside.

Every neighborhood in central Lancaster was within easy walking distance of a park—the city was famous for them. Several streams, as well as the Hocking River, ran through the middle of town. Lancaster was surrounded by fields, hills, and woods. I. J. Collins was right to marvel over the county's name: Old Ebenezer Zane had staked out Lancaster in a beautiful setting.

But just about the only outdoor "playing" took place by way of organized, competitive sports teams. Many older people complained that young parents had succumbed to the fantasy allure of Big Sports, in the hope that their kid would win a soccer, football, or baseball scholarship. Otherwise they'd never be able to afford college. There were more grown men riding bikes around town than young children. The idea of a neighborhood tribe of kids running wild outside with no particular purpose seemed simultaneously exotic, marvelous, and scary—as old-fashioned as the apocryphal stories about Great Grandpa walking five miles to school in a blizzard. All over town, the few kids who did venture outside seemed to go no farther than a front porch, where they constructed invisible protective bubbles with their smartphone screens.

Thinking this pattern might be both physically and mentally unhealthy, the United Way and adult volunteers from partner organizations assembled to show children that playing outside could be fun—though some of the activities, like kids' art and making balloon animals, weren't exactly capture the flag. The Glass Museum showed off Lance McClellan, who'd won the boys' division of the county marbles tournament (his stepsister had won the girls' division), qualifying to go to the nationals in New Jersey. Hutchinson's Company Wrench donated forty bicycles, most of which were given away.

In the summer, many of Lancaster's children spent Monday through Friday in all-day childcare, because their parents—whether they were single, married, or, in fact, the grandparents—worked. Kids who weren't in childcare were often watched over by an older sibling. Few jobs paid enough to allow any income earner to stay home with young children. For many parents, summer was a problem to be solved rather than an opportunity to let children roam.

But there was another reason why so few children ventured outdoors: a gut-deep anxiety that somebody or something lurked somewhere in the shadows, ready to do harm. But for all of its problems—incidents, for instance, like the shots fired at the house on Maple Street—Lancaster was still a safe town.

"We have very courteous drug dealers in Lancaster," Municipal Court judge Patrick Harris told me with a laugh. The fear, he agreed, was "unreasonable."

Nonetheless, the changes of the past thirty years had created a constant low-level, nagging anxiety in Lancaster. It was vague—as if the earth's magnetic field had shifted one degree—but powerful enough to instill gloomy suspicion. "Our whole society is just falling apart," Brad Hutchinson told me, echoing Judge Trimmer.

That was why he mowed his lawn with a pistol on his hip, and why John Oatney had a loaded gun at hand when he heard that family trying to navigate a way to the park behind his house. Since 2004, when Ohio passed a law permitting gun owners to carry concealed weapons, more than fifteen thousand people in the county had been granted licenses, most citing a need for personal protection.

Handguns were once rare in Lancaster. In the previous century, lots of men, and a few teenage boys, had owned rifles for deer hunting, or shotguns for bird hunting, or old, rusty souvenir pistols from one war or another. Nobody could imagine why they'd want to haul a gun around. The idea would have seemed ridiculous.

"We issue a lot of carry-and-conceal firearm permits," Sheriff Dave Phalen told me. "When we started, it was predominantly male, and today it's about half and half, men and women." Phalen believed carrying a gun was "comforting." "I think it gives people a sense of security. Plus, I think there's people who think it's a right: 'I'm gonna be able to exercise a right to be able to carry a firearm.' "

Phalen, an outspoken conservative Christian, favored concealed carry, but he also worried. The night of our conversation, he was scheduled to hold a gun training session for about two hundred local churchgoers. "I don't think it's a good idea to be armed with people in the church," he said. "It's like the airplane: Airplanes go down, but we're not afraid to be on an airplane." But on June 17, a white racist named Dylann Roof walked into the Emanuel African Methodist Episcopal Church, in Charleston, South Carolina, sat down, prayed with some of its members, and then shot and killed nine of them.

"The chances of an incident at your church is, like, almost none," Phalen said. Media coverage, he believed, had inflamed the worry. "So what we're getting is, because on the national news you see this overblown, you're thinking, 'My golly,' you know? And that becomes a reality to people." The mere presence of guns ignited the desire to display them and, if necessary, to use them. "They're saying, 'Hey, we got our CCW permits. We got these guns. We're gonna put 'em in the church. If something happens, we'll be locked and loaded.' I'm thinking, 'You'll get somebody killed.' "

Many stores and bars displayed the universal red-circle-with-a-slash NO GUNS sign. They had to: If they didn't, any CCW holder could legally walk in with a pistol. The signs themselves, though, only made danger seem more possible—a perpetual-motion machine of anxiety.

While many used incidents like the Charleston shooting as a reason to strap on a weapon, opposition to unrestricted gun ownership was equally motivating. Having convinced themselves, or been convinced, that guns were necessary, gun-loving Lancastrians feared that if liberal urban elites had their way, federal forces would come for their weapons. More provocative than even that fear, though, were anti-gun lectures from the metropolitan classes, who didn't know people like Lancastrians, who had proven over and over again for thirty years that they didn't care a whit about them, who sneered at them as bumpkins. Toting a gun was a middle finger in the face of the smarty-pants set.

"I had not been around guns growing up," Jon Hale, the city councilman who commuted to Columbus, told the *Eagle-Gazette*. "My dad didn't hunt, and I wasn't a gun guy. But with the direction our country is going with the talk of 'We're going to get the guns,' we decided to invest in a piece to protect our home."

Confederate flags had sprouted in William T. Sherman's hometown. In the wake of Roof's murderous rampage, and of photos of him exulting in the flag, pressure mounted across the country to stigmatize the stars and bars. In reply, some Lancastrians raised those flags on their houses and in the beds of their pickups. They denied the racist and traitorous interpretations of the flag in favor of disobedience. Just as with guns, it didn't matter that they hadn't been interested in flying the Confederate flag thirty years before.

Sometimes the fear and defiance turned to racism. The Mexicans who came to town to work at Plant 1 had been welcomed, for the most part. Glassworkers who otherwise might have looked upon them with suspicion viewed them instead as fellow factory men trying to make a living. The locals may not have liked the influx of "illegal aliens," but they didn't see it as the Mexicans' fault. As for Sam Solomon, some Anchor Hocking employees liked him and some didn't, but not one, hourly or salaried, ever mentioned his race to me.

Many in Lancaster were well aware of its racial history, and rejected it.

Kellie Ailes, the director of Community Action, told a story about a conference she'd attended during which groups of social service administrators were tasked with solving a math problem about finance. Worried that a black man in her group would be unable to solve the problem, she offered her help. But he'd already solved it. A minor misunderstanding rooted in good intention, one might think. But though the conference had taken place long before, she broke down in tears, sobbing, when recalling the incident, shamed by her assumption and dreading even the possibility that she harbored unrecognized prejudice.

Raised to be midwestern-neighborly, good-hearted, and fair-dealing—but in a near-all-white town that had once been the master of its own fate (or at least seemingly so), Lancastrians were navigating a much more diverse and uncertain world. The town, Mayor Dave Smith told me during a break in a city council meeting, was "growing up."

But the old Copperhead strain that had popularized the Klan a hundred years before still existed. There was the skinny, scruffy-faced man in a sleeveless Lynrd Skynrd T-shirt who'd sidled up to the barstool next to mine at Old Bill Bailey's. It was about four in the afternoon on a Saturday. "I been drinkin' all day," he said, and I believed him. An unlit cigarette held in a gap where three missing teeth used to be bounced like Toscanini's baton as he spoke. He told me he was partying with his roommate, who was about to move out of their shabby apartment nearby. Then, after an awkward silence, he turned to me and said, "Did you hear they wanted Michelle Obama to pose for one of them centerfolds?"

"No," I said. "Do you think she'll do it?" "Prob-lee," he said. "It's fer *National Geographic*." He cackled with so much enthusiasm, he coughed up beery nicotine phlegm. Racism in other parts of town was subtler. It revealed itself in conversations about "strangers" and "newcomers."

The roots of racism in those who expressed it were more tangled than simple hatred sparked by skin color. Lower-class whites were cut off from all the college campus rhetoric about "white privilege," but they wouldn't have understood it anyway, because they, with good reason, didn't feel privileged. Most of them hadn't done anything wrong, but they believed some malevolent force had reached into their community and punished them. Somebody, they thought, was screwing them out of the good-life lottery. Somebody *was* screwing them. It just wasn't who they thought.

"They're racist because they look at those people as getting all the breaks," Harris explained. " 'Why do they get all the breaks? My life sucks. Why don't I get breaks like they do? They get into all the best schools 'cause they're black. I wish I could go into a job interview and be black.' I'm always like, 'Then do it. Trust me, you may find out that was not the best choice you ever made.' So, yeah, there's a huge amount of racism in this community." But it was resentment based on "that perception that African Americans are getting special treatment."

Harris considered the possibility that guns, race, the belief that the drug problem could be pinned on blacks and Mexicans in Columbus or Detroit, the generalized fear that turned parents into ever-vigilant kid guardians, might be the result of a strategy. Referring to Lancaster's tax-starved schools, he said, "Of course, you could be really cynical, which I get sometimes, and say, 'Well, that's one reason to keep 'em stupid.'" Harris, raised a Catholic, continued. "It's the old Catholic philosophy of the Middle Ages: Don't let 'em learn to read, because as long as we're telling them what the Book says, then they'll listen to us." He blamed the dominance of the local Republican Party hierarchy. He was the only Democrat serving as a city-or county-wide elected official. He managed to win by running as a Republican, then switched parties. "It doesn't make any sense at all. I believe it's because you convince people that it's all Obama's fault, it's all the Democrats' fault, it's all this or that, and they'll believe it."

Trying to explain that the roots of Lancaster's problematic changes were deep and old was a futile exercise. A few people who were executives at Anchor at the time remembered Icahn, but nobody else did. Almost nobody knew the true story of the Newell takeover and of the shady dealings of Newell's felonious financier, Gary Driggs. Cerberus had come and gone so quickly that the episode blurred. The vast majority of Lancastrians couldn't name Monomoy, to say nothing of Barington Capital, Wexford Management, or the Clinton Group. They didn't follow the intricacies of carried interest, the decline of union power, Wall Street lobbying, or the political contributions made by the predatory-lending industry. It wasn't that they were rubes, as so many big-city liberals took comfort in believing. It was that they had lives to lead and work to do. Both the national and the local press, which might have once briefed them on how The System had been turned on its head, were themselves eviscerated by digital culture, by their own insular preoccupation with themselves, and by the drum-beat message from cable news and Internet propaganda to never trust "the media."

John Oatney didn't follow politics. He voted because he was a good American who felt it was his duty to do so. When he did, he usually voted for Democrats, because he'd been raised to believe the Democrats looked out for poor people, and he'd never had much money. But then he returned to the Lord. A nice man at church named Tom began educating John. Among other things, Tom told John that he could not call himself a Christian and vote for Democrats. Also, "Obama was a mean and evil person" who was trying "to drive the country down to where it will be easy for somebody from the Middle East, or somebody, to come and harm us, or take over."

John hadn't been aware of any of this until Tom explained it. Tom told him not to feel bad about not knowing. John had just been kept in the dark by watching 4, 6, and 10, the major network TV channels in Columbus. Those stations weren't allowed to tell it like it really was, Tom said. Instead John needed to watch cable news. When John replied that he had "poor boy" TV—that is, no cable—Tom said he had to get himself somewhere so he could see the cable channels that told the truth.

By the end of the day, July 4 didn't feel like much of a happy birthday. But, finally, a crowd of several thousand gathered at the fairgrounds for the traditional fireworks show. They surrounded the racetrack made famous by gas-illuminated harness racing and Peggy Cummins. The fireworks burst, sparkled, and flashed. Rousing, coordinated music blared over hundreds of radios. The booms were loud. Little kids covered their ears with their hands. A few people chanted, "U.S.A.! U.S.A.!" And then everybody went home.

Just before the festival started, the Rotarians gathered for their regular Monday meeting at The Lodge, the former Elks hall, on Main Hill, which had been turned into a bar and restaurant. A woman stood before them to speak the invocation. As everyone bowed their heads, she spoke to God. "This is an exciting time for our community. We pray for our director, Joe, and our conductor, Gary. Please lay your hands on our orchestra members." Her voice cracked. Tears streamed down her face. She read from Psalm 150: "Praise him with stringed instruments and pipe. Praise him with resounding cymbals."

"Our" director, "our" conductor, "our" musicians. There wasn't much left of what *Forbes* had found, and Lancaster stood to lose more still: The hospital the town had built for itself—now its largest employer—which had just celebrated the completion of a $38 million expansion, was under attack. Big regional corporate health systems, following a grow-or-die mandate, wanted to steal its independence by absorbing it into their chains. The festival, though, was wholly Lancaster's. "It's about community, it's about people," orchestra conductor Gary Sheldon told the Rotarians.

The festival couldn't start soon enough for Joe Piccolo. In late June, he'd told me, "If I am still pushing against an immovable wall in two years, I am not going down with the ship." The board was reluctant to accept the changes he wanted to make, he said, but the operation needed to change. Hundreds of volunteers made up the workforce, but that squadron was graying. A few part-time paid employees served in crucial positions, but two women in the office were in ill health, and there were no contingency plans for replacing them. A small minority of aging donors wielded too much control. Lancaster itself was just too old-fashioned. Piccolo was getting heat for hiring Blues Traveler, but young people weren't interested in orchestral music. The festival had to look to the future.

His other frustrations were minor, though many and varied. There was a snafu over rental buses to shuttle ticket holders to the big concert site at OU Lancaster. A group of ministers had hired a nationally recognized Christian singer to appear during the festival period, piggybacking on the sanctioned events Piccolo was trying to sell. Tickets to that event cost $15 or $20. Lancaster's consumer buck would go only so far.

And Christians weren't his only competition. When nearby communities witnessed the success of Lancaster's festival as it grew in popularity, some of them decided to mount their own. Pickerington, a once-tiny farming village in northwestern Fairfield County that had become a Columbus bedroom community over the past thirty years, started the Violet Festival in 1997. This year, the graying rock band Kansas would appear there, on the same weekend Blues Traveler was performing in Lancaster. Dublin, closer to Columbus, was holding its Irish Festival. And the Ohio State Fair was being held July 29 through August 9. Reba McEntire, Meghan Trainor, Patti LaBelle, Alabama, Peter Frampton, Cheap Trick, Dru Hill, and Deep Purple were all slated to appear.

One day, while visiting with him in his office, I commented on a picture of J. Robert Oppenheimer displayed on a computer screen. Oppenheimer's fedora, as well as the cigarette punctuating his gaunt face, reminded Piccolo that Oppenheimer overcame every obstacle to lead the creation of the atomic bomb.

"But, Joe," I said, "he later regretted it."

"Well, we try not to think about that."

By the opening-night concert, a program of Mussorgsky inside St. Mary's Church, controversies had receded into the background. The day had dawned brightly—sunny and warm. Phones in the box office rang with more persistence. And now a sellout crowd of seven hundred had crammed into St. Mary's, one of Lancaster's grandest and oldest churches.

Piccolo seemed to be everywhere at once, huffing and perspiring outside the church, in the back of the church, in the sacristy at the front of the church. Spotting a couple of older female volunteers handing out programs, he dashed up to them and offered to take a handful. But he offended them. Didn't he think they were doing a good job? Did he want to take over?

"I was only trying to help," Piccolo pleaded. But he'd underestimated the importance of their involvement. They'd helped for years. The small bit they contributed to the success of the festival in their community gave them purpose and ownership at a time when there was so little of either.

Joe Boyer didn't get to hear the Mussorgsky; he worked the night shift that night. He'd work nights all through the festival, so he wouldn't see any of the events. Brian Gossett and Aaron Shonk didn't attend, either. Instead they had some friends over to the Colfax cabin. Aaron built a big fire in the backyard and cued up big band music and some blues on a boom box. Sitting around by a fire, drinking some beer, being as loud as they wanted—that's why they'd moved out there. The cheap rent was important, too, of course, and Colfax was a straight shot down 22 to work at Drew, but nights like this were what they'd been looking for.

Brian was in a mood to chill. Over the July 4 weekend, he and Mike had gone to a rave out in the country, and they'd had fun, but he came home deciding that he'd had enough of the rave-fest scene. "I was sitting on this bench, and Mike was sitting near me, across from me, and he's like, 'Are you waiting in line?' And I didn't know what he meant. I looked down, and there's this circle of people sitting on the ground, waiting their turn to inject themselves." He motioned to the skin between his thumb and forefinger. "And that's so fucking retarded." Flakka (akin to meth and moon rocks), sass (related to MDMA), ketamine, and heroin were wrecking everything. He may have been a libertarian when it came to drugs, but people didn't use any sense at all. "Like, what are they going to do with those needles, man? Leave 'em on the ground? That just goes to show they're not responsible enough to even be doing that shit in the first place."

The topic of his own generation led him to tattoos. "Fuck tattoos!" he said, with real anger. "This one time, Renee came home, and she had this big picture down her side, and, I mean, it was really good, looked great, but I told her, 'If you like it, why not hang it on the wall?'"

When Brian first moved in and showed me around the tiny space he'd picked as his bedroom—a side-entrance mud porch just off the small kitchen—a print of a Picasso nude from the Blue Period lay on his bed. A 401(k) enrollment form lay next to the art. I had picked up the 401(k) brochure and smiled.

"They're gonna get me, man," he'd said, referring to The System. His parents had lost a significant portion of their life savings in the 2008 financial collapse. Brian was still angry about it.

"You're going mainstream," I joked. "Well, they say it's like free money," he said. "I don't like it, but . . ." He shrugged. Now the Picasso was hung up behind his bed, but he still hadn't enrolled in the 401(k). He was thinking about it.

The work at Drew was okay—mindless, with the personalities in the warehouse a little hard to take, but he liked it better than he'd thought he might. His first performance review was positive and came with a raise. He still missed Anchor, though.

They hadn't yet installed a landline phone, and since Brian refused to get a cell phone, the only way to reach him was to drive out and knock on his door. If you made the trip, it meant you really wanted to see him. Brian still didn't get the point of the twenty-first century.

He left the fireside and walked back into the little house. Before everyone arrived, he'd been tuning the heads of his drum set, and he wanted to finish the job. He asked me if I knew anything about Dave Brubeck, whose jazz he'd recently discovered. I was a fan, I told him. To Brian, something about "Take Five" sounded honest and cool. With jazz on his mind, he slipped an old Lionel Hampton record out of its sleeve and placed it gently on a little turntable he'd set up on the kitchen counter, then picked up a small tool to tighten the skins of his drums. Swingy vibes, interrupted every few seconds by Brian's tap on a drumhead, wafted out into the hot night, blending with the crackling fire and crickets at the corner of a country crossroads surrounded by fields of tall cornstalks.

The stage and band shell rose up out of the field by the creek. Portable toilets stood ready for duty. Generators, lights, and speakers loomed from eight-story scaffolds. The sun was out, and the grounds, swampy just three days before, had dried enough. The creek had returned to a normal level. The crew was exhausted. One member had reported for work a few days before at 8:30 a.m., carrying morning doughnuts to share, only to discover that it was 8:30 at night. They'd worked through wind and rain this year, but now they sat under the shade of a blue tarpaulin, sipping from beer bottles and surveying the work they counted as good.

Piccolo, though, stood by the stage like a nervous cat. "People in this town don't realize how dire the budget situation is," he said. "We couldn't have survived another rain event." But he didn't seem soothed by the sunshine. His new problem was sound. Mo Pitney would be fine, but Thompson Square had been very loud during the sound check. The orchestra was irritated. Nobody would be able to hear a note they played under Thompson Square's volume. With Blues Traveler already having refused to play with the orchestra, Piccolo faced the prospect of both the audience and the orchestra calling for his head. "I guess tonight will decide if I have good judgment," he said.

The sun was still high when people began finding their tables and staking out their real estate on the hillside. Sundresses, madras shirts, and khaki pants were favored at the dining tables, while jeans, shorts, and T-shirts were in vogue on the hill. Eric Brown, Rosemary Hajost, Mayor Dave Smith, and Jen Walters were all there, along with about three thousand other Lancastrians and visitors from around the county. None of Anchor's top management attended: They hadn't come to the festival in years.

Caterers set up meals on the tables. People sitting in the grass opened coolers. Everybody was happy to be there, no matter where they sat. Maples and sassafras, ripe with fat, green leaves, formed woody curtains around the perimeter of the hillside. As the sun descended, the sky glowed, illuminating a few wispy, friendly clouds with orange-red highlights.

When the percussive downbeat and rapid-fire string notes of Aaron Copland's "Hoedown" arrowed through the dusk, thousands of Midwest smiles lit thousands of faces. A few small children in short pants bobbled with unsteady toddler rhythm in front of parents with guardrail arms stretched out, just in case. Lovers looked at each other and kissed.

The orchestra played Hungarian Dance No. 5, by Brahms. Everybody nodded in recognition. Some knew it as Brahms, others as the soundtrack for a dozen different TV commercials. Rimsky-Korsakov's *Capriccio Espagnol* was less familiar to most, but it was joyous, like summer, and showcased the talents of individual musicians—Lancaster's own musicians for these two weeks—even more effectively than the more famous compositions.

The two big country acts would follow—Mo Pitney (young, charming, and unpretentious) and Thompson Square (loud, slick, and canned)—but right then, nobody cared about the night's headliners. Nobody cared about trying to book Taylor Swift or about drawing people from out of town as a way to boost economic development. They cared about being out in their town with their friends, milling about and seeing people they hadn't seen in a while, listening to music they wouldn't normally listen to, as they admired the skill of musicians who'd devoted their lives to making art. They wanted to drink a glass of wine or a beer and eat a fried chicken leg. They wanted to share all of this with one another.

Over the successive days and nights, the weather continued to cooperate—for the most part. Artwork hung in banks, stores, churches, restaurants, the library. More than fifty musical and other events—whether at a charge or free—went off as scheduled, most of them attracting audiences. None of them were held on the west side.

When the day of the big Saturday finale arrived, a crowd once again gathered at the tables and the hillside: Once again, a nice day turned into an ideal Ohio evening. There'd been backstage drama—a Blues Traveler member somehow wound up stranded in Columbus, for example—but by show time everything was ready.

Piccolo cleaned himself up, put on a new shirt, and stepped on the stage to introduce Sheldon. The orchestra played Sheldon's arrangements of Journey, Aerosmith, and Radiohead songs, followed by an intermission.

During the pause, I ran into festival cofounder Eleanor Hood. "Are you happy?" I asked.

"Relieved," she said. She cried the way people do when pressure is suddenly lifted. She and her friend Barbara Hunzicker had started the festival thirty years before, as if they'd foreseen what the town would face and wanted to manufacture a balm to soothe it. "We really needed this. This is the best night we've had in five years or so. Thank this," she said, pointing at the sky.

The festival would live on. But from the moment Blues Traveler took the stage, Piccolo's future with it began to seem ever more tenuous. The band played a lousy set—too loud, garbled, shambling—but that wasn't really the problem. Like Lancaster itself, the festival had become mired in an uncertain search for what it should become: old people's (and donor-class) music versus kids' music, big versus small, Lancaster PR versus an event for the community.

There was one other problem Piccolo knew he faced but couldn't control: As pleasant and successful (Blues Traveler not withstanding) as it was, the festival did nothing to solve any of Lancaster's problems. It didn't attract any new businesses, and it never would. Lancaster was now just one of many communities with arts and music fests; it had no more claim to being an "arts center" than any other place. Towns all over the Midwest were brewing beer, hosting new coffeehouses, and establishing vegan restaurants as ways to promote their leisure-hipness. Even as the festival unspooled under the bright skies, the economic forecast darkened.

The Lodge, where the Rotarians met, announced it would close for good. The owners had tried to sell the building and lease it back as a way to continue operating, but they couldn't find a buyer for one of the grandest buildings in a prime location on Lancaster's main street.

On July 30, two nights before the festival finale, at about 10:00 p.m., Michele Ritchlin, the director of the West After School Program, received a text on her phone from the Ohio Department of Education. She held her breath, anxious over how many of her grant applications had been successful. All were denied.

She thought of the teachers. They made either $10 or $13 per hour, with no benefits. Ritchlin had hoped to give raises to some, or a full-time position to Dawn Shonk, a relative by marriage to Aaron, who worked part-time. Then she wondered if she would have a job herself, and if the program would even survive.

"How do you replace $200,000 a year?" she asked herself. She couldn't just ask one of Lancaster's wealthy to drop a check in her lap. The pool of well-off people had become much shallower than it once was, so the same handful was tapped over and over from every nonprofit in town. Yet the need for the program was more profound than ever.

The day after Ritchlin received the bad news, I ran into Rosemary Hajost at the festival offices. I asked if she'd heard about the grants. She hadn't, and when I told her the bad news, she said, "This will be devastating." But then she locked her jaw and looked at me with undiminished gumption. "Maybe we should just go back to our roots: ladies with pencils and books and pieces of paper!"

THIRTEEN

Maximum Value

August 2015

Sam Solomon's father showed no mercy when they played nine-ball. He was a shark prowling a green velvet sea. Solomon loved the game, but no matter how much he practiced, he wasn't competitive until his dad aged into reading glasses. Even then, Solomon lost more often than he won.

The rule in their games was always "call your shots." Solomon could sink a miraculous double bank, side pocket, but if he hadn't called it before the stick hit the cue ball, his father would disallow it.

Now, as Solomon sat at the long conference table in a room adjacent to his office with Colin Walker, Erika Schoenberger, and Anthony Reisig, he impressed on them the importance of calling their shots. The next day, board directors would come into town for the meetings. This rehearsal of their presentations would be their chance to convince the board that Solomon's strategic plan for the future was the right one, and that they were the team to execute it.

Calling the shots—being as clear as they could be about what they expected to happen—was so important because Solomon wanted credit for good results. The more credit management received, the bigger Solomon's "operational bubble," the space within which he could manage the company. "If we don't tell them what actions we'll be taking," Solomon told his team, "they'll be telling us." The bigger the bubble, the better the chance of finding a forever home for EveryWare Global and Anchor Hocking.

Long-term value creation was the path he wanted to walk, but Solomon recognized his position. Other than WAMCO's seat, all the other board seats were occupied by proxy hired hands, which made for a weak board. Solomon was already a weak CEO, because the board was entirely new and hadn't hired him, and what little track record he had was inked with default and bankruptcy. A weak CEO answering to a weak board could be disastrous.

In the face of weakness, he planned to project strength through data. He had no intention of pleading, "Don't you want to be my mommy and daddy?" Instead, he'd appeal to their sense of value—as in money—and ask them to decide, sooner rather than later, how long they wanted to stay in the game.

Going into bankruptcy, the value of the debt to the twenty-six shareholders who had a stake was essentially zero. After bankruptcy, the value of the debt was roughly $50 million, and soon, Solomon believed, maybe $100 million. "So yesterday you assholes were splitting one-thirtieth of zero. Today you are splitting about fifty, okay?" Solomon said, preparing—in less diplomatic language than he planned to use—what he would tell the board. "So, because I happen to know how accounting works, I know that when you closed your books last fiscal year, you took your loss. Every penny that you recover this year is found money in your bonus program. So if you really don't want to be here, get the fuck out. Don't come play like debt in an equity chair. So it's not a 'Do you wanna?' It's 'This is the ride. This is what it can deliver. This is the timetable in investment required. Are you in or out?'"

The interests of the management team, the board, and the employees would all seem to be aligned under the rubric "maximizing value." But while maximizing value was easily defined in nine-ball, business was different. With Monomoy, maximizing value meant maximizing cash for themselves and their institutional limited partners in as short a time as possible. If their time horizon was two years, then spending money on anything that would not show a payoff for three years would do nothing to maximize the value. Plant maintenance, marketing, and research were deemed worthless. The fact that Monomoy wound up owning Anchor

Hocking for over six years aggravated the effects of all those deferred expenditures. The tanks kept aging, after all.

Maximizing value for Solomon and the three other top managers meant building the perceived worth of EveryWare Global to $300 million, then $400 million, and on to $1 billion. He insisted he could create a billion-dollar company faster than anybody imagined because EveryWare had such a huge potential. He envisioned Anchor Hocking's—and, to a lesser degree, Oneida's—return to strength, followed by a series of compatible acquisitions. The brands, the distribution channels, the sales force already existed. He could scale it up with each new acquisition—"and you can do it over and over and over again, and you'll grow in hundred-and three-hundred-million-dollar bites at the apple."

But what did maximizing value mean to the lenders? Some might want out now, some later. Some might want to settle for avoiding a loss, some might hope for a gain. To give the board a basis on which to advise its lender clients, the team was trying to forecast cash flow and EBITDA numbers in increments of one, three, and five years. That way, Nationwide or Voya, for example, could choose how long they wanted to remain owners. Solomon seemed to be hoping that the lenders, tempted by the projections, might ignore their instinct to recover their cash as fast as possible in a "liquidity event," and instead give the team a few years to build the value of the company before selling out. But at least one board member, representing about 16 percent of the shares, wanted to be able to go to his bosses and explain how they could get out of EveryWare within sixteen months.

EveryWare was already fielding interest from potential buyers. Going into bankruptcy, the then-board discussed the possibility of a sale to Libbey. But, aware of the Federal Trade Commission's past objections when Newell tried to sell to Libbey, it abandoned the idea. Now that it was out of bankruptcy, Solomon believed he could, if the lenders demanded a sale, deal the company in a matter of weeks. The team would dutifully report any such interest at the board meeting, but, Solomon said, "If I can figure out a way to do what we need to do on that floor for the guy in the furnace room in a way that maximizes the value for these guys"—the new owners—"and allows him to keep doing what he's doing? We'll likely maximize his value as an individual contributor as well. If I don't do this, and these guys decide to liquidate, then we are all screwed."

Solomon had a powerful self-interest, of course: his share of the company. He and the others weren't sticking around a crippled, old-time outfit located in a small, declining town for just a few hundred thousand dollars at the end of the road. They hoped for millions. "You can consider it as a fair reward for salvaging what's currently circa-2000 jobs," Solomon said. "What if we actually build a platform for scalable growth and turn it into many more than that? The positive impact that you have sorta multiplies out. That seems like a fair trade, versus 'We failed miserably, everybody gets to go home, we shutter the place.'"

The lenders had been burned by Monomoy. Solomon believed the board's view of the company now was top-down and clouded by murky numbers from the past. It wasn't aware of all that had transpired, including what decisions Solomon had already made to turn the company around. So the team had prepared a slide: a "2013 Adjusted EBITDA Reconciliation" to make their case that 2013's reported $51.1 million was bogus. They planned to project to the board a final 2015 adjusted EBITDA of $23.6 million—less than half the reported 2013 amount. (The shutdown-ravaged 2014 number was $11.9 million.) If they could convince the board that the $51.1 million reported for 2013 should have been much less, their $23.6 million wouldn't look like such a big drop, especially considering the millions spent on the bankruptcy.

They would tell the board that, by 2020, they expected a "return to 50"—$50.9 million in adjusted EBITDA on revenue of $439.5 million. The owners wouldn't have to invest another dime to get there, but they could get there faster by financing some "tuck-in" acquisitions.

All through July, the team had prepared 150 pages of PowerPoint slides: charts, bar graphs, diagrams, financial tables. They examined the competitive landscape. They detailed "How We Will Win" through service, pricing, manufacturing, marketing.

After the overview of the strategy, Solomon called on the members of his team to dry-run their presentations. He had faith in them, but he imagined his role as CEO to be a combination of coach and mentor. As each person spoke, he judged, focusing on how well they grasped not only their own silo of responsibility but on how they linked that silo to those of the others.

Walker was the oldest, and most experienced, executive aside from

Solomon. A Canadian who commuted from Ontario to Lancaster on Monday and returned on Friday, Walker—in charge of sales and marketing—had worked in banking, then had a long run at Cott, a Canadian maker of private-label beverages. He'd arrived at EveryWare via John Sheppard, who had worked at Cott.

Reisig, the operations chief, was the only one to live in Lancaster. He'd moved his family to town in February because he wanted to be close to the factory, and because he thought it was important to be seen as a local resident. He'd worked in manufacturing-supply-chain management for aerospace, telecommunications, and computer printer companies.

Schoenberger was the daughter of a Baptist minister. Her father, she said, sought the sacred in the "nitty-gritty of showing up and being a faithful worker and doing all the right things." Her mother was a grade school teacher. Shoenberger was born in Chicago and homeschooled until the fourth grade. The family moved to Kent, Ohio, a short drive southeast from Cleveland, where she entered public school. After law school at Ohio State, she joined a large Columbus law firm that had EveryWare as a client. She'd helped the company interview Kerri Cardenas Love for the job of general counsel. Cardenas Love then recruited Schoenberger to the company. Schoenberger had been comfortable at the firm, but the idea of working for a struggling company in transition intrigued her, because she realized she'd gain experience in a much broader array of business law. Plus, Cardenas Love had told her that EveryWare was going to move its headquarters out of Lancaster to Columbus, and that Cardenas Love was about to rise to become chief administrative officer—a de facto CEO—since Sheppard spent most of his time traveling, fluffing investors, and mounting road shows for the IPO. That would place Schoenberger in position to become general counsel. Had Schoenberger known that EveryWare was a house of cards about to collapse amid accusations and recriminations, she'd never have left the firm, but there she was. Now she found herself a one-fourth member of the 10 percent club.

Perhaps because she was the youngest, at thirty-six, and had the least corporate experience, or perhaps because Solomon spotted her raw talent, his coach-player relationship with Schoenberger was more obvious than it was with Walker or Reisig. She was his special project.

In addition to her other duties, Schoenberger handled human resources, which meant she also handled safety. When the board members had made their quick first trip to Lancaster in June and toured Plant 1, they came away shocked. Though management had tried to explain to the board members the nature of glass production, Walker recalled that "they didn't listen. So they just assumed, because they saw that it was scary—it was burning, it was fire, it was hot, there'd been a fire in the plant—here must be all hell." Plant 1's age, the jerry-rigging that had gone on over the years, and the fact that machines were packed closely together didn't help.

Safety became the board's priority. Now it was up to Schoenberger to explain to them that safety was everybody's priority, and that they'd made progress. The company did have a safety problem. Plant 1's injury rate was slightly higher than the glass industry average, and Monaca's was higher still. But the number of lost-time accidents had been cut in half since 2014, Schoenberger rehearsed, and the whole company was creating an improved safety culture.

"'Alas! We *do* need consultants!'" Solomon said in a mocking imitation of an expected board response. "What if they want safety consultants?" he challenged Schoenberger.

The care and feeding of more consultants, she suggested, would be asking a lot of the small number of team members who were focused on doing their jobs digging the company out of the bankruptcy hole. "They ain't sticking around for another consultant," Walker chimed in.

Okay, Solomon said. The bottom line to the board should be: "We were awful. Now we're average." He turned to Schoenberger. The board chairman is insecure, he said. "So let silence be your friend." Don't volunteer information. Don't try to fill in space. You'll only give them rope.

Around the table they went. CFO Bob Ginnan discussed the possibility that the board would demand a "value consultant" to determine how much the company was worth. He practiced his IT presentation. The system had been created for a billion-dollar business and hadn't been updated through multiple owners. It was ancient.

Walker explained how EveryWare was constrained by the "second-tier" Oneida and Anchor brands and the old glass plants in Lancaster and Monaca. To make a run at Libbey's food service business, they needed either brands or lower cost—and right now they had neither.

Reisig described options he would present to the board to make operations more profitable. Metaphorical money leaked from every meta-phorical crack, from inefficient machines to the amount UPS charged for shipping. A new machine was about to be installed to put lids on canning jars. At the moment, that was done by hand, so some employees might lose jobs, but perhaps they could be shifted to other work.

As the meeting went on, it became clear that even as the management team talked about adding value and maximizing value, there wouldn't be much difference in the lives of Lancaster workers or the town. Any hope they might have had that they would emerge from the scalding trauma of the past decades was as empty as the sample glass jars on the conference room table. Under the strategic plan Solomon and his crew had formulated, employment would stabilize, but there'd be no hiring surge, no expansion of overall work. And while, under their hypothetical plan, glass would probably be made in Lancaster for five, maybe ten, more years, by 2030 Plant 1 might go cold.

While the years of underinvestment had crippled Plant 1's ability to make certain items like high-quality stemware, it remained an industry leader in heavy glass—bakeware, measuring cups, storage containers. If that was where the profit could be found, then that was what Anchor would make. One or more of the H-28s that Brian Gossett used to operate would have to go to make room for press machines to make kitchenware. Employment would not necessarily fall, but it wouldn't expand, either. Once that was accomplished, Reisig said, "we should take our shopping cart around the world" and outsource production of ware once made in Lancaster to Mexico and China.

Of course, there was always the option to sell now. Organizations had called Pierce Avenue to express interest in buying all or part of EveryWare Global. The list read like a sinner's samsara.

Anchor Glass, the old Anchor Hocking container division that had been sold off to Naimoli and Simon and then tossed like a medicine ball from one investment group to another through one bankruptcy after another, wanted to explore the purchase of the Monaca plant. Anchor Glass was now owned by KPS Capital Partners, the outfit Monomoy's founders had left to start their shop. KPS bought Anchor Glass in 2014 from Ardagh Group, a global glass manufacturer. Ardagh had bought it in 2012 for $880 million from another PE shop called Wayzata Investment Partners. The deal for the 2014 sale from Ardagh to KPS was for $573.5 million—$435 million in Anchor Glass debt and $138.5 million anted up by KPS. KPS soon recouped its money. In 2015, Anchor Glass took out a $465 million loan and provided a dividend recap to KPS in the amount of $145 million. In May 2016, Anchor Glass provided yet another dividend recap to KPS and a PE partner, AlpInvest, of $148 million. The money came from another $140 million loan to Anchor Glass provided by Credit Suisse's Cayman Islands Branch. KPS called this an "upsizing" of Anchor Glass's term loan.

Libbey phoned to investigate buying Oneida. It wasn't interested in Anchor Hocking.

Arc, the international glassware company that had absorbed Durand, Anchor Hocking's old French rival, called David Weinstein, the new board chairman, to talk about a deal. Arc told Weinstein it wanted to close down Lancaster.

Two small private equity outfits, California-based Aurora Resurgence and Manhattan-based Staple Street Capital, expressed interest in making an acquisition. Before starting Staple Street, its founders had worked at the Carlyle Group and Cerberus, as had two of the three members of Staple Street's executive board. One of those executive board members, William Kennard, former U.S. ambassador to the European Union, had once been chairman of the Federal Communications Commission. His role at Staple Street was to "focus on the communications and media sectors."

Diamond Capital Partners, a mergers-and-acquisitions advisory firm, called Pierce Avenue on behalf of "qualified buyers." The buyers were looking to acquire businesses like EveryWare's.

The most serious inquiry came from U.S. Glass, a shell company formed by Wayzata Investment Partners, the group that had sold Anchor Glass to Ardagh in 2012. The strategy, a Wayzata rep said, would be to "pull apart assets" by either retaining or shutting down the glass plants in Lancaster and Monaca and selling off Oneida.

Solomon didn't like any of these potential deals—not yet. "Why would you blow it up?" he said. "That's stupid. And if you wanted to sell off all the pieces, then you should have just stayed in bankruptcy longer, reduced your expenses more, and sold off the pieces then. So, to me, if you sell it off in the next eighteen months, then we screwed up two months ago" in bankruptcy. But it wasn't up to him. It was up to the board.

Lancaster and its workforce had no idea that any of these options were being considered, or even that a board meeting was about to occur. The town knew the company had emerged from bankruptcy and that Solomon predicted better times—and that was it. Everyone assumed that the now private EveryWare had returned to a sort of status quo.

On August 6, the board met alone with Solomon for twenty minutes in the Anchor Hocking showroom on Pierce Avenue. Surrounded by cake plates and covers, bar glasses, mixing bowls, and canisters, Solomon began giving an overview of what the members would hear in the management presentations.

He didn't get far before the board hectored about safety. At one point, Solomon said, "We're not interested in being lectured." The general meeting didn't go much better, from Solomon's point of view. "It was a shitty meeting," he said. "You've got a bunch of turnaround guys trying to run their turnaround playbooks on a company that has already turned—a bunch of people not prepared to listen."

To his frustration, much of the effort expended throughout July to prepare the pages of charts, graphs, justifications, and plans proved fruitless. Safety consultants would be hired at a cost of several hundred thousand dollars. "That would have been enough to restore the benefits and salaries we denied employees. But we're gonna make 'em safe!" Solomon said with wounded sarcasm. The process would be disruptive. Solomon wouldn't travel to smooth relations with out-of-town suppliers and customers still angry over the service lapses and missed payments of the past year. There'd be extra work for everybody. And the union members would see the consultants and wonder how much money the company was paying for them. In a meeting between management and the unions in July, union leaders had been upset over the company's decision to fix potholes in the parking lot, arguing that whatever cash had gone into blacktop ought to have gone to them instead.

You know the way the world works?" Brian asked. It's like that old Warner Bros. cartoon with Ralph the wolf and Sam the sheepdog. All day long, Ralph tried to eat the sheep, and all day long, Sam beat the crap out of Ralph. The sheep were clueless. They just stood around, mindlessly eating grass. And then the work whistle blew, and Sam and Ralph punched out and walked off for a beer: best pals, two sides of the same system.

He put on a new Flaming Lips album—in vinyl form, of course—and continued folding his laundry. The comment Aaron had made a while back about smartphones and not having anything to hide? Well, that had stuck in his head. How could Aaron be so naive? Brian took no assurance from anything any government official, any politician, any businessman said. Promises of privacy protection were empty. "Dude, that's like the government pointing a gun at your head and saying, 'That's cool, because we're not gonna pull the trigger. Don't worry, dude. Yeah, we've got a gun pointed at you, but it's okay, we won't shoot.'"

The summer was almost over, and Brian used the calendar as another excuse for self-recrimination. He'd wasted most of it. He'd moved some stuff around inside the studio on Main Street but hadn't made any art at all. He and I ought to drive up to Columbus, he suggested. A gallery crawl was coming up. He'd like to see what people were making up there. Maybe he'd take in a little inspiration.

Whenever he was over on the west side and drove by Plant 1's machine shop, he missed working there all over again. Then he'd hear about some guy smashing a digit or getting burned and he'd be glad he wasn't there. Work at Drew wasn't going well. He liked the company fine, and they liked him fine, and he'd received another small raise, but his pay was barely keeping him afloat. The rent in Colfax hacked him off, too. Aaron was cool, but Brian was thinking of moving back in with his mom and dad. He'd committed to stay a year, and he wouldn't leave Aaron in a lurch, but he'd just about made up his mind to go when his year was up. As misanthropic as Brian could be, the isolation was even starting to get to him. When he wasn't driving down to Athens to party with Mike, he spent most days working, coming home, and jamming on his drums, lost in his own beat.

The mother stood up in the courtroom gallery to address Judge Trimmer. Her hoodie slumped off one shoulder. Her jeans were loose, her T-shirt untucked. None of that mattered. She was too drained from weeping and worry. "I love my son dearly, but I don't think he's ready to be out," she told Trimmer. Her son sat at the defense table next to his court-appointed lawyer. He looked humbled and hurt.

He'd been sent to prison for making meth, gotten out, tried a treatment program at the Recovery Center, worked some construction jobs, used again, and run from the cops—who'd found weed, but could have found cocaine or heroin if they'd stopped him at a different time. He'd been using those, too. He glanced at his mother, the woman who had just said she'd rather have him go to jail than come home, and then up at Trimmer. "I don't want to die from using," he said.

Trimmer let a few moments of silence pass. "Getting addicted is the most selfish thing a person can do with his life," he scolded. "Look at your momma! You put her through hell."

Trimmer returned to the mother. Was there anything she would like to add? "I should want him home," she said, starting to cry. "But I just can't. This town is horrible." She sat down and rocked herself back and forth on the gallery bench.

With his mother closing the door on him, the young man, twenty-one years old, told Trimmer that perhaps he could move to the homeless shelter at Community Action, the place Kellie Ailes ran. He didn't want to go back to jail. For the moment, though, that was exactly where he was going: back to county, across Main Street from the courthouse.

He passed Jason Roach walking in the other direction. Dressed in jail scrubs, his hands and feet shackled, Jason shuffled across Main Street, then down the courthouse's second-floor hallway, sounding like Jacob Marley on Christmas Eve.

He was escorted by Deputy Mike Myers. I said hello to Myers as he and Jason walked down the hall and asked how he was doing. "Living the dream," Myers said. "Another day in paradise." He'd been cutting hay on a farm all weekend and now suffered from a stuffy head. Myers knew Jason from Jason's past stints in county. Myers was friendly with many people he escorted to court. He'd lost track of the number of old school pals in chains he'd perp-walked.

Trimmer had seen Jason before, and he wasn't pleased to see him again now. "Every time I get out," he told Trimmer, "I get out to nothin'. I got to get into some kind of program."

Jason's plea was moot. The arraignment had barely begun when the DA and the defense attorney asked to meet with Trimmer in his chambers. There was an issue to discuss. As it would turn out, the defense had raised a question about the legality of the MCU's placement of the GPS device on Jason's SUV, and of the traffic stop on Memorial Drive.

While the two sides haggled in Trimmer's chambers, Jason fretted out loud to Deputy Myers. There was a plea deal on the table, and if he didn't take it, prosecutors were threatening to go harder on Jessica. "I'm not gonna let her go to prison," Jason said. "Nothing comes easy, man," Myers said. "Nothing in this life comes easy."

The meeting in the chambers was inconclusive. There were complications. More negotiation would be required. Jason shuffled back across Main Street, his chains clanking in the road.

Now that he was in jail, uncertain of his ultimate penalty but certain he was going to prison, Jason could only sit and wonder what his post-prison future would look like—where he would go, how he would live. A couple of guys in county asked him to cut their hair. "I have a real passion for hairstyling," he said. Maybe once he got out, he could open his own shop. Minutes later, he said, "When I get out of prison, I will do what I have to do to survive." If he had to go back to dealing, and go hard, he would. "I felt like I was on top of the world" when he was bringing all that dope down from Columbus, he said. "I could buy for my wife, my kids—anything I wanted." Then he talked about earning a high school equivalency diploma in prison, returning to Lancaster, raising his family in the shadow of Mount Pleasant. He wasn't going to work at any McDonald's or Wendy's. That was for damn sure.

With the festival over and the summer coming to a close, the talk out at the country club bar turned to winter plans, the presidential election, and the stock market. As on most Fridays, a core group of friends gathered for drinks and dinner, including Leonard Gorsuch, the developer; a prominent attorney and his wife; a couple of small-business owners; and a few women whose husbands were once part of the group but had passed away. Other couples and individuals straggled in, too. Tina, the woman who worked three jobs—the hospital and two bartending gigs—flitted in and out. She was on duty. Jeannette, a woman who believed the tonic part of a gin and tonic was more like a suggestion than a requirement, tended the bar.

The place still felt empty, but the club had managed to survive by hosting public events, like a couple of golf tournaments and, now that The Lodge downtown had closed up, Rotary meetings. A book on the club's one-hundred-year history sat at the edge of the bar, and, leafing through it, you could see crowds of fancy-dressed attendees at the Governor's Ball, an annual formal no longer held; smiling couples with outrageously graphic golf pants and skirts, posing before tee-off at Scotch Foursome events; and swim meets packed with parents and kid swimmers.

Older people talked about their children and their grandchildren, bragged over their children's business successes. Somewhat younger people bragged over their children just starting their senior year of high school, or entering college. None of them seemed to have any expectation that these children would ever be coming back to Lancaster to live.

The older crowd looked past Lancaster, mostly. A few were still active civically—a board member of the West After School Program was there, as were Cameo League members—and more donated money to local causes. They still loved the town. But Lancaster had become a place they resided in, often part-time, but no longer fully inhabited, any more than they inhabited Marco Island, Florida, in the winter. They vacationed in Europe. They played golf in Scottsdale. They had plugged themselves into the global economy.

Jeannette handed a drink to the attorney. He turned back to Gorsuch and said, "I'm mostly in cash right now," referring to his investment allocations. They debated whether or not the market was overvalued, and what effect the election would have on it.

Hillary Clinton, of course, would be a disaster. Their governor, John Kasich, had formally announced his run at the presidency the month before and was still the preferred candidate. Kasich was conservative enough, and he was a former Lehman Brothers executive. The fact that Lehman's collapse had helped precipitate the Great Recession didn't besmirch Kasich in their eyes. He'd be good for them.

A younger group, less wealthy than Gorsuch's crowd, talked up Trump. He'd announced his presidential bid in June by declaring, "The American Dream is dead," and blaming politicians of every stripe for killing it. They

didn't mention any particular policy they liked, aside from Trump's promise to destroy Obamacare and his hatred of Mexican immigrants—"They're
sending people that have lots of problems, and they're bringing those problems with us. They're bringing drugs. They're bringing crime. They're
rapists"—which they cited approvingly.

They gave the impression of being afraid more than angry. In Lancaster,
or at least among these few people on one night at the country club, Trump
was the candidate for people who feared—even hated—an aggrieved working class and the poor. They were afraid they'd never live the life Gorsuch
lived. Sending their kids to college, and paying for it, was going to be a
sacrifice. It wasn't supposed to be that way. And now they were surrounded
by actual poor people, fellow townsmen-turned-strangers, who were dragging their town down around them.

School had just started, and about half the West School kids in the
after-school program who'd gone to the center on Garfield Avenue
every afternoon had been shifted out of West School and into one of the
brand-new ones. They were both excited and uneasy. Some of them wound
up at Tarhe Trails Elementary, a new school named for Chief Tarhe of
the Wyandots. It was located in a tract-house subdivision on Lancaster's
northwest border. There, they mixed with children from higher-income
families—Columbus commuters, many of them. That was a deliberate
strategy on the part of administrators to create a more diverse income stew.

A few families from both ends of the spectrum objected. Wealthier parents fretted about bad influences emanating from the west-side kids.
West-side parents feared their kids would face snobbery. They also didn't
like the distance from the neighborhood. The west side was troubled, but
it was their home.

The budget crisis that resulted from the denial of its grant applications
divided the board of the West After School Program for the first time since
its founding. Some members wanted to fire the grant writer Ritchlin had
hired; others didn't. Ritchlin was trying to figure out where the grant applications had gone wrong. Was the district not poor enough? Not racially
diverse enough? Not urban enough? Urban school programs received more
grants. Ritchlin believed politics weighted the decision-making because

urban areas had more representation in the state legislature, and so more clout with state education officials. She felt Lancaster and other small towns were being forgotten—again.

She was frustrated, and uncertain just how to proceed. There'd be cutbacks, for sure. The board had squirreled away some emergency funds in past years. They could rent out part of the center's building. A few thousand here and a few thousand there would get them through 2015. What would happen after that was anybody's guess.

Solomon had had three weeks to nurse the wounds inflicted at the board meeting. He didn't like it any better, but he'd moved on to management mode. At a meeting with union leaders to explain the coming changes, he'd listened to their gripes. Up to this point, the gripes had been mundane: What about the Popsicles they were supposed to receive on hot summer days? What about the boot allotment new hires were supposed to be paid so they could buy high-quality, steel-toe work boots? What about the dress code at the DC? But then Solomon announced that a paste-mold machine—an H-28—was going to go. They zeroed in on the news like bird dogs. Would it mean job losses?

Solomon explained that the company didn't plan to eliminate all drinkware, just some of it. If they stopped making it entirely, "Walmart goes away, Target goes away." But the strategy now was going to focus on heavy glass, like baking dishes. That could mean eliminating a burnoff, the machine that put the rims on glasses. "That's my local!" one man said.

Jobs were secure, Solomon reassured him, but they might change. H-28 operators might have to become press operators. In fact, Anchor Hocking was looking to hire replacements for workers who'd left or been fired.

Workforce stability had been a major headache for Reisig. The turnover, especially at the cold end, the sluer, was high. People failed drug tests. Managers had recently caught a guy injecting heroin in a bathroom. But most people quit because the pay was low, the work was hard, and the benefits were lousy.

"You can get a 401(k) at McDonald's," one worker said. "Getting money out of them young people—they want the dollars, because there is no company contribution." Skilled workers, like millwrights, didn't want to work there.

A woman spoke up to say that she'd heard bank employees were getting 401(k)s—it was unclear what bank she referred to—so shouldn't *they* be getting their 401(k)s back? Weren't they bank employees now? Didn't the banks own them?

The pathos of the question escaped even the woman who'd asked it. Anchor Hocking workers once enjoyed company-paid defined pension plans with no required employee contribution. Thousands of Lancastrians lived secure retirement lives, with opportunities to contribute to the town and to their own families, thanks to those pensions. Then the pensions turned into 401(k)s. Then the company reduced its contribution. Then it stopped making any contribution at all. Now she asked for just that little bit back, and if she were to get it, she'd deem that progress.

She wasn't going to get it. There wasn't any money for it. Solomon and Schoenberger—who, as the executive in charge of HR, dealt with benefits—knew this was not the time for a fight, or even for an attempt to explain the difference between a plant worker and a bank employee, or that the company wasn't really owned by banks but by other finance players, or how something she might have read about a big American bank restoring 401(k)s didn't apply anyway. Instead, they said they understood. Their hope was to make them all whole from the concessions the workers had given up to save their jobs in 2014.

Both of them were sincere, but both of them, and especially Solomon, were motivated as much by the need to keep labor peace as by any sense of justice. Solomon had long ago honed his ability to divide his mind between the business-game strategist and the kid who had spent time in tobacco fields.

Schoenberger was still learning. She hadn't yet reconciled her upbringing as the daughter of a minister and a socially conscious schoolteacher with the corporate attorney she'd become. She wanted to believe that, even in the modern business landscape, and in light of everything she'd experienced since arriving in Lancaster, it was possible to blend them, to do good by doing well.

"I just feel compelled to stay and fight, somehow," she told me. When EveryWare went south, she could have returned to her glass-tower law firm in downtown Columbus, had clients come and go, and made a very nice living. "This somehow seems more meaningful." The money that awaited her if the company could be sold for $300 million or more was also a powerful lure—she didn't claim to be a saint. But she knew there was a "giant system" around her, The System Brian hated. She understood she was "a cog in the whole thing." But she hoped she could tilt the scales of that system, just a little, toward the good. "I do want to do better, for them," she said of the employees, "and if there's things we can do better, move faster than we are . . . Unfortunately, none of it's going to, you know, it's hard to overcome twenty years."

As I drove west on Main Street to Lloyd's pretrial hearing, I passed Mark walking in the same direction. He was hunched with his little fedora on his head, puffing a cigarette like it was the last cigarette in the world. I pulled over to say hello.

Mark leaned into the passenger window, jumpy with agitation. His probation officer had told Mark he'd seen him out one night past his curfew, and that he had not been attending NA or AA meetings, as ordered by the court for his ILC. "He says I'm going to jail!"

"I haven't been out past ten. All I do is work. I've never failed a drug test. I did sixteen hours of community service recently. That oughta make this fucker happy!"

"You're shaking," I said.

"I've been chain-smoking all day!"

His probation officer told a different story. He reported that Mark had tested positive for morphine on August 13. Mark was also not attending regular meetings, the parole officer claimed. Mark insisted he was, but that AA wasn't doing him any good anyway, since half the people there were using.

When I pulled up to the courthouse, I spotted Ashley's Ford, with its Hello Kitty license-plate frames, parked across the street. There was a new addition to the back window: a big sticker with script lettering that read, BITCHMOBILE. She was waiting for her children, she said—it was time for her visitation. She'd moved out of the trailer and into a rental house on the east side, near East School. She received a rent subsidy to help her afford it. The house and neighborhood would provide a better environment for her children, and she hoped she might regain custody soon.

Moments later, I saw Lloyd in Berens's courtroom. His cheeks were hollow, his eyes sunken into his skull. The tattoos on his neck and his Vandyke beard looked like they belonged to some other, younger guy from some other, different time. We said hello, then Lloyd listened to the counts. There were six in all. The prosecution offered to remove permitting and possession charges if Lloyd would plead guilty to two trafficking counts and a tampering-with-evidence charge—the running toilet with the diamond rings in his bathroom. Lloyd's lawyer, the same man who'd loaned him money and been paid back in full, said Lloyd would consider it.

The next day, Mark was booked into the Fairfield County Jail. He'd bunk with Jason Roach.

FOURTEEN

Falling Out

October 2015

She was tall, and about fifteen years old, with a strong, fine-featured face and long brown hair. If she'd grown up in Encino, California, she might have been standing on a San Fernando Valley sound stage, working on a Disney Channel set. She'd have hundreds of thousands of Twitter followers. But she grew up in Fairfield County, Ohio, so she stood ankle-deep in sawdust inside the round cattle barn, a landmark built in 1906. She wore white jeans, a white shirt, and rubber farm boots. An enormous dairy cow—black and white, almost five feet tall from head to hoof—stood next to her, in a line with five other teenagers and five other cows, ready for the Senior Division dairy judging. She'd raised hers from a newborn calf—fed it, brushed it, nursed it. And now, suddenly, just as the judging began, the cow acted up. It tossed its head, bumped her, pulled against the chain she held. This was a very annoyed cow, and the 110-pound girl could do little to get the 1,500 pounds of it under control. She was tough, so she tried—but failed—to hide her mortification. Her father half-jogged into the arena and helped her muscle the cow away, out of the line. He put his arm around her shoulders, and as the two of them walked the disobedient animal back to its stall, her tears flowed.

The county fair was the one constant. For 165 years, it was the one event everybody—rich or poor, liberal or conservative—attended. The Civil War

World War I, the Great Depression, and World War II couldn't stop it. The fair was as unchanging as the sandstone monolith of Mount Pleasant, overlooking the grounds. People who'd left town for college, found jobs and established their lives in cities, from New York to San Francisco, returned for the fair. Passing through the gates was like stepping into a time machine that hurtled them back to their childhoods, when the most important thing in the world was tossing a wooden ring around the top of a bamboo cane or winning a blue ribbon for raising the best Holstein in the county. The fair was still a place where controversy could erupt over whether or not the Amanda-Clearcreek school's chicken noodle soup had been made with store-bought noodles. How had it lasted so long in an America bedazzled by digital pop culture, where five minutes ago might as well be five years ago, where everything is show biz and everybody a brand?

Dave Benson believed the fair's unchanging focus on animals, dirt, and what people could do with the stuff that grew out of the dirt had saved it. To him, the fair was a living ode. "We have a lot of pride in Fairfield County," he said. "That person who baked that pie wants to let people know she is the best cherry pie maker in Fairfield County. That quilter wants others to know how talented she is, how imaginative she is. The man with his collection of antiques wants people to know how interested he is in preserving items that are no longer here. People bring in something from a 1950s fair—a little banner, or Anchor Hocking glass—they want to show people they have pride in those items. People displaying their apples want others to know how bright and shiny they are. The hog farmer showing hogs has pride in his hogs."

The fair, he said, was about "cooperation, smiling, and community. And reminiscing." Benson was the fair manager. He'd run it for the past twenty-four years. He calculated the budget in his small office, with Peggy Cummins looking over his shoulder from the *Green Grass of Wyoming* poster on the wall. He made schedules. He helped clean the restrooms. His walkie-talkie chirped constantly between 5:00 a.m. and midnight. Just the other day, some people from Medina, Ohio, had come to the fair, found Benson, and commended him on how clean and tidy the grounds looked. He lived for such moments.

Benson had spent thirty-three years working for the Ohio Department of Transportation, but he was raised on a farm just outside of town: three hundred acres of dairy cows, hogs, corn, wheat, and a few chickens. There weren't many farms that small anymore. The land that hadn't been sub-divided into tract houses had been consolidated into spreads of over a thousand acres. You couldn't make a living working three hundred acres, raising a little of this and a little of that. In a globalized world where soybean prices in Brazil affected import markets in China, you needed computerized combines, crop specialization, and the economy of scale to make it in agriculture. You had to be big.

Benson's father and mother both exhibited at the county fair in the 1920s. He exhibited in the 1950s. His children exhibited. And, while he didn't make a career of farming, he held a tight grip on his nostalgia for what the fair had given him and his family. That's why, though he was officially only a part-time employee of the fair board—he always laughed when he said "part-time"—he worked sixteen-hour days. He was seventy-six years old. "I do it to give back to the community," he said, "for what it gave me as a child. And because I love to do it."

Whenever he got the chance, Benson told local politicians that the county fair was the cherry on top of Lancaster's fudge sundae. He didn't mean to imply that the fair was an economic boon. Money was never the point: Though it pumped a little into the town, the fair, with a budget of about $900,000, operated as a break-even event. He meant that the fair gave individuals a way to define themselves as members of the community at a time when there were few other ways to do so.

Anchor Hocking and Lancaster's other industries were once as much a part of the fair as they were a part of every other aspect of life in town. Anchor Hocking provided thousands of glass items at big discounts to the *Eagle-Gazette* so the paper could give them away to fairgoers who signed up for subscriptions at the paper's fair booth. During a 1962 strike, the paper announced that the annual tradition would be suspended "to avoid any potential controversy or illusion of 'taking sides.'" New subscribers would receive a voucher, their glass delivered after the strike was settled. Anchor had its own big booth every year.

Benson missed Anchor's presence, and Lancaster Glass's presence, and all the others, but he'd adjusted. "We lost a lot of industry in this town," he said. "But we didn't lose the fair."

At 8:15 on the morning of Wednesday, October 14, as Benson was help-ing set up a big tent where those attending the animal auctions could relax, an Anchor Hocking employee arrived at work and opened an e-mail. As she read the few terse sentences, her face sank and she began to cry.

The e-mail had been sent at 6:00 a.m. under Erika Schoenberger's name: "I am writing you today to inform you that Sam Solomon and the Board of Directors have decided to go in different directions." Schoenberger offered no explanation, no reasons, no context. Sean Gumbs, a consultant from FTI—the firm board member Brian Kushner worked for—had already taken over as an interim CEO.

Merger, IPO, shutdowns, a WARN notice, bankruptcy, a revolving C-suite door: The employee had had enough. She sniffled and said, "I don't know how I can get through this." The company was in the middle of the pre-Christmas-season rush, a time when her work was at its most hectic. Some people were quitting. She managed a quick little laugh, saying she'd checked her 401(k) balance. She wasn't old enough to leave, but she was too old to try another career. She broke down. "I just wanted to believe in something again," she sputtered.

Schoenberger wasn't in much better shape. She sat in her office, her eyes red and swollen. Like the girl in the show ring, she tried to muster her professional composure. The past few days had been among the most difficult of her tumultuous tenure at EveryWare Global. Over the weekend, the board had looped her into its discussions about Solomon—who'd become her friend and mentor. As the company's general counsel, she could say nothing to anyone. On Monday, the board chairman had phoned to inform her of its decision to fire Solomon. When her phone rang, she was at a veterinarian's office having the family dog put down.

Now she had to submerge the person she was with the reality of her new corporate life. She defaulted to automatic, falling back on off-the-shelf press release bromides about no one person being indispensable, about moving the company forward—all of it belied by the distress on her face.

Her turmoil wasn't just about Solomon's fate. He'd drilled into his whole team that consultants could offer nothing but bills and expense account charges, and now a consultant—a turnaround consultant—had arrived as a temporary CEO. She'd taken Gumbs out to dinner at the Cherry Street Pub on Tuesday night, when he arrived in town. He seemed nice enough, and he didn't say anything alarming. But she believed his presence had to be bad news.

"I just see value here," she said, over and over. By "value" she meant what Solomon had meant, combined with her own lingering social concern.

Solomon saw value through a business lens, first and foremost. "So maybe we won't maintain it quite as well," he'd once said of a hypothetical private equity owner of an old industrial business like Anchor Hocking. "Maybe that's capital we don't have to spend. And maybe I'll turn that cash into a multiple. And so, again, the interesting thing for me is that, in order for that value to be extracted, someone had to create it. Someone had to create it! And clearly, this company spent decade after decade building that value position, and it takes a fraction of that time to completely erode it." To him, long-term value building was a better business play. Social good naturally followed.

To Schoenberger, value in the business sense and value in the social sense walked side by side. She hadn't quite figured out exactly how to integrate the two, only that they should be integrated.

Now she was forced to confront the truth that the fate of EveryWare Global, of the Anchor Hocking and Oneida employees, and of the towns where they lived barely registered on the new owner group's radar. Such topics were abstractions to it, and they always would be to faraway people convinced that they were the smartest people in the room, whose loftiest goal was making the most money in the shortest time.

The official word was that Solomon had resigned, but that, of course, was a convenient fiction. Weinstein had walked into Solomon's office on Tuesday morning and informed him of the board's decision.

Solomon knew it was coming. He'd received an e-mail on Monday that alerted him to a special board meeting to be held in Lancaster the next day. That was news to him. A regular meeting had been slated for the following week. No pressing matters had arisen to prompt an earlier one. His own job had to be the reason for it.

He was angry. He'd always been privately contemptuous of the board.

In his judgment, by the time you were in late middle age, if you were sitting on the board of a company like EveryWare, you were a second-stringer. Every time the board refused to acknowledge the company's real situation, and its possible future under his strategic plan, they confirmed that judgment. For its part, the board obviously didn't believe that Solomon was the guy who could increase the value of the company for the equity owners they represented. They'd been talking past each other for three months. Irritation from the August meeting had spilled over into a subsequent September meeting in the New York offices of the company's law firm, international giant Milbank, Tweed, Hadley & McCloy.

"Everybody is pissed off," Solomon had told me after that September meeting. "They are pissed we are stupid, and we are pissed they are stupid." At that meeting, the board talked of cuts and more SKU reductions. "We disabused them of that," Solomon said. "Cuts aren't the answer. We have to grow our way out." He and the board had spent almost no time talking about EveryWare Global's actual performance, which Solomon believed was good, considering its starting point. The company had just beaten the budget for the third quarter.

But he was still being haunted by Monomoy and that $51.1 million EBITDA figure reported for the 2013 year. From Solomon's point of view, the board was fixated on it, partly because the equity owners had lent money based on it. The board members, hired by the equity owners, seemed to believe it was their mission to get EveryWare performing to at least that level—maybe better, and sooner rather than later—so they could sell, recoup the money, maybe even make a little profit for their owner-bosses.

Solomon thought equity wasn't paying attention. EveryWare Global was a small line item to them. If they could visualize his billion-dollar dream, they'd buy into it, but they didn't care enough to look. He also harbored another galling thought. Some people within the company suggested that the board didn't want "to listen to what a black man had to say."

That was a rare comment from Solomon. He was plenty race-conscious: You don't grow up the son of a former North Carolina field hand, and you don't become a black CEO in corporate America, without having spent a lot of time navigating racial minefields. But though he sometimes cracked wise, he usually kept thoughts about the possible racial motivations of others to himself.

As it happened, Sean Gumbs, the FTI consultant the board had just hired, was black, and Solomon was surprised to learn that. And when he heard about it, he was dismissive. "He is being told what to do," Solomon said. "There'll be a bazillion calls a day" between the CEO's office and the board chairman. "He's not creating anything; he'll be taking directions."

Much like Solomon, Gumbs was a quintessential high achiever. But he'd followed a straighter path by checking every box required to reach the top of the ivy-covered Great American Meritocracy: the son of immigrants from the Caribbean, a graduate of the ultracompetitive Stuyvesant High School, in New York City, of the University of Pennsylvania, of Harvard, where he earned an M.B.A. He and Solomon had been members of the same African American fraternity, Alpha Phi Alpha, though they'd never met. He'd married a professional woman, and lived in a pricey Manhattan apartment, his kids attending the most rigorous New York schools.

Among many other assignments for FTI, Gumbs still sat on the board of MF Global, former New Jersey senator Jon Corzine's hedge fund, which collapsed in 2011. There, he was the primary finance adviser to former FBI director Louis Freeh—who oversaw the MF aftermath and supervised attempts to recover investors' money. He'd never been the CEO of anything, interim or otherwise. But after FTI was approached by the EveryWare board to help it find a temporary CEO, he volunteered.

Simultaneously with Schoenberger's e-mail, another one had been sent to employees under Gumbs's name. "Over the coming weeks, I will travel to several of our operational locations and meeting [sic] with many of you to hear your ideas on where we need to invest in people, infrastructure and systems to grow and achieve EveryWare Global's full potential. The purpose of my 'listening tour' isn't to create a laundry list of projects that never get done—it is to meet with you, the dedicated employees of this company and to identify a short list of investments that we can execute to have a rapid and positive impact on our business."

Solomon mocked the listening-tour idea. "We don't need a listening tour," he said, as if he still ran the company. "We need to get shit done." Nobody could figure out just what Gumbs was supposed to do. For years, the employees watched Newell, Cerberus, and Monomoy walk through the factories and offices, to "listen." They wondered what the hell those people were listening for.

As for Lancaster, nobody knew that Solomon had been fired. There was no press release, no announcement, no word at all. The *Eagle-Gazette* never reported it. Months later, some in Lancaster still weren't aware of it. Most Plant 1 workers didn't know, either—they didn't sit at desks with computers and e-mail access. Chris Cruit, Joe Boyer, and Swink had no idea for days—for weeks, in some cases—that the company they worked for had a new CEO. Even Chris Nagle, the union leader, didn't learn the news for two days.

Cruit thought Solomon's firing was just one more thing to worry about. He was already anxious about his own job. Anchor had begun removing H-28s, and Cruit was a burn-off man. No H-28, no burn-off. His wrestling school was attracting enough kids—and a few adults—for him to almost break even, but there was no way he could afford to leave the $16-an-hour wage he was making at Anchor.

Nobody in Plant 1 was going to shed any tears over Solomon. Eighteen months after the 2014 shutdown, the fact that Lancaster gave concessions when Monaca didn't still rankled. Solomon had been CEO at the time. So the way Plant 1 saw it, Solomon had screwed them. Monomoy was too vague a target to focus their ire on. Boyer didn't care one way or the other that Sam Solomon had been fired. "I don't see that he did anything for us," he said. As for Gumbs, Boyer suspected the listening tour and the promise of coming fixes might be "blowing smoke up our rear ends."

The average Anchor plant worker had long ago learned to ignore management turmoil. If the factory was open when they came to work, they still had jobs. If it wasn't, they didn't. "He's another cheerleader," Nagle said of Gumbs. "He's just one that's, like, he found his pom-poms, as if he's gonna do something. Until he does something, he's nothin' to us."

Five days after Solomon's departure, somebody in Plant 1 fired up one of the air compressors that had been out of commission for a very long time. About twelve hundred gallons of water flooded into the air system, shutting the whole place down until about one o'clock in the morning: the same ol' same ol'.

Mark Kraft stared at his smartphone screen, so focused on Mobile-Patrol he was oblivious to the dozens of fairgoers walking all around him. He'd been working a booth for the family business and was now taking a smoke break. As he strolled around the midway, bent over his screen, he looked pale and, if it were even possible, skinnier than usual.

He'd been released from the county jail on Labor Day, September 7, after a week's stay. He'd spent most of that time with Jason.

Jail had proven to be interesting and educational. He was surprised by the amount of drugs he could find in county—dope and pills, mainly. And meds. Lots of meds. "They dole that shit out to everybody that's been in there for more than thirty days. All you've got to do is say you're depressed and you can't sleep, and they fucking pump you full of sugar, bro." He learned how to make a rope out of toilet paper, how to play spades, how to play the legal system.

"I'm telling you, bro, I went in there with a Ph.D. in being a junkie and came out half a jailhouse lawyer after listening to these guys talk for a week." He did not, however, learn much about himself, and he couldn't figure out what lesson he was supposed to have gleaned from the experience. The whole thing seemed like a waste of his time and the taxpayers' resources.

He suspected that the real purpose of his brief incarceration had been to rat out Jason, Lloyd, and anybody else in town he could think of to snitch on. "The MCU guys were all like, 'Where are you getting it?' and 'We'll give you a deal.' That's all they wanted from me, man."

Mark didn't trust them or anybody else. Like Brian, he didn't trust anything or anyone. The MCU's interrogations made Mark a suspect in the eyes of the other inmates. People accused of felonies couldn't find jobs after being released from jail or prison. That was an immutable law of the universe. Yet Mark had a job. How'd he keep his job? How'd he get an ILC if he wasn't squealing for the cops? Some of the other inmates harassed him. They threatened to take his "hygiene"—the soap, toothpaste, and snacks inmates could buy with money on their "books," an account established by an inmate or his family.

Inmate accounts and phone calls were quite a profitable racket. A $10 deposit yielded $7 for the inmate and $3 for the company providing the deposit service. Phone calls, operated by another company, were outrageously expensive, about a dollar a minute. Most inmates and their families were poor. But, as the dollar stores and out-of-own apartment owners, the car-title lenders and Monomoy Capital Partners all knew, poverty was big business.

Jason had looked out for him, though, so Mark felt an obligation to re-
ciprocate. When Jason asked him to seek out Jessica, who'd been released
with an ankle monitor, pending adjudication of her conveyance charge,
Mark agreed. Jason was freaked out by the thought that Jessica would be
out and cheating on him, maybe to get drugs. Jason wanted her to know
his feelings hadn't changed: He wrote letters that Mark promised to
deliver. In return for the favor, Jason offered Mark the number of his
Columbus hookup.

On Sunday, September 20, Jessica cut off her ankle bracelet and went
on the lam. A few days later, Jason said, "She'll be on drugs and cheating on
me." He'd cried the whole night before. He was so distraught, inmates had
gathered around to pray with him.

All of Jessica's charges had been dismissed except for the conveyance
charge. Chances were good that she wouldn't spend any time in jail for that.
She'd likely receive probation and treatment. Jason would take the fall for
the trafficking. She ran, she told me, because she didn't have a place to stay
when she was released. Her probation officer said she'd have to find a place.
She tried her mother, but their relationship was fractured, and her probation officer forbade her from staying there anyway. She tried the homeless
shelter at Community Action, but, she said, she was turned away. Fearing
she'd go back to jail, she disappeared.

Jessica took their things and headed for Zanesville. She had a friend there
who was on Suboxone. I sent a text message to Jessica. She returned the
message, typing, "Idk a Jess you have the wrong#." But it was her all right.

Jessica was still AWOL, and Jason still had had no word from her by
the time he was sentenced by Trimmer on October 5. The defense and the
prosecution had worked out a deal to send Jason to state prison for just
over two years, including the time he'd already spent in county jail since
his July arrest.

Dennis Lowe, the new MCU chief who'd replaced Eric Brown, was
furious with the district attorney's office over the agreement. Jason was
the biggest fish they'd caught all year. And all of Jason's promises to help
the cops shut down Lancaster's drug trade had fizzled. Two years seemed
like nothing in light of the amounts of dope Jason had been bringing into
town. In the coming months, stories citing anonymous law enforcement
sources would appear in the newspaper. These stories accused the DA of,

among other things, cutting easy deals for criminals; Jason Roach would be cited as an example. The DA would lose his bid for reelection.

"I am really embarrassed to be here right now," Jason told Trimmer. "I've been . . . I don't really even know what to say. I'm gonna take this time that you are givin' me and try to better myself. I mean, as you know, I've had a drug problem, struggled with it, and I am sick of it. I don't want it no more. I mean, I am almost forty years old. And I'm tired of it. That's it."

"Mr. Roach, we've known each other quite a few years now," Trimmer said. He was disappointed in Roach, who'd once been part of a diversion program. There wasn't much he could do about the plea deal, but he could verbally flay Jason. As he spoke, Trimmer slowly ginned himself into a dudgeon.

"You are part of a much larger problem," the judge said. "And it's *disgusting*, Mr. Roach." His voice rose until he was almost shouting. "You've become such a huge part of this true problem we have in our society. Not only that, but you are doing it while you have three children in your presence! And you are using a *diaper* bag to contain some of the illegal contraband. And not only that, you're doing it with the children's *mother*!"

Trimmer lectured, shamed, berated like an angry father until he was spent. He looked at a photo of the three children. "Your children are adorable, Mr. Roach. Mr. Roach, I'm not foolin' around with you anymore. Enough is enough. You are really being a burden on society. And I don't appreciate it."

"Sorry," Jason mumbled.

"I'm so disappointed in you." As Trimmer rose to leave the bench, Jason half-shouted, "Sorry, Judge Trimmer!"

Trimmer turned around and shook his head. "Oh, Mr. Roach."

Lloyd's sentencing by Berens hadn't been so fervid—Berens was a more laconic presence on the bench. Lloyd and his lawyer, Andrew Sanderson, sat down to read the papers detailing the agreement Sanderson had negotiated. Sanderson had to squint to see the words. "You're getting old," Lloyd joked. "You need glasses. I need glasses, too."

"Yes, Lloyd," Sanderson answered. "You *are* getting old. It's time for you to be done with this shit."

Lloyd balked at the stretch he'd have to serve—four and a half years, double Jason's term. Sanderson reminded him that they'd gone over all of it before, but Lloyd grumbled about "some trumped-up shit." "Go to trial, Lloyd," a frustrated Sanderson said. "I wouldn't do it, but go ahead. Go to trial." Sanderson liked Lloyd, and Lloyd trusted Sanderson, but it was time for tough love. They retreated to a room off the courtroom to have their argument.

Most Fairfield County juries were staunch police supporters, but Lora Manon, the prosecutor, was sometimes surprised by how much sympathy they showed for defendants. She figured the sympathy stemmed from so many of their own relatives or friends having been through the system after facing drug charges. She wasn't from Lancaster, and couldn't understand why so many people still lived there when they didn't have any good reason—in her outsider's view—to stay. There was nothing there economically for them. Drugs were pervasive in all classes, not just among the poor. What they ought to do, she said, was "fly like the wind."

Lloyd, of course, took the deal. During sentencing, Berens issued a perfunctory sermon. Lloyd and I nodded to each other, and he was led out into the chilly, rainy morning to shuffle back across the street. I'd been the only lay witness to Lloyd's fate. No relative, no friend had come to offer a supportive glance. "There are lots of people who you think are your friends when you have drugs," Lloyd had told me.

Mark walked past the Ping-Pong-ball-in-the-goldfish-bowl booth, the ring toss, the guess-your-weight stand, swearing off the drama of Lancaster's drug life. He didn't take Jason up on the offer of the connect. He wasn't any more enlightened as to why he was a junkie, though, or why he was terrified of asking too many questions.

That was the hardest part about staying sober, his own thoughts. He especially hated thinking of his old BMX buddy, Ryan.

Ryan had moved to Columbus to be with his girl. She got pregnant, but the relationship soured. Worse, Ryan got popped by the cops one May, three years ago. He was out on bail that July, but facing prison time, a heartbroken addict with a conviction. So Ryan lay down in the bathtub of his apartment, held a shotgun under his chin, and blew the top of his head off. He was twenty-three.

The fucked-up thing was that Ryan lived for a few days. Mark had gone to visit him at the hospital. Lots of kids showed up, because Ryan was a good dude. Mark had held Ryan's hand. He noticed dried blood caked under Ryan's nostrils. He tried to dab the blood away, but a nurse stopped him. The dried blood was helping to hold Ryan's brain matter in his head, she said. After a few days, relatives ordered the life support be stopped.

Back when he and Ryan were selling weed around Lancaster, Ryan bought Mark a fancy $600 watch for no reason at all. So Mark bought Ryan a similar watch, and those watches became their bro thing. Ryan's fiancée gave Ryan's watch to Mark. He still had it. He never wore it. The watch was too sad.

But he couldn't shut it all down on his own. He'd close his eyes, and his brain would rev: mental tires spinning, but going nowhere, until he could smell the dope, visualize the needle going into his arm, taste the metal flavor in his mouth, feel the warmth. Mark hadn't been out of jail long before he shot up with his buddy Nick.

Ryan had chosen his off-ramp. Mark often thought about taking his own. "I'll tell you something I never told anybody," he said one afternoon. "I'll be, like, watching a movie, and see these people get unrealistically high—OD or something—and I have this feeling of envy, like, 'Oh my God, why can't that happen to me?' For the longest time I've thought, 'If I am gonna die, I wanna die like that.' The times I was getting ready to get high, I wished I would have fallen out. I wished I would have got that high so it would just be over, that I would cease to exist, be done with it."

Politicking was always as much a part of the fair tradition as harness racing and quilting. With the November election two weeks away, 2015 wasn't different, just quieter. Mayoral candidates appeared, and yard signs popped up all around the fairgrounds perimeter, but nobody doubted who'd win. Brian Kuhn was the Republican candidate, so, barring some sudden revelation of malfeasance or shady dealings, he'd be the next mayor.

Not much would change with the election, though a lot needed chang-

ing. All three of the declared candidates talked about economic development, but none offered any coherent plan for going about it. Lancaster
didn't even have a full-time economic development director—the man with
that title worked at the gas company.

The county had just hired a new director—a former employee of the
newspaper—but he issued the same chamber-of-commerce happy talk as
his predecessors. "It's an honor to work for the people of Fairfield County,"
he said when his appointment was announced. "We have so many things
to offer businesses looking to relocate. Great schools, a skilled workforce,
two amazing industrial parks, and a high quality of life. Fairfield County's
location makes it prime for economic growth in the next decade."

The industrial parks existed, but none of the rest of this was true.
Company Wrench founder Brad Hutchinson, for example, wanted to hire
skilled workers but couldn't find them. "We were getting frustrated,
because we felt like the schools either weren't listening or weren't paying
attention," he said. "One guy, who runs the welding program at [a] school,
said, 'I'm gonna tell you, black-and-white, what the issue is.' He says, 'I've
got twenty kids in my class today. You drug-test all of your people, right?'
I said, 'Yep.' He said, 'Sixteen of my kids can't pass a drug test, I guaran-
tee you. So that gives me four kids to work with. Two of the four can't read
a tape measure, but they got shoved into my class because they were struggling, and [the school] felt like, in order to try and get 'em to graduate, we
needed to tuck these kids somewhere where they are out of sight, out of
mind, and they ended up in my program. So I got two kids that really stand
out and are excellent welders, and fifty employers, just like you, who are
screaming to get candidates.' "

Some schools no longer offered trade programs, which meant that Lancaster, a town once filled with skilled labor, had an extremely shallow pool
of it. Hutchinson was constantly annoying the local boosters by saying such
things out loud. But other small-business people agreed with Hutchinson.

Over beers in a tavern called Bootleggers, a man who was the second
generation of his family running a hardware supply business in town said
he sold 144 broom handles at a time to Anchor Hocking, and nuts, bolts,
and other industrial hardware to Diamond Power. Orders from both companies totaled a fraction of what they once did. Rumors were flying around
town that Diamond Power might cut back even more, or close up altogether.

"I'll wait to sell my business until it's worth absolutely nothing, shrewd businessman that I am!" He laughed like a crazy man. A friend of his, a real estate speculator with deep local roots, said houses that used to sell for $120,000 now sold for $85,000. "This is a dead town," he said. "A dead little dying town."

The schools were a brightening beacon, though. It was two months into the school year, and the new buildings were proving popular. Lancaster was justly proud of them. Despite those feelings, though, an operational tax levy to support them was no sure bet to pass in the coming election. The slogan IT'S NOT A NEW TAX! appeared all over town. You could almost see school administrators and teachers on their knees, pleading with voters to understand that the levy was only a renewal of the same tax citizens had passed by a hair several years before. It was as if they felt they were asking people to vote in favor of German measles instead of to maintain and improve their own schools.

The kids in the West After School Program were more rambunctious than usual, thanks to the changed schools and the distraction of the fair. They were making Dawn Shonk a little crazy at Tarhe Trails, but she was an old pro and would get them settled down soon. Michele Ritchlin and the board of the program had grown more confident they'd make it through the school year, despite losing out on the state grants. In September, the board had created a new fund-raising committee, but nobody was kidding themselves that the few thousands of dollars they'd raise would plug the gap left by the lost grants. Ritchlin increased the program's after-school childcare business. By October, 223 kids across the city were in childcare with the program. The idea had never really been to run childcare centers—the purpose had been to tutor and teach—but childcare helped pay the bills. She was still afraid of the future. Lancaster's Head Start program had once occupied the same building she now occupied. Head Start had lost its grants, too, and closed up. A good heart and the best intentions hadn't kept the lights on.

By the time the fair ended, trees blazed gold, red, and purple. Farmers had rolled hay into giant spools scattered over their fields. There'd be no more warm days until spring.

Six days later, Joe Piccolo resigned from his post as the Lancaster Festival's executive director. He'd already left town and turned off his cell phone. The board president called the resignation sudden and surprising, but expressed the usual best wishes and job-well-dones. Piccolo left a similar statement behind.

He'd had enough. He loved the festival and was sincere in his wish that it succeed, but he was tired of the resistance to change he found in Lancaster. "I cannot justify spending the future pushing against an immovable object," he said. For example, when he'd tried to shift dates for certain 2016 events to make it easier for people to attend more of them, the board had rejected the idea. "The response I received was as if I was suggesting that we sell marijuana at Rising Park Day," he said. He wanted to increase the festival's appeal to young people. "My biggest issue was trying to combat the desire to hold on for dear life to the past." The festival wanted to believe it was living in a 1990s world, he said. A native or near-native Lancastrian who could serve as a figurehead to carry out board decisions should take over his old job, he believed. Piccolo moved back to northern Ohio, where he'd pursue an M.B.A. He still hoped to make a career of arts management.

Until it could find a permanent replacement, Dave Gallimore, the old Chief of Lancaster Glass, would serve as an interim director. Lancaster had made a habit of calling on Gallimore: He'd done the same the year before, when the board fired Piccolo's predecessor, and he'd also once served as temporary economic development director. There weren't many of Gallimore's ilk left in Lancaster.

Brian didn't go to the fair. He spent the time working and going on an unsuccessful hunt at Hilltop with Brant. They didn't get a deer. They'd risen well before dawn and were sitting high up in the tree stands by sunrise. But it was a freezing morning, and Brian spent about three hours shivering while trying to sit still with his crossbow. "Then my ADD kicked in," he said, and he and Brant gave up. They'd try again in a couple of weeks.

That night, Brian and some friends did some drinking and poker playing at Colfax. He and his buddy Chris spent the next morning nursing hangovers by watching TV preachers. They switched channels between one speaking in English and one speaking in Spanish, both begging viewers for money. Brian and Chris mocked the preachers like drunken hecklers at a comedy club.

When I left them, I needled Brian. "Keep opening those boxes!" I said, referring to his work at Drew. "I think a little of Brian just died when you said that," Chris said. "Yeah, dude," Brian said. "A piece of my heart just fell on the floor."

Judge Patrick Harris stepped down from the Municipal Court bench the day after Joe Piccolo resigned from the festival. He'd decided to move to Florida to be with the woman he loved. His friends threw him a little send-off at the Ale House 1890.

Eric Brown was there, dressed in his black leather motorcycle jacket. He'd ridden his Harley-Davidson—one last ride before he put the bike away until spring. He was just back from Atlanta, and was about to leave for Chicago to attend the International Association of Chiefs of Police convention, where he'd have to schmooze with law enforcement officials from all over the world. The traveling and glad-handing were big parts of his new job, and he was having trouble getting used to them. He'd been required to play politician at the MCU in order to attract funding and to juggle the concerns of the MCU's member agencies. The stakes and the playing field were both bigger now, though, and they weren't balanced by time in the field. He was a cop turned bureaucrat, and the shift chafed. Lately, he'd been trying to defeat a ballot measure that would legalize medical marijuana in Ohio. Brown didn't have strong moral objections to marijuana, but he foresaw thousands of people who already had a tough time finding a job toking their way into unemployment by failing employer drug screenings.

I mentioned that I'd been spending time with Lloyd. Brown was already gone from the MCU when Lloyd was arrested in July, but of course he knew Lloyd from his many years in local policing. He smiled, bowed his head, chuckled, and, with a mix of amusement and sympathy, said, "Oh, Lloyd. Lloyd, Lloyd, Lloyd. Dumber than a post."

"You went to the fair, I hope," he said. "You had to go to the fair." My going seemed important to him. I assured him I'd gone, that no self-respecting former Lancastrian would fail to go. Then I told him about the girl and her cow. He smiled, as if reassured. "See?" he said. "That's pure. That's something that's so pure."

FIFTEEN

The Future in Play

January 2016

A couple Brian knew walked into the Cherry Street Pub and sat on the barstools next to him. "Hey, man," Brian said. They talked for a minute about a house out in a county village the couple was thinking of buying and fixing up. Russ, the bartender, placed a short glass of whiskey in front of Brian, then greeted another customer by name.

The backbar behind Russ, a giant floor-to-ceiling wooden structure with a mirror in the middle and half-pillars on either end, was crowded with bottles and knickknacks that would seem thematically disconnected if you weren't from Lancaster. It had functioned as a backbar since the 1920s, when it began its life in a nearby tavern. There was a time when glassworkers walking home several miles from the old Black Cat or Lancaster Lens would stop in that tavern for a rest and a rye. One night, a man with a bellyful of booze continued his journey in a blizzard so fierce he became lost in the snow, only to serendipitously wind up back at the tavern, where he spent the night sleeping it off on the bar. Maybe it happened. Maybe it didn't. No matter. The spirit was true. After the tavern closed, the backbar was stored in a barn. Then a man named Johnny Johnson opened his eponymously named restaurant—a diner, really—in the building now occupied by the Cherry Street Pub. Johnson rescued the backbar by installing it in his new place. Now Brian, glassman turned warehouseman, sipped his whiskey and looked at the same enormous hunk of oak.

Kevin "Max" McGee posed, tough-chinned and squinty-eyed in a three-inch-high cutout picture mounted on a wooden stand. He stood guard over the booze in his green-and-white (Go Irish!) 1973 William V. Fisher Catholic High School football uniform. McGee had been friends with Cherry Street owner Billy Smith since they were kids. They'd been part of an east-side Fifth Avenue troop that used to shoot hoops up against each other's garages, drink a little beer, make a little trouble.

The old JOHNSON'S neon sign shone over a row of booths. Black-and-white photos of Lancaster scenes and people, and a carved portrait of Sherman, reminded everybody what a long history they all shared. A picture of McGee's dad in his World War II infantry uniform hung by a corner. He had installed a phone system for Anchor Hocking in the 1960s. An old Anchor Hocking logo sign—an antique, two-armed anchor overlaid by an ornate serif-font "H"—occupied a center space on the back wall.

Over on Pierce Avenue, Sean Gumbs, three months into his sojourn as temporary CEO, had finished his listening tour and his quick study of the American glass industry. He was now convinced that EveryWare—that is, Anchor Hocking and, to a lesser degree, Oneida—shouldn't be in the shape it was in. These were viable businesses, and always had been.

But only now were the debt-to-equity owners seeing what Gumbs, and Solomon before him, saw. They had turned $250 million of debt into equity during the bankruptcy in May and now were just "getting a sense of it," Gumbs said. "Then, in the next breath, it's, 'Well, what's the potential of what I have?' I think the current equity holders—and the largest equity holders are on the board—they got it. There is potential in this business."

Gumbs—short, slight, in glasses and a pile vest over an open-collar shirt—was a twenty-first-century wandering samurai of capitalism. Smartphones and Ivy-covered degrees were his weapons. "I have a particular set of skills," he told me.

"Like Liam Neeson?" I offered, laughing. "As in *Taken*? The movies?"

"I literally don't watch movies," he said flatly before picking up where he left off. "So I think that those skill sets can be applied in lots of places."

He had applied them in many companies in many industries, but his work was never about the product or the company or the place. It was about the game. Through intense focus on the game, he'd mastered it. That's why he earned the kinds of fees outfits like FTI and A&M charged. Everything he'd learned over the past three months convinced him that Anchor Hocking had survived decades of blows for a reason. Despite the depredations, Plant 1 and Monaca kept rising from the mat because "if people could have figured out a way to do this overseas in a cost-effective way, they would have done it. It's not necessarily like other forms of manufacturing in the U.S. that have gone away."

There was no lack of interest in exploiting low-cost foreign labor. Libbey, for example, owned manufacturing plants in Monterrey, Mexico, and Langfang, China. Libbey used a $40.9 million low-interest loan from the China Construction Bank to build the new Langfang factory, which produced tableware both for the Chinese domestic market and for export outside of China. By one estimate, there were four hundred glass furnaces in Asia. As little as the Anchor Plant 1 employees were paid, there were people around the world willing to do similar work for much less. As a result, margins on the kinds of glass Anchor Hocking made were still falling as producers raced each other to the bottom.

The power of American big-box retailers like Walmart exacerbated the situation. The American flag on Anchor Hocking packaging was nice, but Americans wanted cheap stuff—and the harder they shopped for the cheapest stuff, the more they helped drive down the wages of people who made stuff. And the lower those wages dropped, the more a desire for cheap morphed into the self-fulfilling necessity of cheap.

Even so, Gumbs couldn't be shaken from his belief that EveryWare, led by Anchor Hocking, could book profits and grow its value. That didn't mean the equity owners wouldn't sell it. They would. Anchor Hocking had been in play since Carl Icahn greenmailed it, and it would continue to be in play. But the board seemed convinced that investing some capital in repairs, safety, and a small amount of new technology was the smart way to grow back to at least a $250 million valuation, and maybe a little more. Spending, improving customer and supplier relationships, and making better margins on sales would take a while. So owners of the majority of the stake were likely to hold on for at least a year. Of course, if U.S. Glass or Arc, for example, were to back a truck packed with $300 million up to the door on Pierce Avenue, they'd sell. But Gumbs believed that selling out now would be a losing move.

He sounded a lot like Solomon. But Solomon had a bias toward growing through acquisition. Now, nobody talked about acquisitions, or a billion-dollar future. The goal was to get the place cleaned up, make it profitable, then sell.

Solomon had lost the safety argument. Now Gumbs was charged by the board with making safety a top priority. Gumbs said the board obsessed over safety because keeping workers safe was the right thing to do. But its desire to move faster on safety than it perceived Solomon to have been moving may also have been motivated by a desire to sell—few investors want to buy a hazardous plant. In the three months since Gumbs had arrived, the safety consultants Solomon had hoped to avoid hiring had held employee training sessions.

Swink sat through one of them, but he mostly tuned out. The way he saw it, the whole plant was a safety hazard. Everybody knew that. So there wasn't any point in talking about all sorts of scientific procedures to create a safety culture. He just wanted to get back to work, to operating his press.

The company had installed a fire alarm just above Swink's machine. With his ear protection on, he couldn't hear the alarm. But it also strobed, so at least he could see it. He wasn't sure what he was supposed to do if he saw the flashing light, but now he'd know something was on fire that wasn't supposed to be.

As much as they bitched about the hazards, safety was not the top priority for the workers. Joe Boyer, for instance, was still nursing his knees. They creaked like two rusty gate hinges. Especially the right knee. It zinged him with every step he took. When he was a teenager, he'd gone night-fishing by the Hocking River. While pumping up a Coleman lantern, he slipped and ripped something in there. He didn't know what, exactly. After a while, the knee seemed to heal up and it didn't bother him for years. Then, at the end of last summer, he'd spent part of a shift working up on a machine. He stepped off it, kept supervising his shops, went home. In the middle of the night, his throbbing knee woke him up. "It just give out on me," he said.

On his days off, he liked to spend a few hours out in his garage working on his blue '71 Plymouth Barracuda. He'd raced the car at amateur tracks around central Ohio, but gave it up a few years ago because he never seemed to have time. Like a lot of Plant 1 workers, Boyer was often "forced"—held over after a shift to work another two or three hours of overtime because the plant was shorthanded. He was exhausted all the time. When he wasn't working, he wanted to sleep. He didn't even have time to keep his yard in shape, to say nothing of the 'Cuda. But he so missed working on it, he took the opportunity during the 2014 shutdown to pull off the cover and turn wrenches. He'd put a 430-cubic-inch engine under the hood and a bottle of nitrous oxide in the back. After his knee flared up, he couldn't spend more than an hour at a time in the garage. He had to save himself for the plant. Also, his back was killing him.

Boyer thought about seeing a doctor for the knees, but because of the high deductible on the company health insurance, he already owed too much in medical bills. He'd been in the hospital for the gastric reflux check. His premiums for the company health insurance were rising, too, because the company had just raised them. He figured it took about $254 per paycheck, about $500 a month, or about one week's worth of take-home wages to pay his share of the monthly payment. He marveled that the young rookies Anchor was trying to hire could afford the premiums at all on the wages they made. Some didn't. They opted out of the company plan and paid the penalty under the Affordable Care Act for not having health insurance.

Boyer took a Vicodin for the knees and it helped a little, but he hated swallowing those damn things. They were dangerous. He'd seen too many guys in Plant 1 on Vicodin or Percocet or OxyContin practically sleepwalking through a shift. Boyer took aspirin instead, but they were pretty worthless. He worked in pain all through the autumn and into the winter.

The knees were a little better now. He finally did call a doctor, who suggested he try some NSAID cream on his back. And as his back started feeling better, the knees improved, so he figured they were connected somehow. One of these days, he'd go see a specialist. But he couldn't afford it yet.

On October 13, the day Sam Solomon was fired, the unions filed a grievance with the National Labor Relations Board accusing EveryWare of
"unilaterally implement[ing] new health insurance benefits for bargaining
unit employees without bargaining in good faith with the Union as the parties never agreed to the changes nor reached impasse." The grievance was
only the most recent in a long string of complaints to the NLRB that had
accelerated during Monomoy's ownership.

The new health insurance costs mixed with the still-raw anger over the
2014 concessions in a fermenting pool of grudges that drowned any safety
concerns. Morale was as low as it had ever been. Some employees had
stopped caring. "You'd have to be a fuckin' idiot to get fired over there,"
Swink said.

As Boyer suggested, drug use in the plant was common. Some guys,
misjudging Swink—a solid six-foot-tall rock 'n' roller with steel gauges in
his earlobes, a steel spike through his bottom lip, a wispy beard on his
chin, and an Iron Cross inked in the crook between his left thumb and
forefinger—would invite him to snort Percs or Oxys behind the machines.
He always refused. His own father drank himself to death, and he hated
most drugs.

"I actually think we'll strike this year," Chris Nagle said. "Unless we
get something substantial back, with the insurance costs and everything
goin' on, I think we will go on the street."

He'd sent that message to Gumbs. "He thinks we can't do anything,"
Nagle said of Gumbs's reply. "I said, 'Okay, contract comes, don't bring a
knife to a gunfight.'" Nagle hadn't seen such a mean mood in decades.
"He's got the people pissed off now to where they don't care. They can't
afford the insurance and to live, too, so you might as well strike, you know?
They don't have any money comin' in anyway."

He'd told Solomon, and now he'd told Gumbs, that union members
were having to choose between health care and feeding their children.
They had to tell their kids they couldn't play school sports because the public schools now charged fees to kids who wanted to play a sport.

The small equipment changes inside the plant—the removal of an H-28,
some new mold-design gear, the upcoming tank rebuild—were all well and
good, but workers made connections between that investment and their
own wages and benefits. "Our 6 percent is payin' for that equipment,"

Nagle said, referring to the concessions from 2014. The factory men understood better than anybody the need to upgrade the plant, but any upgrades weren't going to put food on the table. The company's decision to pay for a new roof on the Pierce Avenue offices didn't help the mood, either. The roof didn't cost all that much, but, like the parking lot pothole repair, the symbolism grated. "We're still telling our kids they can't eat today, but you're getting a new roof on the building to keep the accounting people dry," Nagle said.

New hires made $12 per hour, about a hundredth of the hourly fee charged by the law firm partners who represented EveryWare during the bankruptcy. Such workers made $96 per day, or $480 per forty-hour week, or about $2,000 per month. They made more if they were forced, or worked holiday shifts, but that money wasn't guaranteed. After deductions, health insurance premiums, and union dues, Nagle estimated that some workers took home under $10,000 per year if they bought into the health insurance plan. That's why many didn't.

Sure, Nagle argued, you could say, as many in Lancaster did, that having any job is better than having no job at all. "But you can't afford to work there, because you can't afford the company insurance."

Though it was only January, and the contract didn't expire until October, Nagle was already telling his members to borrow $10,000 out of their own 401(k)s and set it aside to help them ride out a strike. Like Dale Lamb before him, Nagle knew that nobody really won a strike. "But some days you gotta put your foot in the sand and say, 'We've had enough.' And that's what I tell Sean." There was so much simmering antagonism in the plant that some workers felt like they had nothing to lose. "The company thinks they are making us weaker," Nagle said, "but they're making us stronger. If we do strike, it will put the dead in this corporation."

Gumbs hadn't made it through Penn and Harvard and the balls-out world of high finance without being perceptive. He knew he had a problem. Just before Thanksgiving, the company had handed out $15 Walmart gift cards. In the old days, the company used to pull a big semi full of frozen turkeys up to the plant and hand them to workers at the end of pre-Thanksgiving shifts, but nothing like that had happened for a long time—and not at all during the tenures of many employees. Some scoffed at the

$15 card as a lame attempt to make nice. Others, like Joe Boyer, viewed it as an overture.

Now Gumbs and Erika Schoenberger were compiling a service-award list in another play to boost morale. Anchor Hocking used to give out service awards at milestone anniversaries—ten years, twenty, twenty-five, on and on—and then print the employees' names and photos in *AnchorScope*, the newsletter that went to everybody's mailbox every three months. Like the turkeys, the awards hadn't been given out in years.

As he looked over the list, Gumbs could barely believe what he was seeing. Between Anchor Hocking and Oneida, EveryWare Global had about three hundred employees who'd worked for one or the other of the two companies for at least twenty years. Anchor Hocking had about half a dozen employees who'd worked for the company for at least fifty years.

"The dedication of those people, and what they've gone through," Gumbs marveled. "I mean, two decades for me is . . . staying in place is a structure I have . . ." Gumbs was at a loss for how to describe it.

While Gumbs and Schoenberger were working out service-award lists on Pierce Avenue, Mark Kraft was attending yet another group meeting. This one, however, was different.

Mark had spent the year since his arrest kidding himself. For Mark, being a junkie was like an identity he possessed. He may have begun to hate it, but it was his. When Eric Brown and the MCU broke through his door, he said, "it was taken away from me. I resented that." So, once the dope sickness passed, he kept trying to act as if he was in control of his own destiny.

Sucking a Perc 30 up his nose, swallowing Xanaxes, shooting up in June and again in September—he tried to tell himself they were his decisions. After all, he wasn't always high. He'd gone weeks without using. He went to work. He returned to his parents' house, where he'd been living since his bust. Sure, he'd call himself a junkie, but then he'd say, "Don't worry," or, "Yeah, yeah, yeah," whenever anybody suggested his obsessive Mobile-Patrol scanning, his continuing flirtation with the drama of Lancaster's drug culture, or his use might hint at self-deception.

He'd walk out of a meeting with his probation officer and think, "I should get high," and then he'd think, "How fucked up is that?" And then he'd try to forget about using—but life sort of sucked without dope. Even the week in jail couldn't stop him from shooting up just days after his release.

In late October, Mark ran into Nick, his addict buddy, and Nick's girlfriend at Walmart. Nick was pretty spun out. His girlfriend was a wreck, wraith-thin, with scabs on her face. She'd been cute once. She hadn't been much into drugs before she hooked up with Nick. Mark was so concerned for her that he spoke to his parents, who knew the girl's family, for advice.

Not long after, in November, Nick asked if he could spend a few days in the King Street house. Mark, who was still living with his parents, had allowed Nick to stay there once before. That was a clear violation of Mark's probation—"Yes, I'm a dumbass," he'd said at the time. But Mark agreed again, because he was worried about what Nick and his girl might be doing if he left them on the streets—and not at all, he insisted, because Nick was sure to bring dope.

On November 13, the MCU rushed the door again and found a crack pipe and gear for shooting dope. When the police took Nick to jail, he wrote out a statement saying that Mark had supplied the equipment and sold him drugs.

Mark stared at Nick's handwriting, dumbfounded. He denied supplying drugs to Nick, and he denied knowing anything about the gear. But it was his house, after all, so on November 17 he was booked back into jail. On that day, he failed a drug test. Mark insisted he hadn't used, didn't piss dirty, had been clean since September. The probation officer, though, declared that Mark "tested positive for Morphine and after he was given several chances to admit to the usage, the Defendant did admit to using Heroin."

Really, the date he used, when he tested positive, why he tested positive, whether he'd used or not—none of that mattered. What mattered was that even as Mark called himself a junkie, felt shame and regret, wanted so badly to be free—not just from dope but from himself and his world—that he fantasized about killing himself, he could not admit that he was not at all the chill dude in the hipster fedora that he pretended to be. He was an addict with a yoke around his neck, and it was killing him.

After a few days in the jail on Main Street, Mark was transferred to the jail annex on BIS Road. There, he got high four days straight. "You can buy dope. It's fucking everywhere. On day twelve, I still had no bond, so I said 'Fuck it' and bought some Suboxone. I'm not gonna lie. I did get high."

Mark claimed that people threw cans of tobacco dip with pills hidden inside over the fence. Trustees would collect the cans and sell the pills for $160 per pill, $80 for a half, $40 for a quarter. "It's quite a system," Mark said. "There was people selling Percs in there, fucking needles in there. How the fuck do they do that? I don't know. I wasn't using anybody's dirty needles."

The last day of his incarceration, December 3, "Somebody in our pod bought some really good cocaine. So I do this fat line of cocaine, and instantly I get this call to go to court. I think I'm going in front of a judge, but I was getting out on bond. I was trippin' a little bit. The amount of drugs going through that jail is insane. I was completely appalled."

When he checked back on his house on King Street, he found a note clipped to his porch mailbox. Any more trouble, any more drugs, the note threatened, and Mark would one day drive up to the curb and find the house gone. Just gone. "Somebody threatened to burn my fucking house down!" he said. "Fuckers!"

With some persuading from his lawyer and his father, Mark decided to attend an in-patient drug rehab center in northern Ohio. He was motivated more by fear of the reinstatement of his original felony charge than by recognition that he could not control his addiction. He hoped that if he showed an earnest effort, Judge Berens would maintain the ILC. As a sign of his sincerity, he paid the insurance deductible himself.

Mark checked in January 11, almost one year to the day since his original arrest. Ten days into his stay, he began to see the reality of his life. He felt depressed, afraid he'd always be known as a junkie. If that was so, he thought, his life was over.

The next day, Mark sounded more optimistic. He admitted that, while he'd been calling himself a junkie and used the word "addict," he was just now realizing how fucked up he was. He felt better physically. "I want you to see me in a good place," he said.

He hated to say it, because he didn't like cops—and, in a different way from Brian, he hated The System—but Eric Brown and the MCU team might have saved his life. "I was forced to get sober because of the arrest. I did a lot of meetings and tried to stay sober best I could, but I always had this or that fuckup."

He was afraid of Lancaster, though. Even though he was over a hundred miles away, Lancaster remained as close as his smartphone screen. "Five days ago, I got a text saying, 'Hey, I got a fuckin' script of Xanies,'" Mark said, referring to Xanax. "Facebook, texting me, I'm still in this loop of what's going on down there. I try to get away from it, and it's still right there. I am scared to go back to Lancaster, man. I realize now that I've been up here, that's all I know. What I was doing this last year, this whole sober thing, I feel like I want it more now, and if I don't change people, places, things, it'll blow up in my face."

Mark had been home from rehab for two days when he ran into a kid, Dakota, and Dakota's pregnant girlfriend in the parking lot of a doctor's office. "Hey, you still fuck around?" Dakota asked. "No," Mark answered. "I got some really good weed," Dakota said.

The next day was warm for late January, so Mark went to Rising Park with his little sister. He said hello to a girl he knew, who asked, "What have you been up to?" Mark told her he'd just returned from rehab. After a little small talk, she said, "Can you get me some Percs or anything?" "What the fuck's the matter with you?" he asked.

He'd finally admitted the truth. "I didn't think I was an addict. I might have called myself a junkie." Now, though, he said, the truth had given him willpower. "I kept fuckin' up, and now I realize that, if it's in front of me, I am powerless to it. So the key is not to have it in front of me."

Mark had been sent home with Suboxone. Whereas he once got high on Suboxone, he now hated having to take it. He remained with his parents. His mother counted the pills every day to be sure Mark wasn't selling any. In the past, he would have rebelled at the scrutiny, but now he accepted it.

Like his dope, he both loved and hated Lancaster. The generations of his family, all the interconnections with people—he'd never have that again if he left it for good. Lancaster was a community, for better or worse—and, as weird as it sounded, as hard as it was to believe, it was his community, too. There was no other place on earth where that statement could ever be true the way it was true about Lancaster.

Meanwhile, Lloyd was adjusting to prison, again. Though he didn't like it, he said he was glad to be there, glad to be sentenced to four years. Not that it was fair that he got four and Jason only two, but he tried not to think about that part. He figured it would take at least that long before he was ready to come back to Lancaster. "I want to get real disgusted with myself," he said. There were plenty of drugs for sale on the inside, but so far he'd avoided them. He hadn't heard from his family or had any visitors except me. He'd put some pounds on his frame and had been working out. His arms were beefier than they'd been the day he was sentenced. Some of his teeth were missing. He hadn't sat in a dentist's chair since childhood, maybe, but now the prison dentist was pulling the worst ivories one by one and fitting him for dentures. He was taking some GED courses and had enrolled in a community college prison program. He thought he'd like to become a drug counselor. Learning was hard for him, he said, because he hadn't used his brain in twenty years.

From the control of prison, Lloyd could envision plans and a future, but he knew better than anybody else could how such dreams fall apart. He'd had them before. He would return to town, of course: Where else was he going to go? But nobody was going to stand in line to hire Lloyd. And Lancaster cops would be waiting for him. He hoped they wouldn't hassle him too bad.

Lloyd stuttered and paused, his eyes glistening, when he spoke about Lancaster's police, but not because he feared them. A Lancaster cop named Randy Bartow had done Lloyd a favor once. It was one of the few times in his life anybody had.

One day, Lloyd had walked out of the county courthouse, looking agitated and angry after appearing on some charge or other. Bartow, who was entering the building, stopped him and said, "Hey Lloyd, what's wrong?" Lloyd explained that his girlfriend's ex-boyfriend was keeping the girlfriend's belongings in his house and preventing her from moving them out. Lloyd was headed over there right then to confront the dude. Bartow, knowing Lloyd and knowing there'd be a beatdown, told Lloyd to sit on the bench outside the courthouse. "Give me a little time," Bartow said. Bartow drove away, and about twenty minutes later returned with the girlfriend's stuff. In 2012, Bartow's own girlfriend's ex-husband broke into her house and shot her and Bartow dead, then killed himself. "He was a good cop," Lloyd said.

While Lloyd and Jason were in state prison and Mark was in rehab, Jessica Cantrell sat in county jail. She'd turned herself in on November 17, the same day Mark was booked. She'd had time to think during her two months on the run, and her subsequent two months in jail. "I love him to death," she said of Jason. "He tries, but he keeps lying about stuff. He's really brought me down. Look at me now."

For sure she would have to move away from Lancaster. Nobody in town would give you a job if you'd been in her kind of trouble. Maybe she would go back to Louisiana. She could be a nurse.

Jason learned about Jessica through the grapevine that connects Lancaster to the state's prisons—most Lancastrians would be surprised to know just how many of their fellow townsfolk shuttled back and forth between them. He wasn't sure where he stood with her. He tried not to think too much about it. Like Lloyd, he enrolled in some prison education courses, though he didn't have a future career in mind. Hairstyling was now out. Maybe he could buy "one of them food trucks that's got, like, the grills and the coolers and stuff like that." He'd also talk about the cleaning business, the landscaping business, maybe working for his brother-in-law hanging rain gutters. He could work under the table, not pay any taxes, still collect the disability payments he was receiving for his bad back. That'd be cool.

Lancaster itself was in turmoil. The past year had not proven to be the bright new start the town hoped it would be. The largest private employer went bankrupt, the drug plague showed no sign of abating, the festival director abruptly quit. But the year hadn't been a disaster, either. Anchor Hocking's "parent"—a term that still annoyed the people who hated to think of Anchor Hocking having a parent—had rebirthed it from bankruptcy with much less debt. New elementary schools had opened, and in the November election voters approved—by a narrow margin—the continuation of the levy to operate them. Lancastrians could reach into that mixed bag, pull something out, and justify either optimism or despair.

But then, on December 30, Bridget Kuhn, the newly elected mayor's wife, was indicted on fifty criminal charges related to her embezzlement of more than $350,000 from clients of her bookkeeping business. She'd used the money to feed her gambling habit. Unbeknownst to most people in town, Bridget, a small-town bookkeeper married to a CPA, was regarded as a high roller by the Ohio Casino Control Commission.

Brian Kuhn had joined his wife on some of her casino excursions. And, back in May, Kuhn had informed the county Republican Party that he was having a little business trouble: a matter of discrepancies in payroll accounts managed by the firm he owned. The party hid the information from the public and let the election proceed. The out-of-town special prosecutor brought in to conduct the investigation into Bridget Kuhn refused to say whether or not Brian Kuhn was under suspicion as a party to her crimes.

As if the mayor's troubles weren't bad enough, all through January, the city council members continued their dysfunctional feuding. The new jail that had so agitated one council faction for over a year was now well under construction, but they refused to let the issue drop. The council president had tried to make council committee appointments to oversee the city's departments, but other members objected. At a subsequent meeting, rebellious council members made their own committee assignments. So, as the new year began, Lancaster had a new mayor's wife under indictment, a mayor under suspicion, and a city council mired in a petty, childish spat. All this was printed in newspapers and carried by TV stations statewide. Once again, the amateurish shenanigans and outright criminality of Lancaster's own pols had made the town a regional laughingstock.

In the coming months, Mark would stay sober. But Berens would reinstate his felony and enter a conviction with a fine and a suspended year in state prison. If Mark slipped again, he'd join Lloyd and Jason. Mark was angry about the felony, upset that even as the black-and-blue scars on his arms faded, the felony would remain. He struggled to adopt a Zen attitude about it, and hoped that someday there'd be a way to erase the conviction, and his past.

Carly would be picked up for a probation violation. Mark would feel sad for her. By then, he'd be nearly weaned off Suboxone and looking forward to a trip with his grandfather. He'd have to always be alert, but as time passed, he would come to believe that he'd left heroin behind for good.

Not much would change for John and Wendy Oatney. Between John's learning disability and his menacing conviction, finding a job began to seem like an impossible dream. Having heard that there was work in Kentucky, he considered driving there and sleeping in his car until he could convince somebody to take him on, but he reconsidered and kept looking around Fairfield County. Eventually, he'd find work unloading trucks at a discount store for $8.50 an hour. Wendy would get a raise to $9.70 an hour. The police would return John's gun.

The Lancaster Festival would name Ken Culver as the new executive director. Culver once worked as an Anchor Hocking PR man before the sale to Newell. He'd served as a city councilman and volunteered at the Glass Museum. Joe Piccolo had been right: Picking a local who understood Lancaster, and who would let Lancaster be Lancaster, would prove to be the better choice. The weather would be touch-and-go for the 2016 edition of the festival, but the skies would clear at critical moments, and a big crowd would pay to see the veteran country singer Vince Gill, who would happily perform with the orchestra.

Dave Benson would announce his retirement from the fair.

Ashley would call me to say she'd been evicted from the east-side house and that she'd "lost" the Bitchmobile. She'd tell a confusing story about an ex-boyfriend I'd met, who smoked crack in her bathroom and stole money from her. She stayed at the Relax Inn for a little while, but her monthly $600 of SSI money didn't last, so she slept outside in an alley. She was on her way to another Ohio town, where, she said, she had a friend who might take her in.

The young girl from the trailer park, the one Ashley said was growing up too fast, would run away from home. She would leave a note for her mother.

Mayor Brian Kuhn would be indicted on two felony counts of failing to file state income tax returns. He would refuse to resign his office. His wife would plead guilty to theft and be sentenced to four years in state prison.

The city council members would continue to fight among themselves. Both sides would file dueling lawsuits, at an indeterminate cost to the city's taxpayers.

Michele Ritchlin would create Homework Club, a scholarship system funded by local donors to supplement the diminished budget available to pay for kids whose families could not afford the after-school program. Thirty-six businesses and individuals would donate, including Nancy Frick and her husband, Paul. And in July 2016, Ritchlin would receive the call she'd hoped for: The program would receive two grants of $200,000 each— two of only twenty-six grants approved from 202 applications. The program's target population, the state would decide, was poorer than it had thought. Ritchlin, who once described herself as an anti-tax, Ayn Rand libertarian, would laugh at the obvious contradiction and say that even in the face of new realities, her old beliefs died hard.

That was true of Lancaster as a whole. It had become a town that lived on federal and state government money. But many refused to acknowledge the connection, because, as Mark Kraft could tell them, denial was comforting. The system they believed in was not The System that actually prevailed. That past system had been destroyed, or driven to the brink of destruction, in part by buccaneering free-market finance and Friedmanism. Acknowledging that fact was as painful as a devout religionist losing faith, something cosmopolitan liberals refused to empathize with. Abandoning Lancaster's old moderate conservative pragmatism to blame sin, laziness, scientists, immigrants, unions, and any number of other enemies of the American Way allowed the illusion that *Forbes* magazine had helped establish to remain a viable belief, one to be resurrected, not mourned.

Sam Solomon would stay sore about his dismissal. He would take his time finding his "new passion in life"—but until he found it, he would mentor and coach businesspeople. A biographical sketch for his appearance as a keynote speaker at a National Women Business Owners Corporation conference would say that he "recently completed a turnaround of EveryWare Global that required raising new capital, restructuring debt, reigniting the new product development engine and returning the company to profitability."

The board of EveryWare Global would hire Patrick Lockwood-Taylor, a former Procter & Gamble executive, as CEO. Taylor, an Englishman who'd worked around the world on behalf of P&G brands, would tell me that the board was "compassionate and genuinely intrigued by what is possible. They agree on three things: the fantastic brands—iconic. Two, we have a duty to improve safety. And, three, they have committed to, and have invested capital into, the plant for improved efficiency and safety."

The employees in Lancaster would take a skeptical view. Lockwood-Taylor had never been a CEO. He'd left a large multinational like P&G to become one at a small, unprofitable (Solomon's bio notwithstanding) company. Maybe he was just punching his CEO ticket on his way to some bigger, fancier job. Or maybe he meant it when he said that he knew all about Milton Friedman's doctrine of profits above all—community be damned—and rejected it.

In a series of three videos he made for company employees, he would acknowledge that tough union negotiations were still to come, but that all workers were "owners" of the company. Nobody bought that part. "Many of you remember the heyday of these great companies and brands," he would say. "I want to get back to that feeling that we are the best in the industry and be proud of this company." When the organization is prospering, he'd say, "the community is prospering. I want us to get back to that." They would hope that was true. Lockwood-Taylor would not say that the board was entertaining offers to sell.

Why did they stay? That was the obvious question. Why didn't they take Lora Manon's advice and fly like the wind away from Lancaster? Some people had come down from Columbus to buy a cheaper house in a tract at the edge of town, so their presence wasn't mysterious. Chris Cruit, Joe Boyer, Chris Nagle—they were easy to explain, too. They had a lot of years in Plant 1, and unless they wanted to try for a job in Toledo, at Libbey, there probably wasn't another place in the country where their skills would transfer.

But why did Rebekah Krutsch stay? Rebekah was a waitress at Cherry Street Pub. Even now, she was skittering back and forth behind Brian, hustling to deliver food orders.

The past decade in Lancaster had been a bumpy ride. The home she and her ex-husband once owned fell into foreclosure during the Great

Recession. The financial strain contributed to their divorce. She had four children, who lived with her on the west side near Plant 1. But Rebekah had a lot going for her, too. She was pretty, with a carved face and a mass of curly red hair. She had a college degree. She made art—wire constructions on painted canvases—which she sometimes sold for extra money. Waitressing was her second job. During the day, she worked for the Recovery Center as a drug education teacher in the local schools, a full-time position for which she estimated she took home about $24,000 per year. Her waitressing added another $1,000 per month, income that kept her off food stamps. The government-subsidized health insurance that so many criticized helped a lot. She knew she could probably find work making more money elsewhere, and she was more acutely aware of Lancaster's ugly side than many others were. But when I asked why she didn't move away, she looked at me with wide, pitying eyes and said, "This is my *town*"—as if my asking the question meant I'd been deprived of the quiet power of belonging to a place.

Lancaster people were good people. "There's a lot of love and passion here," she said. "You see it where we are sitting. I wait tables in it. I work in it every day in the schools. The teachers and staff love it. If they didn't love it, they wouldn't be there. Those junior highs, Ewing and Sherman, are falling apart. Literally falling apart. I walk into Sherman and Ewing when they reopen in the late summer and it's stifling. But they love their schools. I'm not going anywhere. I like my town."

She sounded like Gerry Stebelton, the lawyer and former state representative whose firm took over the old Anchor Hocking headquarters, and whose mother had spent decades in the Anchor sluer. He had something to show me, he'd said. So we walked into a corner office overlooking trees, the statue of Sherman, Main Street, Broad Street, and the big golden sandstone City Hall. One day, he told me, he'd stood right where we stood. As it happened, it was a day much like the day we spoke, with the sun illuminating City Hall under a blue sky. He was on the phone with somebody from New York, or maybe it was Chicago, and the next thing he knew he choked up, and an involuntary "My God!" came out of his mouth. The voice on the other end asked what had happened. "Nothing," Stebelton said. "I'm just looking at the most beautiful sight in the world."

Many Lancastrians felt the same way. But the festival's hundreds of volunteers; the people who gave to Community Action, the Fairfield County Foundation, the United Way, Foundation Dinners, Maywood Mission, their churches; the ladies (and a few men) of the Cameo League and the Heritage Association; Loving Lending, which had helped John and Wendy Oatney; the tutors and board members of the West Side After School Program; and a lot of other bighearted, strong-willed people would be mocked by opinionistas like Kevin D. Williamson in a sneering screed published in March 2016 in *National Review*, a leading conservative journal:

> The problem isn't that Americans cannot sustain families, but that they do not wish to. If you spend time in hardscrabble, white upstate New York, or eastern Kentucky, or my own native West Texas, and you take an honest look at the welfare dependency, the drug and alcohol addiction, the family anarchy—which is to say, the whelping of human children with all the respect and wisdom of a stray dog—you will come to an awful realization. It wasn't Beijing. It wasn't even Washington, as bad as Washington can be. It wasn't immigrants from Mexico, excessive and problematic as our current immigration levels are. It wasn't any of that. Nothing happened to them. There wasn't some awful disaster. There wasn't a war or a famine or a plague or a foreign occupation. Even the economic changes of the past few decades do very little to explain the dysfunction and negligence—and the incomprehensible malice— of poor white America. So the gypsum business in Garbutt ain't what it used to be. There is more to life in the 21st century than wallboard and cheap sentimentality about how the Man closed the factories down. The truth about these dysfunctional, downscale communities is that they deserve to die. Economically, they are negative assets. Morally, they are indefensible. Forget all your cheap theatrical Bruce Springsteen crap. Forget your sanctimony about struggling Rust Belt factory towns and your conspiracy theories about the wily Orientals stealing our jobs. Forget your goddamned gypsum, and, if he has a problem with that, forget Ed Burke, too. The white American underclass is in thrall to a vicious, selfish culture whose main products are misery and used heroin needles. Donald Trump's speeches make them feel good. So does

OxyContin. What they need isn't analgesics, literal or political. They need real opportunity, which means that they need real change, which means that they need U-Haul.

For decades, politicians—Republicans and Democrats both—and pundits had all been spewing empty platitudes of praise for "the heartland," "real America," and "small-town values." Then, with shameless hypocrisy, they supported the very policies that helped destroy thriving small towns.

Corporate elites said they needed free-trade agreements, so they got them. Manufacturers said they needed tax breaks and public-money incentives in order to keep their plants operating in the United States, so they got them. Banks and financiers needed looser regulations, so they got them. Employers said they needed weaker unions—or no unions at all—so they got them. Private equity firms said they needed carried interest and secrecy, so they got them. Everybody, including Lancastrians themselves, said they needed lower taxes, so they got them. What did Lancaster and a hundred other towns like it get? Job losses, slashed wages, poor civic leadership, social dysfunction, drugs.

Having helped wreck small towns, some conservatives were now telling the people in them to pack up and leave. The reality of "Real America" had become a "negative asset."

The "vicious, selfish culture" didn't come from small towns, or even from Hollywood or "the media." It came from a thirty-five-year program of exploitation and value destruction in the service of "returns." America had fetishized cash until it became synonymous with virtue.

"This is a success-driven culture, right?" Sam Solomon once said. "This is America, so we tend to really harp on winners. And as long as you are winning—skipping your stone across the pond—that's what gets reported, and we quickly forget the losers." Somebody who plodded along, slowly building, was forgotten. "That's not interesting at all. So it's a little bit of that culture that we've created. That's what works in America."

If you worked for $10, $12, $15 an hour, you were a loser, and you knew people thought of you as a loser. They didn't want to see you, didn't want to know you, didn't want their children to play with your children. So they built bigger and bigger houses behind sturdier and sturdier gates. What's more, your life would never be better. The path Dale Lamb had walked, and four generations of glassworkers before him had walked, had become a dead end.

People like Kevin Williamson, and some in Lancaster, too, preached the gospel of personal responsibility. A prominent local doctor expressed outrage after he'd tried to hire an unemployed job seeker to mow his lawn for $30. The man turned him down. This was proof, the doctor argued, that the underclass just wanted to lie around collecting welfare.

Thirty dollars, though, wasn't a path to anywhere. But the attitude was part of the gospel, and who could argue with it? Of course people should act responsibly. They should do what's best for themselves and the commonweal.

"Have you no morals, man?" Pickering asks Alfred Doolittle in Shaw's *Pygmalion*. "Can't afford them, Governor," he responds. "Neither could you if you was as poor as me."

The greater the income inequality, and the fewer decent-paying jobs there are for people with high school diplomas (or less), the greater the chances that a young woman won't marry the father of her baby. Why would she? Middle-class morality may be a luxury she can't afford. A young man with no job—or a job at Sonic making minimum wage—could very well turn out to be more of a burden than a help. What help would Ashley's baby daddy be to Ashley? He lived in the same Dogpatch trailer park she lived in. But she might want a baby, or perhaps just not take care not to have a baby, because a child might be the one person in her life she could love who would love her back. And America esteems motherhood. Ashley might be a poor, school-dropout addict—the daughter of a poor, uneducated addict—but at least she could be a mother.

Brian Gossett understood. "These people, they've got nothing else, man. So instead of saying, 'Well, I'll be a worker at this place,' or, 'I'll be that,' it's like, 'Okay, I'm a heroin addict. And I have tattoos.'"

Even Judge David Trimmer, an adherent of a strict interpretation of the personal-responsibility gospel, had to acknowledge that having no job, or a lousy job, was not going to give a thirty-five-year-old man much purpose in life. So many times, people wandered through his courtroom like nomads. "I always tell them, 'You're like a leaf blowing from a tree. Which direction do you go? It depends on where the wind is going.' That's how most of them live their lives. I ask them, 'What's your purpose in life?' And they say, 'I don't know.' 'You don't even love yourself, do you?' 'No.' "

Trimmer and the doctor still believed in a world with an intact social contract. But the social contract was shattered long ago. They wanted Lancaster to uphold its end of a bargain that had been made obsolete by over three decades of greed.

Monomoy Capital Partners, Carl Icahn, Cerberus Capital Management, Newell, Wexford, Barington, Clinton—none of them bore any personal responsibility. A&M and $1,200-per-hour lawyers didn't bear any personal responsibility. They didn't get a lecture or a jail sentence: They got rich. The politicians—from both parties—who enabled their behavior and that of the payday- and car-title-loan vultures, and the voters of Lancaster who refused to invest in the future of their town as previous generations had done (even as they cheered Ohio State football coach Urban Meyer, who took $6.1 million per year in public money), didn't bear any personal responsibility.

With the fracturing of the social contract, trust and social cohesion fractured, too. Even Brad Hutchinson, a man who had millions of reasons to believe in The System, had no faith in politicians or big business. "I think that most politicians, if not all politicians, are crooked as the day is long," Hutchinson said. "They don't have on their minds what's best for the people." Business leaders had no ethics, either. "There's disconnect everywhere. On every level of society. Everybody's out for number one. Take care of yourself. Zero respect for anybody else."

So it wasn't just the poor or the working class who felt disaffected, and it wasn't just about money or income inequality. The whole culture had changed. Brian was from a middle-class family, but he didn't believe in any institution or person in authority. He didn't feel like he was part of anything bigger than himself. Aside from his mother and father, and his brother, Mike, he was alone.

Telling Lancaster to surrender and call U-Haul made it easy for America to ignore its Lancasters. Sure, there was a lot of talk about such places and the people in them, but few wanted to spend much time learning about how they'd been left behind by the financialization and digitalization of American life. Silicon Valley kept promising nirvana but delivering new ways to gossip, even while disconnecting people from each other and their real communities. Politicians soothed the blows of globalization with promises to retrain and educate, but none of that happened for Lancaster's working class.

To so blithely dismiss the value of community was to pretend there was no loss. But there was, and the effects of that loss continued to ripple throughout the town.

Lancaster, as a place, would survive; it was too big to dry up like a Texas crossroads bypassed by the interstate. Maybe it would sell scones and coffee to visitors and one day complete a transformation, already well under way, into a Columbus bedroom community with organic delis and rehabilitated loft apartments in the old Essex Wire building. Or maybe it would slide into deeper dysfunction. For sure it could never go back, no matter how much some in town wanted to believe Lancaster could recapture at least the spirit of what it once was. Whatever its future, Lancaster would be a lonelier place than the one Nancy George had found.

When Anchor Hocking quality control supervisors tested the strength and shatter patterns of baking dishes, they used a tap-style punch and hammer. They placed the baking dish on a wooden block within the bounds of a walled frame, held the punch in the center of the dish, and hammered at it—gently at first, then with increasing power, hit after hit, until the dish fragmented into isosceles shards. If the glass had been melted, formed, and tempered just right, it would shatter along lines of stress. You can see the stress lines in an intact dish by holding it under polarized light. You can't see them with the naked eye.

B rian took another sip of whiskey and explained his idea for the trees. The pair of them would be slightly abstract, with leaves big enough for writing on. As guests walked into Bayat and Victoria's wedding ceremony, or maybe the reception, they'd use a gold marker to write their names on the leaves. Afterwards, Brian would have the trees framed and present them to Bayat and Victoria as keepsakes. He'd been working on the trees for a few days now, up in the studio. It was the first art he'd made in months. He lifted his glass and said he was excited about getting back to work creating something.

The studio was clean and organized, his drawing tables neater than they'd ever been. He'd also hung up a few pieces of art—a couple of prints of Renaissance paintings, and the December 31 issue of the *Eagle-Gazette*. That was the one with the big picture of Bridget Kuhn being arraigned in court. He'd turned the paper into an icon to remind him that he wasn't crazy at all; his view of The System had been the right one all along.

He'd also been decorating at his parents' house—repainting a room, buying a new mattress. In a few days, he'd be moved out of the Colfax place. Aaron was cool with his leaving. Brian had paid up for January so as not to leave Aaron with a full tab. Besides, Aaron had started spending a lot of his time up in Pickerington with his girlfriend and would probably be leaving Colfax, too.

Brian emptied out the Colfax freezer by taking the backstrap from the deer he took with the crossbow—he and Brant had had a successful hunt in November—and grilling it at Hilltop for some friends. The meat was delicious. Hilltop hadn't changed. The rocks we'd collected in December 2014 lay where we'd dropped them. The hillbilly cabin was going to remain a dream, but his affection for Hilltop was undiminished. He liked taking naps in the woods and feeling a little disoriented when he woke to the sounds of the trees in the wind. He was never more comfortable with himself than when he was at Hilltop, on land where that early Gossett had made a home.

In December, Mike took a bus trip out to Colorado to snowboard with a busload of kids from school. Brian was a little envious, but proud of his brother. Soon Mike would graduate from Ohio University. Brian wished he'd figured out a way to get to college, too, and to finish, but "at least one of us made it," he said. He knew now that Mike might move away from Lancaster and never go into the silkscreen T-shirt business, or the skateboard graphics business. "I can't imagine what it'd be like to lose him," Brian said.

He planned to stay at Drew. He still hadn't signed up for the 401(k), but maybe there'd be some way he could make a career there. Anchor Hocking was still on his mind, though. "You know," he said, "Anchor was the only job I've ever really been proud of."

Brian took another sip, then spotted somebody staring into a phone. "I hate Facebook," he said. "I have to be careful who hears me say that. Hating Facebook makes you an evil person." He laughed. "Everybody is alone.

Like, even these big houses: In them, you're in the same house, but you're still alone."

Somewhere—he couldn't remember exactly, but it was probably NPR, because he liked to listen to it on his way home from work—he'd heard about some experiment on rats where the dude put some rats in cages by themselves and other rats in this, like, park with a bunch of other rats. And then he gave all the rats plain water and something like dope or something, and the rats could drink whatever they wanted. The rats in the cages totally went for the dope. They'd take so much, they'd kill themselves. The rats who hung out with all the other rats in a park hardly took any drugs, because they weren't lonely. Lancaster, he said, was like a cage. "We don't have a population problem," he said. "We have a consumption problem."

People consumed to distract themselves. If it wasn't dope, it was real estate, cars, cash, Facebook, politics, screens, religion, rote patriotism, stupid movies, dumbass music.

Brian mentioned Mike's trip to Colorado again and said it might be nice to move out west someday. The fact was, though, that he still loved Lancaster. Hilltop was Lancaster. The old buildings were Lancaster. The generations of Gossetts were Lancaster. The picture of Bridget Kuhn on the studio's wall proved he loved it enough to be offended, if not surprised.

A football game had been playing on the flat-screen TV above the bar, some postseason all-star game, most likely. Brian hadn't been paying attention—he wasn't much of a sports fan. But an odd tableau drew his eye: There was a cute girl in small red shorts jumping around with frenetic enthusiasm. She was backed by NFL cheerleaders wearing sexy uniforms and giant, almost insane smiles, their perfect rows of perfect white teeth frozen and miraculous. And around the girl and the cheerleaders, a group of gospel singers shook with fervor as they sang to empty seats. He stared for a few seconds and then said, "The United States of America, dude."

We decided to stay for another drink. The food at Cherry Street was pretty good. Billy and Lorena seemed to know everybody who walked through the door, and you could almost always find somebody you knew to chat with under the pictures and signs and memorabilia. Besides, it was cold outside.

A NOTE ON NAMES AND SOURCES

All names in *Glass House* are real with the following exceptions: The names of minor children have been changed. The names of several people identified by first name only have been changed, but most have not. I reluctantly granted the wish of several people who asked to remain anonymous. In two cases, I chose to grant anonymity to people who did not ask for it; these people are identified only by occupation.

ACKNOWLEDGMENTS

It was my belief that Lancaster had an important story to tell. Telling it would have been impossible without the generous cooperation of its people, its officials, and its various agencies, both governmental and charitable. Lancaster allowed me into its life with much more generosity and openness than even I had expected. I thank all those people whose names appear in this book, and those many whose names do not.

Key logistical and/or research assistance was provided by the board of the West After School Program, Lancaster police chief Don McDaniel and officer Ray Hambel, court reporter Janice Fry, the staff of the Fairfield County Board of Elections, the staff of the Fairfield County District Library, the Fairfield County District Attorney's office, Stuart Stevens, James Linehan, Eleanor Hood, Milton Taylor, John McGraw, John and Mary Snider, the Barrows family, Lisa and Evan Murphy, and Doug Barber.

Photographer Shelley Metcalf shot the image of Plant 1. Amanda Allen created the map of Lancaster. Thanks to both for putting up with me.

The important role played by local newspapers is illustrated by the number of *Eagle*, *Gazette*, and *Eagle-Gazette* stories referenced herein, from 1900 to the present. Please support your local paper.

My buddy Smokey was a most welcoming landlord, efficient taxi service, television and fast food concierge, and a font of information. There are not enough chicken wings in the world to compensate.

Sam Solomon admitted me into the company he was trying to save, and willingly revealed himself in the process. He answered every question I asked without obfuscation. Because he did, he provided a rare peek into the workings of a troubled company. This book would not have been possible without him. I am convinced Anchor Hocking would have folded long ago without the presence of Janet Rayburn. I thank all the executives and workers of Anchor Hocking, past and present, including my friendly nemesis, Erika Schoenberger.

Thanks also to the many bartenders of Lancaster.

Rosemary Batt of Cornell University, Mike McMahon, Victor Fleischer of the University of San Diego School of Law, Denny Garvis of Washington and Lee University, and Debra Riley—experts in the fields of private equity, banking, investment tax law, business journalism, and bankruptcy law, respectively—provided valuable insights, tips, and welcome critiques. Suzy Spencer, who read and critiqued drafts of early chapters, helped set a course.

Serendipity led me to my fellow former Lancastrian Beth (Taylor) Urban, who patiently transcribed many hours of interviews for paltry wages and kept my secrets. Susan Heard's attention to textual detail—also at paltry wages—made me look like a better grammarian than I am. Alex Heard provided early, and continued, encouragement. Nicole Payne combed through the text, seeking out factual errors and confusions—again, for paltry wages. (I am an exploitive employer.) All errors are mine, of course.

Elisabeth Dyssegaard of St. Martin's is the bravest book editor I've ever encountered: She bought a book having no idea how events would unfold. I'm grateful for her faith, and for the continued faith of Michelle Tessler. Laura Apperson of St. Martin's helped keep the work flowing despite my frustrations. Copyeditor Will Palmer and legal advisor Henry Kaufman kept me out of trouble.

During the course of reporting and writing this book, my mother, Agnes "Bobby" Alexander, and then my brother, Bruce Alexander, also a writer, died. They both helped instill in me a belief that stories are among the most valuable artifacts a society can produce.

One day, early in my Lancaster sojourn, while I sat in the bar of the old hotel, a man named Andy Ogilvie, whose father would have been, and should have been, the CEO of Anchor Hocking had he not died at too early an age, and whom I had not seen in at least thirty-five years, and barely knew when I grew up there, walked into the room, looked at me for a moment and said, "That's gotta be an Alexander." I was proud to say yes, and grateful to be from Lancaster.

NOTES

The information in this book was obtained through scores of interviews, more than 3,500 documents, and my own experience and reporting in Lancaster, past and present. The following books provided important background and insights: *The Way We Never Were: American Families and the Nostalgia Trap* (revised and updated), by Stephanie Coontz (New York: Basic Books, 2016); *Private Equity at Work: When Wall Street Manages Main Street*, by Eileen Appelbaum and Rosemary Batt (New York: Russell Sage Foundation, 2014); *The Future of Nostalgia*, by Svetlana Boym (New York: Basic Books, 2001); *Dreamland: The True Tale of America's Opiate Epidemic*, by Sam Quinones (New York: Bloomsbury Press, 2015).

The following selected notes are not a complete list of sources or attributions.

INTRODUCTION. THE CEO

1   *He'd signed his new employment contract:* EveryWare Global Inc. Employment Agreement, February 21, 2014.

3   *stood at a whiteboard:* Sam Solomon, interview with the author, September 24, 2015.

ONE. GLASS HOUSE: DECEMBER 2014

5   *A 2,400-degree lava-like ribbon of glass flowed out of Tank 3:* Tours of Anchor Hocking Plant 1, July 16, 2015, and January 28, 2016.

6   *Brian was awed by what he saw:* Brian Gossett, interview with the author, December 13, 2014.

8   *Brian had a reputation as a complainer:* Chris Nagle, interview with the author, September 28, 2015.

8   *"That place is run . . . let's say jerry-rigged":* Joe Boyer, interview with the author, July 24, 2015.

8   *it had a reputation around the industry for being a "shit hole":* Mike Shook, interview with the author, September 24, 2015.

9   *Lloyd Romine was moving, little by little:* Lloyd Romine, personal communication

with the author, January 28, 2016; Jason Roach, interview with the author, September 24, 2015.

10 *His own lawyer liked him so much he loaned him money:* Andrew Sanderson, interview with the author, November 12, 2015.

10 *He once skipped out on bail and took off to Florida:* Lloyd Romine, interview with the author, February 1, 2016.

11 *somebody knocked on the door of Mark Kraft's house: State of Ohio v. Carly Donn Bowman,* 15CRA00081ABCD (Fairfield County Municipal Court).

11 *Mark's grandparents raised a family in that house:* Mark Kraft, interviews with the author, various dates.

13 *Wendy Oatney was working the late shift at Taco Bell:* Wendy and John Oatney, interviews with the author, various dates.

14 *Cargotec, a Finnish company:* "Business Development," Cargotec 2012 annual report, http://annualreport2012.cargotec.com/en/hiab/business-development.

18 *Ohio Reform Farm at its founding in 1856: Lancaster Eagle-Gazette,* June 3, 1950, "Sesquicentennial Edition."

18 *turned into a state prison for adults, the Southeastern Correctional Institution:* Southeastern Correctional Complex, Ohio Department of Rehabilitation and Correction, http://www.drc.ohio.gov/public/sci.htm.

TWO. THE ALL-AMERICAN TOWN: 1947–1982

21 *every school kid in Lancaster could tell you at least part of the story:* Ruth Wolfley Drinkle, *Heritage of Architecture and Arts: Fairfield County, Ohio* (Lancaster, OH: Fairfield Heritage Association, 1978), 3–21.

21 *Richard Outcault:* "Richard Felton Outcault," *Encyclopedia Britannica,* https://www.britannica.com/biography/Richard-Felton-Outcault.

22 Forbes *devoted most of its thirtieth-anniversary issue: Forbes,* November 15, 1947, various articles.

22 *Two days after graduating from Princeton:* Malcolm Forbes biography, Bryant College Commencement program, May 22, 1976; "Roberta Laidlaw Englewood Bride," *New York Times,* September 22, 1946; "Forbes, B. C.," American National Biography Online, http://www.anb.org/articles/16/16-03558.html.

23 *forming a municipal gas company: Lancaster Eagle-Gazette,* June 3, 1950, "Sesquicentennial Edition."

23 *By 1890, a company called Highland Manufacturing:* Lancaster City Directory, 1904–1905.

25 *Lancaster Lens was placed in the Statue of Liberty's torch:* http://www.lancasterglasscorp.com/; Ohio Glass Museum display, Lancaster, Ohio.

25 *Godman sold out to the Irving Drew Shoe Company: Lancaster Eagle-Gazette,* June 3, 1950, "Sesquicentennial Edition."

26 *two young newlyweds, Nancy and Herb George:* Nancy (George) Frick, interview with the author, May 15, 2015.

28 *another major employer, Diamond Power: Lancaster Eagle-Gazette,* June 3, 1950, "Sesquicentennial Edition."

28 *General Mills opened a plant:* Kevin Hunt, "Bugles in the 'Mad Men' Era," *Taste of General Mills* blog, April 5, 2012, http://www.blog.generalmills.com/2012/04/bugles-in-the-mad-men-era.

31 *there were the perks, too, like the company softball: AnchorScope* newsletters, various
    years, Ohio Glass Museum archives.

32 *Lancaster was streaked with Copperheads:* Gerry Stebelton, interview with the
    author, October 19, 2015.

32 *segregationist George Wallace attracted 1,574 votes:* Abstract of Votes Cast for Offices
    in Fairfield County, Ohio, at the General Election Held, November 5, 1968;
    Fairfield County Board of Elections.

32 *In the 1920s, Lancaster fell into the grip of a resurgent Ku Klux Klan:* John Acton,
    interview with the author, August 7, 2015.

32 *the parks department drained the pool, then refilled it:* James Miller, interview with
    the author, December 9, 2014.

33 *expended much of its energy harassing Catholics:* Dr. Hubert Eyman, Sr., interview
    with Ruth Drinkle, May 27, 1981, Fairfield County District Library Historical
    Collection.

34 *He rented a room in a Lancaster boardinghouse called the Kreider:* Lancaster City
    Directory, 1903–1904.

34 *Born in Maryland in 1874:* Margaret M. Iwen, *Mr. Collins: Father of Anchor Hocking*
    (n.p.: self-published, 2010).

34 *a Pinkerton strikebreaker named Edward Good:* Cy Fulton, interview with Ruth Drinkle
    and Ginny Fetters, September 13, 1982, Fairfield County District Library, Historical
    Collection; Pittsburgh City Directory, RL Polk and Company, January 1, 1900.

34 *Good later headed another Pittsburgh detective agency:* Political advertisement,
    Pittsburgh *Gazette Times*, November 2, 1913, 4.

34 *In 1894 Collins went to work in the factory at the Phoenix Glass Company:* Drafts of
    Anchor Hocking corporate history, c. 1954, Ohio Glass Museum archives.

35 *fallen under the control of a trust engineered by the National Carbon Company:* Tariff
    Hearings Before the Committee on Ways and Means, 1908–1909. Hugo Reisinger:
    "Now, I wish to explain to you one of the actions of the carbon trust. Knowing they
    have absolutely no competition on these low-grade carbons (as I stated before, they
    control every factory; some independent carbon works were built after the
    organization of the National Carbon Company, a few of which I can mention: The
    Consumers' Carbon Company, of Lancaster, Ohio; Dickey-Sutton Carbon Com-
    pany, of Lancaster, Ohio; the United States Carbon Company, of Cleveland, and
    others; all of them have since passed into the control of the National Carbon
    Company."

35 *In late 1905, he and a group of partners:* "The Hocking Glass Co.," *Lancaster Daily
    Eagle*, November 1905.

35 *Fulton successfully tapped a relative for $5,000:* "Thomas Fulton Dies During Fire at
    Home," *Lancaster Eagle-Gazette*, January 7, 1955, 1; Cy Fulton, interview with Ruth
    Drinkle and Ginny Fetters, September 13, 1982, Fairfield County District Library,
    Historical Collection.

35 *Collins hired a young military engineer named William Fisher:* Drafts of Anchor
    Hocking corporate history, c. 1954, Ohio Glass Museum archives.

36 *Ellsworth Boyer, employee number 87:* Ellsworth Boyer, interview with Joan P.
    Haller, October 24, 1982, Fairfield County District Library, Historical Collection.

36 *W. Robert Taylor quit school:* W. Robert Taylor, interview with Joan Haller,
    November 4, 1981, Fairfield County District Library, Historical Collection.

36 *"They just dropped in their tracks":* Alice McAnespie, interview with Joan Haller, 1988, Fairfield County District Library, Historical Collection.

36 *Ollie Smith was hired on in the early 1930s:* Ollie Smith, interview with Joan Haller, Fairfield County District Library, Historical Collection.

37 *In 1918, the average manufacturing wage in the United States was fifty-three cents per hour:* Hourly wages for selected industries, United States, 1935, "100 Years of U.S. Consumer Spending," U.S. Bureau of Labor Statistics, May 2006.

37 *Employees, many of them women, worked from 6:30 a.m. to 5:30 p.m.:* Emit Clark, interview with Fairfield Heritage Association, June 8, 1981.

37 *American Flint Glass Workers' Union (the "Flints") was in Lancaster as early as 1904:* "Lancaster Union 127, AFGWU Is Arranging for the Celebration of the Glorious Fourth—an Announcement," *Lancaster Gazette,* June 1904.

37 *"The question in my mind is 'What must be done?'":* Claude Tucker, *The American Flint,* 3 (June 1912): 6–7.

38 *Collins hired scab labor from out of town:* Harry H. Cook, "Hocking Glass Company Trouble," *History of the American Flint Glass Workers' Union,* part 2, p. 23 (Protest to President D. A. Hayes of the G. B. B. A.), Toledo, Ohio, April 22, 1911.

38 *Six Lancaster shoe workers went to state prison for the assault:* "Twenty Years Ago," *Lancaster Eagle-Gazette* (date unknown).

38 *The union struck, and struck again:* "Local Shoe Workers Will Seek Another Meeting with Miller," *Lancaster Daily Eagle,* March 20, 1934.

38 *Irving Drew Shoe Company, which had moved from Portsmouth, Ohio:* "About Us," Irving Drew Shoe Corporation, http://www.drewshoe.com/aboutus.aspx.

38 *Congress passed the National Labor Relations Act:* "The 1935 Passage of the Wagner Act," National Labor Relations Board, https://www.nlrb.gov/who-we-are/our-history/1935-passage-wagner-act.

39 *Anchor Hocking reported consolidated net sales of $64,399,742:* Anchor Hocking Glass Corporation, annual report, 1946.

39 *in 1950 invented late-night television with* Broadway Open House: "Take Trail Shots at Amsterdam Spot," *The Billboard,* November 25, 1950, 3.

39 *A hundred robed and hooded Klansmen presided at his graveside funeral:* "Ku Klux Klan Hold Services for Merrill Deaver" *Lancaster Daily Gazette,* March 17, 1924.

40 *created the Community Hotel Company of Lancaster:* James Miller, interview with the author, December 9, 2014; "Hotel Lancaster, Best of Size in Midwest Opened," *Lancaster Eagle-Gazette,* June 3, 1950, "Sesquicentennial Edition."

40 *Lancaster voted in 1914 to tax itself so it could build a public hospital:* Carl Burnett Jr., "FMC Plans Events in Buildup to 100th Anniversary," *Lancaster Eagle-Gazette,* October 3, 2015.

41 *"I gave them all those jobs":* Jonathon Nussbaum, interview with the author, August 6, 2015.

THREE. TRIGGERING EVENTS: JULY 1987

42 *"It sounds trite, but it was one big family":* Peter Roane, interview with the author, April 19, 2016.

43 *When Sam Walton realized that Anchor shipped its ware in its own fleet:* Dick Ellwood, interview with the author, May 13, 2015.

43 *But by 1980, imports were beginning to attack Anchor Hocking at home:* Ben Martin, interview with the author, July 11, 2015.

44 *a decision to turn the sales force into salaried employees:* Ken Culver, interview with the author, July 21, 2015; Bob Heath, interview with the author, May 15, 2015.

45 *sixteen million Anchor-made commemorative* Empire Strikes Back *glasses: Anchor-Scope* newsletter, October 1980, Ohio Glass Museum Archives.

45 *In the spring of 1982, a sharp-eyed employee in the company's finance department:* Sam Hurley, interview with the author, May 16, 2015.

46 *George Barber would later say his endorsement of Topper:* Ward Swift, interview with the author, October 5, 2015.

46 *On August 17, 1982, Anchor repurchased Icahn's shares: SEC News Digest*, August 27, 1982.

47 *University of Chicago economist Milton Friedman published: American Conservative Thought in the Twentieth Century*, ed. William F. Buckley (Indianapolis: Bobbs-Merrill, 1970).

48 *Friedman framed some of his theories in less academic language:* Milton Friedman, "The Social Responsibility of Business Is to Increase Its Profits," *New York Times Magazine*, September 12, 1970.

49 *threw the government's support behind tactics like Icahn's:* Michael Blumstein, "Baxter Rejects Call to Curb Mergers," *New York Times*, June 3, 1983.

50 *In early 1983, a Kidder, Peabody banker introduced Naimoli:* Vincent Naimoli, interview with the author, October 8, 2015.

50 *The deal turned out to be an early example of modern financial engineering:* Donald L. Barlett and James B. Steele, *America: What Went Wrong?* (Kansas City, MO: Andrews McMeel, 1992) (originally a series in the *Philadelphia Inquirer*); Zachary R. Mider and Jeffrey McCracken, "Wayzata's Anchor Glass Said to Seek Buyer, May Fetch $1 Billion," *Bloomberg News*, September 22, 2010.

51 *the board instituted a golden-parachute scheme:* Anchor Hocking shareholder proxy packet, May 20, 1987.

51 *Cartoons soon appeared on bulletin boards:* Ken Culver, interview with the author, July 21, 2015.

51 *Local and state economic development officials provided $8.5 million:* Andrew Herod, "Local Political Practice in Response to a Manufacturing Plant Closure: How Geography Complicates Class Analysis," *Antipode* 23:4 (1991): 385–402.

53 *The plant manager told his bosses at headquarters, "You missed out":* Ken Culver, interview with the author, July 21, 2015.

53 *Western loaned Newell $42 million:* "Western Financial Purchases Shares of Wisconsin Firm," *Arizona Republic*, October 30, 1982.

53 *Ferguson's father, Leonard, had been CEO and chairman of Newell:* David Young, "Father, Children in Battle over Millions," *Chicago Tribune*, May 7, 1997.

54 *In May of 1986, Ferguson met with Ray Topper:* Anchor Hocking shareholder proxy packet, May 20, 1987.

54 *On July 3, Topper demanded that the unions at Plant 1 enter into early negotiations:* "Anchor's Distribution Center, West Side Facility May Close," *Lancaster Eagle-Gazette*, July 5, 1986, 1.

54 *On July 31, Anchor's board adopted a stockholder-rights plan:* Anchor Hocking shareholder proxy packet, May 20, 1987.

55   *Union men attacked people:* Dale Lamb, interview with the author, May 8, 2015.

55   *The strike ended on October 22:* "Workers Back on Job; Concessions Enough? Only Time Will Tell," *Lancaster Eagle-Gazette*, October 22, 1986, 1.

55   *the board of directors of Anchor Hocking voted to approve Newell's offer:* "Anchor Board Approves Merger," *Lancaster Eagle-Gazette*, February 24, 1987, 1.

55   *A story went around that Topper cried:* Dick Ellwood, interview with the author, May 13, 2015.

56   *"You could see they were thinking, 'My God!'":* Sam Hurley, interview with the author, May 16, 2015.

56   *About three thousand people streamed through:* Gerry Stebelton, interview with the author, October 19, 2015.

56   *Newell shut down the Clarksburg plant:* "Showdown in West Virginia," *Chicago Tribune*, November 16, 1987.

56   *Then it secretly sent Anchor employees:* Mike Shook, interview with the author, September 24, 2015; Doug Ingram, interview with the author, May 11, 2015.

57   *Western Savings and Loan collapsed . . . Driggs resigned as president and CEO:* Newell Company, Securities and Exchange Commission filing 13-D, March 2, 1998.

62   *critics like Felix Rohatyn:* Fred R. Bleakley, "Surge in Company Takeovers Causes Widespread Concern," *New York Times*, July 3, 1984.

62   *"means for translating private impulse to the public good":* Ann Crittenden, "The Age of 'Me-First' Management," *New York Times*, August 19, 1984.

FOUR. NEWELLIZATION: MARCH 2004

64   *This was certainly the view of Vermont American:* W. Joseph Campbell, "The 2 Sides of Stanleys Suitor," *Hartford Courant*, April 20, 1992; *Newell Co. v. Vermont American Corp.*, 89 C 5202, October 13, 1989 (Illinois Northern District Court).

66   *Joe Boyer walked a picket line:* Joe Boyer, interview with the author, July 24, 2015.

67   *At the insistence, and through the persistence, of an Anchor attorney:* Sam Hurley, interview with the author, May 16, 2015; James Miller, interview with the author, June 30, 2015.

68–69   *a vote to increase Lancaster property taxes to support the schools failed:* Abstract of Votes, Lancaster City Schools proposed tax levy, November 8, 1988.

69   *According to a state "report card" of school districts:* Walt Williams, "County Schools Show Some Improvement," *Lancaster Eagle-Gazette*, January 13, 2002, 7.

69   *In 1991, the fire department employed seventy-four firefighters:* Spencer Remo- quillo, "Fire Chief Plans for Growing City," *Lancaster Eagle-Gazette*, May 21, 2016.

69   *a new task force called the Major Crimes Unit:* Jennifer Lawson, "Crimes Unit Has Busted Nine Labs," *Lancaster Eagle-Gazette*, December 17, 2001, 1.

70   *formed the Fairfield County Foundation in 1989:* Amy Eyman, interview with the author, July 7, 2015.

70   *In 1990, it even made a run at Lancaster Glass:* "Lancaster Colony Corporation History," Funding Universe, http://www.fundinguniverse.com/company -histories/lancaster-colony-corporation-history.

71   *The merger, completed in 1999, nearly killed the company:* David Harding, Sam Rovit, and Catherine Lemire, "Staying Cool When Deal Pressures Mount," Bain and Company, December 1, 2004; "Newell Rubbermaid: Why It'll Bounce Back," *Bloomberg*, October 19, 2003; David Harding and Sam Rovit, "Building Deals on Bedrock," *Harvard Business Review*, September 2004.

72   *the board hired forty-two-year-old Joseph Galli:* Joann S. Lublin, "A CEO Gets Rare Second Act," *Wall Street Journal*, February 3, 2009; "Black and Decker Timeline," *Baltimore Sun*, March 14, 2010.

73   *Galli shut down Mirro's offices and factories in Manitowoc:* Charlie Mathews, "Mirro Worker Says Goodbye After 41 Years," *Manitowoc Herald Times Reporter*, September 11, 2003; "Mirro Plans to Close Manitowoc Plant," *Milwaukee Business Journal*, January 27, 2003.

73   *it sold control of Drew to Wexford Management: Footwear News*, November 30, 1998; Securities and Exchange Commission Form 10-QSB BCAM International, November 16, 1998.

74   *Wexford announced it would close the Drew factory:* Ohio Department of Job and Family Services, WARN Notice filings, 2001.

74   *The Federal Trade Commission thought so:* Carl Burnett, Jr., "FTC Questions Sale," *Lancaster Eagle-Gazette*, December 20, 2001, 1.

75   *Republicans in the legislature gerrymandered:* Linda Roderick Miller, interview with the author, July 14, 2015.

75   *In April 2002, a U.S. district court judge ruled in favor of the FTC: United States of America Before Federal Trade Commission, in the Matter of Libbey Inc., a Corporation, and Newell Rubbermaid, Inc., a Corporation*, docket no. 9301, May 9, 2002; Federal Trade Commission, "Libbey, Inc. Settles FTC's Administrative Litigation," August 21, 2002.

76   *Newell fired 175 factory workers:* Carl Burnett, Jr., "Anchor Hocking to Cut Jobs," *Lancaster Eagle-Gazette*, December 4, 2002, 1.

76   *On February 27, 2003, the Lancaster Board of Education voted to approve a deal:* Carl Burnett, Jr., "$30 Million for Anchor," *Lancaster Eagle-Gazette*, February 20, 2003, 1; Carl Burnett, Jr., "Anchor President Thanks City," *Lancaster Eagle-Gazette*, February 25, 2003, 1; Jess Andrews, "Schools Save Anchor Hocking," *Lancaster Eagle-Gazette*, February 28, 2003, 1.

77   *In February 2004, the district cut another $1 million out of its budget:* Lancaster City School District, Single Audit, Fiscal Year Ended June 30, 2004.

78   *Newell signed a purchase agreement to sell Anchor Hocking:* Securities and Exchange Commission Form 8K, Newell Corporation, April 13, 2004.

FIVE. HOOK, LINE, AND SINKER: APRIL 2007

80   *Ohio's own economic development guru made a swing:* Rami Yoakum, "Big Industry in Southern Ohio Is Over," *Lancaster Eagle-Gazette*, January 13, 2002, 6.

82   *A Princeton grad, Feinberg:* Liz Moyer, "How Chrysler Put the Bite on Cerberus," *Forbes*, May 1, 2009; Katie Benner and Geoff Colvin, "Cerberus: Inside the Wall Street Power-House": *Fortune*, August 5, 2007; Matthew Karnitschnig and Lingling Wei, "Economy Conspires to Dog Cerberus," *Wall Street Journal*, November 20, 2007; Emily Thornton et al., "What's Bigger Than Cisco, Coke, or McDonald's?" *Bloomberg*, October 2, 2005.

83   *Donald Rumsfeld invested between $1 million and $5 million:* Steven Lee Myers,
          "Rumsfeld to Pay Big Price to Avoid Conflicts," *New York Times,* January 29,
          2001.

84   *opened a $200 million revolving loan with Wachovia . . . and a revolving credit
          line for $210 million from Madeleine:* Affidavit of Randal Rombeiro, in re: Global
          Home Products LLC debtors, 06-10349 (United States Bankruptcy Court for
          the District of Delaware).

84   *These dividends appeared to have amounted to about $841,000:* Monthly
          Operating Report, in re: Global Home Products LLC debtors, 06-10340.

86   *Cerberus shut—without notice—an Anchor Glass Container bottle plant:* Joe
          Napsha, "Bill Would Tighten Rules Governing Warning on Closures, Layoffs,"
          Pittsburgh Tribune, October 3, 2009.

86   *GHP sought the first in a series of forbearances:* First Amended Disclosure
          Statement in Support of Joint Plan of Reorganization of Global Home Products,
          LLC, et al., Under Chapter 11 of the Bankruptcy Code, in re: Global Home
          Products LLC debtors, Case No. 06-10340.

86–87   *Newell transferred $43,885,449 in 401(k) savings plan funds:* Securities and
          Exchange Commission Form 11-K, June 29, 2005.

87   *Cerberus shorted the 401(k) account by an estimated $5,749,809:* First Amended
          Disclosure Statement in Support of Joint Plan of Reorganization of Global
          Home Products, LLC, et al., Under Chapter 11 of the Bankruptcy Code, in re:
          Global Home Products LLC debtors, Case No. 06-10340; "PBGC Protects
          Pensions at Anchor Hocking," PBGC press release, April 12, 2007.

87   *company pension plans were each at least $50 million underfunded:* "Companies
          Report a Record $353.7 Billion Pension Shortfall in Latest Filings with PBGC,"
          PBGC press release, June 7, 2005.

89   *Cerberus announced it wanted to scratch the health care plan:* Carl Burnett, Jr.,
          "Anchor Hocking, Union, Square Off," *Lancaster Eagle-Gazette,* December 3, 2006.

89   *GHP worker Brenda Stone despaired:* Letter from Brenda Stone to Honorable
          Kevin Gross, U.S. Bankruptcy Court for the District of Delaware, January 16,
          2008.

91   *The Pension Benefit Guaranty Corporation negotiated a settlement:* Motion
          Pursuant to 11 U.S.C. §§ 105 and 363 and Bankruptcy Rule 9019 for Approval
          of Compromise of Controversy Between Pension Benefit Guaranty Corporation
          and the Debtor, Anchor Hocking CG Operating Company LLC. Regarding
          Pension Plan Claims, in re: Global Home Products LLC debtors, 06-10340.

94   *By the mid-1990s, Lancaster Glass was among the highest-margin performers:* Dave
          Gallimore, interview with the author, May 12, 2015.

96   *Mitarotonda had two demands:* "Barington Blasts Lancaster Anti-Takeover
          Mechanisms," *Alternative Investment News,* July 2, 2007.

96   *the companies making up the Standard & Poor's 500 spent 54 percent of their
          earnings:* William Lazonick, "Profits Without Prosperity," *Harvard Business
          Review,* September 2014.

96   *Lancaster Colony said it would buy back at least two million of its own shares:*
          "Lancaster Colony Reaches Accord with Investor," *Columbus Business Journal,*
          October 10, 2007; Securities and Exchange Commission Exhibit 99.1, Lancaster
          Colony Corporation, October 9, 2007.

SIX. THE CHEESE, THE CEO, AND LANCASTER'S YEAR: JANUARY 2015

100 *About three out of every five pregnant women who came to the hospital:* Charlie Dresbach, interview with the author, October 19, 2015.

100–101 *were eligible for free or reduced-cost lunches:* Lancaster Food Service Department Report, November 4, 2015.

101 *Almost half—44 percent—of Lancaster households led by a single woman:* Scott Spangler, United Way of Fairfield County, e-mail to the author, May 31, 2016.

103 *The number was now over two thousand per month:* Kellie Ailes, interview with the author, July 29, 2015.

109 *A group of Ohio State University urban-planning students:* Chad Gibson et al., "Downtown Lancaster," report, Spring 2013.

SEVEN. THE SHUTDOWN: FEBRUARY 2015

123 *EveryWare Global hauled the weight of $290 million:* Securities and Exchange Commission Form DEF 14A, September 17, 2014.

124 *the results Solomon saw in March didn't show $60 million in EBITDA:* Securities and Exchange Commission Form 10K, EveryWare Global, Inc., for the fiscal year ended: December 31, 2013.

129 *In 1933, its payroll of 2,565 employees amounted to $1.8 million:* Anchor Hocking advertisement, *Lancaster Daily Gazette*, March 28, 1934.

130 *EveryWare sent a WARN:* EveryWare Global Inc., Conditional Notice Pursuant to Worker Adjustment and Retraining Notification Act, June 6, 2014.

130 *Cerberus was forced to pay workers $480,000:* Joe Napsha, "Bill Would Tighten Rules Governing Warning on Closures, Layoffs," *Pittsburgh Tribune*, October 3, 2009.

130 *Monomoy bought Kurdziel Industries:* "Monomoy Capital Partners Acquires Kurdziel Industries and Creates Carlton Creek Ironworks," press release, July 14, 2008.

132 *making him CEO and president of EveryWare Global:* Securities and Exchange Commission Exhibit 10.1, EveryWare Global Inc., "Employment Agreement," February 21, 2014; Securities and Exchange Commission Form 8K, EveryWare Global Inc., June 9, 2014.

135 *CFO Bernard Peters resigned on September 17:* Securities and Exchange Commission Form 8K, September 17, 2014.

135 *In 2013, his first year, Peters made $1,128,998:* Securities and Exchange Commission Form 14A, EveryWare Global Inc.

135 *The company agreed to pay A&M $31,680 per week:* Securities and Exchange Commission filing, Exhibit 10.1, Agreement Letter dated September 23, 2014.

EIGHT. THE BANKRUPTCY: MARCH 2015

138 *tariffs had dropped on imported glassware:* "Glass and Glassware," Harmonized Tariff Schedule of the United States, chap. 70.

139 *Stephen Presser, Daniel Collin, Justin Hillenbrand, and Philip Von Burg founded Monomoy:* Securities and Exchange Commission Form D, Section 4(6), filed November 14, 2005.

139 *Their first fund, Monomoy Capital Partners, LP, raised $280 million:* Monomoy Capital Partners Investor Profile, Pitchbook Data Inc.

140 *To purchase Anchor Hocking, Monomoy invested $6.5 million:* EveryWare Company Profile, Pitchbook Data Inc.; Monomoy Capital Partners Investor Profile, Pitchbook Data Inc.

141 *The buyer was an entity called NL Ventures VI West Fair, LLC:* Fairfield County, Ohio, Property Record Card Parcel: 0531004000; John Covaleski, "Texas Firm Raises $100 Mln-Plus for Net-Lease Properties Fund," CommercialRealEstate Direct.com; AICVentures.com.

141 *Anchor agreed to pay $2.3 million per year:* Securities and Exchange Commission Form 14A, ROI Acquisition Corp.

142 *Monomoy arranged for Anchor Hocking to buy Lancaster Colony's Indiana Glass plant in Sapulpa, Oklahoma:* Securities and Exchange Commission Form 10-Q, Lancaster Colony Corporation, for the quarterly period ended December 31, 2007.

142 *In early 2008, Anchor Hocking closed the Sapulpa plant:* "Oklahoma Glass Manufacturing Plant to Close," Associated Press, February 1, 2008.

143 *In 2008, federal authorities arrested only sixty-nine people:* Cornelius Frolik, "Illegal Immigration Arrests Grow," *Dayton Daily News,* July 18, 2012.

144 *two business incentive loans from the state of Ohio:* Tamaria L. Kulemeka, "Anchor Hocking Gets $10M Loans from State," *Lancaster Eagle-Gazette,* December 5, 2007.

145 *The fees increased year after year:* Securities and Exchange Commission Form 14A, 2013 preliminary proxy statement, ROI Acquisition Corp.

145 *Monomoy had Anchor Hocking borrow $45 million:* "Anchor Hocking Recapitalization Completed," William Blair & Co. press release, October 6, 2011; Securities and Exchange Commission Form 14A, 2013 preliminary proxy statement, ROI Acquisition Corp.

146 *Monomoy had more ammunition this time:* Monomoy Capital Partners Investor Profile, Pitchbook Data Inc.

146 *what sources told the* New York Times *amounted to $100 million:* Kevin Roose, "Private Equity Firm Sees a Future in Flatware," *New York Times,* January 5, 2012.

146 *Monomoy had to sweeten the deal:* Kerry Kantin and Kelly Thompson, "EveryWare Rolls Out Investor-Friendly Revisions to TL," Standard & Poor's LCD Daily Wrap-up, March 2, 2012.

147 *Monomoy foisted a new advisory agreement onto EveryWare:* Advisory Agreement, March 23, 2012.

147 *As of December 31, 2012, the plan was underfunded:* Securities and Exchange Commission Form 14A, 2013 preliminary proxy statement, ROI Acquisition Corp.

149 *He and his wife, Lori, liked to jet in from New Jersey:* Alexandra Beckstett, "Shared Passion: George and Lori Hall Embrace the Racing Life," *Keeneland,* Summer 2012.

149 *former NBA star Jamal Mashburn:* Securities and Exchange Commission, ROI Acquisition Corp Prospectus, October 14, 2011.

150 *Monomoy demanded $100 million in cash:* Securities and Exchange Commission Form 14A, preliminary proxy statement, ROI Acquisition Corp.

151 *"we believe in the business, we believe in its people":* Securities and Exchange Commission Form 8-K, ROI Acquisition Corp., February 1, 2013.

155   *Jefferies offered advice on at least five occasions:* Declaration of Richard
       Morgner, in re: EveryWare Global, Inc., et al, Case No. 15-10743, in the
       United States Bankruptcy Court, District of Delaware.

NINE. PUMP IT AND DUMP IT: APRIL 2015

159   *On April 1, 2014, EveryWare settled out of court:* Securities and Exchange
       Commission Form 14A, EveryWare Global, Inc., "Settlement Agreement,"
       April 14, 2014.
159   *the IBEW mounted a class action lawsuit:* In re: EveryWare Global, Inc.
       Securities Litigation, United States District Court Southern District of Ohio,
       Case No. 14-1838.
162   *Kwasteniet, for example, billed $1,030 per hour:* EveryWare Global, Inc., et al,
       Case No. 15-10743, in the United States Bankruptcy Court, District of
       Delaware Exhibit F, Summary of Total Fees Incurred and Hours Billed
       During the Fee Period, filed July 17, 2015.

TEN. TURN IT AROUND, OR TURN IT UP?: MAY 2015

187   *Lancaster's congressman, Steve Stivers, received $80,700:* Americans for
       Financial Reform, "Payday Pay-to-Play," June 2015.
188   *NCP and its founders were also generous contributors to Dave Yost:* http://
       www6.sos.state.oh.us/ords/f?p=119:30:0::NO:RP::
190   *The state of Ohio took in $298 million from keno:* Ohio Lottery Commission,
       Comprehensive Annual Financial Report for the Fiscal Years Ended June 30,
       2014 and 2013.

ELEVEN. HOPE FOR A FOREVER HOME: JUNE 2015

194   *John Kasich signed new legislation that cut $2 billion worth of income taxes:*
       Julie Carr Smyth, "Kasich Signs $71B, 2-Year Budget After Vetoing 44 Items,"
       Associated Press, July 1, 2015.

TWELVE. PUTTING THE BABY BACK TOGETHER: JULY 2015

221   *World Kitchen, saddled with $812 million of debt, quickly declared bankruptcy:*
       Securities and Exchange Commission Form T-3, WKI Holding Company,
       Inc., Application for Qualification of Indenture Under the Indenture Act of
       1939.

THIRTEEN. MAXIMUM VALUE: AUGUST 2015

242–243   *The deal for the 2014 sale from Ardagh to KPS:* Moody's Investors Service,
          "Approximately $335 Million in Rated Debt Securities Affected," May 7, 2014.
243   *In 2015, Anchor Glass took out a $465 million loan:* Luisa Beltran, "Anchor
       Glass to Pay $145 Mln Dividend to Shareholders, Including KPS," *PE Hub*,
       June 11, 2015.

FOURTEEN. FALLING OUT: OCTOBER 2015

267   *The county had just hired a new director:* Carl Burnett, Jr., "Fairfield County
       Appoints Development Director," *Lancaster Eagle-Gazette*, October 27, 2015.

FIFTEEN. THE FUTURE IN PLAY: JANUARY 2016

274 *Libbey used a $40.9 million low-interest loan from the China Construction Bank:*
Securities and Exchange Commission Form 10-K, Libbey, Inc., "Annual Report for
the Fiscal Year Ended, December 31, 2014."

274 *there were four hundred glass furnaces in Asia:* Patrick Lockwood-Taylor, employee
video presentation, June 2016.

285 *Kuhn had informed the county Republican Party that he was having a little business
trouble:* Trista Thurston, "State Investigation Has Ties to Kuhn," *Lancaster
Eagle-Gazette*, June 21, 2016.

292 *the greater the chances that a young woman won't marry the father:* Stephanie Coontz,
The Way We Never Were: American Families and the Nostalgia Trap, revised and
updated (New York: Basic Books, 2016), 400–406.

INDEX